Popular Culture in the Age of White Flight

AMERICAN CROSSROADS

Edited by Earl Lewis, George Lipsitz, Peggy Pascoe, George Sánchez, and Dana Takagi

Popular Culture in the Age of White Flight

Fear and Fantasy in Suburban Los Angeles

ERIC AVILA

University of California Press

BERKELEY   LOS ANGELES   LONDON

University of California Press
Berkeley and Los Angeles, California

University of California Press, Ltd.
London, England
First paperback printing 2006
© 2004 by the Regents of the University of California

Library of Congress Cataloging-in-Publication Data
Avila, Eric, 1968–
    Popular culture in the age of white flight : fear and fantasy in
suburban Los Angeles / Eric Avila.
        p.   cm.—(American crossroads ; 13)
    Includes bibliographical references (p.) and index.
    ISBN 978-0-520-24811-3 (pbk. : alk. paper)
    1. Los Angeles (Calif.)—Civilization—20th century.   2. Popular
culture—California—Los Angeles—History—20th century.   3. Los
Angeles (Calif.)—Social conditions—20th century.   4. Public spaces—
California—Los Angeles—History—20th century.   5. Los Angeles
(Calif.)—Race relations.   6. Whites—Race identity—California—Los
Angeles.   7. Suburban life—California—Los Angeles—History—20th
century.   8. Migration, Internal—California—Los Angeles Region—
History—20th century.   9. African Americans—California—Los
Angeles—Social conditions—20th century.   10. City and town life—
California—Los Angeles—History—20th century.   I. Title.   II. Series.
F869.L85A95   2004
979.4'94—dc22   2003019072

Manufactured in the United States of America
19 18 17 16 15 14
10 9 8 7 6 5 4

To my parents, Teresa and Edward Avila.

The metropolis itself may be described as a World's Fair in continuous operation.

LEWIS MUMFORD

Cities, like dreams, are made of desires and fears.

ITALO CALVINO

Contents

Illustrations

Preface

Essentially, cultural history is the history of stories that people tell about themselves and their world. Such stories are manifested and transmitted in a variety of ways, the sum of which we broadly define as *culture*. This book takes a set of stories as conveyed through film, photography, architecture, literature, art, and other disparate media that emerged within a particular regional and historical context and considers how they help us to understand a transformative moment in the history of the American city. The cacophonous stories that constitute culture support a variety of human purposes, and they do both more and less than simply provide meaning to abstract social and natural forces. Sometimes, they just entertain. This book, however, looks beyond entertainment to consider how the simultaneity of these stories in space and time corresponded to the spatial and racial reconfiguration of urban life in post–World War II America and how these stories conveyed a particular way of seeing that process. The new cultural forms that emerged within the context of the spectacular rise of Los Angeles in the thirty years between 1940 and 1970 encompassed a struggle over the very identity of the city and its constituent social groups.

I argue that despite popular culture's capacity to incorporate diverse and often contradictory meanings within its fold, the cultural forms explored in the following chapters privileged a particular way of seeing the city and its people. This way of seeing became the basis for a new political subjectivity that prized an inclusive white identity among a heterogeneous suburban public. In making this argument, *Popular Culture in the Age of White Flight* contributes to the critical study of whiteness, a growing (though increasingly unwieldy) body of scholarship that considers the evolution of a white racial identity in the United States and its varied significance to diverse peoples. Studying whiteness means eschewing the idea that a white race of people exists in order to understand how and why immigrants to the United States and their descendants came to know themselves as white. Accordingly, unlike many works within contemporary ethnic studies, no one group dominates the following narrative, which assumes that relations between diverse racial and ethnic groups are mutually constitutive. Because no one group's history can be understood apart from that of others, this book aims for a synthetic approach to the study of race and ethnicity in postwar America.

Historically removed from the entrenched ethnic and class hierarchies that defined social relations in older American cities, Los Angeles provides an ideal setting for understanding the process of white racial formation. Until recently, Los Angeles has remained outside the purview of urban historians, who privileged New York, Chicago, and even San Francisco as "true" cities and refused to grapple with the sociospatial idiosyncrasies of Southern California's development. This is changing, however, as more scholars, goaded by the international attention heaped upon Mike Davis's *City of Quartz*, inquire into the myriad processes that birthed in Southern California one of the world's largest conurbations. Still, anyone studying the history of this city cannot avoid that persistent question about the exceptionality of Los Angeles, as if everything that happens in Los Angeles has not happened and cannot happen anywhere else. Let me try to confront this question at the very outset of this project: Like all cities, Los Angeles maintains a distinct identity that materialized under a unique set of political, economic, social, and geographic circumstances. And yet, to greater and lesser degrees, the city also mirrors larger processes that shape the development of cities in the United States, the West, and beyond. This book acknowledges the unique aspects of Southern California's growth while recognizing how such growth was linked to a larger set of developments that fundamentally altered the historic balance among cities and regions within the United States after World War II.

Race is a primary category of analysis in this study of popular culture; space is another. Space, like time, is an arbiter of social relations, and the identities that we inhabit—race, class, gender, sexuality—are codified within a set of spaces that we describe as neighborhoods, homes, cities, streets, suburbs, parks, factories, office buildings, freeways, and so on. More than providing a physical setting for the formation of such identities, space—its organization, construction, destruction, and representation— plays an active role in shaping social consciousness. This book adopts the recent spatial turn within the humanities and social sciences, often linked to the emergence of postmodern theory, to illuminate the racial turn that dawned upon American society and culture in the decades following World War II. In the age of urban renewal, highway construction, and suburbanization, the spatial reorganization of the American city gave rise to a new racial awareness that, for better or for worse, still grips our collective imagination.

Ultimately, this study emphasizes the suburban character of postwar popular culture. Emphasizing the urban qualities of suburban life, scholars today question whether there is in fact a substantial difference between cities and their suburbs, but the cultural history of postwar America reveals a popular quest for a more ordered alternative to the historic and much feared disorder of the modern city and its culture. Walt Disney, for example, understood that quest and used his insight to build arguably the most significant landmark in American cultural history. In their pursuit of new cultural experiences, postwar Americans opted for something different—an emergent sociospatial order that promised a respite from the well-known dangers and inconveniences of the modern city: congestion, crime, pollution, anonymity, promiscuity, and diversity. That search for order provided an underlying impetus for the post–World War II phase of mass suburbanization and it is the subject of this book.

Finally, although I generally shun the self-reflexive move in history, let me offer a quick word as to how I came to this topic, if only to shed light upon why I chose to write about these cultural phenomena and my complex relationship to them. Although I grew up in suburban San Diego, in a neighborhood more or less bourgeois (or at least affluent by the standards to which my Chicano family was accustomed), as a child I felt a cultural allegiance to Los Angeles. My father and grandfather were avid Dodgers fans. Vin Scully, Steve Sax, and Fernando Valenzuela were household names. And once a year, our extended family made a pilgrimage to Disneyland, a tradition my mother had enjoyed as a child in the late 1950s (her experiences, as well as those of her mother, who also grew up in Los Angeles, surface in the chapters that follow). Those experiences cultivated my early enthusiasm for Los Angeles and the Southern California "way of life." My long-standing interest in film and film culture, moreover, heightened my attraction to Los Angeles, which I, like many non-Angelenos, thought of as the place where movies and movie stars come from. Although I knew Los Angeles through baseball, theme parks, movies, television, magazines, radio (I avidly tuned in to KROQ in the '80s, listening to the likes of New Order, X, and Duran Duran), advertisements, shopping malls, and, most of all, freeway off-ramps, the illusions about the city I conjured through my early engagement with mass culture have been extinguished by sobering discoveries of theories about false consciousness, racialization, and commodity fetishism, and my attraction to Los Angeles' glamour has been tempered by an awareness of the city's many failures. Still, for me, the city's allure remains intact, but for more complex reasons than those I knew years ago.

Acknowledgments

From what I'm told, Berkeley is not what is used to be, but it nonetheless remains a center of American intellectual life in the United States and continues to draw a broad array of diverse thinkers. Between 1986 and 1997, I had the privilege of working with a cluster of Berkeley's brightest stars. During my first research seminar as a graduate student in the Department of History, Gunther Barth introduced me to the study of the modern city and its culture and emphasized not only the intricacies of historical research, but also the necessities of good writing skills. If there was one lesson in graduate school that I have taken to heart, it was Barth's insistence that history is an art, not a science, and that historians use the raw materials of the archive to render their portrait of the past with as much foresight, skill, and diligence as artists working in other mediums do. Waldo Martin supplied helpful insights along the way and sustained my commitment to a timely completion of the dissertation. On the historiographic front of modern Europe, Martin Jay, Susanna Barrows, and Reginald Zelnik sparked my interest in the broader history of Western modernity and its culture. Elsewhere within Berkeley's intellectual universe, Richard Walker and Michael Johns taught me to understand space as an arbiter of social relations, while Paul Groth attuned my thinking to the centrality of landscape within cultural history. David Karnes turned me on to the cultural history of Los Angeles as an undergraduate, and Patricia Penn Hilden generously lent her enthusiasm to my project and graciously shared her own experiences growing up as a mixed-race child in Southern California's version of "White City."

Most of all, Lawrence Levine supervised the execution of the dissertation and, in doing so, brought his deep historical knowledge, constructive criticism, and broad perspective to bear upon this project from its conception as a dissertation abstract to its completion as a book manuscript. Larry taught me how to take popular culture seriously and to think and write like a cultural historian. He also provided a formative learning experience by bringing together a lively bunch of graduate students through his dissertation group. Many thanks to Sara Weber, Leif Brown, Sam Weinstein, Jay Cook, Brigitte Koenig, Michael Thompson, Phil Soffer, Cecilia O'Leary, and Cornelia Sears, who offered their helpful insights and provided communal support throughout the process of writing the dissertation. Larry and his wife, Cornelia Levine, opened their home to us on myriad occasions, creating an intellectual community that was stimulating and, most of all, fun.

Southern California, and UCLA in particular, has been an ideal setting in which to transform this project from a dissertation into a book. I have the privilege of working in the Department of Chicano Studies, where my colleagues Abel Valenzuela, Alicia Gaspar de Alba, Reynaldo Macías, Otto Santa Ana, Judy Baca, and María Cristina Pons have provided much encouragement along the way. Raymund Paredes and Scott Waugh deserve special thanks for their commitment to my professional well-being at UCLA. Elena Mohseni and Olivia Díaz provided critical support and much encouragement. In the Department of History, Steve Aron demonstrated an early enthusiasm for my project, and Henry Yu, Gary Nash, Tom Hines, and the U.S. History Colloquium supplied helpful advice along the way. Daniel Bernardi and Chon Noriega sharpened my ability to use film as primary source evidence. Many graduate and undergraduate students at UCLA, particularly Kristen Guzman and Mike Amezcua, supplied excellent advice and critical assistance. Thanks also to a host of scholars and colleagues beyond UCLA: Becky Nicolaides, Mike Willard, Robert Self, Don Parson, Gilbert Estrada, Frank Wilkinson, Danny Widener, Mark Wild, and the Western History Group at the Autry Museum of Western Heritage. Ryan Moore brought his deep theoretical insights to my support, and Sarah Schrank provided much enthusiasm and critical assistance at the last-minute finish. George Sánchez supplied invaluable insights all along, as did Robin Kelley and Peggy Pascoe. I also had the good fortune of stumbling upon the ethnic studies department at the University of California, San Diego, a model for what ethnic studies can and should be. In particular, Ramon Gutiérrez lent his intellectual support and personal friendship during my transition from graduate student to professor, and George Lipsitz saw the potential for this project early on. His command of American cultural history is mind-blowing, and his dedication to the health of ethnic studies is inspiring. My gratitude to him is without limits. The loss of my dear friend Clark Davis brought a deep and sudden grief toward the completion of this book. In my anxious moments about the fate of this project, I could always turn to Clark for intellectual affirmation and moral support. His untimely death has depleted our scholarly community of a brilliant mind, and his warmth and generosity are sorely missed.

Financial support came from the University of California Heller Fund and the Graduate Opportunity Program at UC Berkeley. The Ford Foundation delivered a much-appreciated postdoctoral fellowship during my third year at UCLA, and the Institute of American Cultures and the Academic Senate Fund at UCLA supplied additional financial assistance. My research was further aided by the staffs of the National Archives Annex in College Park, Maryland; the Library of Congress Manuscripts Division; the Huntington Library; the Bancroft Library; the Anaheim History Room; the Margaret Herrick Library of the Academy of Motion Picture Arts and Sciences; the Southern California Library for Social Research; and the Special Collections Library of California State University, Los Angeles. Special thanks to Octavio Olvera at the Special Collections Library of UCLA's Young Research Library, Dave Smith at the Walt Disney Archives, Matt Roth at the Automobile Club of Southern California, Dacy Taube at USC's Regional History Center, and Carolyn Kozo Cole at the Los Angeles Public Library.

Monica McCormick at the University of California Press tapped me on the shoulder during the final stages of the dissertation, and her enthusiasm for my project since then has been a great source of inspiration. Thanks also to Randy Heyman, Laura Harger, and Madeleine Adams for moving the process along.

Finally, a few people, programs, and institutions deserve special mention. First, I owe much gratitude to the affirmative action programs that were in place during my schooling years. Affirmative action may be a relic of a more amicable moment in race relations, but in my time, it sustained a colorful mix of talented scholars at the highest levels of education and ensured a vital commingling of diverse perspectives and experiences. Moreover, I feel profound respect for the University of California, which provided a stellar education, a diverse environment, and a lifetime job opportunity, and continues to stand as an example of what public education can be. Special thanks to Anthony Macias, whom I met back in the day at Berkeley and who is now, thankfully, a colleague in ethnic studies at the University of California, Riverside. Through the many highs and occasional lows, Anthony has been a tough reader, a deft editor, and a great friend. My brother, Chris, supplied his outrageous humor, keeping it real all along. Kirk Vaughn provided generous reading assistance, insightful criticism, and faithful companionship throughout this entire process. At the day's end, however, all honor and glory go to Teresa and Edward Avila, whose parental capacity for love and support is infinite and inspiring. I remember cringing as a youth when they called my teachers to inquire into my classroom performance. I hope this book answers their calls: It is for them and their efforts.

1 Chocolate Cities and Vanilla Suburbs
Race, Space, and the New "New Mass Culture"
of Postwar America

In 1964, the *New York Times* published an article titled "Coney Island Slump Grows Worse," drawing attention to the plight of the long-standing amusement park. Amid empty roller coasters and deserted bingo parlors, an "air of desertion" permeated Coney Island, whose patronage had declined steadily since World War II. The *Times* identified a number of factors that had facilitated the park's decline, including "unsafe subways," "young hoodlums," and "bad weather." One problem, however, stood out. "Concessionaire after concessionaire" reported that "the growing influx of Negro visitors to the area" was the most critical obstacle to Coney Island's resuscitation. African Americans, who comprised "half the weekend tourists" at Coney Island by the early 1960s, aroused suspicion that their prominence "has discouraged some white persons from visiting the area." Three years later, the first of Coney Island's great amusement parks, Steeplechase Park, became the last, closing its doors forever.[1]

Chicago's Riverview Park met a similar fate at roughly the same time. Billed as "the world's largest amusement park," Riverview stood on 140 acres of land on the city's northwest side. Whereas Riverview enticed an ethnically diverse array of pleasure seekers throughout its sixty-four-year popularity, the amusement park could not withstand the changing demographics that ensued in the era of racial desegregation. As African Americans began to integrate themselves into Chicago's public life, Riverview Park lost much of its appeal. By the 1960s, Riverview began a rapid decline as the park became the grounds for racial and gang violence. Shortly before Riverview Park shut down on October 3, 1967, the *Chicago Tribune* later reported, the park's "natural defenses began to crumble. Racial tension increased in Chicago and soon ran rampant inside the park."[2]

Amusement parks were not the only venue for popular entertainment that fell by the wayside during the post–World War II period. Urban baseball parks that grew alongside amusement parks such as Coney Island and Riverview Park encountered similar crises. Philadelphia's Shibe Park, for example, once hailed as the crown jewel of ballparks, lost much of its appeal among baseball fans during the 1950s. In 1970, Bob Carpenter, owner of the Philadelphia Phillies, removed his team from its inner-city locale. The owner based his decision on his conviction that baseball was no longer a "paying proposition" at Shibe Park and that the park's location in "an undesirable neighborhood" meant that white baseball fans "would not come to a black neighborhood" to see a ball game.[3] Similarly, Brooklyn's Ebbets Field, where the Brooklyn Dodgers had resided since 1913, underwent demolition in 1960. In 1957, the Dodgers' owner, Walter O'Malley, had announced his infamous decision to move his team west to Los Angeles, blaming an uncooperative city government in New York for his decision. While many Brooklyn residents despised O'Malley for taking away their beloved Dodgers, others understood his decision as part of a larger neighborhood transformation. "I guess O'Malley was like everyone else," recalled one former Brooklyn Dodgers fan. "As long as you're not my neighbor . . . it was okay. But once [blacks] started to live in the neighborhood, it was time to move out."[4]

Ebbets Field, Riverview Park, Coney Island, and their counterparts in other American cities all depended on the streetcar to bring a steady influx of pleasure seekers and sports enthusiasts, but that too became a relic after World War II. The mass adoption of the automobile began during the 1920s, but by the postwar period, public and private agencies concentrated their resources on the construction of an elaborate network of highways, leaving streetcars to fall into disrepair. The disappearance of the streetcar undermined the popularity of urban ballparks, amusement parks, and other urban cultural institutions whose inner-city location lost favor with a new generation of motorists whose daily activities became increasingly dictated by the availability of parking space. As the iron tracks of the streetcar gave way to the concrete ribbons of freeways within the nation's cities, Americans parted with yet another cultural venue that had served the needs of a heterogeneous urban public.[5]

What does it mean that these institutions began to vanish from the American cultural scene at roughly the same time? And what does it mean that people used race to explain their declining popularity? What cultural institutions emerged in their place, and how did they surmount the racial tensions that overcame places like Coney Island and Ebbets Field? To approach an answer to such questions requires an understanding of the larger spatial and historical contexts in which these landmarks surfaced. The amusement park, the ballpark, and the streetcar belonged to a generation of urban cultural institutions that surfaced during the second half of the nineteenth century. Their unique development unfolded under the purview of the modern industrial city, which came of age during a distinct moment within the history of capitalist urbanization. In the United States, New York debuted as the modern city's most vibrant incarnation, but Detroit, Chicago, St. Louis, and, further west, Denver and San Francisco also rose to prominence as major urban centers during the nineteenth century. These cities reflected the stage of technological development that delimited the spatial organization of the modern city, with its centralized pattern of urban development and its intense concentration of people and wealth.[6]

In this context, a heterogeneous urban public forged a new kind of culture. Streetcars, amusement parks, ballparks, parks, museums, world's fairs, department stores, nickelodeons, and, later on, the movies constituted the "new mass culture" that drew on available technologies to create a set of new sensations and experiences that satisfied the changing cultural appetites of an expanding urban public. Recently, a generation of urban cultural historians identified the contours of this new mass culture, emphasizing the ways in which it mirrored the transition from a Victorian cultural order that insisted upon the strict separation of classes, races, and sexes to a new cultural order that sanctioned promiscuous interactions among a heterogeneous assortment of urban strangers. The agglomeration of men and women from all classes and ethnicities, otherwise known as the crowd, within the city's venues of work and play created a "heterosocial" world of urban strangers that came to characterize urban public life well into the twentieth century.[7]

The inclusiveness of modern city culture, however, was predicated on the strict exclusion of African Americans and, to a lesser extent, other racial groups. European immigrants to the American city at the turn of the twentieth century converged on the shared spaces of work, housing, and leisure, but African Americans encountered rigid racial barriers that blocked their access to white neighborhoods and jobs in cities of both the North and the South. Their exclusion extended to the public venues of the new mass culture. Blacks sat in the balconies of movie theaters, just as they sat in the back of streetcars. The operators of amusement parks, nickelodeons, dance halls, and ballparks typically adopted a whites-only policy, forcing African Americans to pursue their appetite for diversion in separate and sometimes inferior cultural facilities. When African Americans did appear in such venues, it was generally through a set of vicious misrepresentations that emphasized the innate degeneracy of "darkies" and "coons." The cosmopolitan culture of the turn-of-the-century metropolis was thus achieved only by aggressively excluding and stereotyping African Americans and by upholding entrenched patterns of racial segregation. In short, the new mass culture reinforced a mutually constitutive relationship between *public* and *white*.[8]

A century later, however, the reconfiguration of the American city initiated the decline of both the new mass culture and its urban context and inaugurated a new paradigm of race and space. The New Deal and the subsequent outbreak of World War II profoundly unsettled the spatial and racial organization of American society. The intersection of technological innovations, government policies, demographic upheaval, and other factors linked not by causality but rather by coincidence anticipated the arrival of the postwar urban region, which did not fully materialize until the 1950s and 1960s. Suburbanization, a mode of urbanization in which cities extend outward rather than upward to accommodate the spatial appetites of homeowners, retailers, and industrialists, reached a pinnacle in the years between 1945 and 1970. During the 1950s, for example, suburbs grew at a rate ten times faster than that of central cities, while the nation's suburban population jumped from 35.1 to 75.6 million between 1950 and 1970.[9] Under the patronage of a federal government that subsidized residential and industrial decentralization through an elaborate set of policies, the modern industrial city and its concentrated panoply of factories, tenement houses, and streetcars began to give way to the "postindustrial" urban region and its scattered array of industrial parks, detached single-family homes, automobiles, and freeways.[10]

Postwar suburbanization sanctioned the formation of a new racial geography that spatialized a starker contrast between white and black. Jim Crow effectively blocked black access to public life at the turn of the century, but the wartime convergence of economic opportunities in urban centers incorporated nonwhite social groups into the public spaces of the American city on an unprecedented scale. In particular, World War II initiated yet another mass migration of African Americans into the nation's cities, arguably the most significant demographic shift of the twentieth century. Fleeing a legacy of poverty and racism in the South, millions of African Americans converged on urban centers in the Northeast, Midwest, and Far West, where the wartime economy was at its most vibrant. Black migrants to the cities met substantial hostility there: a spate of race riots during the early 1940s signaled the intense level of competition among racially diverse peoples in search of steady employment and affordable housing.[11]

If *black* became increasingly synonymous with *urban* during the war years and thereafter, suburban development after World War II sanctioned the formation of a new "white" identity. The gains won by labor groups during the 1930s and 1940s created the basis for a postwar truce between labor and capital, ensconcing workers and their families in the comforts of a thriving consumer economy that centered on suburban home ownership. Federal lending agencies such as the Veterans Administration and the Federal Housing Administration underwrote the largest mass-based opportunity for home ownership in national history. But as a racial privilege sustained by redlining, blockbusting, restrictive covenants, and municipal incorporation, as well as by outright violence, federally sponsored suburbanization removed an expanding category of "white" Americans from what deteriorated into inner-city reservations of racialized poverty.[12] The collusion of public policy and private practices enforced a spatial distinction between "black" cities and "white" suburbs and gave shape to what the Kerner Commission, a presidential commission appointed to assess the causes of the 1965 Watts Riots in Los Angeles, identified as "two societies, one black, one white—separate and unequal."[13]

Less than a decade after the Kerner Commission had issued its grave assessment of postwar segregation, George Clinton, the virtuoso leader of the theatrical funk ensemble Parliament, offered a more flavorful account of that same process. In 1975, Clinton wrote the song "Chocolate City" to construe black urbanization as a "takeover" of the nation's cities: "There's a lot of chocolate cites around. We've got Newark, we've got Gary. Somebody told me we've got L.A., but you're the capital, D.C." In what became his signature funk sound, Clinton delivered a wake-up call to white America to signal that it could not maintain its distance from black America much longer: "Movin' in and on ya, gainin' on ya! Can't you feel my breath, heh . . . All up around your neck, heh heh." Striking a chord of defiant pride, "Chocolate City" envisioned black urbanization as nothing less than a national insurrection led by James Brown, Aretha Franklin, and other luminaries of Afro-American culture. In contrast to the disparaging and often dehumanizing portraits of the racialized inner city issued by the nation's leading social scientists, "Chocolate City" asserts the strength of the black ghetto as a bulwark against the hostility of a racist society: "A chocolate city is no dream / It's my piece of the rock and I dig you, CC / God bless Chocolate City and its (gainin' on ya!) vanilla suburbs."[14]

"Chocolate City" reflects one discursive (and indeed subversive) response to the spatial and racial polarization that defined urban life after World War II, but there were many others. Whereas Parliament's hit provides a cultural clue to the urbanization of black identity after World War II, this book explores the cultural expressions that mirrored the suburbanization of white culture and consciousness during the postwar period. Through a tradition of racial segregation, chocolate cities have been present throughout various stages of urban history in the United States, but vanilla suburbs did not become a broadly inclusive way of life until the decades following World War II. Postwar suburbanization nurtured the development of a more expansive white identity, one that extended to various social groups who removed themselves from the racialized spaces of the inner city vis-à-vis home ownership. What role popular culture played in the formation of a suburban white identity, and how that identity was created, consumed, and contested by various social groups, is the subject of this book.[15]

As the civil rights movement gathered steam and the challenge to racial segregation inserted African Americans and other nonwhite social groups into the public spaces of industrial urbanism, a *new* "new mass culture" took shape, one that reflected and reinforced the burgeoning racial order of the postwar urban region. Movies, theme parks, freeways, ballparks, television, and shopping malls highlighted the cultural landscape of chocolate cities and vanilla suburbs and shaped the development of a racialized political culture in a period of intense social change. In the process of developing land on the perimeter of the metropolis, an expanding generation of suburban Americans exercised their preference for a landscape that epitomized homogeneity, containment, and predictability, one that marked a safe contrast to the heterosocial, unpredictable, and often dangerous cultural experiences of industrial urbanism. These values underlie the new spatial culture of suburbia: in enclosed theme parks that directed the movement and gaze of its public, in self-contained housing subdivisions planned according to the disciplined lines of the grid system, and in freeways that channeled the flow of traffic along a uniform line of movement, above and around the inner city.

The reconfiguration of race and space in postwar America and the accompanying transition from public to private modes of entertainment anticipated the formation of a new political culture that gestated in suburban Southern California as far back as the late 1940s. That seemingly apolitical sites such as theme parks, freeways, ballparks, and motion pictures evidenced a changing political sensibility becomes clearer in the following chapters, in part through the recurring presence of a man who spearheaded the assault on what is now commonly described as the New Deal order. In the midst of his political metamorphosis from New Deal liberal to tax-cutting conservative, Ronald Reagan mastered new media technologies to affiliate himself with the spectacles of Southern California's new "new mass culture." He appeared on live television to advocate the building of Dodger Stadium in the Chavez Ravine; he aided the House Un-American Activities Committee (HUAC) in its search for subversive influences in Hollywood; he emceed the televised ceremonies for the opening of Disneyland in 1955; and a recently completed freeway in suburban Los Angeles bears his name. In his thirty-year ascent to the White House, Reagan espoused patriarchy, privatization, patriotism, law and order, hard work, and self-help, modeling a new political subjectivity set against the tenets of New Deal liberalism and personifying the values incubated within the spaces wrought by suburbanization, urban renewal, and highway construction.[16]

Each chapter of this book explores an aspect of the new "new mass culture" to understand the formation of an inclusive suburban white identity after World War II and its political sensibility. Chapter 2 considers the setting: Los Angeles in the decades between 1940 and 1970. Though Los Angeles harbored its own versions of the new mass culture that dated back to the turn of the century, the region's accelerated pattern of suburban development after World War II sanctioned a new set of cultural institutions that marked a clear departure from, if not an outright rejection of, the heterosocial experiences of industrial urbanism. For several reasons, Los Angeles provides an ideal context for studying the post–World War II formation of (sub)urban popular culture. First, although suburbanization profoundly transformed the nature of urban life throughout the nation, Los Angeles debuted as the "it" city of postwar America, accommodating a vast influx of newcomers and garnering a disproportionate share of federal investments. In the decades following World War II, Los Angeles became the prototypical example of the postwar urban region, exhibiting a broader pattern of Sunbelt urbanization taking shape in the South and Far West. Second, the unique social mix of Los Angeles, conditioned by its proximity to Mexico and the Pacific Ocean, provides a fascinating context for understanding how diverse peoples—midwesterners, Jews, Italians, "Okies" and "Arkies," Mexicans, Chinese, Japanese, Native Americans, African Americans—confronted the racial binary that shaped the reality and representation of the postwar urban region. Third, the rise of Los Angeles in the early decades of the twentieth century coincided with the national ascendance of the new mass culture, while the development of a powerful "culture industry" profoundly shaped the texture of urban life in twentieth-century Southern California. These factors sited an emerging political culture that upheld a privatized, consumer-oriented subjectivity premised upon patriarchy, whiteness, and suburban home ownership.

Chapters 3 and 4 explore the dialectic between inner-city decline and suburban growth through the lens of popular culture. Just as whiteness has historically defined itself relative to blackness, the cultural manifestations of vanilla suburbs relied on the lurid imagery of chocolate cities.[17] Chapter 3 explores the relationship between urban identity and cinematic representation, focusing primarily on representations of Los Angeles in film noir. Although noir's seductive style and aesthetic innovations have drawn much attention from film scholars, few have situated noir in a sociohistorical framework. As white flight and industrial decentralization denuded the physical and social landscape of the inner city, Hollywood marketed spectacles of urban decline as mass entertainment. Set amid the littered streets, dark alleys, and decaying buildings of the downtown, film noir represented the postwar crisis of the public city through its narratives of social disorder and psychological malaise. Translated literally as "black film," film noir anticipated the racial turn that informed the white suburban backlash against New Deal liberalism in the 1960s. Its implicit and explicit racial connotations dramatized popular anxieties about the "blackening" of the postwar American city and underscored the imperative for what became a central tenet in the ideology of the New Right: law and order. This chapter concludes with a consideration of the urban science fiction film, which posited a menacing vision of urban chaos. Its portrait of aliens invading and annihilating Los Angeles alludes to the racialized "imagination of disaster" that informed popular perceptions of urban life during the postwar period.[18]

If noir dramatized the postwar crisis of the public city, Disneyland encapsulated the utopian aspirations of the suburban society, which brings us to chapter 4. The amusement park marked a cultural focal point of industrial urbanism, but Walt Disney reinvented it based on his dissatisfaction with Coney Island and its generation of amusement parks. Disney's selection of Anaheim as the site for building Disneyland suited the burgeoning culture of suburban whiteness that during the postwar period inundated places such as Orange County, a region that favored the political likes of Ronald Reagan and Barry Goldwater during the 1960s. For a suburban public deeply unfamiliar with its new environment, yet seeking alternatives to the modern city and its culture, Disneyland provided answers to troubling questions about identity, community, and city that preoccupied postwar Americans. Through its emphasis upon race as a central "theme," its regimented ordering of space, its insistence on family entertainment, and its privileging of a small-town midwestern sensibility, Disneyland repudiated the slums of noir imagination, supplied a usable past, present, and future for Southern

California's transient and mobile population, and modeled popular idealizations of race and space in the age of white flight.

The remaining chapters take up the simultaneous debut of other cultural institutions of the postwar urban region, exploring how they embodied some of the more complex negotiations that ensued in that decentralized social landscape. If Disneyland and film noir reflected and reinforced the formation of a suburban white consciousness, the construction of Dodger Stadium and the implementation of a freeway system revealed the subtle tensions embedded within that process. Chapter 5 explores the arrival of the Brooklyn Dodgers in Los Angeles in 1957 and the subsequent construction of Dodger Stadium in the Chavez Ravine to consider the relationship between popular culture and another salient feature of postwar urbanization: urban renewal. Like suburbanization, urban renewal hastened the racial and spatial polarization of postwar Southern California, and the imposition of Dodger Stadium upon a working-class Chicano community nourished the regional development of a racialized political culture. The westward migration of the Brooklyn Dodgers signified the shifting paradigms of race and space in postwar America, as racial succession dislodged the Brooklyn Dodgers from Ebbets Field and racial dislocation under the guise of urban renewal placed them in Los Angeles' Chavez Ravine. As the nation's first racially integrated ball club, the Dodgers elicited the patronage of various racial and ethnic groups, but the substitution of Dodger Stadium for Ebbets Field reveals not only the westward drift of cultural capital, but also how the spatial culture of postwar suburbia redefined the public experience of spectator sports as well as that of the inner city itself.

The substitution of Dodger Stadium for Ebbets Field was part of a larger transformation in the experience of public life, not unlike the way in which the postwar displacement of streetcars by freeways introduced a new way of moving through the city. Chapter 6 begins with a brief consideration of the disappearance of the streetcar from the streets of Los Angeles during the 1930s and 1940s and then considers its substitution by a unified network of freeways. A chapter on freeways in a book about popular culture may seem anomalous, but, designed to accommodate popular demands for autonomous mobility, the freeway became a defining cultural experience of the postwar urban region. Unlike the streetcar, which promoted contact among urban dwellers and provided a window onto the city's distinct neighborhoods, the freeway severed the commuter from his urban context and furthered the distance, literally and figuratively, between chocolate cities and vanilla suburbs. The freeway's production, however, elicited a complex reaction from an expanding public. Within the expansive terrain of the dominant culture, the freeway joined theme parks, shopping malls, and housing developments as a centerpiece of a new suburban good life, celebrated for its progress and modernity. Working-class communities of color, however, utilized a more meager set of cultural resources to posit a countervision of freeways, which prefigured the outrage that informed the social movements among blacks and Chicanos during the 1960s.

These cultural shifts—from Coney Island to Disneyland, Ebbets Field to Dodger Stadium, streetcars to freeways—paralleled two other cultural developments that are beyond the scope of this study. First, television rose as a powerful cultural phenomenon during the postwar period, and it fit squarely within the spatial culture of postwar suburbia. Recent scholarship has situated television in the cultural context of postwar America, and this study draws upon those insights. As postwar suburbanization encapsulated American consumers within the private space of the home, television offered a simulation of public experience minus the risks that accompanied an evening out on the town. Moreover, by placing an electronic box at the center of domestic space, television reinforced the cultural emphasis on the nuclear family that resonated throughout the cultural milieu of postwar America. To reiterate Marshall McLuhan's insistence that "the medium is the message," the private experience of watching television reinforced the postwar retreat from public life not unlike the way in which theme parks, freeways, and ballparks removed suburban audiences from the landscape of daily life in the city.[19]

Second, the debut of the shopping mall after World War II introduced a new consumer realm that removed shoppers from the city's bustle. Between the late nineteenth and mid-twentieth centuries, the experience of shopping underwent a major transformation similar to that explored in the following chapters. The introduction of the department store during the late nineteenth century reinforced the centralization of consumer culture, as retailers concentrated their activity within the central business districts of American cities. The advent of suburban shopping malls, however, followed the accelerated pattern of decentralization of urban life after World War II and weakened the commercial life of the nation's inner cities. Shopping malls, like theme parks, offered a more particularized notion of community that appealed to white suburban consumers. As with the cultural institutions explored in this book, Lizabeth Cohen argues that the shopping mall "sought perhaps to contradictorily legitimize itself as a true community center and to define that community in exclusionary socio-economic and racial terms."[20]

Although television and shopping malls are not the focus of separate chapters, their presence in the making of postwar popular culture is referenced throughout this book, which emphasizes the overlapping experiences of decentralized urbanization. Although various aspects of the history of theme parks, films, ballparks, and freeways have been explored elsewhere, they have not been considered as part of a larger (sub)urban cultural system in which each constituent part implies a relationship with the others. Viewed alongside one another, the seemingly disparate cultural institutions of the decentralized urban region provide a window onto how the postwar American public experienced and understood the manifestation of chocolate cities and vanilla suburbs in multifaceted ways.[21]

WHITE CITY, WHITE CULTURE, WHITE CONSCIOUSNESS

To a certain extent, the following chapters convey the genealogy of American popular culture as they articulate the many "family resemblances" between the institutions of the new "new mass culture" and their antecedents. An important precedent that illuminates the relationship between urban form and popular culture is Chicago's World's Columbian Exposition of 1893, more familiarly known as "White City." Scholars of White City brought the insights of cultural history to urban history and, in doing so, provided a framework for understanding the "mythography" of the city— a set of cultural representations that present an idealized portrait of urban life through architecture, literature, photography, and film.[22] By exploring the myths, spectacles, and fantasies of urban life that resonate throughout the history of American culture—from John Winthrop's "city upon a hill" to Daniel Burnham's White City to Universal Studio's City Walk—urban historians can begin to understand how urban practices, policies, and politics are entangled in a web of cultural convictions.[23]

White City debuted in Chicago in 1893, and it attained national prominence amid the westward drift of American culture and society, but its latter-day incarnation shifted further west to Los Angeles, where national resources and global capital gravitated during the postwar period. Like White City, Disneyland, Dodger Stadium, freeways, and movies offered a set of spatial fantasies that asserted what city life should (and should not) be and upheld traditional models of social order after an extended duration of economic turmoil and global conflict. Unlike White City, however, the fantasy was not confined to the fairgrounds. Freeways insinuated themselves into the daily lives of every Southern Californian who possessed an automobile. They debuted in miniature as one of Disneyland's many attractions.

Main Street, USA, became a template for a new generation of suburban shopping malls, while Hollywood crafted its noir look upon the streets of downtown Los Angeles. Whereas White City contrasted sharply with the disorder of the "real" Chicago, Disneyland, Dodger Stadium, Hollywood, and freeways modeled a new sociospatial order that took shape along the suburban periphery of Southern California urban centers.[24]

White City also had its sideshow counterpart, the Midway Plaisance, which offered a dizzying array of carnivalesque distractions as a concession to the public's appetite for fun and amusement. The stark juxtaposition of the White City and the Midway symbolized a key tension within American culture at the turn of the twentieth century, when the Victorian insistence upon uplift and refinement began to give way to the titillating sensations of the new mass culture.[25] Cultural historians generally regard the Midway as a harbinger of a twentieth-century mass culture that eventually displaced the didactic model of urban culture associated with the Victorian metropolis, but the cultural institutions of the postwar urban region revealed how elements of both White City and the Midway could be channeled into a singular cultural experience, synthesizing disciplined order and exuberant chaos, didactic idealizations and physical sensation. Walt Disney, for example, made certain compromises in response to the public's craving for sensational distractions, but he avoided the rampant sensuality of the new mass culture by subordinating the carnivalesque within a spatial regime dominated by more earnest ideals such as progress, patriotism, and patriarchy.

By subsuming the Midway's ruckus within the White City's order, Disney and his counterparts helped to resurrect a racialized vision of suburban modernity, one that dominated the promotional imagery of Southern California as far back as the Progressive era. Progressive reformers such as Dana Bartlett idealized Los Angeles as "the Better City," positing a vision of the young metropolis as both a suburban retreat from the polyglot congestion of the modern city and a more respectable alternative to the degraded culture of industrial urbanism. Much to their chagrin, however, Southern California's growth during the Progressive era coincided with the denouement of a new consumer culture that emphasized leisure, gratification, and sensual experience, while the rise of Hollywood as that culture's dominant institution brought to Los Angeles the corruptions and excesses that typified modern life.[26] Nathanael West made this shrewd observation in his 1939 novel, *The Day of the Locust*, which presented a caustic indictment of how the pretension and moral laxity of Hollywood had poisoned Southern California's cultural milieu.

West's bleak vision of Hollywood and Los Angeles prefigured the arrival of film noir, which tendered a cinematic eulogy to the Progressives' notion of a "Better City" in Southern California, but the postwar suburban boom offered a second chance for such a vision. Initially, suburbanization in Southern California remained the privilege of elites and the city's burgeoning middle class, but the decades following World War II witnessed mass suburbanization on an unprecedented scale and rekindled earlier aspirations to a social order based on class harmony, suburban respectability, and racial homogeneity.[27] For the engineers and entrepreneurs of the new "new mass culture," Southern California's suburban boom signaled the opportunity to finally realize the sociospatial order that men such as Dana Bartlett had only dreamt about. No less hostile to cities like New York and Chicago, no less suspicious of their culture, and no less obsessed with order, respectability, and tradition than turn-of-the-century Progressives, Walt Disney and his ilk undertook the responsibility of restoring Southern California's "Better City."

Popular culture played no small part in that effort. *Popular culture* has somewhat different connotations than *mass culture*, but within the history of the United States, both implicate the market as the mediator between cultural producers and the consuming public.[28] The problem with popular culture—especially in the Southern California context—is not its definition but its interpretation. How the market has shaped the regional culture is the subject of much debate and some distortion. A leftist tradition finds clues to the absolute power of capital everywhere in Southern California's built environment. One variant of this perspective regards the city as a junkyard of cheap commodities ruled by the developer's imperative to build according to the proverbial bottom line, while another holds that ruling-class hegemony is safely guarded in the city's militarized landscape. Whether it is seen as the Frankfurt School's administered world, Herbert Marcuse's one-dimensional society, or Mike Davis's carceral city, Los Angeles provides the Left with a textbook example of capitalist domination.[29] Beginning in the 1960s, however, a new generation of urban theorists, most notably Reyner Banham, introduced a much different perspective, drawing inspiration from Robert Venturi's famous maxim that "we can all learn from Las Vegas." Banham and his disciples shed a more appreciative light upon Los Angeles, discerning a democratic brand of urbanism that catered to popular tastes and values. The unbridled course of the market economy, it followed, bestowed a greater freedom of choice on the consumer, obliterating established cultural hierarchies and validating vernacular traditions.[30]

Both perspectives entail their own pitfalls, yet both convey some important truths about Los Angeles and its culture that make their way into the following chapters. Overemphasizing capitalist hegemony ignores the participatory process by which consumers shape the production of culture through the very act of consumption and negates the possibilities for resistance to and the refashioning of mass-produced objects. On the other hand, reading Los Angeles entirely in the vernacular invites a false optimism that misinterprets *popular* as *democratic* and overlooks the hierarchies of power embedded in all cultural forms.[31] The mass cultural landscapes explored in the following chapters reveal popular values, attitudes, and reactions, and their very popularity suggests a shared set of assumptions among producers and consumers about the identity of the city and its public. In this capacity, the success of Walt Disney, Walter O'Malley, and Ronald Reagan as men of their time (and place) rested upon their ability, as well as their privilege, to market a set of values that appealed to an expanding suburban public in search of new meanings by which to identify themselves and their unfamiliar environment.

But on what grounds? Southern California's pattern of suburban decentralization during the postwar period reinforced race as a common denominator in the dialectic between the production and consumption of the new "new mass culture." It enabled Walt Disney to inundate Disneyland with stereotypical representations of mammies and Indian "savages." It allowed Walter O'Malley to build his stadium atop a working-class Chicano community. It granted the imposition of freeways in the middle of expanding ghettos and barrios, and it empowered men such as Ronald Reagan to mobilize white suburban homeowners as a political constituency. The whiteness of Southern California's version of White City was both literal and figurative, and it took shape through a set of cultural practices and material processes that birthed a new paradigm of race and space in the postwar urban region. Whereas the planners of the Columbian Exposition sought to sublimate the class tensions that plagued industrial urbanism in an architectural syntax of order and harmony, the cultural custodians of postwar Los Angeles innovated a spatial order that obfuscated, albeit momentarily, the simmering racial tensions of the postwar urban region.

Typically, *white flight* describes a structural process by which postwar suburbanization helped the racial resegregation of the United States, dividing presumably white suburbs from concentrations of racialized poverty.[32] But the cultural corollary to this development has been overlooked. White flight entailed a renegotiation of racial and spatial identities, implying a cultural process in which an expanding middle class of myriad ethnic backgrounds came to discover itself as white. Unlike previous accounts of white flight, which take for granted a broad category of white people who suburbanized after World War II, this book utilizes recent advances in critical race theory, showing how a heterogeneous public embraced a classless but deeply racialized fantasy of suburban whiteness, and focusing upon the texts and spectacles that licensed broader access to that newfangled identity.[33]

White flight structured the contours of postwar popular culture as a kind of master narrative, and no city seemed better suited for that structure than Los Angeles. Like New York, Los Angeles evidenced the familiar pattern by which white ethnic groups abandoned older inner-city neighborhoods for newer suburban communities. Jews, for example, who initially established themselves in the city's Eastside neighborhoods during the 1920s, moved to newly developed portions of the more affluent Westside a generation later.[34] Unlike New York, however, whose white population actually declined during the 1950s, Los Angeles garnered an influx of westering Americans during the '40s, '50s, and '60s, and the city itself became a suburban refuge for those in search of more prosperous alternatives to the modern city and its culture. As the dominant icons of a Southern California way of life, Hollywood, Disneyland, Dodger Stadium, and the freeway repudiated the slums of the noir past and was a birthplace of the culture of suburban whiteness that enveloped a generation of diverse Americans who sought their place in the California sun.

Recent explorations in the history of white racial formation describe the process by which ethnic and racial identities change over time, but how such identities change across space remains relatively unknown. The racially and ethnically heterogeneous culture of the industrial metropolis at the turn of the twentieth century, for example, encouraged European immigrants to imagine new identities. Whatever parochial and regional loyalties survived the trans-Atlantic voyage, they soon coexisted alongside newly constructed national self-definitions. In New York, Boston, Chicago, and elsewhere, people from County Galway and County Kildare became Irishmen; those from Mecklenburg and Wurttemberg became Germans; and those from Calabria and Campania became Italians.[35] But what happened to these broader identities in the course of moving from the Atlantic to the Pacific? Were they broadened even further in the course of westward migration? Did the distinctions among Italians, Jews, Germans, and Irish endure in cities such as Los Angeles, with its multiracial mix of peoples from Mexico, Asia, and the American South? That the Jewish film magnate Jack Warner could maintain a staunch whites-only hiring policy at Warner Brothers, for example, suggests how Southern California's brand of whiteness was sought by Europe's most denigrated ethnicities.

The reassertion of space in critical social theory designates how social identities are situated within a set of spatial practices.[36] In the period of white flight, the reorganization of social space reconfigured American race relations, a process with as yet unresolved consequences. White flight did not extinguish the traditions, values, and practices of distinctive Euro-American cultures, but it *privatized* them, secluding them within the detached and cellular spaces of the suburban landscape. While the streets of the modern industrial city provided a conspicuous setting for public expressions of social and sexual identity among ethnically distinct groups of European immigrants and their descendants, the interior settings of the postwar urban region—homes, shopping malls, theme parks, freeways, automobiles—minimized the visibility of (or perhaps necessity for) such expressions. White flight entailed an exchange of the heterosocial public world of the modern city, in which Jewish, Italian, and Irish immigrants imparted distinct markings of their culture to the urban landscape, for the mass-produced, uniform, and what some critics decried as monotonous landscapes of the 1950s suburbs. In that process, the landscapes of American cities became identified less by ethnic heterogeneity and more by the racial distinctions that characterized chocolate cities and vanilla suburbs.

This book combines spatial and racial ways of thinking to articulate the complex relationship between racial segregation and racial representation. Exactly what role did the Other play in the postwar formation of a white suburban identity? Of course, he upheld dominant racial hierarchies through his savage, subservient, or otherwise inferior representation, and his presence in Southern California's new "new mass culture" recalled the myriad ethnic notions that white Americans have adopted in their claim to whiteness. He did more than that, however. A new generation of race-conscious cultural historians has begun to illuminate the ways in which images of the Other helped to resolve some of the ideological dilemmas that accompanied the process of becoming white. If, as Richard Dyer argues, whiteness "is emptiness, absence, denial or even a kind of death," racial representations in postwar popular culture often served to fill some kind of spiritual vacancy or emotional void in the soulless landscapes of suburbia. In an age of organization men and lonely crowds, the Other and its representation could bring a modicum of relief, perhaps even comfort, to a rapidly expanding white middle class uncertain about its new identities and communities.[37]

In the chapters that follow, therefore, we shall discover the Janus-faced role the Other played in a burgeoning white suburban consciousness: from "savage" Indians posing a stark contrast to the progress of modern freeways, to "authentic" Indians greeting visitors to Disneyland; from black "mammies" serving pancakes in restaurants mimicking Southern plantations, to black athletes dazzling white audiences with their athletic skills. Popular culture in the age of white flight also voyeuristically dwelled on the spaces of racial Otherness. Mysterious Chinatowns, African jungles, Mexican pueblos, and decrepit slums held a distinct fascination for an expanding category of white Americans who ensconced themselves within the racially homogeneous spaces of suburbia. The sum of these representations does not present a tidy portrait of white hegemony, but rather exhibits a range of conflicting emotions—admiration, curiosity, envy, fear, contempt, condescension—that people felt about the changes that engulfed postwar American society.

Race, of course, cannot be understood apart from other social configurations such as gender and class. Elaine Tyler May has illustrated the domestic implications of containment, a principle that guided American politics and culture during the Cold War. If film noir successfully indicted the American city for its failure to contain the subversive energies of women, blacks, and Communists, then suburban development provided an insular space where such energies could be kept at bay. As urban modernity had weakened traditional racial and sexual boundaries, postwar suburban development reinstated the gendered distinctions between private and public life that had withered under the forces of urbanization, and it created a market for a new brand of family entertainment that surfaced at places such as Disneyland and Dodger Stadium. The following chapters illuminate how the cultural configuration of suburban whiteness upheld the patriarchal white nuclear family as a social ideal and how this ideal accompanied popular notions of racial hierarchy.[38]

Suburban popular culture also included a powerful fantasy of classlessness that supported representations of racial and sexual hierarchy. For the cultural custodians of Southern California's postwar urban region, like their Progressive predecessors, class tensions were anathema to their conception of the American Way. A wave of labor unrest during the mid-1940s unsettled any aspirations to class harmony in the United States, but the postwar democratization of suburban home ownership sanctioned the rise of an expanding white workforce that enjoyed the fruits of an expanding consumer society. In the consumer fantasies entertained by a new generation of suburban homeowners, class and class conflict disappeared from the popular vocabulary. Although a handful of intellectuals decried the development of a "mass society" during the postwar period, Disneyland, Dodger Stadium, and freeways accommodated an even broader mass of consumers, proffering an illusion of classlessness that not only obscured the distinctions between wealthy suburbs and working-class suburbs, but also obfuscated the darker shade of an inner-city working class that subsequently turned to race as a rallying point for social justice.[39]

As the following chapters illustrate, the classless fantasy that underlay the construction of suburban popular culture not only focused on a shining vision of suburban homeownership, but also fixated on a distinctly noir vision of the slums. Film noir, of course, offered the most tangible representation of the urban slum in postwar popular culture, but streetcars, amusement parks, and nickelodeons all comprised a broader "slum tradition" in the suburban imagination. They provided a vivid and often unnerving counterpoint to the disciplined landscapes of postwar suburbia; they embodied the potential for subversion, disorder, and social breakdown; and they offered a metaphor for what was left behind in the age of white flight.

Culture, like war, is politics by other means, and as race surfaced as a primary basis of political conflict in Southern California and, ultimately, the United States, it attained a heightened saliency in the representational realm of popular culture. By the postwar period, Los Angeles had finally shed its notorious identity as an open-shop town, but the racial violence that had marred the regional landscape since the Mexican-American War only intensified. Though a long history of racist practices precipitated the formation of a black ghetto in postwar Los Angeles, the Watts riots of 1965 brought a violent climax to the region's "racial turn," in which Southern California's political culture evidenced a primary struggle between urban nonwhite peoples and suburban white homeowners. Conditioned by such racial distinctions, postwar suburbanization spawned a social movement based on what George Lipsitz describes as a "possessive investment in whiteness," in which white home ownership became the basis of a new political identity that materialized in suburban Southern California after World War II.[40]

The idea that culture harbors a set of myths that have powerful meanings and real effects rests upon a set of theoretical formulations that support the following exploration of urban development in Southern California in the decades following World War II. As a set of collective representations, popular culture in the age of white flight maintained a symbolic world of meaning that nurtured the development of a white suburban consciousness. Such consciousness, in turn, provided the basis for the development of an "anxious, tightfisted conservatism" that revolved around a sequence of racialized social issues.[41] This political constituency practiced the kind of identity politics typically associated with African Americans and Chicanos, but white suburban homeowners predicated their struggle against fair housing legislation, busing, immigration, welfare, and affirmative action on the very whiteness of their communities. Materializing within the new spaces wrought by urban renewal and suburbanization, the new "new mass culture" provided a mythic space where this constituency could first imagine itself into being.[42]

Ultimately, it is the struggle to dominate, not the domination itself, that provides our analytical focus. Politics, whether in city halls or dance halls, connotes struggle, and popular culture in the age of white flight encompassed a set of struggles to define the identity of the postwar urban region and its scattered communities. Urban planners, civic officials, corporate executives, law enforcement, media moguls, housing developers, suburban families, and inner-city minorities (at least those who comprised a "minority" back then) are among the competing social interests that populate the following narrative, and their clashing efforts to define, defend, or defy the hegemony of suburban whiteness reverberated throughout Southern California's sprawling cultural landscape. Using popular culture as evidence about the sociospatial transformation of postwar American society offers a glimpse into the more subtle interplay of conflict, contestation, and even consensus, allowing for a greater degree of complexity than that which informs dominant accounts of Southern California's distinct brand of (sub)urbanism. In the tradition of Carey McWilliams and Mike Davis, the following chapters acknowledge the city's uneven distribution of power and emphasize how such inequalities structured the reality and representation of postwar Los Angeles. But the exertion of power from above always incites resistance from below, and the presence of alternative visions, discourses, and subjectivities within postwar popular culture illuminates the highly contested cultural terrain of the postwar urban region. The dynamic tension between domination and resistance—as well as between conflict and consensus—has been largely absent from historical and contemporary perspectives on Los Angeles, but as the city emerged as the world capital of popular culture during the postwar period, such tensions surfaced in striking and unexpected ways.

2   The Nation's "White Spot"

Racializing Postwar Los Angeles

Los Angeles is not what it was supposed to be. At the dawn of the twenty-first century, Los Angeles ranks among the largest and most polyglot concentrations of humankind anywhere in the world. Sheltering the nation's largest population of Mexicans, Koreans, Vietnamese, Salvadorans, and Thais, Los Angeles has become a cultural kaleidoscope of global proportions. Its Little Saigon, Little Tokyo, Little India, Little Armenia, Koreatown, and Thai Town, as well as its urban and suburban Chinatowns, anchor immigrant newcomers to the region and bring the cosmopolitan flavor of London, New York, Tokyo, and Hong Kong to Southern California. Any lingering complaints about Los Angeles' reputation for shallow suburban conformity are muted by the cacophony of some 150 languages. In our age of alleged multiculturalism, Southern Californians can finally bask in the self-congratulatory paeans to their city as the world's premier global city.

This was not, however, the case a century ago. At the outset of the twentieth century, Los Angeles entertained a set of racialized fantasies that depicted the region as a southwestern outpost of white supremacy. Local boosters ensured that their version of the city myth appealed to whites only and acknowledged the presence of nonwhite peoples only to the extent of their capacity to provide cheap but invisible labor. Such efforts operated alongside promotions of Southern California as a refuge from the "immigrant problem" that plagued other cities, and the earliest patterns of decentralized urbanization signaled the opportunity to create lily-white neighborhoods through racially exclusive practices such as deed restrictions and zoning policies. Los Angeles indeed had its immigrant populations, but city and state officials concocted elaborate but ultimately ineffective "Americanization programs" to minimize the region's social and cultural diversity. Through the combined efforts of housing developers, Progressive reformers, and local boosters, Southern California sustained the development of a white city well into the first three decades of the twentieth century.[1]

World War II, however, unsettled any regional aspirations to white supremacy. The presence of a vital Japanese community threatened a regional sense of wartime security, while a disaffected yet more assertive generation of Chicano youths paraded their distinctive cultural styles before the urban public. More significant, and more challenging to the regional insistence on white supremacy, however, the war initiated the dramatic expansion of Southern California's black community. Blacks were by no means absent from Los Angeles prior to 1940, but the conspicuous presence of a growing black population during the war years and its rapid growth after the war significantly enhanced the region's racial diversity. The early 1940s unleashed what Carey McWilliams identified as a "racial revolution" upon Southern California, dashing once and for all any hope for the realization of a white city in the region.[2]

Or did it? This chapter surveys the social, political, and economic frameworks that structured the formation of a new "new mass culture," one that offered a whitened alternative to the blackened spaces of industrial urbanism. Southern California's new spatial culture took shape under the aegis of accelerated suburbanization and invasive urban renewal programs and effected a virtual "sorting out" of the regional population by race. While such developments wielded a strange new urban configuration that initially baffled planners and the public alike, suburbanization and urban renewal ultimately sanctioned the formation of a sociospatial order that reified the contrast between chocolate cities and vanilla suburbs in Southern California and heightened the salience of race in the regional culture. Against this backdrop, a suburban popular culture materialized, positing a racialized vision of the city as "the nation's white spot" and as the very image of "whiteness, flatness, and spread."[3] Ultimately, we shall discover, this vision flickered momentarily during the post–World War II period, yet lasted long enough to incite a profound shift in the course of American politics and culture.

THE BETTER CITY: A BLUEPRINT FOR RACE AND SPACE IN PROGRESSIVE LOS ANGELES

Key to understanding the cultural formation of a white city in postwar Los Angeles is Southern California's particular legacy of race relations. Since the U.S. conquest of California in 1848, civic boosters and public officials have struggled to overcome their self-consciousness about Los Angeles' Mexican heritage by emphasizing a regional tradition of white supremacy. Joseph Widney, an early president of the University of Southern California, argued in *Race Life of the Aryan Peoples* (1907) that Los Angeles was destined to become the world capital of Aryan supremacy, and Abbot Kinney, a speculator and developer who established the region's first theme park at Venice Beach, crusaded for Anglo-Saxon racial purity through eugenics. The most compelling image of whiteness in Southern California, however, was what Carey McWilliams first identified as the "Spanish Fantasy Heritage," a romanticized vision of the city's Hispano past that masked the brutalities of a racialized conquest. For a brief moment at the turn of the twentieth century, such cultural endeavors suited a city with a rapidly expanding Anglo population and helped to distinguish Los Angeles from older polyglot cities that teemed with "un-American" immigrants.[4]

Southern California's myth of a white city had its variations. Beginning in the late nineteenth century, the migrants who populated American Los Angeles were not Europeans, but white midwesterners removed from their European roots who sought refuge from the drudgery of rural life. Between 1910 and 1930, Americans born outside California contributed three-quarters of the region's demographic growth. The midwestern flavor of the regional culture drew on the influx of Americans from Kansas, Nebraska, Iowa, Indiana, Illinois, and Missouri, who established state societies that offered cultural life preservers for thousands of uprooted midwesterners. Of course, the "midwestern myth" of Los Angeles in the early decades of the twentieth century obscured the region's social diversity, but it did so by promoting an image of the city as the bastion of middlebrow, middle-class, midwestern whiteness.[5]

The Progressive era reinforced the "whitening" of the regional culture and society. Unlike urban reformers in other cities who struggled against both immigrant labor groups and powerful corporate interests to implement social and political reform, the Los Angeles Progressives readily assumed power in an open-shop city that did not teem with immigrant populations and agitated workers. Nonetheless, Southern California at the turn of the twentieth century harbored the growth of racial and ethnic communities that challenged the Progressives' melting-pot vision of an Anglo American civic culture. Against the city's growing Japanese, Mexican, and African American communities, Los Angeles Progressives supported an array of measures designed to ensure racial and ethnic homogeneity. Sharing a prevalent antipathy to Asians in turn-of-the-century California, Progressive reformers in Los Angeles generally favored restrictions on immigration, including the Alien Land Act of 1913 and the Immigration Act of 1924. African Americans were generally excluded from the Progressive agenda, as exemplified by the exclusion of black women from the Los Angeles Women's Suffrage League, while the city's burgeoning Mexican population incited the creation of a set of Americanization programs by which foreigners were expected to shed their cultural differences and assimilate into the mainstream of social and cultural life.[6]

The Los Angeles Progressives situated their ambition for racial and ethnic homogeneity within a spatial vision that would distinguish their city from its older urban counterparts. While the conspicuous presence of immigrant and racialized groups in New York, Chicago, and San Francisco reinforced a growing perception of cities as bastions of cultural diversity and social mixing, Los Angeles Progressives recognized the region's capacity for suburban development as a "whiter" alternative to the polyglot congestion of the modern city. No better exposition of the Progressives' racialized suburban vision of Los Angeles emerged at the outset of the twentieth century than Dana Bartlett's *The Better City*. Bartlett, who came to Los Angeles in 1908 as a social-gospel minister/reformer, wrote *The Better City* to assert his vision of Los Angeles as a suburban retreat from the "noise and rush of modern commercialism," designed for "a people within whose veins run the red blood of the hardy Northmen." Praising the region's hospitable climate, Bartlett recognized a "tendency [toward] open and not to[o] crowded quarters," where the "laying out of new subdivisions far out beyond the city limits makes cheap and desirable home sites obtainable for a multitude of working men."[7]

Closely linked to the Progressives' vision of suburban homogeneity was an emphasis on family and domestic life. In cities throughout the nation, Progressive reform coalitions identified the family and home as bulwarks against the corrupting forces of urban modernity, and in Southern California, local Progressive reformers sought to implement a more "perfect family life" through suburban decentralization. Bartlett's vision of Los Angeles as a "city of homes" and a "city without slums" would provide a suitable environment for "only healthy, happy families." The California bungalow came to symbolize Progressive aspirations to white suburban domesticity. To reinforce their efforts to create a family-friendly environment, Los Angeles Progressives also passed a series of antivice measures between 1909 and 1915, which targeted the degrading influences of alcohol, gambling, and prostitution on Southern California's burgeoning civic culture. With some mockery, Willard Huntington Wright associated these efforts with a small-town earnestness that defined the ethos of Progressive Los Angeles. In Wright's view, Los Angeles was created by the

> rural pietist obsessed with the spirit of village fellowship, of suburban respectability. . . . The inhabitants of Los Angeles are culled mainly from the smaller cities of the Middle West—"leading citizens" from Wichita; honorary pall bearers from Emmetsburg; Good Templares from Sedalia; honest Spinsters from Grundy Center. . . . These good folks brought with them a complete stock of rural beliefs, pieties, superstitions, and habits. . . . Everyone is interested in everyone else. Snooping is the popular pastime, gossiping the popular practice.[8]

With its emphasis on domesticity, class harmony, and racial and ethnic homogeneity, the brand of "suburban respectability" that dominated the Progressives' vision of Los Angeles also included an ambition to achieve material progress. Despite their adherence to some aspects of an older Victorian social code, Progressives did not want to turn back the clock. Rather, they maintained aspirations to civic development that reflected a most material conception of progress. Bartlett lauded the industrious spirit in Los Angeles that produced streets, railroads, harbors, and other amenities of modern civilization. Like his Progressive counterparts in Los Angeles, Bartlett equated growth with progress but kept faith that progress could ensue without the moral corruption that seemed endemic to city life. "It is well to remember that the desire for mere wealth and outward greatness has proved the ruin of many a city," Bartlett cautioned, but his exhortation of civic development in turn-of-the-century Los Angeles conveyed his belief that material progress and moral uplift were compatible and that the fusion of these ideals was the key to creating a "better Los Angeles."[9]

Because of Southern California's distance from European points of entry into the United States and because of its conspicuous and enduring Hispano legacy, the promotion of Los Angeles during the Progressive era reflected a racial project that rendered the city's Spanish and Mexican past as a touristic fantasy packaged for mass consumption and targeted the city's racial and ethnic groups as candidates for either total assimilation or outright exclusion. This racial vision of Los Angeles encompassed both a moral repudiation of the sensual pleasures of urban life and civic commitment to infrastructural growth and material progress. Such ideals suited the decentralized patterns of growth beginning to take shape in the region, and, with limited but substantial success, Los Angeles Progressives pursued a racialized vision of suburban modernity that defined popular notions of Los Angeles well into the 1920s. The following decades, however, profoundly challenged that vision and threatened the prospects for making Los Angeles a white city.

THE SOUTHLAND SWINGS: INDUSTRIAL URBANISM
DURING THE DEPRESSION AND BEYOND

By the 1930s, the notion of Los Angeles as the "seaport of Iowa" clashed with the increasingly multicultural reality of the city. Racial segregation was present throughout every stage of Southern California's development, but by drawing racially and ethnically diverse peoples to the region, the industrialization of the regional economy during the second quarter of the twentieth century reinforced the heterosociality of public life and undermined the Progressives' effort to create a racially and ethnically homogeneous society. Throughout the 1930s and into the 1940s, Southern California sustained the development of a New Deal political culture, which coalesced in public spaces such as factories, street fronts, streetcars, nightclubs, amusement parks, ethnic neighborhoods, community centers, and parks. Ironically, however, while the region's New Deal moment cultivated the sort of heterosocial public life that defied the Progressives' insistence on suburban homogeneity, federal officials in the Roosevelt administration created a blueprint for the spatial and racial polarization of the postwar urban region.

The Depression, of course, curtailed regional development, but contrary to the experience of its urban counterparts elsewhere, Los Angeles exhibited patterns of demographic and economic growth throughout the 1930s. In that decade, Los Angeles' population increased by six hundred thousand inhabitants, with more than 87 percent of that increase due to net migration. Also in contrast to the national pattern, industrial employment in Los Angeles rose sharply, particularly during the second half of the 1930s, when the city added an embryonic aircraft industry to its expanding manufacturing economy. By 1939, Los Angeles County ranked first nationally in agricultural income, as well as in the production of airplanes and motion pictures, second in auto assembling and retail trade, fourth in women's apparel, and fifth in the overall value of industrial production.[10] The region's industrial maturation during the 1920s and '30s was concentrated in distinct communities of the regional landscape, where a semblance of the heterosocial world of the modern city took shape.

Boyle Heights, for example, bustled in those decades, as its proximity to industrial activity along the southeastern periphery of downtown Los Angeles sustained the formation of a commercially vibrant, heterogeneous community. Initially, the neighborhood took shape in the 1880s as an enclave of white-collar workers, but during the early decades of the twentieth century, it became an initial point of settlement for Eastern European

Jews, who numbered more than thirty-five thousand by the mid-1930s. Jews settled alongside other social groups, including Mexican Americans, who began to concentrate in Boyle Heights during the 1930s. Jews and Mexicans shared Boyle Heights with African and Japanese Americans, whose collective presence conferred on the neighborhood the distinction of being a "U.N. in Microcosm."[11]

Similarly, Watts before World War II witnessed a diverse concentration of native Angelenos and newcomers to the region. As of 1920, most Watts settlers were of European descent—Germans, Scots, Greeks, Italians, and Jews—but the town also included several hundred blacks and Japanese. Mexican workers employed by the Pacific Electric Railway established a *colonia,* a settlement for laborers and their families, in Watts, known as "Spanish camp" among the non-Spanish-speaking inhabitants of the area. Although Watts was seven miles south of downtown Los Angeles, the inter-urban lines of the Pacific Electric ensured easy access to centers of employment and entertainment. The Watts Junction, where the Long Beach–Santa Ana line connected with the San Pedro–Redondo line, anchored a heterogeneous working-class population who depended on the rail lines for travel throughout Southern California.[12] In his youth, the tenor saxophonist William "Brother" Woodman Jr. moved with his family from Mississippi to Watts, where he recalled finding a congenial social environment. "We all got along very well. There were whites, Mexicans, Orientals, Jewish people. That's why, at that time, I didn't really understand about prejudice."[13]

Watts and Boyle Heights nurtured political alliances among their working-class inhabitants. The 1930s strengthened a regional tradition of interethnic cooperation among workers that dated back to the establishment of alliances such as the Japanese Mexican Labor Association in 1903 in rural El Monte. During the Depression years and well into the following decade, Mexican American men and women struggled alongside blacks, Jews, and whites to improve the workplace conditions for longshoremen and cannery and defense workers, and to elect public officials who defended the interests of the city's working class. The 1933 Dressmakers' Strike, for example, involved the cooperative efforts of Mexican American, African American, and Russian Molokan women, who organized under the International Ladies Garment Workers Union (ILGWU) and successfully struck for higher wages and improved working conditions. Other strikes among longshoremen, cannery workers, and aircraft employees reflected the collective efforts of employees who set aside racial and ethnic differences to advocate their mutual class interests.[14]

Such interactions, however, did not preclude vicious episodes of racial hostility during the Depression. The repatriation and deportation campaigns of the early 1930s signaled renewed hostility to the growing presence of Mexicans and Mexican Americans in Southern California, particularly among poorer whites whose sense of entitlement to jobs and government assistance rested upon an ingrained sense of white supremacy. The spectacle of Mexican Americans applying for state and federal assistance irked those who supported the city's effort to deport foreigners, even if those "foreigners" happened to be American citizens. Between those who voluntarily repatriated to Mexico, discouraged by the entrenchment of racial discrimination in Southern California, and those forced onto trains and shipped across the Mexican border, Los Angeles lost approximately one-third of its Mexican population in the first half of the 1930s.[15] Thus even at the height of its multicultural moment, Los Angeles witnessed some particularly intense episodes of racial hostility and demonstrated a growing level of discomfort with the city's racial and ethnic diversity.

Still, blacks, Mexicans, whites, and other ethnic groups mingled in Los Angeles' nighttime venues, even as Mexicans were rounded up and deported to Mexico during the day. During the 1930s and 1940s, the reigning Swing Era sheltered a scattered array of racially integrated music venues. Along the coast, the Venice Pier and the Santa Monica Ballroom attracted working-class youths who sought a moment's release from the demands of work. In Long Beach, the Nu Pike Amusement Park drew crowds from all parts of the city. Downtown, Duke Ellington performed "Jump for Joy," an all-black musical revue, before integrated audiences at the Mayan Theater, and at Shep's Playhouse in Little Tokyo, Gerald Wilson, Coleman Hawkins, and other jazz greats performed before audiences of black and white war workers. In Hollywood, moreover, the Canteen on Sunset Boulevard sanctioned racially mixed dancing throughout the 1940s, and the Palladium on Sunset Boulevard also offered a racially mixed venue. These institutions highlighted the cultural landscape of industrial Los Angeles and reproduced a semblance of the "diverse and pluralistic street culture" that defined public life in older industrial cities such as New York and Chicago.[16]

Such interactions took shape in a political culture dominated by New Deal reforms, ushered in with the 1938 election of Fletcher Bowron as mayor of Los Angeles. Bowron's political posture reflected both the interests of labor and minority groups and the reformist stance of Los Angeles Progressives, as he won City Hall on a campaign to clean up the corruption of the previous mayoral administration. His abolition of the notorious Red Squad, the intelligence bureau of the Los Angeles Police Department that monitored the activities of labor organizations, signaled the end of the open shop in Los Angeles. Bowron carried the support of political agencies in Los Angeles that reflected the city's myriad social interests—the Congress of Industrial Organizations (CIO), the League of Women Voters, El Congreso de Personas que Hablan Español, the Los Angeles chapters of the Urban League, the National Association for the Advancement of Colored People (NAACP), and the Community Service Organization. These organizations comprised the New Deal coalition that reigned in the city's political climate during the 1930s and early 1940s.[17]

Another local figure who assumed political prominence in this period was Edward Roybal, Los Angeles' first Chicano city councilman since 1881. Roybal symbolized a new generation of Chicano political leadership that ascended during the labor struggles of the 1930s and affiliated itself with the New Deal reforms of the Democratic Party. In 1949, with the assistance of the Community Service Organization, a Mexican American civic unity organization inspired by the work of the Chicago community activist Saul Alinski, Roybal captured the council seat representing the city's Ninth District. His candidacy won the support of labor groups such as the CIO Political Action Committee, the ILGWU, and several American Federation of Labor (AF of L) locals, as well as the various racial and ethnic constituencies of neighborhoods such as Bunker Hill and Boyle Heights. Beatrice Griffith, for example, noted the historical significance of Roybal's election: "For the first time in Los Angeles history, various nationality groups combined their forces to work unanimously for a councilmanic election. . . . Persons of Negro, Jewish, as well as Japanese, Chinese, Italian, Filipino, and Russian ancestry went into their own neighborhoods and plugged Roybal. Their various language newspapers often gave free space to the campaign."[18] Despite the racial and ethnic diversity of Roybal's supporters during the 1940s, however, Roybal increasingly personified the political engagement of East Los Angeles' expanding Chicano community. His outspoken stance against freeway construction, police brutality, and urban renewal programs illuminated Chicano opposition to the political culture that dominated Southern California in the age of white flight.[19]

Roybal and Bowron converged on a set of issues that constituted Southern California's period of New Deal reform. One issue in particular was that of public housing. During the 1930s, the constituent groups who rallied behind Southern California's New Deal coalition expressed their support for public housing. Women's groups, inheriting the legacy of the settlement house movement of the late nineteenth century, endorsed public housing, as did minority groups such as the NAACP, which, as a key element of the New Deal alliance, demanded access to improved housing conditions for African Americans. Additionally, labor unions, most notably the AF of L and the CIO, also advocated public housing as a means of reviving a depressed construction industry and an opportunity to improve housing conditions for struggling families. Allied within the New Deal "hegemonic bloc" that governed American society during the 1930s and well into the following decade, these groups shared a commitment to public housing in a city historically dominated by the private housing market.[20]

Public housing and other New Deal issues, however, were suddenly shelved with the U.S. entry into World War II. Often regarded as a watershed in Los Angeles history, the war inaugurated the region's most explosive period of economic and demographic growth. While the war effort rescued the nation from economic misery, it sparked a "second gold rush" in California as the massive influx of federal dollars into regional defense production created a wealth of new jobs. Southern California garnered a disproportionate share of federal defense contracts, as its location on the Pacific coast and its preexisting industrial infrastructure proved ideal for the strategic armament of the West Coast. Between 1941 and 1945, the infusion of seventy billion federal dollars into the regional economy initiated the development of what eventually became the nation's largest military-industrial complex.[21] In 1943, the region's peak year of production, a quarter-million workers found employment in aircraft production, shipbuilding, oil refining, tank assembly, and aluminum, synthetic rubber, and machine tool production.

Federal investment in the regional economy triggered a dramatic population increase that endured well beyond the early 1940s. The city's population jumped from 1.5 million to approximately 1.8 million between 1940 and 1946, reaching just under two million by 1950. The war years provided a foundation for continued demographic growth throughout the postwar period. Los Angeles' population reached 2.5 million in 1960, climbing to 2.8 million in 1970. County growth was even more dramatic. In 1940, the population of Los Angeles County was 2.79 million; it nearly doubled to 4.2 million a decade later, and grew to six million by 1960 and seven million by 1970. This surge in population, coupled with the parallel growth of the surrounding four counties, transformed Los Angeles into a "regional metropolis" fueled by "mass suburbanization on a scale never before encountered."[22]

World War II sparked this growth, forcing Southern Californians to confront the radical diversification of their social environment. The demand for labor in the early 1940s compelled an unprecedented integration of workers in war-related industries. Whereas aircraft production and shipbuilding companies had employed few African Americans and Mexican Americans prior to World War II, their numbers rapidly increased on the production line. In

1945, one African American leader calculated that 85 percent of black workers in Los Angeles were employed in war industries, primarily aircraft and ship production. Mexican Americans similarly encountered new employment opportunities during the war years. In 1944, Mexican Americans comprised 10 to 15 percent of Lockheed's workforce, while the California Shipbuilding Corporation alone employed nearly 1,300 Mexican Americans.[23] In *Lonely Crusade*, the black writer Chester Himes noticed Los Angeles' heterogeneous workforce: "Mexicans, Europeans, Orientals, South Americans—and Filipinos, he added to the quartet. Southerners, Northerners, Easterners, Westerners—and Indians—this was manpower. With the curious blend of native and migrant, racial and religious, current and traditional hatreds—this was culture. . . . Niggers alongside nigger-haters. Jews bucketing rivets for Jew-baiters. Native daughters lunching with Orientals."[24]

Himes, however, knew that Los Angeles was not a utopia of interracial harmony. Former county supervisor John Anson Ford recognized the exacerbation of racial tensions during the 1940s: "Perhaps never before had so large a population in America experienced the variety and intensity of racial frictions that marked World War II and its aftermath in Los Angeles County." The internment of Japanese Americans symbolized the most egregious example of the kind of racist xenophobia that defined the social climate of wartime Los Angeles, but other groups found themselves the targets of racial animosity as well. The well-known Zoot Suit Riots of 1943 and the Sleepy Lagoon trial that ensued between 1942 and 1944 proved the extent to which racism against Mexican Americans remained entrenched in the region. The early 1940s marked what Supervisor Ford labeled Southern California's "difficult days of racial readjustment" and illustrated the heightened salience of race in midcentury American society.[25]

Perhaps nothing tested the regional level of racial tolerance more than the wartime and postwar migration of African Americans to Los Angeles. From 1848 through the Great Depression, Los Angeles had sustained a minor but visible black presence. The absence of a sizeable black population led blacks and nonblacks alike to conclude that Los Angeles remained a "ghettoless paradise," but the pouring of poor southern blacks into Southern California during the war years prefigured the formation of a black ghetto in Los Angeles. Between 1940 and 1946, Los Angeles' black population more than doubled, growing from 63,774 to 133,082. By 1950, that number reached 171,209, giving Los Angeles the West's largest concentration of African Americans. The following decade solidified that distinction, as Los Angeles' black population reached 334,916 by 1960, climbing even higher, to 503,606, by 1970.[26]

The blackening of Los Angeles during the war years and their aftermath sparked a reactionary effort to delineate a new set of spatial and racial boundaries that materialized throughout the course of postwar suburbanization. Because many Southern California communities prohibited African American residents, those areas where blacks already resided accommodated the settlement of incoming blacks. The early 1940s thus marked the beginnings of Watts's transition from a multicultural community to a black ghetto and the decline of the kind of interracial interactions that surfaced in the city's industrial communities. Throughout the postwar period, the blackening of the South Central portion of the city provoked an effort among white homeowners to discourage blacks from seeking shelter in their neighborhoods. In the Allied Gardens district of Compton, for example, whites threw rotten fruit at the newly purchased homes of incoming black settlers, smearing them with paint, tearing out rose bushes, cutting off electricity, and burning crosses in their front yards. Such turf wars marked a growing consciousness about the color of urban space in Southern California and a reinforcement of the borders that divided white space from black space. As one black migrant to Los Angeles recalled of the city in the 1940s, "You knew your boundaries."[27]

White wartime resistance to black settlement was particularly strong in the industrial suburbs of southeast Los Angeles, such as Huntington Park and South Gate, two communities that flourished during the 1930s with the establishment of industrial branch plants of the Firestone and General Motors corporations. These communities sheltered the initial influx of the Dust Bowl generation of migrants to Southern California, who maintained a strong sense of their whiteness by virtue of their former coexistence with southern blacks. Despite the initial efforts to prevent Okies' and Arkies' settlement in Southern California through the construction of "bum blockades" at the state border with Arizona and Nevada, Huntington Park and South Gate epitomized white suburbia by the outset of the postwar period. The uneasy juxtaposition of these communities with an expanding black neighborhood in the South Central area generated a set of racial frictions that recreated a semblance of southern-style segregation in the far Southwest.

The Okies came to Los Angeles as another "Other" during the Great Depression, but their fate diverged significantly from their black counterparts who came to Los Angeles at roughly the same time. The postwar transformation of Dust Bowl communities such as South Gate, Huntington Park, and Bell Gardens illustrates the larger postwar enfranchisement of the white working class, who became the largest "welfare generation" in the history of the United States, relying on government programs that extended home ownership and education to the mass of American consumers. South Gate, for example, demonstrated the postwar affluence bestowed on the Dust Bowl generation of Okies and Arkies, while nearby Lakewood, heralded as a model of the postwar suburban good life, held a substantial population of southern whites who came to Los Angeles in dire straits during the 1930s. The proximity of these communities to an expanding black ghetto, however, heightened anxieties about neighborhood stability and prefigured the rise of the "silent majority" during the late 1960s. As recent social histories have demonstrated, that identity found its partial roots in the "plain folk Americanism" that white southerners brought with them to places like Los Angeles during the Great Depression.[28]

The war years thus inaugurated Southern California's "racial turn." A firsthand witness to Japanese internment and the Zoot Suit Riots, and legal counsel for the defendants in the Sleepy Lagoon trial, Carey McWilliams described the volatile social mix of wartime Los Angeles as nothing less than a "racial revolution." Within the span of two years during the early 1940s, Los Angeles confronted a new racial landscape that shattered earlier idealizations of the city as the seaport of Iowa or the westernmost outpost of Aryan supremacy. With African Americans abandoning the southern system of apartheid in hopes of a better life in Southern California, Japanese Americans enduring the trauma of evacuation and internment, and Chicano youths arousing popular antipathy and public suspicion, race acquired a new salience in the regional culture. World War II sanctioned racial interactions in both antagonistic and amicable ways, but in the aftermath of that crisis, an expanding generation of white Southern Californians forged a return to racial normalcy that rested upon a distinct set of spatial practices.

RACIALIZING URBAN AMERICA

As the experience of early 1940s Los Angeles suggests, one of the most striking features of midcentury urbanization in the United States was the concentration of African Americans in the vicinity of the downtown core. Black urbanization had been in effect since the aftermath of the Civil War, but the magnitude of that process increased dramatically by the mid-twentieth century. From 1945 to 1964, millions of southern blacks, fleeing an impoverished and deeply segregated South, sought high-paying jobs and opportunities for advancement in the nation's largest cities. Their convergence on the great cities of the Northeast coincided with, and perhaps caused, an emerging pattern of residential suburbanization among whites and white ethnics. Largely excluded from suburban development, African Americans concentrated within the parameters of the inner city and substantially darkened the face of urban America. New York City's white population, for example, decreased by 7 percent while its black population increased by 46 percent. Similarly, whereas Chicago's white population dropped by 13 percent, its black population rose by 65 percent, and Philadelphia's white population experienced a 13 percent decline during the 1950s and its black population a 41 percent increase. Washington, D.C., Detroit, and Newark experienced a transition from a white to a black majority in the course of a single generation. Whereas African Americans throughout American history had remained rural and southern, they became predominantly urban and northern during the postwar period.[29]

The concentration of African Americans within the precincts of northern cities during the postwar period coincided with the onslaught of a postwar urban crisis that crippled the nation's most vital manufacturing centers. The crisis, which fell especially hard on cities such as Detroit, Chicago, New York, Pittsburgh, St. Louis, Philadelphia, and Boston, reflected a complex array of government policies and corporate decisions that halted the centralized pattern of industrial urbanism that had taken shape throughout the nineteenth and early twentieth centuries. In particular, the war effort during the early 1940s initiated an uneven pattern of regional economic development that favored the burgeoning urban centers of the South and West at the expense of the industrial Northeast. The reallocation of federal resources favored the growth of Sunbelt cities such as Miami, Atlanta, Phoenix, Los Angeles, and Oakland and inaugurated the formation of a Rust Belt that extended from the manufacturing centers of the Midwest to the Northeast.[30]

Federal policy played a significant role in the shifting pattern of urban development in postwar America. Federal policies during the war effort not only channeled federal investments away from the urban Northeast, but also actively encouraged industrial decentralization as a defense strategy. The "parallel plant" policy of the Department of Defense, for example, entailed the building of new defense plants outside traditional urban centers. The federal emphasis on industrial decentralization gave shape to a new urban geography that unsettled the economic hierarchy of the nation's cities. Whereas the manufacturing of textiles, automobiles, electrical appliances, motor vehicles, and military hardware had remained concentrated in the urban Northeast throughout the first half of the twentieth century, industrial leaders and corporate executives, following federal incentives to decentralize, sought to maintain a competitive advantage by relocating to suburban areas as well as to the growing centers of the Sunbelt economy. The "runaway shop" became a characteristic feature of the postwar urban economy and entailed the loss of hundreds of thousands of manufacturing jobs in traditional urban centers.[31]

The federal government precipitated the urban crisis in other ways as well. Although chapter 6 will examine more broadly the effects of federally subsidized highway construction on the midcentury reconfiguration of urban life, the architecture of a national transportation policy exacerbated the postwar urban crisis. The Clay Commission, for example, established by President Eisenhower to study the need for highway construction, asserted that suburbs were superior to cities and that new freeways should be used to decentralize urban areas. In support of that endeavor, the Interstate and Defense Highway Act of 1956 authorized funding for the construction of an interstate highway network that would promote decentralization as a military strategy. The construction of beltways and a growing reliance on trucking for freight transport provided incentives for industrial relocation. By the 1960s, new factories lined peripheral highways, boosting the tax bases of suburban communities at the cost of central cities.[32]

Government policies and corporate decisions alone, however, did not determine the fate of American cities during the postwar period. Aspiring homeowners, taking advantage of federal housing initiatives, also hastened the deterioration of the industrial metropolis by relocating to the suburban fringes of American cities. Beginning during the New Deal, federal policy extended suburban home ownership to broader segments of the American public. The Home Owners' Loan Corporation (HOLC), for example, established in 1933, innovated the self-amortizing home loan, allowing Americans of modest means to purchase homes without a substantial down payment. Similarly, the Federal Housing Administration (FHA), established by the 1934 National Housing Act, guaranteed privately financed home loans against default, allowing banks to adopt more liberal lending policies. FHA programs maintained a clear antiurban bias. The terms of FHA loans favored the purchase of single-family dwellings and implemented a set of minimum requirements that all but precluded home ownership in concentrated urban neighborhoods. Deeming crowded neighborhoods, older properties, industrial activity, and what it called "the presence of inharmonious racial or nationality groups" as anathema to secure investment, the FHA's *Underwriting Manual*, a veritable bible among private lending institutions, directed housing loans to the suburban periphery and opened doors for the exodus of people and capital away from urban centers.[33]

Despite the benefits the New Deal bestowed on African Americans and other racial constituencies during the 1930s, housing policy under the Roosevelt administration established a pattern of racial segregation that structured the contours of subsequent urban development. Both the HOLC and the FHA implemented a racially biased set of policies that virtually prevented blacks and other nonwhite groups from attaining suburban home ownership. The HOLC, for example, devised a method of property appraisal, adopted as a national standard by private lending institutions, which maintained an extreme sensitivity to race. Based on an extensive survey of urban neighborhoods, the HOLC assigned a "grade" to each neighborhood—1 being the highest and 4 the lowest. Each number corresponded to both the code letters A, B, C, and D, and to the colors green, blue, yellow, and red, respectively.[34]

The HOLC's assessment of Los Angeles neighborhoods, for example, demonstrates how race factored into government calculations of urban property values. Los Angeles neighborhoods "highly protected by deed restrictions" and those where the "population is homogeneous" were always accorded an A rating, while neighborhoods with "first-grade qualifications" yet within a short distance of "fourth-grade contamination" areas were assigned a B rating. The C neighborhoods in Los Angeles evinced "indication[s] of infiltration of Jewish families" or sheltered a "few Mexicans and Japs." Invariably, neighborhoods that sheltered even a few black families received a D rating and were redlined. Thus, those neighborhoods that sustained the region's heterosocial public life throughout the 1930s and early 1940s were targeted by the HOLC. Watts acquired a "low red" grade, as did Boyle Heights, which HOLC officials identified as a " 'melting pot' area, literally honeycombed with diverse and subversive racial elements."[35]

The FHA, chief underwriter of the postwar suburban boom, used the racially biased ratings established by the HOLC and reinforced the federal government's insistence on racial homogeneity as a precondition for home ownership. "If a neighborhood is to retain stability," the FHA's *Underwriting Manual* stated, "it is necessary that properties shall continue to be occupied by the same social and racial classes. A change in social or racial occupancy generally contributes to the instability and decline in property values." A 1933 report submitted to the FHA by one of its consultants, Homer Hoyt, reveals the FHA's assessment of racial worth and its acknowledgment of the fluid and contingent boundaries of white identity:

> If the entrance of a colored family into a white neighborhood causes
> a general exodus of the white people it is reflected in property values.
> Except in the case of Negroes and Mexicans, however, *these racial and
> national barriers disappear when the individuals of foreign nationality
> groups rise in the economic scale or conform to American standards
> of living. . . .* While the ranking may be scientifically wrong from the

standpoint of inherent racial characteristics, it registers an opinion or prejudice that is reflected in land values; it is the ranking of race and nationalities with respect to the beneficial effect upon land values. Those having the most favorable effect come first on the list and those exerting the most detrimental effect appear last:

1. English, Germans, Scots, Irish, Scandinavians
2. North Italians
3. Bohemians or Czechoslovakians
4. Poles
5. Lithuanians
6. Greeks
7. Russian Jews of lower class
8. South Italians
9. Negroes
10. Mexicans[36]

Thus, FHA officials recognized the inherent instability of ethnic hierarchies, but remained vigilant toward racial distinctions between white and non-white. This recognition provided a material basis for the development of an inclusive white identity predicated on suburban home ownership, and in Southern California, where the FHA maintained a most vital role in shaping regional patterns of suburban development, the settlement of places such as Orange County and the San Fernando Valley created a space where a diverse array of whites and white ethnics could "conform to American standards of living" and remove themselves from the FHA's least-wanted list. The great paradox here is that while the New Deal sustained the development of a heterogeneous public culture in Southern California during the 1930s and into the following decade, it simultaneously planted the seeds for the destruction of that culture by enacting a set of racially biased policies that enabled the racial polarization of the postwar urban region.

VANILLA SUBURBS

To be sure, Los Angeles experienced an urban crisis at midcentury, but it was one of growth, not decay. World War II inflicted a set of growing pains upon Los Angeles, a region long advertised as a bucolic retreat from the tensions of urban life. The booster myths that mediated an image of Los Angeles throughout the 1920s, whatever their distinct nuances, all shared a common emphasis on how Los Angeles stood apart from other American cities. Los

Angeles, unlike New York, Chicago, and San Francisco, lacked the qualities of urban life that, as chapter 3 illustrates, Hollywood subsequently defined as noir: congestion, pollution, anomie, and crime, as well as racial and ethnic mixing. While Southern California's phase of urban development during the 1920s challenged such urban bravado, the wartime boom exposed Dana Bartlett's "Better City" as pure farce. More alarming, the postwar formation of a ghetto and barrio within the city's older neighborhoods signaled the radical urbanization of the region and prompted a search for new patterns of community formation that minimized the sort of interactions that defined previous modes of urban social relations.

The 1940s brought a set of rude awakenings for Southern Californians. The worsening of traffic congestion during the early 1940s, for example, dramatized the crowding of city streets and underscored the need for a highway system that better served the needs of commuters who found themselves driving longer distances to work. In a 1942 survey of 225,000 Southern California workers, the California State Railroad Commission calculated that more than 85 percent traveled to work in cars. Even when efforts were made to ensure the accessibility of places of employment to public transit, workers still asserted their preference for the automobile. Traffic congestion and, in particular, the "promiscuous" mixing of different types of vehicles on the city streets alerted public officials to one aspect of the crisis of growth in Los Angeles and, as chapter 6 will illustrate, heightened the impetus to build a regional network of thoroughfares that provided for the rapid movement of traffic through an expanding regional metropolis.[37]

If Southern California enjoyed fame for its natural setting and hospitable climate, the intense phase of wartime urbanization left its scars on its unblemished landscape. Smog was first discovered in Los Angeles in 1943, when a brown haze settled in the Los Angeles basin, so noxious that the *Los Angeles Times* reported Southern California's "Gas Attack" on its front page. The identification of smog incited public officials to implement an array of measures to limit the proliferation of exhaust in the city's air and to establish municipal agencies to evaluate their success during the 1940s and 1950s. Such efforts notwithstanding, the browning of Southern California's air severed a more mature Los Angeles from its youthful myth as the healthful antidote to a hyperurbanized society.[38]

The war years wreaked further havoc on Los Angeles' infrastructure. Wartime rationing of building materials brought the construction of new housing to a halt, while massive population growth severely strained the city's existing housing stock, particularly in expanding black neighborhoods, where greater numbers of people with severely limited housing opportunities concentrated in unprecedented numbers. The issuing of building permits sank to new lows during the war years, and by July 1943, public officials estimated the city's vacancy rate at a mere 0.4 percent. "I am convinced that the overall housing shortage," mayor Fletcher Bowron confided to a friend in 1945, "is unequaled in any other major city in the United States."[39]

The housing crisis that befell wartime Los Angeles dramatized the need for new housing to both public officials and private developers, who had competing visions about the future course of urban development in Southern California. City officials, particularly those affiliated with Fletcher Bowron's New Deal coalition, emphasized a "public" mode of urban growth that stressed government programs such as public housing to eliminate slum conditions and to provide affordable housing for the city's inhabitants. Their notions clashed with the privatized version of development favored by land developers and corporate interests, who constituted an unofficial, but no less powerful, force in the process of urban development. Ultimately, the market approach trumped the public vision; the defeat of public housing in Cold War Los Angeles illustrates the transition to a new political culture that encouraged the spatial and racial fragmentation of the postwar urban region.

Whatever support fueled the campaign for public housing throughout the 1930s, it garnered opposition from the private sector after World War II, particularly among the real estate, finance, and construction industries. The arrival of the Cold War serendipitously offered interest groups such as the National Association of Real Estate Boards and the Urban Land Institute a potent weapon in the fight against public housing. By decrying housing subsidies as socialist, private real estate interests and their allies waged a powerful assault on the fate of subsidized housing in Southern California and illustrated the virility of red-baiting as a key political strategy during the Cold War.

It is difficult to comprehend the success of the campaign against public housing without understanding the salience of McCarthyism in Southern California's postwar political culture. One might argue that alongside Washington, D.C., where Cold War diplomacy of global scope took shape, Los Angeles arose as the western capital of the Cold War. Perhaps no region of the United States profited more handsomely from federal investments in Cold War defense production than Southern California. After a brief lull in the late 1940s, the Korean War reignited the regional economy and prompted federal orders for more missiles, aircraft, and surveillance technology. Regional dependence on Cold War defense production signaled political opportunities for local Republican strategists such as Richard Nixon, who defeated Helen Gahagan Douglas in the 1950 senate race through a successful media campaign of red-baiting his Democratic opponent. And, as chapter 3 will discuss, Hollywood provided a conspicuous arena for the investigations of the House Un-American Activities Committee (HUAC), which used the film industry as a vehicle to publicize its determination to rid the nation of Communist subversives. Studio executives such as Walt Disney came to the aid of HUAC in its hunt for Communists, purging anyone suspected of socialist politics from the ranks of the film industry and producing films that celebrated a conformist, classless, and consumerist vision of the "American way."[40]

Southern California's virulent strain of McCarthyism spawned a regional political climate that refused to tolerate New Deal programs such as public housing. The anti–public housing forces scored a major victory in 1949, when Los Angeles secured a contract from the federal government, under the Taft Ellender Wagner Act, which promised the construction of ten thousand units of public housing. The Small Property Owners' League immediately retorted by issuing a pamphlet, *Bowron Administration Moving People via Gestapo Housing Authority,* claiming that "government owned tenement housing . . . would accomplish the major step towards Communism." Housing developers such as Fritz Burns, as a spokesman for the Southern California Association of Real Estate Boards and a vigorous opponent of public housing, argued for the "ways and means of meeting and defeating socialism which seems about to engulf us." And the *Los Angeles Times,* historically Southern California's voice of private enterprise and real estate development, decried public housing as outright "socialistic."[41]

Following the example set by HUAC's investigation of Hollywood studios, the foes of public housing also scrutinized the offices of the City Housing Authority (CHA) for any subversive influences. Frank Wilkinson, chief public relations officer for the CHA, in a routine eminent domain hearing for a proposed housing project, refused to answer the question that ended so many careers in Cold War America: "What organizations, political or otherwise, have you been a member of since 1932?" The California State Un-American Activities Committee took Wilkinson's silence as proof of his subversive persuasions and succeeded in ousting him and six other CHA employees.

Furious over the purging of the CHA, Fletcher Bowron remained adamant in his refusal to cancel the city's contract for public housing, which caused his political demise. Public housing was the central issue of the 1953 mayoral campaign, in which Norris Poulson successfully branded Bowron a Communist and won the race. Poulson, a three-term congressman from Los

Angeles and virtually hand-picked by the *Los Angeles Times* to run against Bowron, immediately canceled the city's contract with the federal government for the construction of public housing and restored, for the remainder of the decade, the privatized vision of growth endorsed by the *Times*.[42]

Though a powerful force in the "making" of modern Los Angeles, the *Los Angeles Times* and its allied forces did not simply will the defeat of public housing. Whereas organized labor had endorsed public housing into the 1940s, McCarthyism limited labor's institutional power and halted the enactment of New Deal programs such as public housing. After the 1953 election of Norris Poulson, organized labor in Los Angeles "was almost never in a weaker position," and the labor unions, key constituents in Southern California's New Deal coalition, withdrew their support for public housing. Without labor's support, as the historian Don Parson concludes, public housing could not withstand the red-baiting campaigns marshaled by private real estate interests.[43]

Not that public housing was ever central to the interests of mainstream labor activists. With or without public housing, Southern California's white working-class and middle-class families retained access to government programs that effectively secured their own version of the suburban dream, however modest, and, unlike black community leaders, they did not view public housing as a solution to pressing housing needs. The most severe features of the urban crisis that settled on Southern California during the war years thus remained confined to expanding communities of color, while suburban development exempted white Southern Californians from the many problems that afflicted the inner city. As consumers, the white working class found in FHA and Veterans Administration (VA) assistance programs the means to realize their dream of suburban home ownership. The array of housing options available to them, however, widened Southern California's racial fault lines.

Beginning during the early 1940s, for example, new FHA communities surfaced in the Southern California landscape that marked a distinct departure from the polyglot communities of Watts and Boyle Heights. For example, in 1939, Fritz Burns, probably the most successful among Southern California's "community builders," built Westside Village, a planned community of eight hundred homes near the Douglas Aircraft plant in Santa Monica, to serve the needs of war workers. The success of Westside Village inspired the 1941 creation of a larger development, Westchester, a community of three thousand homes situated alongside the city's main airport and North American Aviation. In 1947, Burns teamed up with the industrial magnate Henry J. Kaiser to form Kaiser Community Homes, which undertook the construction of Panorama City in North Hollywood, located near the Lockheed and Vega plants in Burbank. Largely immune from the side effects of wartime urbanization in Southern California, these new communities followed the decentralized pattern of industrial development that delineated the parameters of postwar suburbanization.[44]

By virtue of their racial exclusivity, however, the new wartime communities sheltered an inclusive white identity on the fringes of the urban core. Toluca Wood, Panorama City, Westchester, and Westside Village all encouraged occupational and class diversity while strictly enforcing racial homogeneity. Fritz Burns, for example, "intentionally programmed" class and occupational diversity into developments such as Westchester and Panorama City, integrating workers, managers, and professionals in the same neighborhood unit. Burns viewed class stratification as un-American but apparently did not hold the same view toward racial segregation. The developer maintained a steadfast policy of Jim Crow, even after the Supreme Court's prohibition of racially restrictive covenants in *Shelley v. Kraemer* in 1948. While the new wartime communities underscored the blurring of class lines along the suburban periphery of the metropolis, ensconcing white workers and their families in the comforts of suburban home ownership, they simultaneously reinforced the pattern by which chocolate cities and vanilla suburbs took shape.

Housing developers, of course, were not solely responsible for the racial exclusivity of the new aircraft communities. While developers built racially exclusionary measures into their new communities, they were sanctioned by a larger culture that maintained racial discrimination at the workplace. White employers at the region's largest aircraft firms remained committed to Jim Crow, and after the labor shortage of the early 1940s had subsided, with white veterans returning home in search of steady employment, they returned to a whites-only policy following the war's conclusion. Their restoration of a white workforce was supported by white workers, many of whom belonged to unions such as the United Auto Workers, which remained determined to provide employment for returning white veterans. Thus, the whiteness of Southern California's new aircraft communities also hinged on the efforts of white employers and their white employees to expel blacks from the aircraft labor force in the aftermath of World War II. Consequently, blacks went from representing approximately 10 percent of the aircraft labor force at the peak of production in 1944–45 to less than 3 percent by 1950.[45]

The FHA, guaranteeing a major share of home loans for Southern California's wartime communities, underwrote the whiteness of the postwar urban region. In many ways, Los Angeles became the FHA's favorite city during the 1940s and 1950s. "Nowhere in the country has activity in FHA loans been so pronounced as in the Los Angeles area," noted the regional director of the FHA in Los Angeles, commenting on the fact that by the early 1940s, California won the largest share of FHA funding for private homes.[46] The FHA's insistence on racial homogeneity, however, structured racial exclusivity in postwar suburban development. Although whites did not flee the more densely concentrated neighborhoods of Los Angeles' inner city for the suburbs, as they did in New York City and its boroughs, Southern California nonetheless exhibited the characteristic spatial and racial fragmentation of the twentieth-century urban populace. The editors of the *California Eagle,* serving Southern California's black community, indicted the FHA for its complicity in this development in 1959: "Whites are moving to suburban areas and leaving the centers of the metropolitan areas to Negroes and other so-called minorities. Negroes aren't moving to the suburbs because they are barred from suburban housing developments. The most important single factor in the discriminatory polices pursued by developers and builders is the indirect support such discrimination gets from FHA and VA."[47]

Federal housing policy had created the basis for the racial segregation of the postwar urban region as far back as the late 1930s, and it was during the 1950s that racial distinctions became even more pronounced in the region's social landscape. Perhaps no community better epitomized Southern California's vanilla suburbs than Lakewood, an "instant city" of 17,500 homes near Long Beach, about fourteen miles south of downtown Los Angeles, which opened in 1951. Lakewood reflected the collaborative efforts of Ben Weingart, Louis Boyar, and Mark Taper, who imagined a self-sufficient residential community with its own schools, recreation grounds, religious facilities, civic center, and, of course, shopping center. Near Douglas Aircraft and alongside Southern California's primary industrial corridor, Lakewood was situated in a growing area where agricultural fields rapidly gave way to residential subdivisions. With the assistance of private investors and one hundred million dollars from the FHA toward construction costs and mortgage guarantees, Weingart, Taper, and Boyar's housing development was the largest undertaking of its kind.

Lakewood's success as a prototypical suburban community reflected an ironic moment of cooperation among diverse peoples who collectively maintained a racially exclusive suburban community. An early promotional brochure touted Lakewood as the "white spot" of Long Beach, a city whose African American population had dramatically increased between 1940 and

1950. It emphasized to potential buyers the use of racial and residential restrictions that ensured Lakewood's standing as a "100% American Family Community."[48] Lakewood's sales staff refused to accept applications from black families, steering them toward the expanding black neighborhoods of South Central Los Angeles. Still, Lakewood's inhabitants varied across religious, class, and regional lines. Jews, Catholics, Okies, engineers, janitors, aircraft plant workers, and their families all found Lakewood amenable to their pursuit of the suburban good life, but their many differences did not preclude their entry into a suburb reserved for whites only.

In Southern California during the postwar period, Jewish men such as Taper, Weingart, and Boyar encountered success as agents of suburbanization in postwar Southern California, and they embodied a new generation of Jewish community builders who "replaced the Jewish film magnate as the entrepreneur par excellence" in postwar Los Angeles. Initially, the land purchased by Lakewood's developers was protected by "restrictions of an all-inclusive nature," which, along with restrictive covenants built into property clauses, prevented the sale of lots to blacks, Mexicans, and Jews. Although Boyar, Taper, and Weingart purchased a suburb in which they could not live, they lifted the restriction and Lakewood welcomed Jewish home buyers upon its opening. "It was often said of this suburb," recalls lifelong Lakewood resident D. J. Waldie in his suburban memoir, "that every other house was either Jewish or Catholic."[49]

The settlement of Jews in Lakewood demonstrates the extent to which postwar suburbanization in Southern California sustained the "whitening" of a social group that endured centuries of racist persecution. Jews came to Los Angeles in the early decades of the twentieth century and, confronted with restrictive covenants that explicitly barred them from Southern California's white neighborhoods, settled in Boyle Heights alongside other racial and ethnic groups. During the 1940s, however, Eastside Jews, by virtue of their commercial success as service providers, began to enjoy a newfound affluence and initiated an exodus out of Boyle Heights to converge on areas west of downtown Los Angeles. The opening to Jews of the Westside, which included communities such as Beverly Hills, Bel Air, Brentwood, Pacific Palisades, and the southern portion of the San Fernando Valley, made that area synonymous with the new affluence that Jews acquired during the postwar period.

The presence of Jewish developers in the making of postwar suburbia offers a glimpse into "how the Jews became white folks" in the sociospatial context of postwar America. Clearly, the atrocities of Nazi Germany forced American and European gentiles to rethink the ancient stereotypes of Jews as a degenerate group. In the United States, the weakening of an entrenched anti-Semitism, coupled with an economic boom, created a national context in which Jews could "become white," but perhaps no region was better suited for that makeover than Los Angeles. Hollywood, as Michael Rogin and others have argued, facilitated the "whitening" of Jews not only through its financial success, but also through its representations of racial otherness. Most significant, however, the combination of undeveloped land, which created unprecedented opportunities for Jewish community builders, and the dramatic expansion of a black presence in the region sustained a growing perception of Jews as white. *U.S. News and World Report,* for example, included Jews in its report on a religious version of white flight in Southern California: "Churches and synagogues have been abandoned by whites, sometimes to be taken over by Negro congregations."[50]

Lakewood's inclusive version of suburban whiteness rested upon a unique administrative structure that accelerated postwar Southern California's fragmentation into a sprawling agglomeration of racially exclusive communities. In 1954, the developers of Lakewood struck a deal with the county of Los Angeles. For minimal costs, the county would provide vital services (fire, police, library) to Lakewood, which incorporated as an independent municipality. The deal between Los Angeles County and the city of Lakewood eliminated the presence of a homegrown bureaucracy and exempted Lakewood's citizens from the burden of supporting public services.[51]

The Lakewood plan initiated a "new trend" in municipal incorporation that promised to "shape up the shapeless boundaries" of the expanding postwar urban region. Whether or not suburbanization entailed a rejection of city life, the incorporation of suburban communities such as Lakewood indeed signaled a repudiation of city government. The *Los Angeles Mirror News,* reporting on the incorporation "craze" that swept suburban Southern California during the 1950s, wondered, "Are big cities obsolete?" Although the Lakewood plan excited concern about the development of a "sprawling, disconnected, haphazard" urban region, the residents of Lakewood and the twenty-five other "cities by contract" between the years of 1954 and 1960 relished the opportunity to assume greater control over municipal affairs.[52]

Local control became a mantra among suburban Southern Californians, who used municipal incorporation as a means of ensuring homogeneous communities and stable property values. By allowing a greater degree of control over zoning and land-use policies, municipal incorporation allowed the residents of Lakewood to create racially homogeneous communities by excluding those populations who tended to rely on rental housing and county services. In this way, the Lakewood plan authorized the "sorting out" of the regional population by race. Although the Los Angeles urban region became increasingly diverse during the postwar period, individual communities in Southern California grew increasingly homogeneous. In 1950, there were thirty-eight cities with populations less than 1 percent black; these cities contained 24 percent of the metropolitan area's population. In 1970, by contrast, there were fifty-eight cities with populations less than 1 percent black, containing 33 percent of the regional population. Both the number of segregated cities and the population residing in those cities increased. Moreover, of the fifty-eight segregated cities, thirty-one were older cities that had successfully retained antiblack patterns. The other segregated cities were the new Lakewood Plan cities. Of the thirty-two created between 1950 and 1970, twenty-eight had populations less than 1 percent black. Thus, Gary Miller concludes, "the Lakewood Plan cities were essentially white political movements."[53]

In addition to its social composition and its political structure, Lakewood's design and construction reflected the larger cultural preoccupation with order shared by a new generation of suburban Americans. Uniformity, efficiency, and predictability were the key imperatives that guided Lakewood's development from the laying of foundations to the sale of homes. A bucket excavator could dig foundations for individual homes in less than fifteen minutes. Workmen laid 2,113 foundations in a hundred days, quickly followed by carpenters who nailed up three-foot foundation forms. Lakewood's developers applied the Fordist principles of mass production to housing construction. Construction crews repeated discrete tasks—pouring concrete, laying floors, raising walls, scaling rafters—synchronizing their efforts in order to move from house to house as quickly as possible. In this way, workers built a hundred homes a day and more than five hundred per week. Whereas "the average number of houses per acre in prewar subdivisions had been about five," one acre of Lakewood yielded eight homes. Consumers could choose one of seven floor plans, each decorated in one of four styles—Maple, Traditional, Modern, and Provincial. Lakewood was not exactly the "bourgeois utopia" that more affluent Americans pursued during the suburban boom of the 1920s, but it offered a modest version of the suburban good life to greater numbers of people.[54] Veterans needed no down payment, and the FHA guaranteed loans at 4 percent interest for up to thirty years. "When the sales office opened on a cloudless Palm Sunday in April 1950," recalled D. J. Waldie, "twenty-five thousand people were waiting."[55]

Lakewood's layout epitomized the efficient organization of space that marked the development of postwar suburbia. Typical of suburban developments built on Southern California's flat terrain, Lakewood was built on the grid system, "a fraction of a larger grid, anchored to one in Los Angeles." Streets intersected at right angles, with avenues running north and south and streets running east and west. The grid also dictated the arrangement of homes. "Each block is divided into the common grid of fifty-by-one-hundred feet lots," wrote D. J. Waldie; "all the houses are about 1,100 square feet." The grid reflects distinct traditions of city planning, and its historical application reflects a solution to the problem of ordering undeveloped land. For the builders of Lakewood, the grid proved the most efficient way of organizing 3,500 acres of Southern California land "that was as good as any other."[56]

At the center of the grid stood an institution that earned a greater prominence in the cultural life of postwar Americans. Lakewood Center, an outdoor pedestrian mall occupying a 154-acre site, featured one hundred businesses and a major department store, making it the largest development of its kind upon its opening in 1950. Unlike downtown commercial districts situated along bustling city streets, Lakewood Center stood at the center of a vast parking lot that accommodated twelve thousand cars, and its one-story buildings faced inward along a central promenade. The designers of Lakewood Center sought ways to manipulate consumer behavior through a rigorous ordering of pedestrian space. They used the principles of department store interior design and drew on existing knowledge about the psychological aspects of shopping to create a self-contained environment wholly dedicated to consumption. The minimally landscaped promenades of Lakewood Center allowed an unobstructed view of window displays, and its understated modernist architecture gave greater prominence to signs and advertisements. Lakewood Center's highly disciplined layout not only established an important precedent for a subsequent generation of regional malls that appeared in Southern California and throughout the nation during the 1950s and 1960s, but also reflected a larger spatial culture that informed the design of freeways, theme parks, ballparks, and, of course, insular suburban communities such as Lakewood itself.[57]

The spatial organization of suburban Southern California reflected a larger demand for social order that seemed imperative at an uncertain time in American history. Contrary to the popular perception of the post–World War II period as "happy days," Americans found themselves preoccupied with a number of global and domestic concerns. The Cold War against the Soviet Union loomed as the gravest threat to the nation, not only provoking fears about nuclear annihilation, but also heightening anxieties about internal subversion. HUAC's hearings, the execution of the Rosenbergs, and the Alger Hiss trial intensified the suspicion that engulfed Americans throughout the postwar period. Other social anxieties compounded Cold War tensions. Juvenile delinquents and working women threatened the primacy of the nuclear family and prompted a renewed emphasis on patriarchal domesticity. The burgeoning civil rights movement, moreover, threatened the tradition of white supremacy in the United States, arousing a growing suspicion of liberal elites who mandated racial integration from their perch in Washington, D.C. White Americans, not far removed from the misery and anxiety of the 1930s and early 1940s, seemed vulnerable, psychically at least, to the profound changes that engulfed the nation and the world throughout the postwar period.[58]

If postwar Americans could not order the chaos of global affairs and internal developments, they could at least take shelter in their own suburban havens. Like Lakewood, Orange County was one such haven during the 1950s, at least for the time being. The county's name reveals its agricultural past, but World War II foretold a very different future. The war channeled a flood of federal defense outlays into the region, bringing an influx of military personnel and their families. The formation in Orange County of what eventually became the nation's largest military-industrial complex fueled the regional economy, spurring activity in the real estate, construction, finance, and service industries. Orange County's population growth after World War II, moreover, was nothing less than astounding. Although the county's population nearly doubled between 1940 and 1950, it underwent its most spectacular growth in the following decades, skyrocketing from 216,224 in 1950 to 703,925 in 1960. By 1970, Orange County sheltered nearly 1.5 million inhabitants, furthering the expanse of Southern California's suburban metropolis. The county's rapid demographic growth, however, did not include racial and ethnic diversity. By 1960, for example, African Americans constituted less than 0.5 percent of the county's overall population.[59] Alongside Mexican Americans, Orange County's black minority remained confined to the older urban centers of the region.

Orange County's characteristics—its racial homogeneity, its dependence on a Cold War economy, its high rates of home ownership, and its flurry of intense real estate development—fostered a distinct political culture that foreshadowed the changing tenor of national politics during the 1970s and 1980s. Orange County residents, many of them newcomers to Southern California, sparked a conservative revival that espoused a strong defense, a weak federal government, virulent anti-Communism, staunch nationalism, and unabashed celebration of laissez-faire capitalism. Conservative churches such as the Central Baptist Church, right-wing organizations such as the

John Birch Society, and local newspapers such as the *Orange County Register* offered a forum where such values were codified into political action. These and other institutions that highlighted Orange County's cultural landscape, including Disneyland, as chapter 4 suggests, reflected and reinforced a burgeoning "middle-class revolt" that crystallized in the suburban spaces of Southern California.[60]

The brand of political conservatism that Orange County's residents adopted hinged in no small part on a growing consciousness of race and racial difference in postwar America. The civil rights movement, at its zenith during the 1960s, surfaced as a major threat to the guarded white identity incubating in the insular suburban spaces of Orange County. Through a number of racially exclusive practices that prevented or discouraged blacks from acquiring housing and employment in the area, Orange County residents exhibited a remarkable racial homogeneity. Their success in that endeavor seemed particularly imperative in the national context of the 1960s. The gains won by the civil rights movement during the 1960s not only intensified opposition to government-sponsored efforts to remedy racial discrimination, but also mobilized a white backlash that catapulted conservative ideologues into public office. Ronald Reagan, for example, successfully mobilized his white suburban constituents in places like Orange County to advance his political ambitions. With 72 percent of its electorate voting for Reagan in the 1966 gubernatorial election, Orange County won recognition as Reagan Country at the height of the civil rights movement. Reagan demonstrated an acute awareness of the racial anxieties of his white suburban constituents. Arousing local animosity to metropolitan Los Angeles and conjuring menacing images of teeming black masses, Reagan warned his Orange County supporters that "the jungle is waiting to take over" in the aftermath of the Watts riots.[61]

One issue in particular codified a suburban brand of identity politics among white homeowners in Orange County and other parts of Southern California. In 1963, the state legislature passed the Rumford Fair Housing Act, which opened housing laws to prevent racial discrimination in the renting or selling of real estate. The Fair Housing Act incurred intense opposition in California, particularly in the southern portion of the state. The following year, white Californians retorted by placing Proposition 14 on the ballot, which would rescind the Fair Housing Act, derided by its opponents as the "Forced Housing Act." California voters approved the proposition in 1964, winning a two-to-one majority in Orange County. Although white suburban Southern Californians thus enjoyed a momentary reprieve from the threat of racial diversity, the California State Supreme Court nullified the proposition that same year, declaring it unconstitutional, and thus gave California conservatives such as Ronald Reagan another issue with which to mobilize white suburban voters, who felt, in Reagan's words, that "if an individual wants to discriminate against Negroes or others in selling or renting his house he has a right to do so."[62]

The unique political culture that took shape in Orange County during the postwar period engendered a political transformation that ultimately shaped the course of national politics during the remainder of the century. The Reagan Revolution of the 1980s saw the realization of a conservative populism that reflected the values of disaffected working-class and lower-middle-class whites, who shifted their political allegiance from the Democratic to the Republican party. Race—racial ideology and racial identity—played a significant role in that shift. Distant from the class-based coalition politics of the New Deal years and disillusioned with the racial liberalism of Lyndon Johnson's Great Society, white Americans of the 1970s and 1980s, predominantly northern Catholics and southern Protestants, channeled their grievances into support for a new political leadership that trumpeted a return to traditional values such as patriarchy, patriotism, law and order, hard work, and self-help, and that promised to end federal "favoritism" toward special interest groups. The Reagan Revolution gripped regional constituencies throughout the nation during the late 1970s and throughout the 1980s, but it first took root in the new suburban communities of Southern California toward the end of the postwar period.[63]

CHOCOLATE CITIES

While Orange County cultivated a suburban brand of white identity politics, inner-city communities experienced an unprecedented degree of racial segregation, which ultimately gave way to a racialized brand of political activism that mirrored that of their white suburban counterparts. By the early 1960s, the patterns of racial segregation in Southern California's social geography had become clear to contemporary observers. The Los Angeles County Commission on Human Relations documented the effects of white flight on the social geography of 1950s Los Angeles. "Of the 334,916 Negroes living in the City of Los Angeles," the report summarized, "313,866, or 93.7 percent live in the Central District." And of the 12,297 blacks who lived outside of Watts, 10,860 "have simply joined members of their race in the segregated areas of San Pedro, Venice and Pacoima." Mexican Americans experienced a similar concentration in the unincorporated territory east of the downtown core. Between 1950 and 1960, the percentage of Latino residents in East Los

Angeles increased from 29.4 percent to 51.5 percent. Such findings led the commission to conclude that Los Angeles was "experiencing the growth of a highly segregated community that can be compared to the most unfortunate of such situations to be found anywhere in the United States."[64]

During the 1950s, Watts and South Central Los Angeles, which had remained two separate black communities through the 1940s, coalesced to form a broader area that became synonymous with the black ghetto. Although the *Los Angeles Times* and other real estate interests waged a fierce battle to obstruct the construction of public housing within the confines of downtown Los Angeles, those groups did not object to three new public housing projects in Watts during the 1950s, which accentuated the poverty endemic to the area. Moreover, the deterioration of housing conditions in that area, exacerbated by a rapidly expanding black population, fostered the conditions typically associated with slums. Whereas African Americans had once touted Los Angeles as a "ghettoless paradise," the structure of racial inequality built into postwar suburbanization ensured that Southern California's suburban good life would remain off-limits to blacks.[65]

The transformation of Watts during the postwar period gave a different set of connotations to that community in the minds of suburban whites. Eldridge Cleaver, for example, who grew up in Watts during the 1950s, recalled how his community's name became an epithet, "the same way as city boys used 'country' as a term of derision. To deride one as 'lame' who did not know what was happening . . . the 'in-crowd' of the time from L.A. would bring a cat down by saying that he had just left Watts." If Watts symbolized the backwardness of country life to some, it began to signify the danger of the city to many whites, particularly following the Watts riots of 1965. In his successive bids for election as mayor of Los Angeles beginning in 1961, Samuel Yorty marshaled white anxieties about Los Angeles' growing black population and exploited images of an overcrowded ghetto bursting with black rage. In his successful 1969 campaign against Tom Bradley, who eventually became Los Angeles' first black mayor, Yorty and his campaign forces associated Bradley with the militant strain of black nationalism that unnerved white America. Circulating black and red flyers that read "Watts power" in white suburban communities and placing late-night phone calls to San Fernando Valley residents from a fictitious "Watts Committee for Bradley," Yorty strategically situated his opponent within a misrepresentation of Watts as the locus of seething black nationalism.[66]

The city's new mayor personified the political transformation of Southern California during the postwar period. Although Yorty had once been a

New Deal Democrat, the Cold War inspired his political metamorphosis as he cofounded California's version of HUAC. Yorty campaigned for Richard Nixon in the 1960 presidential election and later endorsed California's winning gubernatorial candidate, Ronald Reagan, whose political career followed a trajectory similar to Yorty's. His prodevelopment stance shaped his commitment to freeway construction, thereby winning the support of organized labor groups. Perhaps most crucial to his entry into the mayoral office, however, Yorty capitalized on the racial anxieties of white suburbanites who looked with trepidation on the inner city from their suburban enclaves. Yorty's tenure as Los Angeles mayor completed the political transition from the diverse working-class coalitions of the New Deal era to a politics predicated on the racial divisions that took shape in the context of decentralized urbanization. Subsequent chapters of this book, accordingly, explore the cultural dimensions of that transition, identifying the values and mindset that encouraged political leaders such as Yorty and Reagan to abandon the Democratic for the Republican party, not to mention the millions of working-class and lower-middle-class whites who undertook a similar crossing of party lines during the 1960s.[67]

If Watts surfaced as Southern California's ghetto after World War II, East Los Angeles became synonymous with the barrio, which sheltered the nation's largest concentration of Mexicans and Mexican Americans during the postwar period. Although Mexicans have maintained a presence in Eastside communities since the turn of the century, they shared those communal spaces with African Americans, Japanese Americans, Italian Americans, Jews, Russians, and Armenians. The war years, however, initiated the departure of groups that were not ethnically Mexican, leaving their homes to be rented or bought by Mexican immigrants and their children. During the 1940s, for example, Boyle Heights lost its Jewish population and coalesced with other Eastside communities to form a larger Chicano barrio, homogeneous and isolated from the rest of the city.[68]

The departure of the Jews from Boyle Heights left its mark on that community. A group typically associated with service provision in urban ethnic economies, Jews established a vibrant commercial life in East Los Angeles, but their exodus after World War II crippled the economic health of that community. One woman recalled the fate of East Los Angeles in the wake of its version of white flight:

> Everything was decaying and getting worse and worse. When I moved here, there were Japanese and Jewish. It was really a Jewish community. Everything was so green. We had everything—the theater, the drug stores, the little post office in the drug store. But since Jewish people

went, that was the end of the post office. Now, no more post office, no more banks. So we have to go to the one on Brooklyn or go downtown.[69]

The unincorporated status of East Los Angeles, moreover, limited that community's capacity to improve living conditions. Throughout the postwar period, East Los Angeles remained an unincorporated county "island" surrounded by Los Angeles and other municipalities. The concentration of Mexican immigrants and Mexican Americans in East Los Angeles during the postwar period added further strain on existing services and exacerbated the problems that already afflicted the community: poor housing, inadequate public services and facilities, meager employment opportunities, and deteriorating schools. Lacking the advantages of political self-determination and wholly dependent on an unresponsive county burdened with administrative responsibilities elsewhere, Chicanos and Mexican immigrants in East Los Angeles had little means to combat the placement of prisons and industrial waste sites that other communities successfully resisted. At the losing end of the municipal incorporation game, the citizens of East Los Angeles struggled to remedy the deteriorating quality of life in their community.[70]

Even as East Los Angeles witnessed a growing concentration of Mexican and Chicano poverty during the postwar period, however, the barrio did not encompass the experience of Los Angeles' Mexican American community to the same extent that the ghetto characterized the postwar experiences of African Americans in Los Angeles and other American cities. Although some may find such broad comparisons unsettling, historians have emphasized in recent years the "racial indeterminacy" of Mexican Americans, and have illustrated the ways in which that group has used this ambiguity to its advantage. Clearly, the experience of Mexican American soldiers during the war effort heightened a sense of patriotic nationalism in the Chicano community and inculcated a sense of entitlement to the good life that burgeoned in suburban Southern California. Neighborhoods in the San Gabriel Valley such as Pico Rivera cradled a Chicano middle class during the postwar period, while communities such as Lakewood tolerated those families of Mexican descent who willingly identified themselves as "Spanish." Less segregated than African Americans, Mexican Americans in postwar Los Angeles straddled the fence between chocolate cities and vanilla suburbs.[71]

The brief career of pop star Ritchie Valens illuminates some of the ambiguities underlying Mexican American identity in postwar Los Angeles. Valens grew up in Pacoima, a racially and ethnically heterogeneous suburb on the outskirts of the San Fernando Valley. During the late 1950s, Valens, then known to his friends and family as Ritchie Valenzuela, attended San

Fernando High School, which sheltered a striking and seemingly amicable intermixture of Chicano, black, Asian American, and white students. There, Valens earned local recognition by singing for the Silhouettes, a multiracial band popular among white and Chicano car clubs in East Los Angeles. The record producer Bob Keane recognized Valenzuela's potential and, after changing his name to Ritchie Valens, prepared the singer for mass-market appeal. Valens's Anglicized name reflected the racial premises on which Mexican Americans could attain success in show business, but his musical sensibilities drew on the polyphonic sounds of Southern California's diverse social mix. His childhood familiarity with traditional Mexican folk ballads, combined with his appreciation of rhythm and blues, rockabilly, and country western, sparked his talent for creating a unique sound that proved widely popular with a national audience. Valens's two greatest hits, "La Bamba," a traditional Mexican *son jarocho* taught to Valens by his uncle, and "Donna," a song about a failed romance with a white classmate whose father forbade her to go out with "that Mexican," illuminated the singer's transracial appeal and typified the subtle nuances embedded in postwar Mexican American identity.[72]

Valens belonged to a broader musical culture that maintained remnants of the cultural interactions that ensued during Southern California's Swing Era. Despite the overarching pattern of spatial and racial segregation, certain musical venues remained points of contact among black, Chicano, Asian, and white youths. In East Los Angeles, the Angelus Hall, East Los Angeles College, Rainbow Gardens, and the El Monte Legion Stadium featured R&B and rock and roll musicians that attracted predominantly Chicano and black audiences. The Zenda Ballroom downtown and the Hollywood Palladium echoed with the sounds of the Latin jazz that flourished in 1950s Los Angeles, catering to a mixture of blacks, Latinos, and Jews. These venues showcased the new musical styles that captivated the city's diverse populace and, to a certain extent, preserved what remained of the heterosocial New Deal culture that flourished during the 1930s and 1940s.[73]

The popularity of these musical venues illustrates a key strategy by which the region's youth found the means to "cruise around" the hegemonic bloc that enforced spatial and racial segregation, but it also provoked a powerful counter-effort to reinforce the cultural paradigm of chocolate cities and vanilla suburbs.[74] The Los Angeles Police Department (LAPD), under the leadership of chief William Parker, played a key role in this effort. Parker, an elite U.S. Army soldier who fought in World War II, became police chief in 1950 and restructured the police department along military lines. Although Parker managed to weed out the entrenched corruption in the LAPD, his militarization of the department inaugurated an epoch of sour relations between the police department and the black and Chicano communities, which have provided a constant source of trenchant criticism of law enforcement in Los Angeles since the Parker years.[75]

If the LAPD and its infamous Red Squad targeted union organizing in Los Angeles during the reign of the open shop, interracial mixing became the new scourge of law enforcement during the post–World War II period. The trumpeter Art Farmer, for example, recalls police harassment at a "nice club, what we would call black and tan, because black people and white people went there too." Los Angeles police officers, however, broke up the scene "because they said they didn't want this racial mixing there, and if the club didn't change its policy there was going to be trouble."[76] John Dolphin, owner of South Central's R&B record stores, organized a rally of 150 local businessmen who protested the LAPD's practice of turning away white patrons from black businesses on the grounds that it was simply "too dangerous to hang around black neighborhoods."[77] The musician Johnny Otis, who hosted a local television show for Los Angeles bands and their fans, described how the police would harass the youths who participated in the program: "The cops would come and hassle the kids standing in line, ... they see the black and Hispanic and Asian kids and they don't like it. They just didn't want to see that. If it were all Asian and Hispanic and black they wouldn't care, but there were whites there and they're mixing with the blacks and what not." Such tactics on the part of law enforcement so frustrated Otis that he ceased to promote his concerts in Los Angeles. The police effort to prevent interracial mixing within the venues of Los Angeles' nightlife suggests not only the degree to which such mixing persisted throughout the postwar period, but also a reinvigorated determination among city officials to enforce the emerging paradigm of space and race in the postwar urban region.[78]

Police harassment of minority youths had deadlier consequences than the closing of nightclubs. On the evening of August 11, 1965, the California Highway Patrol stopped Marquette Frye and his brother, who were found to be driving under the influence of alcohol. The officers handling the situation were about to release Frye and his brother when less forgiving officers appeared on the scene. The ensuing confrontation between the police and the Frye family aroused the anger of a nearby crowd of observers, all black, who began throwing rocks, bottles, and sticks at the officers as they fled in their cars. From this spark, the worst race riot in American history erupted over the course of five days, leaving thirty-four people (mostly Watts residents) dead, 1,032 injured, 3,952 arrested, and more than forty million dollars in property damage. In the wake of this tragedy, police chief William Parker offered his sensitive assessment of the situation: "One person threw a rock, and then, like monkeys in a zoo, others started throwing rocks."[79]

The racist comparison between African Americans and monkeys notwithstanding, Parker's description of Watts as a "zoo" not only bears an affinity to Reagan's vivid description of Los Angeles' inner city as "the jungle," but also implies the extent to which postwar suburbanization placed Southern California's black community in a virtual state of captivity. Excluded from the region's new suburban developments, African Americans found themselves boxed in by the exclusionary policies of federal agencies, as well as by the violence deployed by white homeowners and racist police officers. As the interracial working-class coalitions of the New Deal era fragmented under the aegis of the Cold War, and as a new pattern of racial segregation surfaced in the postwar American city, black Americans forged new models of political activism that asserted an invigorated sense of black identity and emphasized the distinct needs of the black community. The frustrations embedded in such activism at times exploded in violence, as it did in Los Angeles in August 1965 and throughout the rash of urban uprisings that punctuated the nation's "long hot summer" of the mid-1960s. But while the 1960s codification of identity politics among various racial groups elicited, and continues to elicit, charges of separatism from white liberals and conservatives alike, the logic of such politics mirrored the separatist pattern of decentralized urbanization that overtook American cities in the aftermath of World War II.

DERACINATING DOWNTOWN

The expanding concentration of poverty along the southern and eastern periphery of the city center vivified the crisis that afflicted downtown Los Angeles. Since the turn of the twentieth century, Los Angeles has followed a decentralized pattern of development, but that did not prevent the formation of a centralized urban core as far back as the 1920s, which sustained the concentration of the region's commercial and cultural activities. Office buildings, banks, restaurants, movie palaces, and streetcars lined the thoroughfares of Broadway and Spring Streets, offering some semblance of the centralized city. World War II, however, reversed that development by initiating an accelerated pattern of residential and industrial decentralization, diminishing the commercial and cultural prominence of downtown. By the mid-1950s, urban critics and boosters alike dismissed downtown Los Angeles as a mere "illusion," while national magazines such as *U.S. News and World*

Report underscored the perception of a downtown in decline: "The downtown area in Los Angeles has been hurt badly by the new patterns created by long-distance freeway driving and suburban living. Property values are down. There are more vacancies. Older buildings require repairs and replacements. Many blocks are filled with stores which look like outdoor bargain basements. This is not a problem indigenous to Los Angeles. All big cities have the same trend. But here the figures are especially depressing."[80]

Popular accounts of urban decline in Los Angeles implicated the presence of nonwhite social groups. *U.S. News and World Report,* for example, described a downtown "overrun with shoddy discount houses displaying signs in both English and Spanish."[81] A 1941 Works Progress Administration (WPA) guide to Los Angeles highlighted the disjuncture between the "grimy structures and crumbling adobes of the pueblo period" and the "monumental modern buildings" that began to appear in the downtown scene. "Evidences of the city's dissimilar periods and cultures create a feeling of confusion in this vicinity," the very kind of confusion that troubled a postwar generation of urban planners who sought to impose the modernist principles of order and uniformity on the urban landscape. The same guide identified Main Street as "the principle business street of a district with some 60,000 people of foreign birth—mostly Japanese, Fillipinos, Chinese, Mexicans, Negroes, Jews and Italians," and singled out this space for harboring "diverse types of derelicts and transients."[82] Throughout the postwar period, downtown Los Angeles became identified with the kind of racial heterogeneity that a new generation of suburban Americans abhorred.

American Indians soon became a part of downtown's social mix, particularly during the 1950s. The post–World War II period marked the expansion and urbanization of California's Indian community and, as a result of this process, Los Angeles sheltered the nation's largest concentration of Indians by the mid-1970s. In the early 1950s, the Bureau of Indian Affairs established its "Relocation" Program to generate greater self-sufficiency among Indians by removing them from reservation areas and placing them in jobs in western industrial centers. Though Los Angeles had historically maintained a small Indian presence relative to other racial and ethnic groups, the decades following World War II saw the expansion of an Indian population representing the many tribal affiliations of the Midwest and Southwest. In 1955, Los Angeles County had an Indian population estimated at six thousand; this more than doubled in the span of five years. In the twenty-one-year period between 1955 and 1976, approximately thirty thousand Indians were relocated to Los Angeles, most of whom initially settled as tenants in the low-rent, central city neighborhoods that had not yet been razed by urban renewal programs. Leaving the reservation without money, jobs, work skills, and, in most cases, basic familiarity with English, the 1950s generation of Indian arrivals in Los Angeles remained vulnerable to disease, unemployment, anomie, and, in particular, alcoholism in their confrontation with city life.[83]

The racialized milieu of downtown contrasted sharply with a vision of downtown redevelopment that took shape in Southern California's corporate community. For the business executives and city officials who constituted the downtown establishment of American cities, declining revenues, increasing crime, and the general exodus of a more affluent corps of workers, taxpayers, and consumers proved worrisome. To reverse downtown's downward spiral, business leaders formed alliances with municipal officials and labor groups. The "growth coalitions" that took shape in the nation's cities marshaled an array of public and private resources that transformed the historic function of the central business district. As with postwar suburbanization, the federal government played no small part in this process. As we shall see in chapters 5 and 6, public monies available for the construction of highways made possible the clearing of vast segments of downtown property that had been identified as "blighted," and Title 1 of the 1949 Housing Act authorized municipal governments to purchase, assemble, and clear blighted areas and then sell the bulldozed land to private developers, ostensibly for the purposes of housing. Such power encouraged municipal agencies to mitigate the effects of the postwar urban crisis by marshaling an array of public and private resources to reverse the fate of the postwar American city.[84]

Endowed with federal support, corporate leaders took the initiative in the effort to rebuild the nation's downtowns. In the two decades following World War II, the economic health of the central business district increasingly depended on the presence of national and multinational corporations, especially those affiliated with the expanding FIRE (finance, insurance, and real estate) sector of the economy. These industries dominated urban economies during the postwar period and compelled corporate executives to take an active interest in downtown revitalization. Corporations thus more or less directly sponsored the urban renewal process of the 1950s and 1960s as corporate leaders served on planning agencies and collaborated with city officials to create a downtown infrastructure amenable to the corporate world and its professional legions.[85]

In response to downtown decline, Los Angeles mayor Norris Poulson expressed a sentiment in 1955 shared by many of his mayoral counterparts elsewhere during the postwar period: "Sure we're decentralized here in Los

Angeles, but we've got to support and strengthen the downtown area. It's my notion that no city can be a great city without a strong downtown core."[86] Private businessmen concurred with the mayor's opinion. Walter Braunschweiger, executive vice president of Bank of America and chairman of the Los Angeles Central City Committee, described the imperative to redevelop downtown: "Los Angeles has a remarkable opportunity to proceed with the development of a new downtown. There is a need for new, larger structure and for investors to build buildings and for us to build a city. . . . [T]he plan can enhance the values of the Los Angeles central area as the headquarters for business and as a cultural and recreational center."[87]

In that endeavor, public officials, labor groups, and corporate interests vested in downtown redevelopment established various agencies to remedy inner-city decline. Los Angeles' growth coalition comprised many organizations such as the Greater Los Angeles Plans Incorporated (GLAPI) and the Downtown Businessmen's Association, which represented the support of twenty-five of downtown's most prominent businesses, including Norman Chandler of the Times Mirror Corporation. At a moment when the economic vitality of downtown Los Angeles weakened under the decentralizing force of suburbanization, the city's business elite sought ways to secure the presence of large firms to maintain regional economic development.[88]

Among GLAPI's first tasks was the redevelopment of Bunker Hill (see figure 1), formerly a middle-class residential enclave in the heart of downtown Los Angeles, which by the 1940s sheltered a working-class immigrant community of tenement houses, mom and pop stores, cafes, restaurants, drugstores, shoe-repair shops, and dry-cleaning services. That neighborhood presented an eyesore for city officials and downtown executives who envisioned a sanitized corporate image of downtown Los Angeles. In 1939, the HOLC identified the "blighted" condition of Bunker Hill, noting in particular its racial diversity: "This is one of the older and practically obsolete single family residential sections, having had its beginning 50 years or more ago. Subversive racial elements predominate. . . . [I]t is a slum area and one of the city's melting pots." The HOLC targeted Bunker Hill as a "slum clearance project," but recognized that "definite steps have as yet [not] been taken."[89]

The first plans for Bunker Hill's redevelopment reflected the initial compatibility of public housing with redevelopment, as prescribed by New Deal policy. Architects Robert Alexander and Drayton Bryant, both of whom shared the social vision that informed the planning policies of the New Deal, proposed a redevelopment scheme that ensured the maintenance of the "predominantly residential" character of Bunker Hill, using funds from the

FIGURE 1. Noir Los Angeles, circa 1940: "blight" on Bunker Hill. (Courtesy of the Los Angeles Public Library.)

1949 Housing Act to build eleven apartment buildings "so spaced and oriented as to take full advantage of views, sun and breeze."[90]

The mid-1950s defeat of public housing, however, freed the Los Angeles Community Redevelopment Agency (CRA) to pursue a redevelopment program that did not contain a housing component, one that more closely reflected the corporate-civic vision of GLAPI and the Downtown Businessmen's Association. A sense of betrayal descended on the soon-to-be-displaced residents of Bunker Hill, who waged a campaign against the CRA through letter writing, lawsuits, and public protests. Much of their outrage focused on the apparent contradiction in the logic of the city's probusiness forces, which decried government-subsidized housing as "socialistic," yet welcomed the use of public monies for slum clearance and urban renewal. Without the support of organized labor, which by the 1950s had abandoned New Deal issues such as public housing and had embraced the prodevelopment agenda of the city's corporate interests, the community activists of Bunker Hill found little support for their cause.[91]

Bunker Hill redevelopment would thus proceed without the original housing scheme proposed by Alexander and Bryant. Vested with the broad powers of eminent domain to acquire, administer, sell, and lease property, the Los Angeles CRA condemned Bunker Hill as "blighted" in 1951 and slated the district for redevelopment. The CRA used official reports from fire, police, and health departments, all of which emphasized the dangerous and decrepit conditions of that neighborhood. After the piecemeal acquisition of Bunker Hill properties, the CRA relocated the residents and businesses of Bunker Hill and began site demolition in 1960.[92]

In the course of a single decade, the CRA wiped out one hundred years of organic growth in Bunker Hill. The corporatization of that neighborhood closely followed the discipline of modernist city planning, which embraced the principles of homogeneity, uniformity, and monumentality over diversity, complexity, and locality. Bunker Hill itself was smoothed, homogenized, graded, and degraded. High-rise corporate "monuments" appeared, linked by private pedestrian walkways and plazas. Luxury apartment towers substituted for tenement houses, catering to Bunker Hill's anticipated white-collar clientele. The streets that had sustained Bunker Hill's bustling social life gave way to multilane thoroughfares that bisected vast parking structures. "Superblocks" and "megastructures" highlighted the landscape of the new Bunker Hill and reflected the new spatial order that overtook American inner-city landscapes during the postwar period (see figure 2).[93]

Aware that office towers and luxury apartments alone could not sufficiently anchor a corporate workforce in a revitalized downtown, city officials and corporate elites sought to implement a new cultural infrastructure within downtown's parameters. Their logic reflected an important pattern in the history of urban growth. Cultural institutions such as museums, symphonies, theaters, and universities have historically played an auxiliary, yet important, role in the promotion of urban development. The corporate makeover of the nation's inner cities implicated such institutions of high culture. The early 1960s construction of New York City's Lincoln Center, for example, epitomized the use of high culture in the postwar drama of urban redevelopment.[94]

In their quest to assert the cultural sophistication of their city, civic elites in Los Angeles pursued their own version of Lincoln Center. The construction of the Dorothy Chandler Pavilion and the Mark Taper Forum (together referred to as the Music Center) illustrates the process by which high culture came to displace working-class immigrant culture in downtown spaces such as Bunker Hill. "In a dazzle of diamonds and décolletage, with cinema stars, celebrities and just plain millionaires on hand," the Music Center

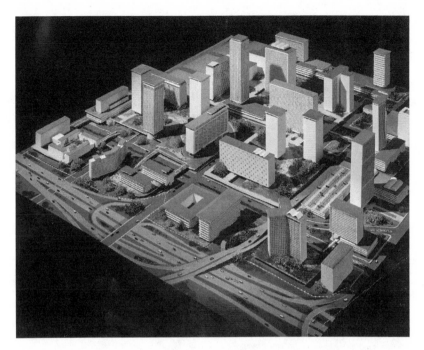

FIGURE 2.   Model for the new Bunker Hill, circa 1950s. (Courtesy of the Los Angeles Public Library.)

opened on December 6, 1964, illustrating the cultural politics of downtown revitalization.[95] As chapter 5 emphasizes, however, downtown's makeover also included more popular cultural institutions, as the construction of Dodger Stadium in nearby Chavez Ravine comprised the popular counterpart to the Music Center, both cultural centerpieces of the "new downtown."

The opening of the Music Center marked a turning point in the regional history of elite formation. Until Dorothy Chandler executed her scheme, the ranks of Southern California's elite remained firmly grounded in WASP identity. To the consternation of the downtown establishment, however, Chandler "crossed over" to the city's burgeoning Westside, to enlist Jewish financial support for her vision of high culture in downtown Los Angeles. She turned to Mark Taper, who saved the day for Mrs. Chandler by handing her a last-minute sum of one million dollars. Taper's contribution symbolized a kind of olive branch that mended the widening rift between Westside Jewish wealth and downtown WASP wealth, and signaled the initial acceptance of Jews into the upper echelons of Southern California society.[96] The

Dorothy Chandler Pavilion and the Mark Taper Forum thus stood as tributes to the ethnic rapprochement between WASPs and Jews in the upper tiers of Southern California's class hierarchy.

Despite the spatial discrepancy between the monumentality of the new downtown and the decentralized, low-density development of its surrounding urban region, the postwar makeover of downtown Los Angeles reveals the extent to which urban planners predicated their redevelopment efforts on a set of values similar to that which guided suburban development. Their efforts to implement homogeneous, uniform spaces within the parameters of downtown and to obliterate the existing spaces of complexity and diversity reflected the same principles that informed the design and construction of communities such as Lakewood, as well as the cultural institutions that sustained their quality of life: shopping malls, theme parks, and freeways. Chapter 5 extends this discussion further, emphasizing the ways in which Dodger Stadium mirrored the postwar suburbanization of the city center, but that process followed a set of principles that guided the organization of urban and suburban space throughout the postwar period.

If suburbanization, at least in its postwar manifestation, implied a racialized process that privileged an inclusive white identity, then the suburbanization of downtown Los Angeles underscored the saliency of race in the midcentury transformation of urban life. Writing to city councilman Edward Roybal in the midst of the Bunker Hill controversy, Maria Gallegos de Hillary thanked the city's first twentieth-century Mexican American official for his outspoken stance against downtown redevelopment: "If it should go through none of us in the old neighborhoods of the town would feel safe.... One would think that this were Russia where a community of individuals can be liquidated at the whim of a planner.... Yo no soy en su distrito, pero soy de tu raza [I am not in your district, but I am of your race]."[97] Such sentiments, while reflecting a sense of ethnic pride, also capture the ways in which urban renewal programs of the 1950s conjured feelings of racial solidarity among those groups adversely affected by the convulsive transformation of American urban life at midcentury.

SUBURBANISM AS A WAY OF LIFE

The spectacular growth of Southern California in the decades following World War II brought national attention to the region. *Newsweek*, for example, declared that "it's still an age of miracles" in its 1953 cover story about Los Angeles and its postwar development. "The most rapidly expanding area on earth," Los Angeles surfaced in the pages of *Newsweek* as "big league country" even before the arrival of the Brooklyn Dodgers in 1957. Other national magazines offered similar glimpses of the "new" Los Angeles. *Life,* for example, ran a 1960 cover story titled "Los Angeles in a New Image," and *National Geographic* showcased an elaborate photo essay on the "Colossus of the West," depicting the same cultural icons that rival magazines highlighted in their coverage of the expanding western metropolis: "Hollywood's gaudy white way," the "ecstatic world" of Disneyland, the "ultramodern" Dodger Stadium, and "the ribbons of freeway."[98]

In the cultural discourse of postwar America, Hollywood, Disneyland, Dodger Stadium, and the freeways symbolized the "new" Los Angeles that took shape in the decades following World War II. In the following chapters, we shall discover how each of these institutions corresponded to the various dimensions of Southern California's postwar transformation that have been considered in the preceding pages. Hollywood, through its rendition of film noir and science fiction, visualized the "blight" that afflicted Southern California's urban core during the mid-1940s, while Disneyland encompassed the utopian aspirations that guided the region's explosive phase of suburban development. Dodger Stadium demonstrated, ostensibly, the regenerative possibilities of urban renewal, while the implementation of a unified network of freeways underscored the centrality of highway construction to the postwar urban experience. Inner-city decline, suburbanization, urban renewal, and highway construction transformed the American city in the decades following World War II, and the combination of these factors wielded a new cultural configuration that defined the "new" Los Angeles in the second half of the twentieth century.

These spatial processes, however, simultaneously engendered a growing awareness of race and racial difference, and this too dominated public discussion in and about the "new" Los Angeles. In 1956, *U.S. News and World Report* soberly reported, "West Coast, Too, Has Its Race Problems." The article described the dramatic expansion of Los Angeles' black community. "Negroes are flocking to Los Angeles from the South," where they "meet hostility from 'Anglo' whites and sometimes, too, Mexican Americans." The national newsmagazine reported this development to its white readership with a faint hint of alarm: "At every hand, in the factories, offices and schools of Los Angeles, you'll find growing numbers of the new Negro— ambitious . . . and aggressive in his demands." Local magazines intensified the spotlight on the "blackening" of postwar Los Angeles. *Los Angeles,* "the magazine of the good life in Southern California," featured an article about the problems facing "our Negro community," while *Frontier* magazine, reflecting the more liberal slant of *The Nation,* which owned it, reported that Los Angeles "may not know it," but it was "spiritually below the Mason Dixon Line."[99]

Thus, to the chagrin of those who, like police chief William Parker, upheld Southern California as the nation's white spot, the "new Negro" became part and parcel of the new Los Angeles. By and large, black newcomers to Los Angeles during and after World War II were excluded from the postwar suburban boom, and their confinement within the parameters of an expanding ghetto garnered heightened awareness of Southern California's "widening black-belt." The "racial revolution" that exploded during the war years thus set the stage for the spatial and racial polarization of Southern California's postwar urban region and anticipated the formation of a racialized political culture that brought a decisive end to Southern California's New Deal order. While postwar Americans could read about the "blackening" of Los Angeles in the pages of newspapers and magazines, they could also witness Hollywood's rendition of that process through the arrival of new film genres that focused on the "black" city and its alien invaders. Film noir and the urban science fiction film delineated a set of representations that dramatized the nation's urban crisis, and Los Angeles, a rapidly expanding metropolis in deep denial about its own urbanity, played a starring role in such representations.

3 The Spectacle of Urban Blight
Hollywood's Rendition of a Black Los Angeles

"See Los Angeles crumble before your very eyes!" promised the *Los Angeles Herald Express* in the headline of its review of *War of the Worlds*, a science fiction thriller about a Martian attack on Los Angeles. Movie audiences reveled in the film's special effects, which dramatized the aliens' annihilation of Los Angeles and the frenzied exodus of the city's inhabitants. *War of the Worlds*, based on the 1898 H. G. Wells novel and a cinematic replay of Orson Welles's infamous radio broadcast of 1939, was the nation's highest-grossing film after its release by Paramount Pictures in 1953, and it inaugurated Hollywood's golden age of science fiction cinema.[1]

The film brought a sigh of relief to the film industry. The 1940s were a time of uncertainty for Hollywood, as a series of financial setbacks and congressional investigations challenged its monopoly on the cultural life of American society. The arrival of television in the late 1940s worsened Hollywood's predicament by offering a privatized alternative to the experience of going out to the movies. The industry's pessimism translated into a set of cinematic representations that dramatized the deterioration of the modern city and its public culture. Film noir arrived in the aftermath of World War II and rendered a bleak portrait of urban decadence, in which the boundaries that fortified traditional social relationships dissolved. By the early 1950s, such images gave way to a more unsettling portrait of urban chaos, as the urban science fiction film portrayed attacks on American cities by hordes of alien invaders. Once a garish symbol of the new mass culture that dominated the public sphere of the industrial metropolis, Hollywood suffered alongside the midcentury decline of that culture and implicated itself in its cinematic obituary for urban America.

Double Indemnity (1944), which initiated the late 1940s cycle of film noir, and the 1953 success of *War of the Worlds* bracketed a transitional moment in the national political culture, in which a privatized conservative ethos displaced New Deal idealism in the polarized climate of the Cold War. The director and actor John Huston sensed this transition from his vantage point in Hollywood, noting that by the late '40s "the high hopes and ideals of much of the Roosevelt years were slipping away."[2] Moreover, Siegfried Kracauer, who had just finished his magnum opus, *From Caligari to Hitler*, which recognized in German Expressionist cinema a latent social need for a totalitarian state, looked at Hollywood's new "horror thrillers" to identify "the sadistic energies at large in our society [that] are specifically suited to provide fuel for fascism."[3] McCarthyism did not produce the brand of fascism that overtook Kracauer's Europe, but film noir's tales of cynical disillusionment and the apocalyptic imagery of science fiction heralded a new political culture that rejected the social vision of New Deal liberalism and evidenced the ideological transformation of American society during the 1950s.

That Los Angeles provided a conspicuous setting for both *Double Indemnity* and *War of the Worlds* suggests how the makers of both film noir and the urban science fiction film found that city an appropriate canvas upon which to render their indictment of the industrial metropolis and its public culture. While the expansion of suburban Southern California provided a mythic space for the construction of a new "white city," the postwar deterioration and racialization of urban communities such as Boyle Heights, Bunker Hill, and Watts offered a decaying foundation upon which to construct a cinematic vision of a black and alien Los Angeles. To identify regional anxieties about the demise of the Progressives' "better city," this chapter considers Hollywood's late-1940s portrait of Southern California's "black city" through the lens of two popular film genres: film noir and the urban science fiction film. The films surveyed in this chapter constituted a cinematic prelude to a new "new mass culture," which took shape in the region's emerging vanilla suburbs and modeled a set of new values that were inimical to the spatial culture of New Deal urbanism. A city caught between a bygone vision of suburban idyll and a "black" portrait of its urban future, Los Angeles encompassed the urban ambivalence of Americans in the age of white flight.[4]

KILLING THE SLUM

As a preamble to understanding how film noir and the urban science fiction film heralded the arrival of a new suburban cultural order, some consideration of the early relationship between cinema and urban modernity is necessary. Unlike Disneyland, Dodger Stadium, and the freeway, which marked a clear and conscious departure from their respective cultural predecessors, Hollywood and the movies at midcentury remained synonymous with the new mass culture that peaked at the turn of the century. From its earliest inception, cinema reproduced the experience of urban modernity that enveloped the burgeoning crowds of consumers and spectators in the cities of Europe and America. If the modern city introduced a set of new sensations and novel distractions through technical innovation and mechanical reproduction, cinema codified those sensations and distractions within a cultural practice that replicated the discontinuous, ephemeral, and frenzied nature of the urban experience. It debuted alongside new technologies such as trains, photography, electric lighting, telegraph, and telephone, and it materialized in a burgeoning consumer culture of spectacular display that included department stores, world expositions, and advertising, as well as more lurid attractions such as phantasmagoria, wax museums, and morgues. Indeed, modern life was "cinematic" before the fact, and it delivered a new experience of space and time that was repackaged on a more intimate scale in the darkened space of the movie theater.[5]

Cinema captured the varied experiences of urban modernity across space and time. Toward the late nineteenth century, Paris emerged as a capital of modern life, and, after its massive restructuring through the interventions of Haussmannization, that city sustained the development of a new visual culture predicated on ephemerality and the accelerated circulation of images, bodies, and glances. If Paris represented a "showplace of visuality and distraction," New York promulgated a hyperstimulating urban experience reinforced by the rapid concentration of sounds, signs, and crowds. In an environment characterized by the "intensification of nervous stimuli," cinema marketed speed, thrill, and sensation as popular entertainment.[6] If Paris and New York implicated cinema in their distinctive cultures of visuality and nervous stimulation, the westward migration of filmmakers at the outset of the twentieth century added yet another dimension to the affinity between the movies and modern life: mass production.

Cinema already dominated the public life of Paris and New York by the time of its arrival in Hollywood. The movies came to Southern California in 1906, when the New York–based Biograph Company became the first to shoot in the Los Angeles area. By 1911, at least ten motion picture companies had established themselves in the region, initiating a trend that codified Southern California's ascendance as the world capital of film production. Film historians have offered various explanations as to why film production shifted from East to West. Obviously, Southern California's temperate climate and varied topography played a crucial role, providing ideal conditions for on-location shooting. The region's open-shop policy, moreover, resulted in lower costs of labor relative to other cities. And the dominance of the Motion Picture Patents Company (MPPC) in East Coast markets hampered the commercial success of independent filmmakers, who sought alternative locations for film production in places such as Southern California, far removed from the domain of powerful agencies like the MPPC.[7]

The prominence of the independent filmmaker at this time underscores the fact that filmmaking largely remained an individual enterprise at the outset of the twentieth century, removed from the corporatist structure of film production that became synonymous with Hollywood and the studio system by the 1920s. In the urban centers of the East Coast and the Midwest, cinema first took root in immigrant, working-class neighborhoods, which popularized those cultural practices that were relatively inexpensive to produce and enjoy. In this context, early American cinema appealed to a marginal yet expanding population of urban consumers who often found reflections of their life circumstances in the representational fare of early film. The film historian Stephen Ross has demonstrated how pre-Hollywood filmmaking reflected an ideological mélange of silent short film, catering to a varied set of class and ethnic constituencies. Class consciousness remained a hallmark of American filmmaking up through the first two decades of the twentieth century, and the manifestation of working-class cinema underscored how early film consciously appealed to immigrant working-class audiences by depicting their own plight.[8]

The 1920s rise of Hollywood, however, precluded cinematic representations of class struggle and guided the politics of filmmaking in a decidedly more conservative direction. Ironically, this development was maneuvered by a bold set of ethnic entrepreneurs, who rose from their immigrant working-class precincts in cities such as Chicago and New York to captain the helm of Hollywood's industrial behemoth. The role of Jewish tradesmen in the making of Hollywood illuminates not only the process by which the film industry situated itself in the dominant structures of power in American society, but also the means by which a generation of ethnic immigrant entrepreneurs and entertainers forged an economic and representational space in which to reinvent themselves and their identities, anticipating the metamorphosis of a social group that up to a certain point retained an affinity with the ethnic, working-class connotations of the immigrant slum. As the world capital of film production, Hollywood came into being through the efforts of Jewish men—such as Jesse Lasky, Carl Laemmle, Adolph Zukor, William Fox, Samuel Goldwyn, Marcus Loew, Louis B.

Mayer, William Fox, Irving Thalberg, Harry, Al, Jack, and Sam Warner, Harry Cohn, Joe and Nick Schenk, and David O. Selznick—who forged the modern motion picture industry through the centralization of film production, distribution, and exhibition. Hollywood's "big eight" studios— Paramount, Fox, MGM, Universal, Warner Brothers, Columbia, United Artists, and RKO—innovated the application of assembly-line factory production to the business of making movies and substantially diminished the opportunities for independent filmmaking. By the mid-1920s, the Big Eight enjoyed a virtual monopoly over film production. Lary May first discovered the now well-known fact that "from 60 firms scattered all over the nation making about 2,000 movies per year in 1912, the 'big eight' made 90 percent of the 800 yearly feature films during the 1920s."[9]

For this generation of Jewish immigrant entrepreneurs, Hollywood supplied an ideal melting pot that codified a more expansive notion of American identity that appealed to an aspiring generation of immigrant Americans and their progeny. Little wonder, then, that Carl Laemmle named his weekly column for his studio trade journal the "Melting Pot," and chose an architectural style laden with racial connotations—Mission Revival—as the most appropriate garb for his Universal City studio, which opened in 1913. Jewish entertainers such as Al Jolson simultaneously repopularized the minstrel show as a staple form of entertainment in 1920s America, which reflected the process by which Hollywood's version of blackface could effectively Americanize immigrant ethnic groups. These examples underscore the way in which the rise of Hollywood and the studio system used cultural significations of racial otherness to assert a racialized vision of American identity, one that materialized under the aegis of an evolving corporate structure that broadened the appeal of the Hollywood product among an expanding mass of consumers.[10]

By the end of the 1920s, after the solidification of the studio system, Hollywood had successfully steered filmmaking away from its diverse, working-class origins toward a standardized form of mass entertainment that catered to a broadening category of middle-class Americans. This shift corresponded to a set of cinematic representations that departed from earlier scenes of class conflict, emphasizing instead cross-class fantasies that embraced more conservative ideals such as consumption and class harmony. Moreover, such fantasies materialized in a new institution that highlighted the commercial precincts of urban America: the movie palace. This venue sanctioned the commingling of classes and ethnic groups in an opulent setting that often mimicked racialized fantasies of Oriental, Egyptian, or Arabian splendor. Sid Grauman's Chinese Theater, for example, opening in

Hollywood in 1924, sported a ninety-foot-high bronze pagoda roof and brought "all the mysteries of the Orient" to the "very heart of the cinema capital of the world." The Chinese Theater modeled the new exoticism that infused the moviegoing experience of the 1920s and reflected the Orientalist cravings of consumers who coalesced under a broader reconfiguration of middle-class whiteness.[11]

If cinema replicated the varied experiences of modern urban life, its subsequent industrialization in 1920s Hollywood demonstrated how mass production and mass consumption defined a distinctly twentieth-century brand of American modernity. The mass production of movies under the new studio system diminished the subversive potential of filmmaking and encouraged Hollywood filmmakers to tailor their product according to dominant conceptions of the social world and its constituent identities. This process empowered marginal social groups to align themselves within the mainstream of social life and to effectively "Americanize" themselves through a set of representational and economic practices that reinforced prevalent notions of patriarchy, racial hierarchy, and classlessness. When Adolph Zukor thus described his ambition "to kill the slum tradition in the movies," he articulated the means by which the rise of Hollywood could support dominant social values and silence any oppositional tendencies.[12] It was not until the late 1940s, however, at the dawn of the postwar suburban boom, that the "slum tradition" was killed once and for all through the arrival of film noir.

BLACK CITY, BLACK FILM

Coined by French film critics in the late 1940s, the term *film noir* denotes a cycle of filmmaking in the United States roughly spanning the ten years following the end of World War II. Defined as a genre, a mood, a sensibility, and a movement, film noir eludes precise definition but includes an array of crime dramas ranging from individual case studies of murder and criminal deviance to more general treatments of gangsters and organized crime. Its origins have been related to various cultural and intellectual influences: Progressive muckraking journalism, hard-boiled detective fiction, German Expressionist cinema, French existentialism, and Freudian psychoanalysis. Although not exclusive to film noir, the stylistic conventions associated with it—compositional imbalance, location and night shooting, voice-over narration, chiaroscuro lighting—arose within the historical circumstances of film production during the 1940s. Wartime restrictions imposed limited budgets and a materials shortage on filmmakers, who experimented with new techniques in lighting, sound, cameras, lenses, and editing.[13]

Noir's thematic emphasis on betrayal, alienation, and disillusionment marked a distinct departure from the standard fare of filmmaking in the United States. The French critics who first identified film noir in the late '40s noted that American films of this period demonstrated a more somber style and a darker tone than the usual American movie of the '30s, which generally conveyed happy endings and an upbeat spirit. By contrast, noir's tales of murder and passion, of ordinary lives gone hopelessly astray, of psychopathic criminals preying upon innocent citizens and of conniving women seducing gullible men, alluded to a changing sensibility among postwar American movie audiences. To these critics, and to their American counterparts, the "new wave" of crime dramas after World War II suggested a shift in the national psyche, a distinct loss of confidence in the vitality of the American dream.[14]

Film noir embraced the modern industrial city as its favored milieu but emphasized the seedy side of urban life. Noir's dark urban vision resonated throughout its titles: *Dark City, City of Fear, The Naked City,* and *Cry of the City.* The noir vision of the city drew on a representational tradition in Western culture. In contrast to the Enlightenment view of the Western city as the site of individual opportunity and the summit of social progress, film noir emphasized the social and psychological consequences of urban modernity. Based initially on the writings of Dashiell Hammett, Raymond Chandler, and James Cain, and with striking parallels to the paintings of Reginald Marsh, George Bellows, and Edward Hopper, noir's erotic portrait of an urban wasteland intimated a deep ambivalence toward the American metropolis. By the 1940s, amid a massive surge of urban industrial growth, film noir translated these literary and artistic visions of urban malaise into a more popular cinematic discourse that appealed to broad audiences.

Towering buildings and neon signs frame noir's narratives of urban malaise, and its characters are often unable to find their way out of the city's nocturnal maze of littered streets, desolate alleys, and dingy sewers. In *D.O.A.* (1950), a small-town accountant indulges in the rowdy nightlife of the big city, only to realize that he has been fatally poisoned. He spends his remaining hours on the streets of Los Angeles in a frantic search for his killer. In *Act of Violence* (1949), Frank Enley returns from the war to live a quiet life in the suburbs with his wife and children, but flees to the abandoned neighborhoods of downtown Los Angeles to evade an avenger from his shady past. And in *The Reckless Moment* (1949), Lucia Harper, an upstanding suburban matron, is drawn into the city's nefarious web to protect the reputation of her daughter. The frame darkens and seems to contract as she drives into the inner city, where meandering grotesques peer ominously through her window. If the noir city traps the innocent, it also shelters the guilty, who lurk in the darkest corners of the metropolis. In *He Walked by Night* (1949), a cop killer prowls the city's byways at night, descending into the sewers to evade police. In *M*, a 1951 remake of Fritz Lang's macabre classic, a child molester hides alone in a shabby Bunker Hill tenement, where detectives find the tiny shoes of his child victims.

Film noir depicted a world in which promiscuous interactions among the city's diverse strangers had disastrous, often deadly consequences. In the maelstrom of city life, the boundaries between good and evil blur, and film noir catalogued the various sorts of transgressions that transpired in the wake of this blurring. In the noir city, emasculating women seduce and manipulate vulnerable men. Waitresses, nurses, truck drivers, and salesmen mock the work ethic by concocting murderous schemes in their pursuit of easy wealth. Murderers, thieves, and mobsters hide from the law in black nightclubs, Turkish baths, and Chinatowns, where their criminality assumes racial connotations. The illicit associations among diverse yet equally shady figures transpire in those spaces of the modern city that suited the striking cinematography of film noir: nightclubs, alleys, sidewalks, tenements, train stations, bathhouses, amusement parks, and office buildings. In the dark and disordered universe of the noir city, the inscribed boundaries between the races, sexes, and classes dissolved.

Noir directors targeted specific urban sites that conveyed their vision of urban malaise. The tenement, for example, is a recurrent noir setting, identified as an appropriate milieu for noir's gallery of urban deviants. Its peeling walls, dingy lighting, rickety stairs, and brick walls frame the encounters between prostitutes and their johns in *Act of Violence* and hide the monstrous fetishes of the child molester in *M*. Similarly, the nightclub shelters the shady dealings and illicit liaisons that transpire in the noir city. In *Criss Cross* (1949) and *D.O.A.*, the nightclub and its exotic music lure the morally susceptible main characters into the city's racial underworld and, ultimately, to their demise. And in *T-Men* (1948), undercover Treasury agents venture into a seedy Ocean Pier nightclub to crack a mob ring of counterfeiters. Noir featured the tenement and the nightclub, both landmarks in the culture of industrial urbanism, as conspicuous venues for the kinds of social transgressions that transpire in the noir city.

Film noir innovated narrative strategies to enhance its portrait of urban chaos. Noir's use of the flashback as a narrative device reinforced the overall emphasis on the disjointed and chaotic texture of modern life. In contrast to contemporary Hollywood narratives, which followed a clear chronological order, film noir favored a twisted and highly convoluted narrative structure in which past and present are haphazardly intertwined through the scattered and often contradictory memories of multiple characters. The flashback is a primary vehicle for this effect. Flashbacks from several points of view and flashbacks within flashbacks enforced a splintered chronology that prevented the straightforward narration of a story. The narratives of *Mildred Pierce* (1945), *Double Indemnity, D.O.A., Criss Cross,* and *Sunset Boulevard* (1950), for example, are conveyed almost entirely through flashbacks.[15]

The flashback signaled a departure from conventional narrative structures in other ways as well. Prior to noir, most Hollywood films had happy endings. Noir, by contrast, not only offered decidedly unhappy endings, but also disclosed those endings at the outset of the films. Thus in *Sunset Boulevard*, we learn that Joe Gillis is dead as he begins to narrate the events that led to his murder. Likewise, a dying Walter Neff calmly relates the story of his fateful involvement with a femme fatale in *Double Indemnity*. Set in the labyrinthine streets and dark alleys of the modern city, the jumbled narratives of film noir reflected and reinforced the perception of the city as the site of danger, chaos, and imminent doom. As we shall see in subsequent chapters, film noir prefigured the need for new cultural institutions such as Disneyland and Dodger Stadium, which reflected a new suburban cultural order that repudiated the disordered culture of the metropolis in favor of a more regimented organization of cultural space.

LOS ANGELES NOIR

Film noir favored New York as the preeminent noir city, but it maintained a tight focus on Los Angeles as well. To a certain extent, noir's unflattering portrait of midcentury Los Angeles reflected the perspective of those who wrote and directed noir films from their vantage point in Hollywood. Fleeing the perils of Nazi Germany, some of Europe's most celebrated artists and intellectuals came to Los Angeles during the war years and brought their aesthetic sensibilities to bear on the style of Hollywood filmmaking during the 1940s. Banished from their cosmopolitan cultural milieu in Paris, Vienna, and Berlin, some of these individuals drew on their experiences in Los Angeles and Hollywood to fashion a critique of twentieth-century mass culture and, by extension, of the Enlightenment and its legacy in the West. Theodor Adorno and Max Horkheimer continued the work of the Frankfurt School, or the Institute for Social Research, in wartime Los Angeles, where they sketched their ominous vision of an all-powerful "Culture Industry." Ironically, Los Angeles' culture industry offered lucrative opportunities for some of Adorno and Horkheimer's compatriots, whose familiarity with German Expressionist cinema laid the groundwork for the creation of Los Angeles noir. Like the Marxist dialecticians, some of noir's most acclaimed directors, namely Billy Wilder *(Double Indemnity, Sunset Boulevard)*, Fritz Lang, Max Ophuls *(The Reckless Moment)*, Robert Siodmak *(Criss Cross)*, Otto Preminger *(Whirlpool)*, and Fred Zimmerman *(Act of Violence)*, found in Los Angeles the makings of a noir vision of urban decline and social anomie.[16]

In whatever ways Los Angeles may have offended the urban sensibilities of cosmopolitan Europeans, the city's landscape at midcentury provided an authentic setting for the creation of Los Angeles noir. By forgoing studio sets in favor of on-location shooting, the directors of *Act of Violence, Mildred Pierce, Double Indemnity, Sunset Boulevard, In a Lonely Place* (1950), *Criss Cross, D.O.A., T-Men,* and *He Walked by Night* incorporated the roughest corners of Los Angeles into their vision of urban decline to refine the look of authenticity in their films. The pressbook for *Criss Cross,* for example, emphasized to theater owners and advertisers that "the air of realism and authenticity which pervades the film is largely due to the fact that all of the outdoor scenes were filmed in their actual locale, which is the old section of Los Angeles."[17] However contrived or illusory movies seem, *Criss Cross* and other cinematic examples of Los Angeles noir illustrate how the city itself, at least its deteriorated portions, provided an authentic setting for dramatizing the malaise that settled on American cities at midcentury.[18]

Noir filmmakers identified particular Los Angeles neighborhoods that modeled the archetypal noir landscape. Bunker Hill, once lauded as an affluent enclave of Los Angeles, bore the visible signs of what planning officials defined as urban blight at midcentury. As early as 1939, the Home Owners' Loan Corporation (HOLC) reports identified Bunker Hill as having "been through all the phases of decline and is now thoroughly blighted." Even more noir was the HOLC's recognition of the "subversive racial elements [that] predominate" in the neighborhood, with "dilapidation and squalor everywhere in evidence."[19] Newcomers to Los Angeles—whether Mexicans from south of the border or Indians from the American Southwest—found Bunker Hill a convenient and affordable place to settle, while the neighborhood simultaneously sheltered a substantial elderly population. After World War II, Bunker Hill continued to decline, as police reports confirmed an increase in crime and cited evidence of a burgeoning narcotics trade. By

1957, the city's Department of Building and Safety identified 60 percent of Bunker Hill's buildings as hazardous.[20] At the outset of the postwar period, a rapidly deteriorating Bunker Hill reminded city officials that the ills of urbanization were catching up with Los Angeles.

Housing officials targeted Bunker Hill as an area ripe for "rehabilitation" and produced their own film noir to garner support for a slum clearance project. In 1949, the City Housing Authority (CHA) of Los Angeles, with the assistance of USC graduate students, produced *And Ten Thousand More*, a short film documenting slum conditions in Los Angeles as part of its campaign in support of public housing. The film depicts a young reporter on an assignment to find out if Los Angeles needs the ten thousand units of public housing requested by mayor Fletcher Bowron. "I got the lowdown, maps, statistics, the whole works," says the reporter in a voice-over narration, then, "like a leg man is supposed to do, I went out and got a look for myself." Unlike the jaded private eyes of Raymond Chandler and Dashiell Hammett novels, who know the dark secrets of the noir city, the earnest reporter of *And Ten Thousand More* is innocent of the depths of squalor at the heart of Los Angeles. Surveying the impoverished neighborhoods of Bunker Hill and the Chavez Ravine, the reporter is shocked to discover "slums tucked in everywhere all over town, where you'd least expect them." As the reporter walks through a dismal landscape of tents, shacks, tenement houses, and factories, the towering image of City Hall looms in the background, identifying the authorities responsible for cleaning up the mess. "What can be done about all this?" asks the reporter, who next visits a public housing site recently completed by the city of Los Angeles. In stark contrast to the filth of inner-city poverty, public housing is presented as a model of domestic tranquility and community stability. By the end of his assignment, the reporter's editor asks, "Does Los Angeles need ten thousand units of public housing?" "Brother," the reporter replies, "and ten thousand more!"[21]

Whereas the CHA created its cinematic vision of Bunker Hill as an imperative for social change, Hollywood filmmakers exploited the remnants of that neighborhood as a setting for titillating tales of perversion and corruption. In *Criss Cross*, Slim Dundee's gang plots a heist in a room of a run-down Bunker Hill hotel. In the background, a window frames a glimpse of the Angel's Flight trolley, which used to transport Bunker Hill dwellers to and from their fashionable residences. In *Kiss Me Deadly* (1955), private investigator Mike Hammer rummages through the byways of Bunker Hill to learn the secrets of a murdered woman. And in *Act of Violence*, when

FIGURE 3.   On-location shooting for *Criss Cross* (1949)
in Bunker Hill. (Courtesy of Universal Studios Licensing
LLLP.)

Frank Enley forsakes his comfortable suburban life in Santa Lisa to escape
his checkered past, he flees to Bunker Hill, where he finds refuge in the desolate apartment of an aging prostitute.[22]

Gangsters, fugitives, private investigators, and prostitutes are not the
only ones who roam the lonely streets of Bunker Hill in film noir. An even
more disturbing vision of Bunker Hill surfaces in *M*, Joseph Losey's 1951
remake of Fritz Lang's 1931 film about a child molester, updated for its Los
Angeles setting. The opening credits appear over a night view of the Angel's
Flight trolley ascending Bunker Hill, where a lone psychopath inhabits a
shabby apartment. Panic engulfs Los Angeles as four little girls have been
murdered and now another is missing. Local police mount a massive sweep
of the city's criminal underworld in their hunt for "M," stumbling upon his
quarters, where they find clues to his heinous crimes. The local mob, ner-

vous that the police might interfere with their business in the search for "M," undertake their own search for the deviant. On the run from both the mob and the police, "M" passes through the Third Street tunnel, past Angel's Flight and other landmarks of a decaying inner city. The mob finds "M" first, and he is taken to an underground parking lot, where a kangaroo court is held to determine the killer's fate. The police arrive on the scene, arresting the mob leadership and taking "M" into their custody.

Film noir cast Bunker Hill as Southern California's heart of darkness, a site that harbored crime, fear, and psychosis. In contrast to the CHA's efforts to film housing conditions in Bunker Hill as a means of inspiring public subsidies for working-class housing, the makers of Los Angeles noir offered no such inspiration and used the landscape as a centerpiece for their narratives of fatalistic despair. Noir's stylized, almost glamorous vision of urban decay repudiated the kind of idealism that informed the creation of social welfare programs such as public housing. Its mood of cynical disillusionment alluded to the larger ideological transformation that began to envelop American society at the outset of the postwar period, in which a weakened New Deal idealism began to give way to a privatized conservative ethos. Nothing symbolized this transformation more poignantly than the defeat of public housing in Los Angeles and other cities across the nation. As conservative forces and private interests marshaled Cold War hysteria to win political influence, branding the remnants of New Deal Progressivism as "Communistic," Americans began to exchange their collective vision of social progress for an individual stake in the privatized world of consumer affluence.

The cinematic fate of Bunker Hill befell other landmarks of Los Angeles noir. Built as a garment factory in 1893 and inspired by the utopian aspirations of Edward Bellamy's *Looking Backward*, the Bradbury Building showcased technological innovation and industrial development in turn-of-the-century Los Angeles. Its interior court, with its glass ceiling, open caged elevators, iron grillwork, and marble flooring, has been lauded as "one of the most magnificent sites of nineteenth-century commercial architecture anywhere in the world." By the mid-twentieth century, however, the forces of urban decline had usurped much of the Bradbury's grandeur. Writing in the late 1960s, the design critic Reyner Banham described the Bradbury as "an unintegrated fragment in a downtown scene that began to disintegrate long ago." Banham may well have been referring to the early 1950s, when the Bradbury starred in noir's vision of urban decline. In *D.O.A*, the Bradbury becomes Los Angeles' "O.K. Corral" at the film's climax, when Frank Bigelow finally guns down his killer in the shadowy recesses of the building's interior court. And in *M*, the unnamed child-killer takes his last victim to a room in the Bradbury, where he hides amid the dismembered limbs of dress shop mannequins.[23]

By implicating elements of Los Angeles' Victorian landscape in its blighted vision of urban decline, film noir underscored the ephemeral nature not only of the urban built environment, but also of the meanings imposed on that environment. To consider how Lewis Leonard Bradbury might have reacted to the sight of his building in film noir, or, perhaps more curious, how the upstanding Victorians who built their ostentatious homes on Bunker Hill would react to images of their neighborhood as a hideout of gangsters and child molesters, is to fathom the shifting perceptions of the city and its landscape across generations. Rapid urbanization in Southern California, sustained by a long-standing commitment to growth and development, betrayed Progressive visions of civic community and asserted new ways of understanding the urban scene. The dawning perception of the American city at midcentury reflected less the whims of moviemakers and the advertisers of their product than the growing physical and emotional distance between Americans and their cities. By fixating on the ruins of "the better city," film noir dramatized how the degraded culture of the modern metropolis overwhelmed the Progressives' civic vision by midcentury and underscored the need for a sociospatial alternative to the chaos of urban modernity, precipitating such transformative urban processes as suburban development, urban renewal, and highway construction. Only a few years prior to the arrival of bulldozers in Bunker Hill, film noir had already annihilated that space in public consciousness.

Film noir incorporated other elements of the better city into its sinister mise-en-scène. If Southern California's Progressives predicated their vision of suburban respectability on the predominance of the single-family home, film noir dramatized the corruption of that vision by midcentury. *Double Indemnity* and *Mildred Pierce*, two well-known Los Angeles noirs based on the novels of James Cain, expose the evil lurking behind the domestic facades of suburban normalcy. In *Double Indemnity*, for example, Phyllis Dietrichson resides in the Los Feliz neighborhood of Los Angeles, in "one of the California Spanish homes that everyone was nuts about." At the outset of *Mildred Pierce*, similarly, a jaded Mildred begins her story by first identifying the setting where her troubles began: "We lived on Corvalis Street, where all the houses looked alike." Highlighting the regional distinctiveness of such suburban images, both homes modeled the Spanish Revival style of architecture that local boosters deployed as part of their "sunshine strategy" to market turn-of-the-twentieth-century Los Angeles as a semitropical suburban paradise.

The images of suburban domesticity in *Double Indemnity* and *Mildred Pierce,* however, barely mask the treachery of the main characters. The sunny exterior of the Dietrichson home, for example, contrasts sharply with its dark, foreboding interior, where Dietrichson and her illicit lover concoct their nefarious plan to murder her husband in such a way as to collect double indemnity on her insurance policy. In the film's violent climax, that darkness enshrouds the final act of violence, in which the two lovers murder each other. Likewise, the appearance of suburban normalcy in *Mildred Pierce* is compromised by Mildred's reckless pursuit of self-sufficiency and especially by her daughter's criminal misdeeds. By posing a stark contrast between setting and narrative, both *Double Indemnity* and *Mildred Pierce* underscore the mid-twentieth-century demise of the Progressive vision of Los Angeles as the better city, emphasizing the corruption of the suburban culture that Progressive reformers once touted as the moral alternative to urban modernity.

The collapse of Southern California's suburban order surfaced in subsequent noir films. Lucia Harper is an upstanding suburban matron in *The Reckless Moment,* "determined to keep scandal away from her doorstep." Her daughter, who becomes romantically linked to a shady art dealer residing in a downtown hotel, stymies her efforts, however. To protect her family's respectable name, and in the prolonged absence of her husband, Lucia oversteps the boundaries of her suburban world, entangling herself in the city's web of corruption to cover up the accidental death of her daughter's boyfriend. In her compromised position, Harper becomes involved with Martin Donnelly, a sort of urban confidence man usually kept at bay from insular suburban communities. Donnelly appears at Harper's doorstep at night, reminding her that, in spite of her suburban distance from the city and its shady characters, "we're all involved with one another, in one way or another." At the film's climactic ending, Donnelly sacrifices his life for Lucia Harper's reputation, and while she mourns his death in secret, she resumes the appearance of suburban respectability in the sanctity of her household.

The illicit intercourse between urban and suburban becomes a central theme of *Act of Violence.* Frank Enley returns from the war to resume his tranquil suburban life with his wife and new baby in Santa Lisa, California. His tranquility is shattered, however, when a figure from his past arrives to avenge Enley's wrongdoings during the war, forcing him to flee his sunny suburban world to retreat into the darkest corners of Los Angeles at night.

On the run, he finds refuge in the shabby Bunker Hill apartment of an aging prostitute, who forces him to abandon his pretensions to suburban respectability by acknowledging his past crimes. By the end of the film, he experiences a shattering loss of innocence, and ultimately he pays with his life to atone for his dark past.

These examples of Los Angeles noir dramatized a spatial transgression in which the boundaries between urban and suburban dissolved. Because of its low-density suburban landscape, Los Angeles supplied the makers of film noir with a particularly ironic setting in which to convey the pervasive ills of urban modernity. Unlike noir films set in other American cities, where the anonymous crowds and neon signs conveyed familiar notions of metropolitan life, Los Angeles noir deployed a contrast between the visual imagery of suburban normalcy and the narrative drama of vice and violence. By focusing on the most cherished icon of Southern California's low-density landscape—the suburban home—*Double Indemnity, Mildred Pierce, The Reckless Moment,* and *Act of Violence* articulated the inability of suburban Los Angeles to shield its occupants from the poisonous culture of the metropolis, shattering any lingering illusions of Los Angeles as the better city but, at the same time, dramatizing an imperative to fortify the boundaries between the suburbs and the "black" city.

REEL BLACK CITIES

In 1943, the National Association of Real Estate Boards issued *Fundamentals of Real Estate Practice,* which advised real estate agents to be wary of those living on the margins of respectability. Along with the bootlegger, the madam, and the gangster, the pamphlet added the "colored man of means" to its list of those who would "instigate a form of blight" in residential neighborhoods. What is striking here is not that real estate agents targeted blacks as a threat to property values, but rather the way in which African Americans are likened to white deviants. In the discourse of the real estate industry at midcentury, African Americans were criminal by virtue of their skin color. By the same token, however, whites who engaged in prostitution, gambling, or murder relinquished their claim to whiteness by virtue of their deviant behavior.

Film noir deployed a similar discourse, dramatizing the fine line between whiteness and blackness within the spatial parameters of the modern city. Black servants, custodians, garage attendants, shoe-shine boys, Pullman porters, and jazz musicians often share the same urban spaces with the morally corrupt white men and women who occupy the noir city. Through its cinematography and its masterful use of light, film noir "blackened" not only those whites who broke the law, but also those who transgressed socially prescribed boundaries. In particular, noir implicated white women who overstepped the boundaries of private life in its blackened cinematic landscapes, adding a racial dimension to its perverse portrayal of sexual relations. As white flight promised to resecure the distance between white and nonwhite and to reassert the gendered division between public and private life, film noir pointed out the consequences for white men and women who transgressed the boundaries of their own whiteness by stepping into the promiscuous world of the black city.[24]

Film noir targeted those urban spaces that sanctioned racial and ethnic transgression. The nightclub and its music provide an exotic setting where the boundaries between whiteness and blackness blur. In *Criss Cross, D.O.A.,* and *In a Lonely Place,* the antiheroes of Los Angeles noir first acquaint themselves with the city's dark underworld in downtown nightclubs. In *Criss Cross,* Steve Thompson wanders into "the old club," hypnotized by the haunting music of Esy Morales and His Rumba Band and reignites a dubious relationship with an old flame. In *D.O.A.,* as Frank Bigelow swings with "jive crazy" women in a San Francisco nightclub, the camera homes in on the face of a black trumpeter and enforces the racial connotations of urban nightlife. And in *In a Lonely Place,* Laurel Gray escapes her troubled relationship with a violent man in a Hollywood nightclub, where she finds comfort in the performance of Hadda Brooks. In her song, Brooks conveys the fears of a woman involved with an unstable man, narrating the inner turmoil of the white protagonist. Film noir's spotlight on such interracial moments pointed to the very real "mixing" that urban nightclubs sanctioned throughout the war years. While law enforcement in Los Angeles and other American cities of the 1940s policed the city's racially mixed venues in their efforts to fortify the boundaries between whiteness and nonwhiteness, film noir sided with the law, implicating the city for its betrayal of a racialized vision of civic order.

The more technical properties of filmmaking shed light on film noir's racial portrait of the American city. In particular, the use of light in film noir bolstered the genre's thematic emphasis on the "blackening" of white deviance. Noir directors and cinematographers pioneered lighting techniques that defined the noir style of filmmaking. Noir, as Richard Dyer observes, is a drama about light or, rather, the metaphorical uses of light in the telling of a story. Drawing on the innovative uses of light in German Expressionist cinema of the 1920s and working under strict rations of industrial materials, noir stylists of the 1940s developed a rigorous conservatism in their use of light to create a foreboding atmosphere in which to situate noir's tales of urban transgression. Darkness pervades the noir screen, always encroaching on the sources of light within the frame, just as the characters of noir are menaced by a hostile world. Noir's antiheroes are often mired in darkness or ensconced in shadows as if to depict the corruption of their souls. In *He Walked by Night,* for example, Roy Martin is a vicious killer who, as the title suggests, prowls about the city at night. Throughout the film, his face is hidden from full view as it is marred by dark shadows, reinforcing his criminality.[25]

The absence of light in film noir underscored the genre's emphasis on racial transgression. *Double Indemnity,* for example, is essentially a tale about a white man's descent into moral blackness. The film's use of racial and ethnic markers, as well as its lighting techniques, underscored the blurring between whiteness and blackness, a blurring central to noir's critique of the city. Walter Neff recounts how, in his lust for a blond housewife, he murdered her husband and concocted an elaborate scheme to collect the maximum reward on the victim's life insurance policy. It is not simply the narrative and cinematic contrast between whiteness and racial and ethnic otherness that frame Neff's account of murder, but rather the way in which Walter Neff and Phyllis Dietrichson transgress the boundaries of their whiteness to enact their vicious scheme.

In his moral descent, Walter Neff crosses the boundaries of his own whiteness. "No visible scars, 'til a while ago, that is," Neff confesses at the outset of *Double Indemnity,* just after Phyllis fires a bullet into his chest. Those scars appear not only on Neff's bloodstained shirt, which registers black on the screen, but also on the complexion of a man so scarred by his own treachery and so mired in shadows that his blackness seems to appear on his skin. Speeding his way along the desolate city streets at night, a wounded Neff enters the offices of the Pacific All Risk Insurance Company, empty except for the black janitors on the night shift. From the outset of *Double Indemnity,* Neff's exclusion from civil society is reinforced by his association with racial Others and by his occupation of racialized spaces. He seems at home in the dark exoticism of the Dietrichson household; he depends on a "colored woman" to look after him; and, more significant, he relies on two racial figures for his alibi on the night of the murder. The first, Charlie, a black janitor, sees Neff coming and going from his apartment through the service stairs and attests to Neff's whereabouts on the night of the murder. The second is the Westwood Jew Lou Schwartz, whose name, as Eric Lott points out, derives from the Yiddish word for "black" and who receives a strategically timed business call from Neff that same evening. As

FIGURE 4.   Frank Enley (Van Heflin) retreats into the
shadows of Bunker Hill in *Act of Violence* (1949). (*Act
of Violence* © 1949 Turner Entertainment Co. A Warner
Bros. Entertainment Company. All Rights Reserved.)

Neff descends into moral darkness, his dependence on racial Others belies
his claim to whiteness.[26]

Double Indemnity also situates the femme fatale in its racialized mise-
en-scène, and, as the landmark film noir to arrive first on the scene in 1944,
the film set a precedent for the genre's racialization of deviant white
women. Noir's disturbing portrait of relations between men and women
corresponded to the sexual upheaval that shook the home front throughout
World War II, and, by focusing on the crisis of the white male, film noir
underscored the imperative to reinforce sexual normalcy at the outset of the
postwar period. Missing from this perspective, however, is the way in which
noir's parade of femmes fatales are "blackened" by virtue of their presence
in the racial milieu of the noir city. Ambitious, snide, and duplicitous, the
white woman of film noir wielded the edgy disposition typically associated

with urban life, but as the city appeared as the heart of darkness at the outset of the postwar suburban boom, the femme fatale of film noir assumed racial connotations not only through her actions, but also through her very image on the screen.

Phyllis Dietrichson, played by Barbara Stanwyck, ranks among the "blackest" white women of film noir. Her platinum-blond hair and fair skin belie her black soul, in much the same way that her sunny abode hides an inner darkness. Upon closer scrutiny, however, Dietrichson's racial habits belie her appearance. When Neff first meets Dietrichson, for example, the housewife is sunbathing to become darker, so much so that she tells Walter, "I need to get my face on straight" before discussing his proposal for a new insurance policy. Neff is brought further under her spell by her "exotic" perfume, which she had purchased in Ensenada, Mexico, where people drink "pink wine" instead of bourbon. That Phyllis inhabits a black world is reinforced by the cinematographer's use of lighting. As noted earlier, Phyllis lives in a California Spanish–style house. The exoticism of the home and the blinding reflection of the California sun from its white stucco walls creates an interior darkness suitable for Phyllis's treachery.

Other white women in film noir, though not the conniving femme fatale portrayed in *Double Indemnity*, cross the boundaries between whiteness and blackness by overstepping the boundaries of their suburban world. Both *The Reckless Moment* and *Mildred Pierce* dramatize the illicit association between women and technology in the racialized context of the noir city. In *The Reckless Moment*, for example, Lucia Harper compromises her reputation of suburban respectability by insinuating herself into the urban world of strangers, not unlike the way in which Mildred Pierce forsakes her role as a docile housewife to pursue her own ambitions. When Mildred finally removes her frilly apron and divorces her husband, she becomes at one with the metropolis, signified poignantly by the garish neon sign that bears her name atop her restaurant. In a decentralized metropolis like Los Angeles, moreover, the automobile is the primary means by which both Mildred and Lucia enter the public realm: they are often seen behind the wheel of their cars, driving intently along the city's boulevards. The image of a woman behind the wheel of a car, even by the late 1940s, contradicted the popular identification of automobiles with masculinity and male mobility. Although women had played integral roles as both producers and consumers of automobiles since the 1920s, film noir exploited the image of women driving to highlight the transgressive connotations of women entering the public realm.[27]

Such mobility, however, forces Lucia Harper and Mildred Pierce to compromise their claim to suburban whiteness. In *Mildred Pierce*, Mildred's black servant, Lottie, provides a racial marker that measures Mildred's whiteness. When Mildred begins working as a waitress after her divorce, her daughter, ashamed of her mother's lowly job, forces Lottie to wear Mildred's waitress uniform, mocking the affinity between Mildred and Lottie. In a more revealing moment, Lottie mistakenly responds to someone shouting for Mildred amid the bustle of Mildred's kitchen. Such affinities disappear, however, when Mildred begins to ascend the class ladder. Moving into the Beragon estate, Mildred requires Lottie to address her as "ma'am" and to wear formal servant's attire. But just as Lottie fumbles in her efforts to play the role of proper servant, Mildred fails to maintain her marriage and wealth, returning to her modest means after her daughter is exposed as a murderer.

Like Mildred Pierce, Lucia Harper relinquishes her white respectability to indulge her independence and her adulterous desire for Martin Donnelly in *The Reckless Moment*. With her husband away, Lucia assumes the responsibility of maintaining order in her household. She enlists the support of her black servant, Sybil, whose marginal visibility in the film obscures her role as Lucia's secret confidante. In the film's climax, Sybil drives Lucia in pursuit of Donnelly after he leaves her home with the body of a man he has just killed in her defense. With Sybil behind the wheel, Lucia demonstrates her loss of autonomy and her covert dependence on her black servant. When Lucia confides to Sybil her true feelings for Donnelly, Sybil seems intuitively aware of the spark between them, uttering that which Lucia is too respectable to say: "I like that Mr. Donnelly." Lucia's confidence in Sybil exposes the depths of interracial friendship and the bonds of womanhood, but only in a moment of transgression. For all of Sybil's importance to Lucia Harper, her subordination is restored at the end of the film, as she returns to the kitchen after Lucia's husband returns home.

Both *Mildred Pierce* and *The Reckless Moment* situate their narratives of racial transgression in a spatial context that demarcates the boundaries between suburb and city. As noir's misguided characters cross those boundaries, they simultaneously cross the racial divide between whiteness and blackness. Frank Bigelow (Edmund O'Brien) makes a similar mistake in *D.O.A.* His trouble begins when he plans a weekend escape from his small suburban town in Southern California to indulge in the racialized nightlife of San Francisco. After a goodbye kiss with his fiancée, whose blond hair and white lacy dress connote the moral purity of a faithful wife, Bigelow joins a party of wild conventioneers in San Francisco, where he cavorts with "jive crazy" women who wear black, enjoy jazz music, and flaunt their independence from home and family. In a drunken stupor at a nightclub, Bigelow is fatally poisoned and spends his remaining days in frantic pursuit of his killer on the city streets at night. Ultimately, *D.O.A.* documents one man's fateful decision to cross a set of spatial, racial, and sexual boundaries and reminds its audience of the dreadful consequences of that decision.

The blackness of the noir city implicated other racial groups besides African Americans. For example, Los Angeles noir deploys Orientalist themes and imagery to reinforce its racialization of white criminality. In Warner Brothers' adaptation of Raymond Chandler's *The Big Sleep* (1946), for example, the private investigator Philip Marlowe follows Arthur Geiger, a pornography producer who poses as a dealer in rare books, whom Marlowe identifies by his "Charlie Chan" moustache. Inside Geiger's Hollywood Hills home, Marlowe winces at the owner's penchant for Chinese antiques and notes to himself, "There's something very queer about this one." It was Los Angeles' actual Chinatown, however, that supplied a stereotypically Asiatic setting for noir's tales of murder and mystery. By the 1940s, what was called Chinatown in Los Angeles was actually an Orientalized version of Olvera Street: a kitschy collection of shops and restaurants that provided a touristic alternative to the real Chinese community that had been razed in the early 1930s for the construction of Union Station. Although, in the aftermath of wartime hostilities toward Asian Americans in Los Angeles, Japanese and Chinese Americans in Southern California had initiated their own departure from the noir city by settling in suburban locales such as Monterey Park and Gardena, film noir pandered to an older perception of Chinatown as the site of danger and mystery.[28] The story told in *T-Men*, for example, is dubbed the "Shanghai Paper Case," and the agents on the trail of counterfeiters are led to Los Angeles' Chinatown in search of clues. As two Treasury agents, or "T-Men," wander through the shadows of Chinatown, vaguely Chinese music reinforces the air of mystery and danger. Other Sinophobic clues surface in *T-Men*. The man in question, known simply as "the Schemer," maintains an "unusual habit" of chewing Chinese herbs, while the blonde moll of the Vantucci mob models her penchant for silk kimonos and fastens tiger lilies to her hair. Such Orientalized images of Los Angeles reinforced a broader perception of black cities that implicated other racial groups such as the Chinese.[29]

In Los Angeles, Mexico and Mexicans stood alongside Chinese and African Americans as symbols of racial otherness, and Southern California's proximity to Mexico added a shade of brown to the racial hue of the noir city. If film noir is a genre about border crossings, Mexico provided a literal setting for such crossings, where refugees from the law seek escape. In *Double Indemnity,* Walter Neff plans to flee to Mexico after executing his plan for murder, and gringo crooks escape south of the border in *Too Late for Tears* (1949), *Hollow Triumph* (1948), *Armored Car Robbery* (1950), *Quicksand* (1950), and *Southside 1-1000* (1950).[30] The sleazy culture of the U.S.-Mexican border is depicted in both *Touch of Evil* (1958) and *Where Danger Lives* (1950), and *Out of the Past* (1947) and *One Way Street* (1950) portray the illicit love affairs that flourish south of the border. In *Double Indemnity* and *Mildred Pierce,* Mexican architecture provides a racialized setting for the treachery of Phyllis Dietrichson and the pathological ambition of Mildred Pierce. Set against a pervasive perception of Mexican criminality that targeted zoot suiters and Chicano youths in general in cities such as Los Angeles, noir's recurring images of Mexico offered an alternative setting for the moral compromises that arise in the noir city.

The racialized milieu of downtown Los Angeles also provided a prominent backdrop for an alternative noir vision, which did not reach mainstream audiences. In 1961, the student filmmaker Kent Mackenzie produced a fictional documentary, *The Exiles,* which portrays twelve hours in the lives of ten young American Indian adults relocated to Los Angeles. As the city sheltered an expanding pool of federally relocated Indians, *The Exiles* dramatizes the urban predicament of uprooted Indians, who seek relief from the city's anonymity in the nightlife spaces of bars, dance halls, liquor stores, and theaters. The city, however, affords little comfort. Depicting scenes of a lonely woman in a movie theater and Indian men walking the streets of downtown in a drunken stupor, *The Exiles* conveys the real-life dilemma of Indians relocated to Los Angeles, who have nothing to do in the alien world of Los Angeles at night. In the film's climactic scene, a group of Indians meet at a scenic spot in the Chavez Ravine, where they perform a ritualized Ghost Dance, drinking and dancing until dawn. Though one Indian woman finds that in Los Angeles, her "prayers are never answered," the scene of the Ghost Dance reflects the attempt to maintain spiritual faith in the secular world of the noir city.

Less polished than a Hollywood product, *The Exiles* nonetheless reflects a noir sensibility in its portrayal of Indian relocation to Los Angeles. Los Angeles is no less "black" in *The Exiles* than it is in Hollywood noir, but the film presents an alternative noir subjectivity that emphasizes the alienation of nonwhite social groups in their encounter with urban modernity. Such perspectives, as noted, did not reach mainstream audiences, who avidly consumed the lavish studio productions that focused on the psychic crisis of the white male. Ultimately, Hollywood's version of noir dramatized a threatened white masculinity and identified the modern city as the locus of that threat, where the racial distinctions between white and nonwhite dissolved. In its spotlight on the "weak man"—acted so memorably by Fred MacMurray, Burt Lancaster, Edmund O'Brien, and others—film noir conveyed the racial and sexual pitfalls that confronted the white male during his unlawful sojourn in the noir city. Mired in the shadows of the black city, vulnerable to the seductions of "black" women, and hypnotized by the sounds of black music, the white male antihero of film noir meets his demise, and Los Angeles, once touted as the very image of suburban whiteness, falls short of its promise to deliver a "better city."

LAW AND ORDER

Although film noir initially emphasized the racial and sexual ambiguities that urban Americans confronted at the outset of the postwar period, the following decade saw a departure from this theme. The "policier" of the 1950s, a subset of film noir, focused on the intricacies of police and detective work in the fight against urban crime. Unlike the films noirs of the mid-1940s, the new policiers used narrative patterns and visual strategies to enforce a clearer distinction between good and evil, upholding law enforcement as a mighty bulwark against the criminal forces that infested the city at night. In their tight focus on the dangerous and sophisticated work of police detectives and undercover agents, *T-Men* and *He Walked by Night* marked a departure from noir's standard fare, anticipating the arrival of the policier in the 1950s.[31] Moving away from the ambiguous and ironic tone that had characterized the early years of film noir, the policier depicted an upstanding portrait of law and order and emphasized the reinscription of the social boundaries that bifurcated the physical and cultural landscape of the postwar urban region.

At the outset of *T-Men*, the film's title appears over the seal of the U.S. Treasury Department, while a stolid narrator's voice describes the "six fingers" of the Treasury Department's "fist": "the intelligence unit, customs agency service, narcotics unit, secret service, alcohol tax, and coast guard." The Treasury Department's fist "hits fair but hard," foreshadowing the tough battle that looms ahead for the undercover T-men who are assigned to the Shanghai Paper Case. Two treasury agents, Anthony Genaro and Dennis O'Brien, pose as mobsters in Los Angeles to break a counterfeiting operation by the Vantucci family. In their pursuit of the mysterious Schemer, the two agents follow a winding path down the mean streets of Los Angeles, where they home in on their suspects. The Schemer discovers the true identity of one T-man and informs the Vantucci mobsters, who shoot Genaro dead in front of his partner. Before he dies, Genaro offers a coded tip to O'Brien, who has infiltrated the mob circle. Armed with new information but barely clinging to his undercover identity, O'Brien breaks the counterfeiting ring with the help of other T-men. Justice prevails, but at a high price.

Similarly, *He Walked by Night* describes a police hunt through "a maze of baffling trails and criminal leads" to apprehend a vicious murderer. The opening scene is a panoramic sweep of Los Angeles at night. A voice-over narration explains, "Because of that vast area, because of a population made up of people from every state in the Union, Los Angeles is the largest police beat in the country and one of the toughest." A police officer is murdered in a foiled robbery attempt. Inside Los Angeles city hall, a towering icon of law and order in the policier, radio dispatchers report the crime to police detectives, who launch an investigation for a killer "hidden away somewhere in the vast city." Their suspect is Roy Martin, a "white male American, 26 or 27," who "looked like such a nice kid," according to an officer who caught a glimpse of him. After a dragnet sweep of the city's shady characters, the police fail to identify Martin, who remains elusive in the shadows of the city. Using various descriptions of the killer, police render a composite sketch of Martin's "fine face" and circulate that drawing throughout a national network of law enforcement officials. A positive identification of Martin leads police to a small bungalow in Hollywood, where they surround the premises. Martin retreats into the sewers, where he is hunted down and shot.

"Police work is not all glamour and excitement and glory," the voice-over narrator comments in *He Walked by Night,* and both *T-Men* and *He Walked by Night* emphasize the "thorough, painstaking, and tedious" work of urban law enforcement. Unlike earlier noir films that indict the city for its corruption of all social relations, the policier portrays the city as a battleground that pits the forces of law and order against the criminal deviants who preside over the city's dark underworld. Indeed, noir's upstanding portrayal of the police bears a resemblance to the restructuring of law enforcement in cities such as Los Angeles, where William Parker became chief of police in 1950. His rectification of the image of the Los Angeles Police Department depended not only on the implementation of the kind of technologically sophisticated weaponry and surveillance equipment that is featured so prominently in *He Walked by Night,* but also on a very public emphasis on the presence of a "lawless criminal army warring against society." For Parker, the police comprised a "containing element" against the criminal underworld, "a thin line of blue which stands between the law-abiding members of society and the criminals who prey upon them."[32]

In its semidocumentary approach to the battles waged by law enforcement against the city's criminal forces, the noir policier of the 1950s rendered a portrait of the contaminated city, infested with lowlife criminals of every sort. Chief Parker himself emphasized the "very dirty business" of law enforcement, and both *T-Men* and *He Walked by Night* dramatize police officials' descent into the depths of urban squalor to stamp out crime. In *T-Men*, O'Brien and Genaro soil themselves to penetrate the inner ring of the city's mob underworld, wandering through a decrepit amusement park, a seedy nightclub, a grimy boxing ring, and other sordid spaces. "Did you ever spend ten nights in a Turkish bath looking for a man?" O'Brien asks his partner. "Well, don't."

The most compelling image of urban squalor, however, arrives with the climactic scene of *He Walked by Night*, in which Roy Martin evades police by descending into perhaps the dirtiest of all urban spaces: the city's sewer system, which the voice-over narrator describes as "seven hundred miles of hidden highways, ideal for the use of someone who needed to hurry from place to place without being seen." The final descent into the sewer conjured a long-standing preoccupation with sewers in nineteenth-century Europe and America. In their discussion of nineteenth-century notions of bourgeois respectability, Peter Stallybrass and Allon White contend that sewers, like streets, remained one of the few linkages between the separate enclaves of wealth and poverty in the metropolis. Despite bourgeois attempts to insulate their social and economic life from that of the city's working class through the construction of private spaces such as clubs, theaters, skyscrapers, or suburbs, sewers remained a "metonymic chain of contagion which led back to the culture of the working class."[33] The sewers thus provided a conduit by which the "unutterable horrors of the city" could reach the city's respectable classes. The climactic scene of *He Walked by Night* thus homes in on Los Angeles' sewers to highlight the transgressive connotations of film noir, dramatizing the suburban imperative to sequester urban criminality within its filthy spaces.

Both *T-Men* and *He Walked by Night* endow such images of public squalor with racial connotations, maintaining a long-standing association among race, cities, and filth.[34] Roy Martin, despite his fine face and his apparent likeness to a nice kid, sacrifices the gleam of his Aryan features to become at one with the shadows of the city. The miserly distribution of light by director of photography John Alton emphasizes the "blackening" of Martin's face and body, suggesting the loss of whiteness that is prerequisite to criminal deviance. The Shanghai Paper Case of *T-Men* offers a lurid tour of the city's spaces of vaguely Chinese racial otherness. Such Orientalized images of the city's underworld contrast sharply with Parker's idealization of Los Angeles as the "white spot of the great cities of America" and underscore the racial polarity between good and evil.[35]

In whatever ways the noir policier of the 1950s departed from the thematic conventions of earlier film noir, it remained faithful to noir's central dictate that the city is the site of violence and danger in American society. Noir's indictment of urban life corresponded to cultural perceptions of cities such as Los Angeles at the outset of the postwar period. *Collier's*, for example, instructed its readers in 1950, "Don't Go Out Alone at Night in L.A.," reporting that "the City of Angels is terrorized by hoodlums."[36] While Los Angeles remained mired in such dismal perceptions at the outset of the postwar period, suburbanization offered a sanctuary from the criminalized and racialized milieu of the city and sanctioned the formation of a political sensibility that emphasized "law and order," an issue that eventually became a staple of suburban California's brand of Republican conservatism. Dramatizing the evil deeds of criminal deviants who overtook the modern American city, film noir, as far back as the late 1940s, foreshadowed the politics of law and order that men such as William Parker advocated and that ultimately propelled politicians such as Ronald Reagan and Pete Wilson into the highest ranks of public office.

BLACK HOLLYWOOD

Perhaps the real-life inspiration for the stalwart detectives of *T-Men* and *He Walked by Night*, Chief William Parker maintained a worldview that, like the noir policier of the early 1950s and (as we shall discover) the thematic imagery of Disneyland, rested on an unambiguous distinction between good and evil. At the outset of his tenure as police chief, at the height of Cold War anxieties, Parker targeted Communists as the evil within and expressed his determination to root out the "communist fifth column within our borders." Parker expressed his dismay "to find adherents to this alien philosophy encamped in our churches, our schools and in our government" and, closer to home, asserted that internal subversives "furnished as much material to our screenwriters as they did to our enemy." By implicating the screenwriter in pervasive suspicions about the "enemy within," Chief Parker showed how Hollywood itself became a target of Cold War anxieties.[37]

The Cold War did not bode well for the film industry. Once in 1947 and again in 1952, the House Un-American Activities Committee (HUAC) conducted highly publicized investigations of possible subversive influences in Hollywood. The rampage of McCarthyism in the industry signaled the destruction of the New Deal spirit that had inspired the unionization of Hollywood writers, actors, and stage employees throughout the 1930s and into the 1940s, forcing studio executives to adjust to the shifting political climate at the outset of the postwar period. Those members of the Hollywood Left who most actively defended the interests of Hollywood workers now found themselves isolated from a film community that repudiated the political tolerance of the New Deal period and came quickly to HUAC's aid in its search for "subversives." The compilation of a secret blacklist that identified suspected Communists cast a pervasive sense of paranoia over the film community and furthered Hollywood's political polarization during the 1950s.[38]

The presence of HUAC in Hollywood only compounded the difficulties that confronted the film industry at the outset of the postwar period. Although the arrival of HUAC in Hollywood secured for management a competitive advantage over its labor force, a number of financial and legal setbacks during the 1940s had severely weakened the studio's monopoly over film production. First, Hollywood lost much of its overseas market in the aftermath of World War II, as European nations struggled to rebuild their domestic economies. Great Britain, France, and Italy levied substantial duties on the importation of American films in the late 1940s to nurture the development of homegrown film industries. Second, and perhaps more disastrous for studio profits, the U.S. Supreme Court ruled against the studios in two antitrust suits in 1944 and 1948, forcing the breakup of the vertically integrated film industry and divorcing the studios from control over the exhibition of motion pictures.[39] John Houseman predicted that after January 1, 1950, the day that "divorcement" went into effect, "moviemaking and real estate shall not be of a single flesh. From now on, in theory at least, Hollywood is on its own."[40]

Moreover, the introduction of television by the late 1940s threatened Hollywood's preeminence. Offering a convenient, affordable, and novel alternative to the public experience of going out to the movies, television threatened to displace the movies as the nation's favorite pastime in the age of white flight. With television's commercial expansion beginning in the late 1940s, the number of television sets in use soared by more than 1,000 percent, from 14,000 in 1947 to 172,000 in 1948. In 1949, that number increased to one million, rising to four million by 1950 and thirty-two million by 1954. By the end of the decade, 90 percent of American homes had television sets, and the number of television stations in the United States increased from five to 517.[41] Television, cultural historians have argued, fit squarely within the reigning ideological emphasis on family and domestic leisure. As suburbanization offered refuge from the noir city and as the prospect of nuclear war encouraged American families to remain safely at home, television became the cultural centerpiece of the white, middle-class suburban home and challenged the cultural hegemony of Hollywood and the movies.[42]

Though Hollywood reigned supreme with the advent of the new mass culture in the early decades of the twentieth century, the age of white flight brought substantial financial loss to the film industry. Between 1946 and 1956, annual box office receipts declined from $1.692 billion to $1.298 billion, or about 23 percent. Declining revenues stemmed largely from a sharp decline in movie attendance, as the national rate of attendance decreased annually by 10 percent for roughly ten years following 1947. Revenues, however, decreased more slowly than attendance, largely because ticket prices rose by nearly 40 percent, from thirty-four cents to fifty cents on the average. On the production level, the ten largest studios saw their gross revenues fall from $968 million in 1946 to $717 million a decade later, a decrease of 26 percent, while combined profits fell even more precipitously during these same years, from $121 million to $32 million, or 74 percent. Such losses invited speculation about Hollywood's crumbling empire.[43] *Life* reported "Trouble in Hollywood" in 1948, describing how "movie makers struggle to offset the effects of foreign costs, loss of foreign revenue and bad films."[44]

Mired in such turmoil, Hollywood began to market its own predicament as entertainment and used the properties of film noir to convey the air of decadence that pervaded the film industry at the outset of the postwar period. In 1950, for example, Columbia Pictures released *In a Lonely Place*, which centered on the psychic turmoil of Dixon Steele, a jaded screenwriter and murder suspect who faces the kind of public scrutiny leveled against the screenwriters indicted by HUAC for politically subversive activity. Emotionally unstable and prone to violent outbursts, Steele struggles to maintain his sanity in the surreal world of the film industry, where various Hollywood types personify the worst qualities of show business. *In a Lonely Place* conveyed the sense of paranoia that descended upon the film industry during HUAC's investigations, but it also exposed Hollywood as a locus for the degraded culture of the noir city—a place teeming with nobodies, has-beens, and wannabes, all conniving after stardom.

The classic example of Hollywood noir is, of course, *Sunset Boulevard*, a drama about the tragic aftermath of fame. Although she dismissed any comparisons between herself and the character she portrayed in the film (Norma Desmond), Gloria Swanson seemed appropriate for the role of a forgotten star who had once reigned as queen of Hollywood in a bygone age. Glorified by films, fan magazines, newspapers, and radio, living in hand-some, if not extravagant, estates, and conspicuously enjoying every amenity of modern life, Swanson personified success as Americans had imagined it in the 1920s. Movie stars, however, like movies, vacuums, cigarettes, and auto-mobiles, are ultimately commodities subject to the marketing decisions of corporate executives, who strive endlessly to gauge the public's fickle tastes. Norma Desmond learns this lesson most painfully in *Sunset Boulevard*, though she fights valiantly, yet vainly, against her own obsolescence. When her screenwriter gigolo tells her, "You used to be big," she quickly retorts, "I am big! It's the pictures that got small." Alienated from the technocratic bureaucracy of the studio system, Norma Desmond has no recourse other than to retreat into a delusion of stardom, sustained by the myriad pho-tographs and mementos that pervade the foreboding interior of her Gothic mansion.[45]

Like other films noirs, *Sunset Boulevard* deploys a set of racial signifiers to convey the exotic blackness of Norma Desmond and the old Hollywood. Desmond's savagery becomes immediately apparent as she makes funeral preparations for her pet chimpanzee, and it is reinforced by her penchant for animal skins, which pervade her wardrobe and interior decor. Her estate models the Spanish Gothic architectural style that defined the exotic milieu of 1920s Hollywood, and its dark interior mirrors the inner blackness of its owner. Betty Schaefer, Joe Gillis's fellow screenwriter at Paramount and his true romantic interest, presents a white alternative to the black Norma Desmond. Her fair demeanor, blond hair, and white clothes present a virtu-ous contrast to Desmond's moral corruption; Norma Desmond's black hair and dark lair underscore the racial connotations of her otherness. Her black-ness provides a racial metaphor by which to understand the postwar decline of Hollywood and other institutions of new mass culture. If the reconfigu-ration of race and space in postwar America society facilitated the "blacken-ing" of the institutions of the new mass culture, *Sunset Boulevard* drama-tized the racialization of Hollywood itself.

The sumptuous decay of Norma Desmond's estate also embodied the postwar condition of an institution that, like the aging starlet herself, once stood at the vibrant center of a new urban nightlife: the movie palace. Although John Houseman warned that it was premature to say "that tall grass will shortly be growing amidst the ruins of Rialtos, Criterions, Granadas, and other abandoned Main Street landmarks from coast to coast," the closing of more than four thousand conventional four-walled theaters between 1946 and 1956 indicated the decline of the movie palace as a focal point of American popular culture.[46] Suburbanization undercut the popu-

FIGURE 5.   Noir in the noir city: the downtown movie theater. (*Act of Violence*
© 1949 Turner Entertainment Co. A Warner Bros. Entertainment Company. All
Rights Reserved.)

larity of the movie palace and introduced more privatized modes of entertainment. By the late 1940s, the drive-in attracted growing numbers of
movie fans, demonstrating a newfound use of the automobile as a venue for
watching movies. The number of drive-ins in the United States multiplied
from sixty in 1945 to fifteen hundred by 1949.[47] Movie theaters continued
to attract audiences, but their new suburban locations precluded the lavish
venues that catered to the urban crowd. Instead, the application of niche
marketing to the exhibition of films brought forth the suburban multiplex,
which targeted a particular demographic group and eliminated the public
lobbies, foyers, atriums, and grand stairways of the movie palace. As an
institution of the new mass culture that debuted alongside amusement
parks and ballparks, the movie palace thus shared the fate that befell Coney
Island and Ebbets Field in the age of white flight.

Film noir may well have been a victim of its own success. At the very
outset of the postwar suburban boom, as Americans began looking toward
suburban communities to secure themselves within the private realm, film

noir dramatized the dangers of the urban milieu and not only reflected but also reinforced a fear of stepping out into the city. Such fears, in turn, aroused Hollywood's own anxieties about its uncertain future, and by the mid-1950s, television offered a convenient and privatized alternative to an urban nightlife that featured the very public experiences of movies, their premieres, and their palaces. Determined to find a means of recapturing its lost audience, Hollywood experimented with various technical innovations to produce a more dazzling spectacle than what the standard feature film offered. Cinerama, Technicolor, and 3D all debuted in the mid-1950s, but despite their initial splash at the box office, the novelty soon wore off.

Eventually, studio filmmakers looked to film genres beyond film noir to offer a more familiar and perhaps more comforting movie experience. Westerns, musicals, war films, and biblical epics lifted American movie fans from the dregs of the noir city and heralded the new political climate of the 1950s. After a brief debut during the silent era of filmmaking, the Western regained much of its popularity at the outset of the Cold War, upholding the traditional myth of rugged individualism in a frontier setting, while rescuing the white male from debilitating entrapment in the noir city. Musicals, particularly the handsome spectacles of MGM's *On the Town* (1949), *Singin' in the Rain* (1952), and *The Bandwagon* (1953), offered a nostalgic retreat from the political uncertainties of the day, emphasizing ritualized romance and traditional gender roles. War films such as *Sands of Iwo Jima* (1949), *From Here to Eternity* (1953), and *Battle Cry* (1955) reiterated the glories of combat and dramatized the U.S. triumph over its enemies abroad. And in a more earnest vein, biblical epics such as *Samson and Delilah* (1949), *The Land of the Pharaohs* (1955), and *The Ten Commandments* (1955) upheld traditional Judeo-Christian values against the onslaught of pagan hordes.[48] Of all the film genres that appeared in the aftermath of film noir, however, the science fiction film recaptured some of the lost enthusiasm for the movies and rendered an even more unsettling portrait of the American city as vulnerable to invasion by a subversive, alien Other. In the disastrous spectacles of science fiction, Los Angeles once again won a starring role.

COMMIES, ALIENS, AND INVISIBLE MEN

Conventional understandings of 1950s science fiction film have looked to the political climate of Cold War America to explore its deeper meanings. Martians, monsters, giant insects, crawling eyes, fifty-foot women, blobs, pods, "its," and other "things" have been commonly understood as cinematic apparitions of Communists and the Red Menace. And rightly so.

Science fiction film provides a window onto the political culture of postwar America, a time when Americans built bomb shelters in their backyards, performed disaster drills frequently, and gazed fixedly at the televised witch hunts of HUAC. Films such as *Invasion of the Body Snatchers* (1956), *It Came from Outer Space* (1953), and *Invasion of the Saucer Men* (1957) provided an arena in which Americans could work out their obsession with Communist subversion and offered a glimpse into the nexus between politics and culture in postwar America.[49]

Given the "racial revolution" of the war years, however, it is not difficult to imagine the presence of another subversive entity latent in the cinematic imagery of science fiction film. In the age of *Brown v. Board of Education*, when the Supreme Court dismantled the racial barriers that bisected public space, Ralph Ellison discerned the possible affinities between black Americans and the aliens of science fiction film. Writing in the early 1950s, amid an onslaught of science fiction thrillers, including *It Came from Outer Space, Zombies from the Stratosphere* (1952), *Them!* (1954), *War of the Worlds, When Worlds Collide* (1951), and *The Thing* (1951), Ellison prefaced his novel *Invisible Man* by declaring, "I am an invisible man. No, I am not a spook like those who haunted Edgar Allen Poe, nor am I one of your Hollywood movie ectoplasms. I am a man of substance . . . and I might even be said to possess a mind." Ellison's effort to deny his likeness to Hollywood movie ectoplasms suggests how African Americans and other racial groups are usually invisible as human beings and often visible only through the disfiguring lens of American popular culture. Ellison's insights resonated within a historical context in which the widening racial divide between white and black America rested upon a set of cultural polarizations that informed the narratives of science fiction film.[50]

Given the social upheaval that American cities experienced at mid-century, Ellison may not have been too far off the mark in recognizing the racial meanings of Hollywood movie ectoplasms. In their description of the social landscape of the city, federal agencies such as the HOLC deployed certain terms that betrayed a perception of racial minority groups as a kind of urban pathogen, threatening white neighborhoods with the prospect of "contamination." HOLC officials deemed communities such as Boyle Heights as "honeycombed with diverse and subversive elements," underscoring a perception of blacks and Mexicans as vermin. Such descriptions reveal the extent to which science fiction cinema, with its discursive emphasis on invasion, infestation, and infiltration, encompassed a set of images and words that found more consequential forms of expression in official assessments of urban property values. This way of seeing the urban landscape intensified amid the racially charged turf wars of the 1940s, in which heightened anxieties about the black invasion of white space inspired a renewed determination to protect the communal spaces of whiteness from the encroachment of blacks and other racial groups.

White flight thus provides a key social context for grasping the meaning of two of the highest-grossing science fiction films in the nation's history, both set conspicuously in Los Angeles. Paramount's *War of the Worlds* and Warner Brothers' *Them!* reveal a perception that Los Angeles was under attack by alien invaders and that suburban domesticity offered a safe alternative to the chaos that had descended upon the postwar American metropolis. In the changing racial geography of the postwar, postindustrial city, the urban science fiction film provided a cultural arena where suburban America could measure its whiteness against the image of the alien Other. In their representational emphasis, visual style, and promotion, *Them!* and *War of the Worlds* recorded popular perceptions of racialized invaders in the age of white flight.

Both *War of the Worlds* and *Them!* are narratives about alien invaders and the destruction they wreak upon American cities. Central to these narratives is a visual distinction between "us" and "them"—between a homogeneous citizenry and the alien Other. *Them!* depicts the invasion of Los Angeles by giant ants, enlarged by overexposure to radiation from atomic bomb testing sites in the desert. Although the film offers an allegory for the dangers of atomic energy, creatures as ordinary as ants represent hideous aliens that invade vulnerable cities and attack their innocent inhabitants. The giant ants, with bulging eyes and deadly mandibles (see figure 6), recall historic stereotypes of racial groups as animalistic and especially alien. Such stereotypes ran particularly high in times of international or domestic crisis. Japanese Americans, for example, were likened to rats in political cartoons of the World War II period. In the late nineteenth century, similarly, when California suffered from economic depression and high unemployment, Chinese immigrants bore the brunt of racist stereotypes, depicted in visual and literary discourse as bats with sharp claws and gnarled fangs. African Americans have endured such vicious representations throughout their history, stereotypified in the national culture most often as simian creatures. Monkeys, bats, rats, and ants have each been likened to various racial groups in American history, setting a cultural precedent for postwar understandings of the affinity between nonhuman and nonwhite.[51]

In *War of the Worlds,* such representations are taken a step further as Martians replace ants as the alien Other. The Martians of *War of the Worlds* land on Earth in search of a more hospitable climate for procreation. Though we know the Martians only by their sleek metal saucers that hover above the

FIGURE 6.   Giant ants wreak havoc in *Them!* (1954).
(*Them!* © 1954 Warner Bros. Pictures, Inc. All Rights
Reserved.)

ground, a few scenes reveal a frighteningly inhuman Other. In one sequence
of images, the noted scientist Dr. Clayton Forrester and his companion,
Sylvia Van Buren, take refuge inside an abandoned home. Although Sylvia
is rarely seen apart from the company of men, she is momentarily separated
from Forrester, distracted by a hunch that the invaders are nearby. As Van
Buren searches the quarters alone, tension mounts as an encounter with the
Martians seems dreadfully imminent. With the camera behind her, Sylvia is
unaware that a Martian is watching her. The camera, in other words, mimics
the predatorial gaze of the alien, as the white woman becomes the object of
the alien's desire. Her whiteness contrasts sharply with the alien physiog-
nomy of the Martian as a long, bright green arm slowly extends toward her.
The *Los Angeles Herald Express* emphasized this graphic scene, noting the
"skinny tentacles" of the Martians, with "vacuum cups at the end of each
finger" and "flesh which looks like a piece of raw pulsating liver."[52]

The vulnerability of the white woman is a common trope in the urban science fiction film—not only in narrative content, but also in the publicity materials used to advertise such films. Take, for example, the garish advertisement poster for *Invasion of the Saucer Men*. The poster is one of the richest images of the entire genre and captures some of white America's deepest anxieties about the Other. The central image of the advertisement is a scantily clad white woman with heaving breasts, flailing in the clutches of a hideous alien monster. In the background is the metropolis, under attack by flying saucers. Again, the alien bears a familiar resemblance to cultural stereotypes of racial minorities, blacks in particular. With their bulging saucer eyes, enormous heads, and dark, almost black skin, the Saucer Men seem more familiar than alien, recalling lurid representations of "coons," "sambos," and "pickaninnies" in American popular culture. The blackness of the aliens provides a sharp contrast to the milky whiteness of the woman's skin. She is helpless in the grip of an alien predatory sexuality, naming historical anxieties about black male lust for white women.[53]

The alien threat to white women had a heightened significance during the postwar period, a time when the national culture reemphasized the sanctity of the nuclear family. Suburbanization, it has been argued, inspired a cultural emphasis on the stability and coherence of the nuclear family. The primacy of the detached, single-family dwelling provided a space in which postwar Americans could cherish their idealization of the nuclear family, while the vastness and unfamiliarity of places such as Levittown and Lakewood engendered a renewed emphasis on "family values" as a respite from the depersonalized, private world of 1950s suburbia. Yet the concerted attempt to preserve the primacy of the nuclear family as the most fundamental unit of American society faced many obstacles. Communists, homosexuals, and racial minorities, for example, were viewed as dangers not so much to the individual or to the society at large, but rather to the stability and coherence of the American family. Moreover, the American family, as a cultural ideal, was almost always coded in the national culture as white. In the racialized climate of postwar America, white flight could therefore be viewed as a collective attempt to maintain the hegemony of the white nuclear family.[54]

War of the Worlds, for example, asserts the divinity of the white family while exposing the potential threat to that institution. In the climactic scene of the film, as masses of Angelenos take refuge inside a church shortly before the imminent holocaust, a white family—mother, father, son, daughter—huddles together in prayer, gazing up toward the image of Christ at the altar. As the camera homes in on their frightened faces, the audience is reminded exactly who is the victim in the narrative of alien aggression. Lighting is thrown on their faces from above, highlighting their fair skin, blond hair, and blue eyes. The sanctity of this image is reinforced through editing, which cuts from images of the family to the image of a white Christ at the altar, the supreme embodiment of Western humanity. Such editing supports a visual association between Christ and the family in a racialized context of whiteness.[55]

And yet, while these films exalt the white family and white womanhood, they simultaneously emphasize the dangerous potential of alien motherhood. *Them!*, for example, is a film about alien motherhood run amok, depicting the nightmare of uncontrolled, mindless reproduction of the Other. The film's climax is loaded with sexual tension, as the "queen" ant takes shelter in the "egg chamber" deep in the bowels of the city's sewers. Again, as in *He Walked by Night*, the sewers become the site of the urban subconscious, where degraded fantasies about white criminality and alien sexuality are intertwined. The queen ant is the nativist's worst nightmare, as she represents alien procreation gone mad—uncontrolled and unstoppable. Such representations of endless reproduction do not simply resonate with postwar anxieties about maternal domination. Rather, they underscored popular fears about alien motherhood in particular. The antagonist is, after all, an insect. Ultimately, climactic tension is resolved as the phallic bazookas of the army incinerate the queen and her eggs, thereby securing the city for white supremacy over the reproduction of the alien Other.[56]

Racial images are coupled with urban images in these films, dramatizing the political and cultural conditions of the nation's age of white flight. Just as white flight implies the movement of white masses away from the city, films such as *Them!* and *War of the Worlds* emphasize the flight of a homogeneous white citizenry from the violent onslaught of the Other. In *Them!*, for example, "UFO reports" confirm that "flying saucers shaped like ants" are heading west toward Los Angeles. Subsequent film images cut to urban crowds frantically preparing for the imminent arrival of "Them." A state of emergency is declared and the National Guard is called on to protect the white citizenry from the "savage and ruthless" invaders. Panic ensues prior to their arrival, as radio and television announce (with an alarming similarity to reports announcing civil unrest in Los Angeles in June 1943, August 1965, and April 1992):

> By direction of the President of the United States, in full agreement with the Governor of the State of California, and the Mayor of Los Angeles, the city of Los Angeles is, in the interests of public safety, hereby claimed to be under martial law. . . . Curfew is at 1800 hours.

Any persons on the street or outside their quarters after six P.M. tonight will be subject to arrest.

Similarly, in *War of the Worlds*, it is the prospect as well as the reality of doomsday that maintains the air of suspense. Though the aliens initially descend on a small California town, it is their slow but steady march toward Los Angeles on which the suspense of the narrative builds. The movement of the Other from the small town to the big city parallels the Great Migration of blacks during the 1940s and 1950s, in which massive numbers of black rural southerners migrated to cities such as Los Angeles. Migration becomes invasion in *War of the Worlds* as the Martians draw nearer to the city. The skies darken upon their arrival and panic descends on the hordes of Angelenos, who flee in desperation. Police cars with loud-speakers patrol the streets of downtown to maintain what little social order is left: "Everybody listen carefully! We must evacuate the city! All major highways have been marked to lead you to shelter and welfare centers in the hills." The very anticipation of doomsday in the urban science fiction film corresponded to the sense of crisis that descended on the postwar American city—a sense that someone or something was on its way, bring-ing crisis and destruction.

Finally, the Martians arrive, laying waste to the city. The realism of such images of destruction is enhanced through the use not only of innovative special effects but also of real and recognizable buildings and landscapes, which promoted audience identification with the crisis on the screen. A spectacular scene depicts the obliteration of Los Angeles city hall, a symbol of municipal authority and civic order, which explodes in a brilliant burst of fire. In other urban science fiction films, the use of the Empire State Building, Times Square, the Washington Monument, or the Golden Gate Bridge serves to name the urban scene and deepen the viewer's familiarity with the events taking place in the film. In each instance, however, the result is always the same: total obliteration of the most poignant symbols of Western progress and American civilization.

One contemporary critic discerned possibilities for pleasure in such ter-rifying images: "Just as listeners willingly mesmerized themselves into being scared half to death by the Welles broadcast, so will viewers take vic-arious pleasure in the terror loosened in the film."[57] Finding a certain poetry in such images, Susan Sontag described this pleasure as the "aesthetics of destruction."[58] Such images of aliens and their onslaught on the city un-doubtedly held an ambiguous fascination for the white suburban audiences of postwar America, who not only recoiled in horror from such a vision of their own destruction, but took a certain delight in that vision as well. Urban, industrial audiences have historically held mixed feelings toward the macabre, the alien, and the exotic, drawing on ambivalent feelings of shock, terror, curiosity, and even delight. The urban science fiction film, with its emphasis on disaster, disorder, and the grotesque, inherits its appeal from carnival sideshows and dime museums, which drew thousands who paid their admission fee to ogle curiosities such as "the FeeJee Mermaid" and "What is it?"[59]

The postwar popularity of films such as *Them!* and *War of the Worlds* revealed the extent to which this fascination persisted, even among suburban audiences of the 1950s. Although suburban audiences found themselves increasingly regimented within new spatial regimes, they maintained a fixation on the baser elements of society. Within a tradition of what the historian Robert Rydell calls "white supremacist entertainment," film noir and urban science fiction film granted a safe space in which audiences could flirt with any unconscious or unspoken attraction to the Other, even as they clung to traditional notions of racial hierarchy in the process of community formation. Their fixation on the city further suggests that even an expanding generation of suburban moviegoers did not say goodbye to the metropolis, or at least its cinematic representation. Film noir offered a momentary reveling in the racial morass of the city at night, and the urban science fiction film simulated the terror of an alien invasion, and while these films upheld an emerging suburban social order, they simultaneously preserved a psychic tie between the city and suburb.

Thus, even as flag-waving white Americans sought to distance themselves from subversive entities such as Communists and blacks during the Cold War era, the Other, in its political or racial manifestations, maintained its centrality in postwar American popular culture and inserted itself into the very heart of Southern California's cultural milieu. This came as no surprise to political scientists such as Michael Rogin and John Shover, who recognized the necessity of blacks, bureaucrats, Communists, and other social demons in Southern California's burgeoning right-wing political culture. In a region unfettered by tradition, where the ties to an organic past are negated by a regional commitment to growth and development and where the possibilities for attaining the suburban good life seem somehow tangible yet always impossible, the presence of the Other, in reality or representation, offered a comforting scapegoat that allowed frustrations to be deflected from the suburban dream onto its perceived enemies. Politics thus become "hallucinatory, since the real source of the anxiety, Southern California itself, can never be faced."[60]

None of this is to say that Hollywood's portrait of urban life in the United States was entirely dismal. Film noir's debut in the mid-1940s coincided with a set of films that celebrated the city's festive culture. *Meet Me in St. Louis* (1944) and *Centennial Summer* (1946) were two musicals that portrayed the mounting excitement and blossoming romance of turn-of-the-century St. Louis and Philadelphia on the eve of a world's fair. *Hello 'Frisco Hello* (1943), *Coney Island* (1943), and *Greenwich Village* (1944) offered similarly lighthearted fare, evoking romantic images of San Francisco and New York during the Gay '90s. American audiences, with their enduring appetite for sentimentality and nostalgia, enjoyed such images of their cities even as they reveled in the squalor of the noir city, suggesting their deep ambivalence toward the city and its culture.

But if the historical setting of the turn-of-the-century American city afforded a generous capacity for nostalgic idealizations and utopian aspirations, the "here and now" of film noir and the urban science fiction film afforded no such comforts. With their penchant for on-location shooting, semidocumentary reportage, and "wondrous" special effects, film noir and the urban science fiction film heightened a perceptual blurring between the reality and representation of urban life in postwar America. The noir vision of the city was not solely the invention of Hollywood, for it was as much the product of the very real changes that overtook American cities at the outset of the postwar period. The combination of economic restructuring and demographic upheaval at midcentury created a literal and figurative setting for the real "black" city that white Americans abandoned in the course of suburbanization. In their wake, Hollywood found the makings of a noir vision, one that situated the city within a larger set of social and political upheavals that engulfed postwar American society.

Hollywood's rendition of the postwar urban crisis implicated distinct social actors, each of whom attained greater recognition in urban public life during the 1930s and early 1940s. Blacks, women, homosexuals, and Communists ran rampant in the noir city, threatening the prospects for a return to the classless vision of white patriarchy that defined suburban idealizations of the American Way. These groups secured some accommodations in the political culture of New Deal liberalism, but their figurative doubles in film noir and the urban science fiction film dramatized their threat to the dawning social order of Cold War America. In a virtual replay of a noir movie, right-wing ideologues such as Ronald Reagan targeted these very groups as subversive entities while hailing the virtues of law and order, as well as home and family. Through their narrative patterns and visual imagery, film noir and the urban science fiction film prefigured this political scenario as far back as the immediate postwar period, but their mise-en-scène cast the city itself as another "enemy within," one that threatened the return to some semblance of racial and sexual normalcy. Ultimately, film noir and the urban science fiction film indicted the modern city for its failure to "contain" the subversive energies latent in American society, be they racial, sexual, or ideological.

By the mid-1940s, Hollywood had fulfilled Adolph Zukor's earlier intention to "kill the slum" through a literal portrait of urban decay and, in doing so, it had further affiliated the American film industry with the set of dominant social values that informed the construction of a new suburban society. That Los Angeles maintained its own "slum tradition" illustrates the extent to which urbanization in Southern California had severely compromised Dana Bartlett's vision of a "better city" and dramatizes how the very urban process of social mixing had desanctified the city of the angels. But the possibilities for redemption were not entirely lost, for the phase of mass suburbanization that settled on the region during the postwar period brought forth an alternative sociospatial order, one very different from the racial and sexual mélange of the modern city. Iterating a fear of going out into the big city, film noir and the urban science fiction film called for a privatized alternative to the public city and anticipated a new spatial experience that promised order, regimentation, and uniformity. By the mid-1950s, Disneyland had burst onto Southern California's cultural scene as a refuge from the noir city. Removed from the city center, the theme park modeled the burgeoning racial and spatial order of the decentralized urban region, offering a more sanitized and more disciplined cultural experience that rescued postwar audiences from the squalid maze of the noir city.

4 "A Rage for Order"

Disneyland and the Suburban Ideal

Los Angeles was the scene of the last fling of thousands of soldiers about to be shipped to the front. Bars and shady amusement centers were generously patronized. Such was the setting for the clash between the men in uniform and the unemployed gangs, many of whose members had adopted the zoot suit costume with oversized coats, baggy trousers, and low-hanging watch chains.

JOHN ANSON FORD, *Thirty Explosive Years in Los Angeles County,* 135

In its portrait of urban blight at midcentury, film noir favored the recurrent imagery of the amusement park. In *T-Men,* the two undercover agents wander through a decrepit amusement park in their search for the Schemer. In the climactic ending to *Strangers on a Train,* a murderous psychopath stalks an ominous fairground at night and a merry-go-round whirls violently out of control. A huge Ferris wheel is the setting for a climactic confrontation between Orson Welles and Joseph Cotten in *The Third Man,* and in *The Lady from Shanghai,* multiple images of a shooting by a femme fatale are refracted through the mirror-maze of a funhouse.

Though it once reigned as a favorite institution among urban Americans at the beginning of the twentieth century, the amusement park lost much of its popularity during the post–World War II period, and the signs of its decline permeated the cinematic landscape of film noir. Answering noir's call for a suburban alternative to the disordered chaos of modern city culture, Disneyland debuted in 1955 as the very antithesis of Coney Island and its urban counterparts. Coney Island was everything that Disneyland was not. In contrast to Coney Island's unruly crowds, Disneyland presented a controlled landscape that orchestrated the movement and vision of park visitors and modeled a regimented organization of space that paralleled the emerging spatial culture of postwar suburbia. And against Coney Island's visual dissonance, Disneyland subordinated all aspects of park design under a set of "themes" that reinforced the perception and experience of order, familiarity, and harmony. Ordered enough to contrast sharply with the chaos of the modern city, yet intimate enough to counter the limitless sprawl of Southern California's expanding urban region, Disneyland presented a compact, reassuring model of order that resembled an updated version of the Progressives' "better city."

An inconspicuous setting in which to discern the transformation of American politics and culture during the postwar period, perhaps, Disneyland nonetheless encapsulated the values built into the design of postwar suburban communities, and it anticipated the burgeoning political culture of suburban whiteness that overcame Southern California during the 1960s and 1970s. Extolling the virtues of consumerism, patriarchy, patriotism, and small-town midwestern whiteness, Disneyland issued a set of cultural motifs that emphasized a retreat from the public culture of New Deal liberalism and instead asserted a privatized, suburban alternative to that culture. Moreover, that Walt Disney chose Orange County as the site for his theme park suggests the affinity between the park and its suburban setting. In Reagan Country, Disney found a physical and cultural environment that accommodated his determination to reassert more traditional notions of an American Way that conformed to popular idealizations of suburban respectability in the age of white flight.

SEX ON THE BEACH

In the lineage of American popular culture, the turn-of-the-twentieth-century amusement park preceded Disneyland, coming of age just as the United States completed its transformation into an urban industrial nation. The amusement park, typified by Coney Island, satisfied the cultural needs of turn-of-the-century Americans, who sought diversion from the demands of modern industrial life. An electric landscape of Ferris wheels, roller coasters, and other mechanical attractions patronized by a motley, sometimes unruly crowd, the amusement park marketed the sensual, even sexual, experiences of the modern city as mass entertainment. Coney Island at the turn of the century reflected a very different set of historical circumstances than those that gave rise to Disneyland in the mid-1950s. Our understanding of those differences can illuminate the degree to which the cultural organization of American life shifted in the transition from the modern industrial city to the postindustrial urban region.

Coney Island highlighted the cultural landscape of that paragon of industrial urbanization, turn-of-the-century New York. Once a desolate stretch of sand dunes, Coney Island became in the second half of the nineteenth century a seaside resort for New York's expanding middle class. The extension of streetcar and railroad lines to Coney Island granted accessibility to growing numbers of pleasure seekers who sought a day's escape from the city.

During the 1850s, horse-drawn streetcars ran to Coney Island from Brooklyn, and in the early 1870s, steamers carried visitors on a two-hour trip from the city for fifty cents. In 1875, Andrew Culver built the Prospect Park and Coney Island Railroad, which increased Coney Island's clientele from thousands annually to millions. Following the completion of Culver's railroad line, a succession of hotels sprang up at Coney Island: the Manhattan Beach (1877), the Brighton Beach (1878), the Oriental (1880), and the Elephant, completed in 1882 and sculpted in the shape of its namesake animal.[1]

As with other cultural institutions located on the outskirts of the modern city, such as ballparks, the owners of streetcar and railroad companies played a major role in the development of Coney Island, using mass transit to ensure a steady influx of New Yorkers. In fact, many of the companies and individuals who built railroads and trolley lines were largely responsible for the popularity of the amusement park. Nowhere was the synergy between mass transit and popular amusement more evident than at Coney Island. The Culver line terminal, for example, opened onto Culver Plaza, where band concerts frequently greeted arriving tourists. Visitors could then proceed to gaze upon the three-hundred-foot Iron Tower, a souvenir of the Philadelphia Centennial Exposition of 1876, with two steam elevators to carry customers to an observation platform. The significance of trolley lines and railroads in the initial development of Coney Island illustrates how the technologies that animate city life shape the contours of urban popular culture. As we shall discover, the transition from the centralized city to the postwar urban region implicated new technologies such as the automobile and the freeway, engendering new cultural forms such as Disneyland.

The accessibility of Coney Island sustained the influx of New York's myriad classes and ethnic groups, who sought release from the regimen of daily life. While Coney Island drew largely on the rising middle class and the more prosperous segments of the working class for its patronage, those who could afford only transit fare still came to Coney Island "merely for the joy of mixing with the crowds on the public street and catching the live sense of humanity and of good humor that is everywhere."[2] New York's expanding working class took a particular interest in Coney Island. In Manhattan around 1905, in two separately conducted surveys of working-class families who could pay little for recreation, subjects frequently mentioned going to Coney Island once or twice a summer.

Just as Coney Island reflected the growing class diversity of the modern industrial city, it encompassed the city's tremendous ethnic diversity as well. Immigration to New York reached unprecedented proportions at the turn of the century, and Irish, German, Italian, and Eastern European Jews soon accompanied Anglo-Saxon Americans in their pursuit of pleasure. As John Kasson suggests, Coney Island held a double appeal for New York City's immigrant population. On the one hand, the amusement park was not that far removed from the immigrant experience, as the air of merriment and festivity at Coney Island held some familiarity for frequenters of street festivals and band concerts, celebrants of Purim, and patrons of Yiddish theater. In this capacity, Coney Island reflected the "slum tradition" that Adolph Zukor recognized in working-class cinema.

On the other hand, the resort provided a means by which newcomers and especially their children could transcend the limitations of family, neighborhood, and tradition to participate in the mainstream of modern American culture. This was particularly true for women, particularly young women, who frequented Coney Island. The heterogeneous and anonymous character of the urban amusement park afforded immigrant and native-born women alike an unprecedented degree of freedom from Victorian sexual mores, even as they faced new forms of oppression in the workplace. As growing numbers of women submitted to the demands of factory work, they found some relief in the city's expanding circuits of leisure and amusement, frequenting the many bars, cabarets, dance halls, saloons, parks, and theaters that catered to workers of both sexes. By 1900, New York's working women made regular excursions to Coney Island to satisfy their need for diversion. Some brought a girlfriend, while others came in groups. Still others ventured alone, where they could often rely on an encounter with a member of the opposite sex, happy to "treat" his newfound companion to a day's amusement. Said one woman of her days spent at Coney Island in its heyday, "It costs only fare down and back, and for the rest of it the boys you 'pick up' 'treat.'" At Coney Island, women could escape the supervision of parents and other relatives to discover a newfound sexual freedom sanctioned by the modern city and its anonymous venues for heterosocial interaction.[3]

In other ways as well, Coney Island reflected the nascent sexual culture of the modern city. Although historians generally distinguish the amusement park from the theme park, the former also had its "themes"—sex, romance, and titillation foremost among them. "Any well seeming youngster may invite any girl to dance" at Coney Island, observed one journalist, "an arrangement long since sanctioned by that maelstrom of proletarian jollity, the 'social,' where tickets . . . connote partners and more partners, till everybody knows everybody else."[4] In addition to its dance halls, Coney Island's amusement parks encouraged physical interaction with strangers of the opposite sex. George Tilyou's Steeplechase Park, the third of Coney

Island's amusement parks, opened in 1897 and incorporated sexuality and romance into its repertoire. For example, its Razzle Dazzle, otherwise known as the Wedding Ring, featured a large circle of laminated wood suspended from a pole, which, when rocked back and forth, caused patrons to stumble into one another, packaging the kind of physical encounters that occurred frequently on city streets as a form of sexual amusement.[5]

Coney Island sustained greater freedom of sexual expression for homosexual men as much as for heterosexual women. In his study of the urban spaces that cultivated a gay male identity, George Chauncey identified the amusement park, in addition to streets, alleys, bars, dance halls, and theaters, as one arena in which that identity took shape. Jimmy Durante, who began his career in show business playing piano in the venues of Coney Island and the Bowery, remembered working in one Coney Island dive where the "entertainers were all boys who danced together and lisped." Coney Island's many bathhouses also provided a setting in which men could enjoy not only the more intimate company of other men, but also the camaraderie that ensued among men attracted to other men. The Washington Baths in the heart of Coney Island hosted a beauty pageant of men competing against other men before a crowd of male onlookers.[6]

Coney Island thus repackaged the sexual cultures that burgeoned on the city streets, promoting various forms of intercourse among an anonymous and heterogeneous crowd of predominantly working-class men and women. Its overwhelming popularity among New York pleasure seekers spawned an entire generation of amusement parks that highlighted the cultural landscape of urban America in the early twentieth century. Made possible by swelling urban populations, the elaboration of transportation systems, and increasing spending power among the working- and middle-class segments of society, amusement parks rapidly proliferated throughout the country. Boston's Paragon Park and Revere Beach, Philadelphia's Willow Grove and nearby Atlantic City, Atlanta's Ponce de Leon Park, Chicago's Riverview Park and White City, Denver's Manhattan Beach and San Francisco's Chutes—these and other amusement parks catered to the growing demand for amusement in an expanding urban industrial democracy.

Los Angeles harbored its own versions of Coney Island. Early in the century, three amusement parks were built on piers extending into the Pacific Ocean, all linked by a train that ran along "several miles of solidly built-up beach frontage lined with amusement concessions, pleasure piers, apartment houses and cottages, saltwater plunges, beach clubs and cafes." Ocean Park Pier, built by Abbot Kinney in 1905 at the south end of Santa Monica Bay, advertised itself as "a vacation in a day," featuring "every sort of jazz attractions from monkey farms to loop-the-loops, dip-the-dips, ride-the-clouds, and go-crazy-in-the-fun-houses." To one contemporary observer, Ocean Park Pier offered "the Coney Island atmosphere—though perhaps some of it is rather of the Atlantic City type."[7]

In the same year Kinney opened Ocean Park Pier, he also built the Venice-of-America attraction, a cultural center promoting "uplifting" cultural events, expounding on the Mediterranean theme that local boosters used to advertise Los Angeles. Although Kinney sponsored "improving lectures, Chautauqua meetings and art exhibits, and provided free transportation from Los Angeles," visitors seemed less interested in cultural uplift than in amusement park attractions, forcing Kinney in 1906 to "convert his dream city into an imitation Coney Island, building a pleasure zone and importing freaks and side shows." Venice Pier, described by a 1907 Pacific Electric brochure as a "Coney Island of the West," featured an indoor saltwater plunge and an array of restaurants, dance halls, roller coasters, fun houses, freak shows, and camel rides.[8] A group of rival entrepreneurs capitalized on the popularity of the coastline among pleasure seekers in Southern California, opening the Santa Monica Pleasure Pier in 1909, which featured the Blue Streak Roller Coaster, a ballroom, and a carousel.

Farther south, the Long Beach Pike opened in 1902, originally named the "Walk of a Thousand Lights" by its developer, Charles R. Drake. It featured a bathhouse, two pavilions, and a bandstand where the nation's first municipally supported band played to audiences all year round. The Pike acquired a roller coaster in 1907 and a merry-go-round in 1911. The Works Progress Administration's guide to Los Angeles described the Pike as a "major local industry" with "shooting galleries, penny arcades, a roller coaster, side shows, a merry-go-round, miniature automobiles, power scooters, and similar amusements for adults and children alike." Typical of nineteenth-century popular culture, the Pike also featured an array of human oddities and exotic side shows, including the Fat Lady, the Sword Swallower, the Fire Eater, the Ubangis from Africa, and the Cross between a Man and a Monkey.[9]

Like Coney Island, the Pike drew a heterogeneous array of pleasure seekers, who crowded into the spaces of the amusement park in search of fun and excitement. Mexican youths in Los Angeles, for example, adopted the Pike as a popular hangout during the 1930s and '40s. Taking advantage of the Long Beach Line of the Pacific Electric Railway, young Mexican American women often ventured to the Pike, where they could escape the strict supervision of relatives and neighbors. For example, my maternal grandmother, Mary Gonzales (later Hernandez), who grew up in Watts during the 1930s and worked in the Firestone tire plant during the early 1940s, recalls venturing to

FIGURE 7.   Coney Island West: selling "sex" at Santa Monica's Ocean Park. (Courtesy of the Los Angeles Public Library.)

the Pike with some of her coworkers who were also young single Chicanas. "We used to take the trolley cars down there to Long Beach and we never knew what to expect, but we always had a good time. It was such a big deal to be there, with everyone out and about . . . no parents, no chaperones."[10]

Gonzales's experiences at the Pike illustrate the way in which Southern California sustained an aspect of the youthful, unsupervised urban culture that defined the experience of the amusement park during the first half of the twentieth century. The amusement park's popularity among urban audiences at the turn of the century signaled a larger transition from the culture of production to the culture of consumption, in which Americans exchanged the values of sobriety and thrift for those of indulgence and personal fulfillment. That transition arose within the precincts of the modern city, in which the entrepreneurs of the new mass culture found ready access to the urban middle class and the largely untapped working class. The modern city, in its venues of amusement parks, movie houses, dance halls, and department stores, showcased the new ethic of consumption for a heterogeneous population of workers, immigrants, women, and other groups previously relegated to the margins of social life. No longer did these groups have to conform to the elitist standards of Victorian respectability. Rather, Coney

Island and its generation of cultural institutions invited audiences to revel in the dissonance, vulgarity, and exuberance of urban industrial culture.

WALT DISNEY'S COUNTERCULTURE

Walt Disney's youth coincided with the peak of the amusement park's popularity in the early decades of the twentieth century. Born in Chicago in 1901, at age five Disney moved with his family to Marceline, Missouri, a small town along the main line of the Atcheson, Topeka and Santa Fe Railroad one hundred miles northeast of Kansas City. In Marceline, Disney encountered a setting that would exert a profound influence on the imagination he would employ in the service of mass entertainment. According to his chief biographers, the young Disney grew enamored with the animals of his father's farm, with the railroad that made daily stops in his town, and with the town of Marceline itself, which inspired not only countless images of small-town life in Disney's films, but also the creation of Main Street, USA, a turn-of-the-century recreation of a small-town commercial thoroughfare and the first of Disneyland's five "lands."[11] Painted in bright pastel colors and complete with a firehouse, an ice creamery, and a "city hall," where Disney himself occasionally resided, Main Street, USA, upheld Disney's faith in the virtues of small-town America and symbolized a nostalgic retreat from the decadence of the noir city.

Disney's infatuation with the virtuous spaces of small-town America revealed the spatial dimensions of his imagination. His preoccupation with the settings that nurtured traditional folk values reflected a deeper conviction that human values and behavior were conditioned by their surroundings, and that proper surroundings cultivated proper values and behavior. That conviction not only dictated the placement of Disneyland in Orange County, but also guided the ordering of space inside the park and determined the park's thematic emphasis on small-town America, the "wild" frontier, and the suburban family home. Not unlike Daniel Burnham's White City, designed to inspire and uplift its onlookers, Walt Disney's Disneyland reflected the use of three-dimensional space for the transmission of cultural values and meanings. This affiliated Disneyland with the underlying principles of the City Beautiful movement, which upheld the capacity of urban architecture and planning to instill a common, or dominant, set of values—particularly a respect for tradition and order—among a diverse and often unruly public.

In 1910, Disney's family moved to Kansas City, where Disney would spend most of his adolescence. There, the young Disney witnessed the civic struggles that accompanied the cultural transition to urban modernity. In the second decade of the twentieth century, a strict moral climate conditioned the administration of amusement in Kansas City. City officials, alarmed by the sudden popularity of movie houses, dance halls, and amusement parks, associated such activities with larger patterns of dependency and delinquency and took measures to address what they identified as "the problem of leisure." Kansas City's Recreation Department assumed the responsibility of monitoring the leisure habits of the urban public. The city's Board of Public Welfare oversaw the Recreation Department, in addition to the Social Services Department, the Parole Board, and the City Correctional Farm. In placing the Recreation Department under the supervision of the Board of Public Welfare, Kansas City officials demonstrated the extent to which they viewed commercial amusements in pathological terms, seeking measures to exert control over the proliferation of such amusements.[12]

Official efforts to regulate commercial amusements in Kansas City reflected the reformist impulse of the Progressive era. Progressive reformers at the turn of the century expressed their dismay at their urban surroundings and embarked on a crusade to clean up American cities. As part of their efforts, Progressives sought to control what they perceived to be the excesses of urban commercial culture through government regulation and expert supervision. The Progressive antipathy to the new mass culture rested upon a larger indictment of the modern industrial city. Jane Addams, for example, one of the nation's most influential social reformers, deplored that the demanding routines of city life bred an almost unconscious desire for escape among city dwellers: " 'Looping the loop' amid shrieks of stimulated terror or dancing in disorderly saloon halls are perhaps the natural reactions to a day spent in noisy factories and in trolley cars whirling through the streets, but," Addams warned, "the city which permits them to be the acme of pleasure and recreation to its young people commits a grievous mistake."[13] Reformers such as Addams voiced their concerns about the effects of the new mass culture on the nation's youth, whose moral conscience seemed threatened by the lure of amusement parks, dance halls, and movie palaces. In Kansas City, such anxieties aroused official concern. Fred R. Johnson, who served as chief executive of the Board of Public Welfare, adopted the reformist stance toward Kansas City's commercial amusements, noting in 1911 "the intimate connections between amusements and immorality. Public dances, questionable picture shows, poorly regulated amusement parks and burlesque houses are prolific sources of corruption."[14]

Thus, Walt Disney came of age in the midst of a cultural struggle between Progressive reformers and the entrepreneurs of the new mass culture. That struggle epitomized the larger effort to come to terms with modernity, which had thrust Americans into a turbulent sea of social, economic, and cultural upheaval. Progressives confronted such upheaval with caution, seeking to restore some sense of the previous social order, while the entrepreneurs of the new mass culture pandered to the popular cravings for newness and sensuality among the expanding crowds of the new metropolis. In the initial stages of his career, Disney joined the ranks of the entrepreneurs, beginning as an apprentice for a small advertising agency in Kansas City, and then working as an animator for the Kansas City Film Ad Company. His subsequent success in Hollywood, however, strengthened Disney's moral outlook and guided his determination to both entertain and educate the public. The tensions that accompanied the transition to urban modernity in the early decades of the twentieth century permeated Disney's work. Awestruck by the burgeoning technologies of mass entertainment, yet deeply suspicious of urban mass culture and its immoral influences, Disney expressed his ambivalence toward urban modernity by using technical innovations to represent traditional ideals, a paradox that came to define the Disney style.[15]

In July 1923, a twenty-two-year-old Disney boarded a train for Los Angeles with only forty dollars in his pocket and a copy of his animated film, *Alice's Wonderland*. Disney's older brother Roy had already established himself in Los Angeles, and the younger sibling reasoned that Southern California's burgeoning film industry harbored opportunities for the talents of an unemployed animator. After selling another *Alice* film to a New York agent, Disney officially established Disney Productions, which expanded to Walt Disney Studio in 1925. Although Disney would soon join the ranks of Hollywood's elite, he discovered that success in the film industry did not demand a sacrifice of his small-town midwestern values. In fact, in Southern California, Disney found himself in company with other displaced midwesterners who shared his nostalgic affinity for small-town ways of life. As the region sustained a long and steady influx of midwesterners beginning at the turn of the century, Southern California's political culture generally reflected a provincial hostility toward immigrants, labor unions, and other elements of cosmopolitan urban culture.[16]

Disney's infatuation with small-town America crystallized during the 1930s, as the showman garnered national enthusiasm over the debut of Mickey Mouse in 1928. Disney, a man "never weaned away from the common bond with the great majority of American small town and country folk, their taste and ideals," adopted a populist cultural politics that extolled the wisdom and dignity of the common man.[17] To identify Disney as a "populist," as historian Stephen Watts reminds us, is not to assign an arbitrary political label to someone who never identified himself as such. Although Disney never crusaded for agrarian reform or campaigned for free silver, his work resonated with themes and sentiments that had permeated populist discourse since the late nineteenth century. Disney's appreciation of American "folks" surfaced in various animated short and feature-length films that dramatized the resilience and tenacity of underdog figures. Such works echoed the cultural tone of the 1930s, a decade when many of the nation's artistic, intellectual, and political leaders rallied behind what Christopher Lasch characterized as a "petty bourgeois populism." Along with the illustrator Norman Rockwell, the politician Huey Long, the folksinger Woody Guthrie, the composer Aaron Copland, the literary critic Van Wyck Brooks, and the painters Thomas Hart Benton and Grant Wood, Disney celebrated the culture of the common man. Their enthusiasm for American folk culture flourished in the New Deal era, in which the federal government supported a number of cultural projects documenting the life experiences and cultural habits of ordinary Americans.[18]

The early 1940s, however, channeled Disney's ideological convictions in a decidedly different direction, as his idealization of the American folk increasingly took on conservative, if not reactionary, overtones. The war and its aftermath heightened Disney's suspicion of multiple conspirators undermining the American way of life. A highly publicized labor strike among Disney animators in 1941, for example, convinced Disney that strike leaders worked on behalf of "Communistic agitation" and that labor unions were un-American. As Disney's hostility to organized labor increased in the course of World War II, his relationship with the federal government also grew increasingly antagonistic. After the bombing of Pearl Harbor, Disney allowed the U.S. Army to use a Burbank studio as a supply base and joined the war effort by producing training films and propaganda cartoons, neither of which the federal government paid for. Slighted by Washington, D.C., and enraged toward labor groups, Disney embraced a more conservative outlook that anticipated a broader transformation in the national political culture.[19]

Disney's political reorientation solidified in the aftermath of World War II. The Cold War aroused anti-Communist hysteria among Americans and prompted a national witch hunt for anyone suspected of Communist sympathies. When HUAC sought to identify Communist influences in the Hollywood film industry in 1947, Walt Disney lent his support to that cause, establishing, along with the actors Gary Cooper and Adolphe Menjou and the writer Ayn Rand, the Motion Picture Alliance for the Preservation of American Ideals to investigate the influence of Communism in the entertainment industry. On October 24, 1947, Disney appeared as a friendly witness before HUAC, assuring members of the committee that although his studios were now "100 percent American," the Disney Studio strike of 1941 had involved "a communist group trying to take over my artists."[20]

Embroiled in highly politicized and even more highly publicized struggles, Disney could not find distraction from his troubles in his work. Disney's film productions of the 1940s, despite their innovative blend of live action with animation, did not win the accolades that Disney had earned a decade earlier. Several films of the time, including *Saludos Amigos* (1943), *The Three Caballeros* (1945), and *Make Mine Music* (1946), elicited the scorn of critics. Whether these critics abandoned Disney in favor of new artists on the cultural scene or their criticism that Disney increasingly relied on slick commercial formulas to sell films held some truth, it can be said that Disney's parting of ways with the critics heightened the showman's growing disdain for "highfalutin'" intellectuals.[21]

Disney's animosity toward labor unions, big government, finance capital, and intellectuals intensified as the Cold War continued, and the egalitarian brand of populism that Disney had espoused in the 1930s increasingly gave way to a reactionary defense of the American Way. An embittered Disney gradually retreated into a vision of a homogenous WASP folk embodying the traditional small-town values of hard work, rugged individualism, tightly knit families, and traditional gender roles. His commitment to that vision surfaced during the Cold War in an outpouring of vaguely historical films that dramatized various strands of Disney's new political outlook. Films such as *Davy Crockett* (1955) and *The Swiss Family Robinson* (1960) illustrated the virtues of frontier Americans removed from modern civilization. *So Dear to My Heart* (1949) and *Pollyanna* (1960) evoked the cohesion of small-town communities and the goodness of small-town folk. While postwar Americans, not unlike Walt Disney himself, were forsaking their small-town roots for the "good life" that burgeoned on the suburban periphery of American cities, the rush to suburbia was fueled in part by the kind of vision that Disney celebrated in film and ultimately enshrined at Disneyland.[22]

The reactionary politics that Disney espoused toward the end of his career, what Richard Schickel described as "the politics of nostalgia," not only reinforced the showman's idealization of small-town life, but also affirmed his long-standing suspicion of cosmopolitan urban culture. In the course of planning Disneyland, Disney articulated a need for an alternative to the Coney Island experience, one that modeled the values that seemed to dissipate in the chaos of urban modernity. The early 1940s left Walt Disney Productions in financial disarray, prompting company leaders to seek alternative venues in which to market Disney products. Following his foray into television, Disney began to think seriously about the creation of an amusement park that would represent a total inversion of the Coney Island experience. Disney himself expressed a "need for something new" but admitted, "I didn't know what it was." Based on his strong revulsion against previous institutions of urban amusement, Disney once remarked that Coney Island and its generation of amusement parks were "dirty, phoney places run by tough looking people." After visiting a dilapidated Coney Island in the course of planning Disneyland in the mid-1940s, Disney recoiled from its "tawdry rides and hostile employees."[23] Subsequent admirers of Disneyland, even New York journalists, affirmed Disney's indictment of Coney Island. Gladwin Hill of the *New York Times,* for example, asserted that Disneyland marked a departure from "the traditionally raucous and ofttimes shoddy amusement park," delighting in the fact that Disneyland eliminated the "ballyhoo men to assault [the visitor's] ears with exhortations to test his strength, skill, courage, [and] digestion, or gawk at freaks or cootch dancers."[24]

Mired in the midcentury mythology of the noir metropolis, Coney Island aroused Disney's long-standing prejudices against cities and cosmopolitan culture. Raised by a strict father who cautioned against the "corruptive influences of a big city," Disney remained suspicious of cities and their culture throughout his life. Even in Los Angeles, a city historically not recognized for its cosmopolitan urbanity, Disney set himself apart from Hollywood's more urbane elite, appearing in denim overalls and plaid flannel shirts at parties in his own home. If Disney distanced himself from Hollywood, he avoided New York City altogether. After his success at Disneyland, when asked to consider New York as the site for a second theme park, he dismissed the suggestion in large part because he doubted the capacity of New Yorkers to embrace the Disney worldview. "He said that audience is not responsive," recalled John Hench, Disneyland's chief architect and Disney's close associate, "that city is different." Hench also elaborated on Disney's conviction that urban modernity preyed on the moral conscience of Americans:

> In modern cities you have to defend yourself constantly and you go counter to everything that we've learned from the past. You tend to isolate yourself from other people . . . you tend to be less aware. You tend to be more withdrawn. This is counter life . . . you really die a little. . . . I think we need something to counteract what modern society—cities—have done to us.[25]

Having to defend yourself constantly became one of the hallmark experiences of city life at the turn of the twentieth century, particularly for women, who were often forced into a defensive posture against the unwanted advances of amorous men at places like Coney Island. One contemporary observer of Coney Island in its heyday noted that the typical shop girl at the amusement park was "keen and knowing, ever on the defensive . . . she distrusts cavaliers not of her own station."[26]

Disney, like the previous generation of Progressive reformers, deplored how the modern city seemed to demand the sacrifice of innocent virtue. The average citizen, he once remarked, "is a victim of civilization whose ideal is the unbotherable, poker-faced man and the attractive, unruffled woman."[27] Disney's revulsion against the poker-faced man and the unruffled woman echoed earlier cultural anxieties about confidence men and painted women in antebellum America. Much like the trickster figure of various folk cultures, the confidence man was the seducer who preyed on the naiveté of strangers, particularly women and the young, for self-aggrandizement. The confidence man, however, unlike the trickster, owed his existence to the modern city in the first half of the nineteenth century, where individuals could lay claim to new and higher social status through deceit and manipulation. In her study of middle-class culture in nineteenth-century America, Karen Haltunnen located cultural anxieties about confidence men and painted women within the rapid expansion of the city and its ambiguous social milieu. Hypocrisy, the art of deceit and manipulation mastered by the confidence man, "paid off in an urban environment." Though removed from the historical context in which middle-class moralists denounced the rise of confidence men and painted women, Walt Disney, in his critique of "phony" amusement parks, poker-faced men, and unruffled women, shared a similar antipathy to the hypocrisy and insincerity that defined social relations in the urban world of strangers.[28]

Continuing a long-standing effort to transmit "uplifting" social values through mass entertainment, Disney renounced the contradictions and uncertainties of modern urban society. The very heterogeneity and dissonance that defined cosmopolitan urban culture inspired Walt Disney to create a counterculture of order, regimentation, and homogeneity. "We design an area to create a certain atmosphere," recalled John Hench about Disneyland, "and we maintain it so that there isn't that visual, thematic, and even functional contradiction that exists outside in cities where everything is all mixed together." To counter the ethnic heterogeneity and sexual ambiguity that characterized the Coney Island experience, Disney and his corps of designers sought to create a landscape where "everything says the same thing."[29] Thus, whatever paradoxes and contradictions defined Disneyland and its brand of mass entertainment, park designers took extreme measures to minimize such ambiguities in their effort to rescue Americans from the degraded cultural habits they had acquired from places like Coney Island and to restore a vision of an unambiguous social order that seemed lost to generations of urban Americans. Main Street, USA, extolled the virtues of small-town life, while Frontierland celebrated the national imperatives of expansion and the ideology of manifest destiny. The emphasis on "family entertainment" at Disneyland asserted the necessity of the patriarchal nuclear family. And the prominence of racialized representations at Disneyland maintained a long-standing preoccupation with race and racial identity, while at the same time affirming a homogeneous vision of whiteness. These representations of social order offered some relief from the dissonance of urban modernity and afforded postwar Americans a comforting distraction from the many uncertainties and anxieties of the day.

ORANGE GROVES TO PARKING LOTS

In search of a setting in which to represent his vision of social order, Walt Disney settled on Orange County, then an agricultural empire just beginning its transition to a suburban refuge from Southern California's urban core. Initially, during the planning phases for Disneyland, Disney assumed that he would build his park in Burbank, adjacent to Walt Disney Studios. Burbank officials, however, shared Disney's dim view of the amusement park and rejected his proposal to build what was then imagined as Disneylandia. One Burbank official asserted, "We don't want the carny atmosphere in Burbank," reflecting the growing distaste for amusement parks after World War II.[30] Unable to convince Burbank officials that he imagined a more uplifting alternative to the typical carny show, Disney called on the Stanford Research Institute (SRI), a think tank established by Stanford University in 1946 to further industrialization and economic progress in the western United States, to identify an alternative site in Southern California for the construction of Disneyland.

After an extensive survey of various sites in the greater Los Angeles area, SRI recommended a parcel of land in Anaheim, not unlike the "ten square miles of indifferent Southern California farmland" upon which Lakewood materialized in the early 1950s.[31] Anaheim, located in Orange County some eleven miles south of downtown Los Angeles, rested alongside the planned route of the Santa Ana Freeway, scheduled for completion in 1955, the same year that Disney targeted for the opening of Disneyland. Until World War II,

Anaheim had remained a sparsely populated agricultural outpost devoted to citrus cultivation. After the war, however, city officials in Anaheim made efforts to boost economic development in the hope that factories and subdivisions would begin to replace ranches and orange groves. The coming of the Santa Ana Freeway would certainly help their cause, providing a direct link between Los Angeles and Anaheim and igniting a prolonged phase of intensive suburban development in Orange County. The characteristics of Disney's ideal site for Disneyland encompassed many of the same qualities that developers sought for the construction of suburban communities. The Anaheim site identified by SRI satisfied Disney's stipulation for one hundred acres of flat land, "with no intensive improvement or buildup" and no nearby oil fields, enjoying excellent weather, accessible to automobile transportation, and removed from land already under government control.[32]

Just as Walter O'Malley coveted the Chavez Ravine as the site for the construction of Dodger Stadium because of its proximity to Los Angeles' new freeways (as we shall discover in chapter 5), Walt Disney and SRI studied the evolving pattern of Southern California's freeways in the search for a site on which to build Disneyland. Because the "southern California area is characterized by preponderant use of private auto transportation," SRI reasoned that "the problem of accessibility [is] thus resolved to the consideration of existing and proposed arterial networks serving the various districts."[33] By the late 1940s, California's Division of Highways had formalized its plans for the southern extension of the Golden State Freeway into the agricultural communities of Orange County, Anaheim and Santa Ana in particular. The coming of the freeway would accelerate residential growth in Anaheim and surrounding towns, placing Disneyland in the midst of an expanding pool of potential customers and employees. One Disneyland official later recalled the significance of the freeway to the search for a site on which to build Disneyland: "The freeway project was such that we could see that the freeways would eventually hit Anaheim as a sort of hub, so that's how we selected Anaheim."[34]

So vital was the freeway to the success of Disneyland that it earned a permanent place inside the park. Among the thirteen original attractions included in the park's opening in 1955, Autopia in Tomorrowland was a "real model freeway," not unlike the "motorways of the world of tomorrow" that highlighted the Futurama exhibit of the 1939 New York World's Fair. Situated between a rocketship ride and the Voyage to the Moon attraction, Autopia demonstrated the centrality of freeways to Disney's optimistic vision of the future. Although Autopia offered its patrons a "real life highway adventure," it also maintained a didactic function, unlike the titillating sensations of Coney Island's attractions, which emphasized pleasure for its own sake. "Constructed to acquaint youngsters with traffic conditions on the highways of tomorrow," Autopia demonstrated Disneyland's capacity to familiarize its guests with the new modes of transportation that served the needs of a rapidly sprawling public.[35]

Disney and SRI predicated the success of Disneyland on the changing patterns of urban development in postwar Southern California, identifying those institutions central to that development. Disney marketed Disneyland to a growing suburban population, who had left the city for many of the same reasons that influenced the placement of Disneyland in Orange County. Removed from the developed areas of Los Angeles, yet attractive to growing numbers of homeowners and business leaders who sought a suburban refuge, Orange County struck Disney as the ideal location. The trend toward decentralization ultimately persuaded Disneyland's designers to choose Anaheim as the home of Disneyland, which, not unlike the Federal Housing Authority's directives for its mortgage guarantees, reflected "the desire to get away from the highly developed central areas." By building Disneyland in Anaheim, Disney tailored his theme park to the changing preferences for home and work in the suburban fringes of the metropolis. By the early 1950s, the outline of a decentralized, regional metropolis had materialized to the extent that SRI concluded in its report to Disney officials that "decentralization is virtually essential" to the future success of Disneyland.[36]

The Anaheim site afforded Disney the opportunity to reinvent the amusement park for a new generation of suburban Americans. Although the placement of Disneyland beyond the frontier of urban development in Southern California reflected the placement of Coney Island in relation to New York City a century earlier, Disney viewed the suburban location of Orange County as an ideal setting for an alternative to the Coney Island experience. Despite Coney Island's origins as a fashionable resort for New York City's leisured class, the exuberant culture of the city's working class ultimately overcame the amusement park, which marketed the spectacle of the modern city in its crowded, electrified venues. Disney designed Disneyland, as we shall see, not only as "a protector" from the chaos and contradictions of the noir city, but also as the very antithesis of the Coney Island experience.[37]

In addition to the location of Disneyland, the layout and design of the theme park also suited Disney's ambition to create an "atmosphere of cleanliness and order." Reacting against what Disney criticized as the "diffuse, unintegrated layout" of Coney Island, Disneyland's designers sought to maximize control over the movement of the crowd through the meticulous organization of space.[38] Whereas Coney Island and its generation of amusement parks had multiple entrances and exits, Disneyland offered only one path by which visitors could come and go. Upon entering the park, visitors began their day in Main Street, a central corridor that channeled pedestrians toward the central hub of the park, "from which the other 'lands' radiate out like spokes in a wheel"—Tomorrowland, Fantasyland, Frontierland, and Adventureland (see figure 8).[39] The spatial organization of Disneyland reflected the designers' intention to process the milling crowd with as little indecision as possible. "Each land is easy to enter and easy to exit," asserted one Disney official in a speech to the Urban Land Institute, a national organization of urban developers, "because everything leads back to the central hub again. The result is a revelation to anyone who has ever experienced the disorientation and confusion built into world's fairs and other expositions."[40]

Through such a meticulous organization of space, the designers of Disneyland kept at bay that monstrous entity that dominated the landscape of the turn-of-the-twentieth-century metropolis: the crowd. In its report on Disneyland's initial success, the *New York Times* noted that although Disneyland "was designed to accommodate 60,000 visitors a day comfortably," the crowd remained surprisingly absent from the park: "A typical Disneyland feature is [the] avoidance of unwieldy crowds, even when hundreds of people are waiting at an attraction. This is accomplished by fences and railings which double back and forth in maze patterns, preventing crowding and without policing."[41] Much to the chagrin of public health officials and social reformers, the crowd made its boisterous debut in the context of urban modernity toward the end of the nineteenth century, but a half-century later, Walt Disney and his corps of designers at Disneyland demonstrated how urban planners could effectively minimize its presence through a new spatial discipline that guided the shifting basis of public life in the postwar, postindustrial urban region.

The "rage for order" that Richard Schickel recognized in the park's landscape also extended to its visual presentation. "Disneyland was the first to use visually compatible elements working as a coordinated theme," boasted a corporate publicity brochure about the park's visual clarity. By organizing the park around a series of themes, park designers could avoid "the contradictory 'hodge-podge' of World's Fairs and amusement parks."[42] To eliminate any distractions from the contrived vistas within the park, Disney buried all water, power, and sewer lines beneath street level. To fully immerse visitors in each of the themes of Disneyland, each land appeared

FIGURE 8.   An aerial view of Disneyland shortly after its opening in 1955. (Courtesy of the *Los Angeles Examiner*/Hearst Newspaper Collection, Department of Special Collections, University of Southern California Library.)

completely self-contained and could not be seen from any other section of the park. Designers also relied on the technique of forced perspective, "a device well-known in motion picture circles," to trick the eye into seeing structures as taller than they really were. Thus, Sleeping Beauty's Castle in Fantasyland and the Matterhorn Bobsleds roller coaster, both proportionally larger at the bottom and smaller at the top, created the illusion of greater height. Similarly, the buildings of Main Street, USA, were scaled to about 90 percent of full size at the ground floor, 80 percent at the second floor, and 60 to 70 percent at the third floor. In sharp contrast to the dissonance that reverberated throughout the landscapes of American cities, the Disneyland environment rested upon the meticulous organization of space, guaranteeing the perfect view every time and ensuring that visitors would see exactly what park designers wanted them to see.[43]

Walt Disney's rage for order also included prescriptions for the hiring of employees. In his disgust for the "hostile employees" and "ballyhoo men" who presided over the Coney Island experience, Disney sought to employ people whom he recognized as "clean and natural without extremes" at Disneyland.[44] Park officials issued a set of guidelines to control the image of their employees, targeting the personal style of urban working-class youths: "no bright nail polish, no bouffants. No heavy perfume or jewelry, no unshined shoes, no low spirits. No corny raffishness ... that's a natural look that doesn't grow quite as naturally as everybody thinks." Disney's chief biographer described the general image of park employees as "blond, blue-eyed ... outdoorsy [and] vacuously pleasant," identified by their "rather standardized" appearance.[45] Disneyland officials expected nothing less. "We tell them right from the start," explained one park official, that "we require conformity."[46]

The carefully managed image of the park and its employees ensured total predictability in the Disneyland experience. Disney's perfection of Audio Animatronic technology, "a computerized system that programs sound and movements of inanimate figures," allowed for the mechanical simulation of humans and animals and eliminated the need for live actors or animals in the park's many attractions. Disney reasoned that Audio Animatronics "permitted guests to see a show performed the same way time and time again."[47] In the Great Moments with Mr. Lincoln exhibit, for example, an Audio Animatronic simulation of Abraham Lincoln offered what one critic labeled "a three-minute package" designed to arouse the sentimental patriotism of viewing audiences. Adventureland's Jungle Cruise, where visitors embarked on a ten-minute excursion into the simulated rivers of Africa, used an array of mechanized animals to ensure that "every boatload of people will see the same thing." In an advanced age of mechanical reproduction, the robotic simulation of exotic animals and past presidents not only destabilized people's perception of space and time, but also ensured an impresario's greatest ambition: the endless repetition of a perfect show.[48]

The predictability of the Disneyland experience played no small part in the tremendous popularity of the park. Disney realized the extent to which Americans craved predictability in their cultural experiences after World War II. The Depression had dramatized the severe unpredictability of the market economy, and the outbreak of World War II had generated an awareness of the precariousness of global order. Both traumas imparted a new quest for predictability, particularly for the great masses of Americans who approached, but had not yet reached, the security of the middle class. D.J. Waldie explains in his Lakewood memoir that "in a suburb that is not exactly middle class, the necessary illusion is predictability."[49] As a master of illusion, Walt Disney aimed to imbue Disneyland with the aura of predictability. In a world rife with uncertainty, suburban Americans sought predictability in the domestic economy, in world affairs, in the design of suburban communities, and, as Disney realized, in entertainment.

"A LIVING SET FOR TELEVISION"

The predictable illusions manufactured at Disneyland paralleled other cultural experiences of the postwar era. Both creators and consumers of Disneyland noted the parallels between a visit to Disneyland and watching a film. "An experienced movie maker himself," noted a tourist brochure about Disneyland, "one of Walt's major considerations in the design and construction of Disneyland was arrangement for visual—and camera—effect."[50] Disney's corps of animators, set designers, and special-effects artists became the chief designers of Disneyland, bringing their skills to work in a three-dimensional medium. As in conventional film or television production, park designers sought to build "an orderly sequence of messages" into the physical landscape of Disneyland. John Hench recalled how park designers likened the design of Disneyland to the production of film: "A film makes sense to the audience because the director takes them from scene one to scene two and so on. If the director were to leap from scene one to scene fifty-two, it would be like sending the audience out for dinner in the middle of a film." Movies and television not only offered Disney a stock of images to exploit in his park, but also provided a framework by which park designers could organize space. Filmmakers and animators, not architects and engineers, possessed the skills necessary to design Disneyland. "However," remarked Hench, "we need something to keep the weather out and to stand and not fall over, so we use engineers and architects."[51] Still, despite their distinctive skills, architects and filmmakers forged an unprecedented partnership in the creation of Disneyland, one that initiated a new spatial culture of celebrity that increasingly defined public life in the United States.

In whatever ways Disney designers incorporated Hollywood "magic" into their plans for Disneyland, the noir vision that had dominated American cinema only a few years prior to Disneyland's opening remained conspicuously absent from the theme park. Noir's dark allure stood in stark contrast to the pristine charm of Main Street, USA, and noir's convoluted narrative structure was countered by the "orderly sequence of messages" built into the overall design of the theme park. Disneyland's meticulous emphasis on spatial order had more affinities with the shopping mall, which also made its debut during the early 1950s, as both highlighted the new suburban society that modeled itself as the very antithesis of the noir city.

Throughout his career, Walt Disney never expressed any affinity for the noir sensibility that his filmmaking counterparts marketed during the mid-1940s. Instead, he embraced a more earnest stance that seemed well suited to the early years of television, another cultural institution that gained prominence in postwar suburban America. Television played a major role in the creation, promotion, and ultimate success of Disneyland, illustrating how the new medium facilitated the shifting cultural paradigms of postwar America. Unlike other Hollywood studio executives during the late 1940s, Walt Disney approached television with an open mind. "When the industry was cussing television and trying to ignore it," Walt Disney's brother and business partner, Roy Disney, remarked, "Walt moved in and worked with it and made it work for him."[52] Television provided Walt Disney with another venue in which to market his brand of popular culture. After successfully producing a Christmas special for television in 1950, Disney realized that his company's other productions could be easily programmed for television. In the early '50s, Disney himself hosted the weekly television series *The Mickey Mouse Club* and *The Adventures of Zorro*, which indicated the showman's future success in the transition to television entertainment. But it was the 1954 popularity of two television programs in particular, the *Disneyland* series and a three-part series about the frontiersman Davy Crockett, that enabled Walt Disney to finance the construction of Disneyland.[53]

In his earliest conceptualization of Disneyland, Walt Disney imagined television would play an important role in the success of his endeavor. Not only could the theme park provide a "living set for television," but television, in turn, also provided the means "to create a new motion picture audience and to encourage the fullest box-office patronage for our forthcoming pictures." Disney also realized the potential of television to advertise Disneyland to national audiences. "I saw that if I was ever going to have my park," Disney once remarked, "here, at last, was a way to tell millions of people about it—with TV."[54] While Disney was still considering Burbank as the site for the construction of his park, the *Burbank Review* anticipated that "Disneyland and its activities will be transmitted by television throughout the country," and imagined the park as "a complete television center with theater, stages, sets and technical equipment."[55] Even after Burbank officials rejected Walt Disney's plan for an amusement park, television still figured into the selection of Anaheim as the site for Disneyland. According to SRI, Anaheim provided a suitable location because, among several other factors, that site afforded a "direct line of sight" to "master transmitters" on Mount Wilson.[56]

Disney's foray into television not only coincided with his plans for Disneyland, but also supplied the capital necessary to build the park and offered a primary means of advertising the park to national audiences. Desperate for additional monies to finance rising construction costs, Disney turned to the American Broadcasting Corporation (ABC), becoming "the first leading Hollywood producer to enter into a formal alliance with television." ABC, then a fledgling network, provided Disney with a half-million dollars up front toward construction costs and agreed to guarantee loans of up to 4.5 million dollars. In return, Disney granted ABC a 35 percent interest in the theme park and agreed to produce a weekly series for the network. The series, *Disneyland*, began in 1954, featuring animated films, documentaries, and "constant bulletins" on the progress of Disneyland's construction.[57]

On July 17, 1955, ABC televised the opening festivities for Disneyland, marking what one contemporary observer considered "the most important development to date in relations between the old and new mass entertainment form." To cover the event for its prime-time broadcast, ABC amassed the "greatest concentration of TV equipment and cameras ever assembled at one place."[58] Art Linkletter, Bob Cummings, and "Ronnie" Reagan, accompanied by "a parade of stars of television and motion pictures," hosted the celebration for ABC. In this first made-for-TV event in the history of live television, a number of difficulties plagued the opening ceremonies. Audio and video portions of telecast went dead intermittently, and the anchors had trouble synchronizing their comments with the images on the screen. The absence of drinking fountains and the scarcity of restrooms aggravated a crowd of twenty-five thousand people already frustrated by long lines and mechanical breakdowns. Disney dismissed the malfunctions by reassuring viewers that "Disneyland will never be completed as long as there is imagination left in the world."[59]

The success of the Davy Crockett series in the mid-1950s cemented the bond between Disneyland and ABC. For the 1954–55 season, Disney produced a three-part series about the life of the frontiersman. In the typical Disney fashion, the writers of the series overlooked Crockett's ambiguous role as a historical figure and instead celebrated his role as "king of the wild frontier." The series offered Disney executives an extraordinary marketing opportunity, as it spawned "The Ballad of Davy Crockett," which went to number one on the hit parade and remained at the top of the charts for several weeks. Coonskin caps also became a national fad, manufactured and distributed by Disney merchandisers to coincide with the airing of the series. The Davy Crockett phenomenon demonstrated the myriad possibilities for profit from a single Disney production. As Disney's head of promotion, Vince Jeffers, boasted, "I could make a good case that the licensing of an article is more profitable than manufacturing it. I often made money out of movies that were a loss at the box office."[60]

The royalties from record sales and coonskin caps helped to finance the ongoing construction of Disneyland, stimulating interest in Frontierland, that section of the theme park celebrating "the faith, courage and ingenuity of the pioneers who blazed the trails across America, from the Revolutionary War to the final taming of the Great Southwest."[61] Fess Parker, the actor chosen to play Crockett for the series, starred as Davy Crockett at the opening celebration of Disneyland, greeting Frontierland visitors on horseback. Although Parker suffered a few indignities that day, including an accidental spraying by lawn sprinklers before television viewers, his presence at Frontierland seemed to confirm for Davy Crockett fans that Disneyland was indeed a "living set for television."[62]

Following the success of the Davy Crockett series, ABC's *Disneyland* aired *Underseas Adventure*, a promotional show about the making of the motion picture *20,000 Leagues under the Sea*, soon to be released by Disney studios. "Nobody complained that we were doing publicity movies," recalled Disney studio executive Bill Walsh.[63] In fact, *Underseas Adventure* won an Emmy award for Disney, and *20,000 Leagues under the Sea*, bolstered by the success of the promotional piece, went on to gross more than six million dollars in its first release, bringing in sponsorships from Coca-Cola and Johnson and Johnson. The success of the film also inspired the creation of Tomorrowland's Submarine Voyage attraction, which debuted in 1959 and reinforced the overlapping experiences between the theme park and television.[64]

For its part, ABC profited handsomely from the success of the park and the television show. The network garnered one-third of the revenues earned by Disneyland, until 1960, when Walt Disney Productions exercised its option to buy back ABC's one-third share of ownership of Disneyland for 7.5 million dollars, a sum fifteen times the size of the network's original investment. In addition, ABC's investment in Disneyland boosted its prominence as a national network for the first time, attracting a flood of national advertisers to its entire schedule.[65]

The partnership between Walt Disney Enterprises and ABC in the creation and success of Disneyland illustrates not only the corporate underpinnings of Disneyland's construction, but also the degree to which the cultural experiences of postindustrial urbanization overlapped. Not unlike television's influence on the national expansion of major-league baseball and Walter O'Malley's decision to move the Brooklyn Dodgers to Los Angeles, the success of Disneyland depended in multiple ways on the park's proximity to Los Angeles' burgeoning television industry. Television supplied the capital necessary to finance the completion of Disneyland and provided a means by which Disney could advertise his park to national viewers. More significant, however, the practice of watching television had significant parallels to the experience of a trip to Disneyland. Like television,

Disneyland was marketed as a form of "family entertainment," and its highly regimented landscape channeled visitors through a series of "lands," each offering a unique thematic program that paralleled the distinct channels of a television set. Moreover, just as television transformed the nature of private life by bringing the outside world into the home, Disneyland, hidden behind a twenty-five-foot earthen berm, codified the experience of interiority into a new form of public amusement. Both Disneyland and television sustained a blurring between interiority and exteriority in ways that reflected the broader cultural shift that descended upon postwar America. As an area of land maintained for public recreation, however, Disneyland remained, at its very essence, a park. But its affinity to the cultural experience of television illustrates a new kind of *privatized* public life that debuted in postwar Southern California, one that precluded the illicit social interactions that transpired in the noir city.

Moreover, ABC's role in the construction of Disneyland underscored the corporate sponsorship of popular amusement in postwar America. In the transition from the manufacturing economy of the nineteenth century to the consumer economy of the twentieth, Americans had attained a greater awareness of the corporations that produced the many goods they consumed in their daily lives. During the postwar era, when that transition resumed after the disruptions of the 1930s and '40s, Americans became even more familiar with the brand names of automobiles, televisions, appliances, and other commodities that sustained the suburban way of life. Since that transition, advertising had remained a constant fact of daily life. Although advertisements had insinuated themselves into the landscape of the modern city at the turn of the century, their presence was no less visible after the postwar retreat into the suburbs. Advertisers simply focused their efforts less on the public space of the city and more on the private space of the home. Postwar Americans thus enjoyed a more intimate familiarity with the corporations that fed their needs for food, clothing, shelter, and entertainment.

Walt Disney brought that intimacy to bear on the experience of Disneyland. The corporate order that overtook the United States in the latter half of the twentieth century became manifest at Disneyland, where every merchant and concessionaire inside the park represented "a wholly-owned subsidiary of a giant corporation."[66] Park management, eager to attract corporate support for Disneyland, reminded corporate executives that Disneyland's audience belonged primarily "in the middle and upper income brackets . . . the heart of the consumer market for major corporations." Corporate names saturated the landscape of Disneyland, from its rides and attractions (Atlantic Richfield's Autopia, Bank of America's It's a Small World, and General Electric's Carousel of Progress) to its many restaurants and concession stands (Casa de Fritos and Aunt Jemima's Kitchen). It is a key paradox of Disneyland that advertising, historically an urban form of communication, sustained Walt Disney's effort to create his vision of a world removed from the influence of cities.[67]

In a moment of heightened anxiety about the increasing power of corporations to condition human experience, Disneyland demonstrated how corporations could model the kind of social order enshrined within the park. The Monsanto Chemical Company, for example, supported Disney's emphasis on the nuclear family and the detached single-family home, sponsoring Tomorrowland's House of the Future. The exhibit, in which visitors could walk through an experimental home designed for "the typical family of four," was designed "to explore the utilization of the special properties of plastics to enhance economy, convenience, and beauty of homes of the future." Other corporations, in turn, took the opportunity to include their products in the plastic home. The Kelvinator Division of American Motors Corporation supplied the home's "food center" with microwave ovens and an "ultrasonic dishwasher." Bell Telephone furnished the House of the Future with telephones that included "preset and push button 'dialing,' hands-free speakers and transmitters [and a] front door viewing screen." And the Armstrong Cork Company, in collaboration with the Crane Company, designed a climate control system that "filters, cools, heats and scents the air in each room." In sponsoring the park's many attractions and exhibits, the nation's most prominent corporations attached a dollar value to their willingness to support the Disneyland premise that corporations could make the world not only more exciting, uplifting, and convenient, but also better-tasting and sweeter-smelling.[68]

The corporate presence at Disneyland suggested that private, not public, authorities possessed the means to effect the kind of social order that Disneyland represented. The affinity between Walt Disney and his Progressive predecessors thus extends only so far. Where turn-of-the-century reformers had called on government policy to safeguard their vision of social order from the excesses of urban commercial culture, Disney, a man suspicious of government bureaucracy, presumed that that social order could be marketed, not legislated. Corporations could provide the "expert supervision" that urban reformers demanded. As a cultural institution of the postindustrial urban region, where shopping malls and corporate plazas increasingly structured civic interaction, Disneyland epitomized the privatization of public life after World War II.

A WHITE WORLD AFTER ALL

The social order that Disney and his corporate sponsors envisioned at Disneyland materialized in the distinct lands of the park. That vision extended to the representation of social groups whose shifting position in postwar American society aroused the aspirations and anxieties of diverse Americans. World War II had exerted a significant force on racialized and gendered groups, propelling blacks and women into public life in unprecedented ways. Their integration into the daily routines of urban life generated an acute awareness of their changing position in society. While that awareness generated a good deal of optimism about the possibility of social change, it also sparked reactionary countermeasures to reassert sexual subordination and racial segregation in the years following World War II. Disneyland's thematic emphasis on racial hierarchy, as well as the nuclear family and suburban domesticity, illustrated Disney's identification with the impulse to restore social order during the postwar era through the resubordination of women and the resegregation of blacks.

Race figured prominently among the many themes of Disneyland. The multiple images of Indians and blacks inside the park reflected Disney's long-standing fascination with racial caricatures and ethnic stereotypes. The animal characters of many of Disney's full-length animated films were often endowed with racial or ethnic characteristics. Si and Am, the mischievous Siamese cats of *Lady and the Tramp* (1955), and Kaa, the villainous serpent of *The Jungle Book* (1967), connoted the vague Orientalism that permeated Disney films. In *Dumbo* (1941), the crows that teach Dumbo how to fly "are too obviously Negro caricatures." And Disney refined his caricature of Latinos in *The Three Caballeros* (1945), inspired by his Goodwill Tour of South America. These animated characters illustrated a latent tendency in Disney's oeuvre to invest certain characters with qualities constitutive of racial and ethnic stereotypes in American culture, leaving the audience to presume that other characters, lacking such qualities, are without race or quite simply, white.[69]

A similar tendency was at work in Disneyland. Frontierland, "a land of hostile Indians and straight shooting pioneers," featured Indians as its main attraction.[70] The *Disneyland News*, a promotional monthly that chronicled the park's development, promised prospective visitors that "you can actually meet full-blooded American Indians and hear stories of the Old West." Like the Igorot Village of the St. Louis World's Fair in 1904, or the Dahomey Village of the Columbian Exposition in Chicago in 1893, where earlier generations of Americans marveled at the exotic spectacle of what was touted as "savagery," Frontierland's Indian Village displayed popular conceptions of indigenous ways of life for tourist consumption. Frontierland's designers promised nothing but authenticity. "Taken as though bodily from a camp on the American Plains of more than 100 years ago," reported the *Disneyland News*, "inverted cones hide covered marvels of primitive engineering." Disneyland also claimed to represent the diversity of Native America. "Disneyland's Indian population numbers twenty full-blooded braves, representing sixteen tribes," including the "Apachee, Winnebago, Shawnee, Hopi, Navajo, Maricopa, Choctaw, Comanche, Pima, Crow and Pawnee."[71]

Despite the few references to "hostile Indians" in the promotional literature for Frontierland, Disneyland generally depicted Indians as friendly, extolling their cooperative and affable nature. The *Disneyland News* even emphasized the degree to which park visitors could interact with the park's resident Indians: "Parents crowd with youngsters and cameras to take pictures of the Chief or one of the other brilliant costumed Indians with their children. Although some hesitate before the strangely dressed red men, they soon lose any shyness before the Indian's winning charm." The long-standing fascination with the noble savage in the West also made its way into the park. In addition to its emphasis on friendly Indians, Frontierland insisted on the contentedness of the American Indian, who "as a child of nature . . . lives from nature and is a happy man."[72] The *New York Times* went so far as to interpret the popularity of the Disneyland Indian as a craving on the part of visitors to actually be Indian: "One of the most amusing and revealing sights at Disneyland is a score of people straining over paddles in a big Indian war canoe, while a real life brave solemnly steers in the stern—a privilege for which the hard working paddlers have paid 50 cents apiece. But for ten minutes they are Indian warriors."[73]

"Playing Indian," as Philip Deloria reminds us, was a vital part of 1950s popular culture. While Frontierland's Indians, particularly in their contrast to the futuristic wonders of Tomorrowland, clearly upheld long-standing distinctions between white progress and nonwhite "savagery," their centrality in the Disneyland experience begs for additional consideration. While low-budget films such as *The Exiles* dramatized the predicament of "real" Indians mired in the dregs of the noir city thanks to federal relocation programs, Disneyland took great strides to showcase an authentic portrait of Indians in their native habitat for the amusement, amazement, and perhaps even adoration of its white suburban audience. If this audience worried about detachment, anomie, alienation, and other buzzwords that circulated within the cultural currents of Cold War America, the presence of Indians in their native habitat—at Disneyland, in Hollywood Westerns, at craft fairs,

FIGURE 9.   American Indian performer at Disneyland,
1955. (Courtesy of the Los Angeles Public Library.)

or in reenactments of powwows—recalled an authentic and vital mode of
being in the world that seemed lost among a generation of consumers whose
freedom of self-expression was increasingly confined to the name brands
that dominated postwar American society.

And yet, while Frontierland offered its foray into racial otherness, it also
reinforced the burgeoning distinction between white and nonwhite that
defined the social landscape of the postwar urban region. Frontierland struck
Disney as the most appropriate place to insert his conception of African
Americans and their place in U.S. history. Along the banks of the Rivers of
America, one could find Aunt Jemima's Kitchen. Sixty-two years after Aunt
Jemima had made her debut as a cultural icon at Chicago's Columbian
Exposition in 1893, Disney created a permanent home for her at Disney-
land. "Relive the days of the Old South," promised an advertisement for the
Aunt Jemima Company to its presumably white audience. Disney designed
the restaurant as a recreation of a southern plantation kitchen, where an

African American woman, dressed as "Aunt Jemima did . . . on the plantation," "was on hand every day to welcome visitors warmly." At the Pancake House, Aunt Jemima "will serve her famed pancakes everyday and also will sing to entertain visitors." The actress playing Aunt Jemima remained one of the few black employees of Disneyland through the 1960s. Finally, in 1968, after substantial pressure from the civil rights group the Congress on Racial Equality, park officials introduced Disneyland's first black "people contact" employee. Until then, Aunt Jemima had been one of the few black faces representing Disneyland to the public, presiding over the recreation of the Old South at Disneyland.[74]

Park designers situated their stereotypes of black Americans alongside a recreation of Europe's first encounters with Africa, connoting larger Western conceptions of non-Western peoples. Adventureland beckoned visitors with "the sound of native chants and tom-toms," enticing them to explore the mysteries of "distant and unknown" lands. The centerpiece of Adventureland was the Jungle Cruise, a boat excursion "along the shorelines of the Congo, Amazon, Nile and other jungle rivers."[75] "It's in the water itself where Adventureland's mysteries lie," promised one press release from Disneyland's public relations division. "Wild animals and native 'savages' attack your craft as it cruises through their jungle privacy."[76]

Of course, Walt Disney cannot take credit for inventing these racial stereotypes. Rather, park designers drew on a tradition of racial stereotyping in the national culture. Generations of Americans could view images of racial otherness at world's fairs and expositions of various sorts. The Plantation Village of the 1897 Tennessee Centennial Exposition in Nashville recreated the life of a southern plantation. Enthralled with that exhibit, the designers of the Omaha World's Fair of 1898 created their own version of the Plantation Village. In the Midway of Chicago's 1893 Columbian Exposition, the Dahomey Village stood apart, geographically and conceptually, from every other national and ethnic village on the fairgrounds. Although a few outspoken Americans such as Frederick Douglass and Ida B. Wells expressed their disgust at the marketing of such gross misrepresentations as authenticity, white Americans of various generations could use such images to reify their own sense of whiteness.[77]

The racial dimensions of the Disneyland experience surfaced not only in those places of the park where images of blacks and Indians prevailed, but also where such images did not appear. Main Street, USA, touted as "everybody's hometown" and "the heartline of America," reflected Walt Disney's populist idealization of a WASP folk.[78] In *The Age of Reform*, Richard Hofstadter detected a latent xenophobia in the populist sensibility, which, while seeking to maintain "the primary contacts of country and village life," also cherished a vision of "an ethnically more homogenous nation."[79] That vision guided the creation of Main Street, USA, where the absence of mammies, Indians, "savages," and the "black tap-dancing shoeshine boys" reified Disney's racialized and deeply nostalgic vision of American "folks." The exclusion of African Americans and their history from the representational syntax of Main Street, USA, was most glaring in the Great Moments with Mr. Lincoln exhibit, which debuted at Disneyland in 1965. The Audio Animatronic Lincoln recited a speech designed to elicit the patriotic sentiments of Disneyland audiences, making no mention of slavery or the Civil War. Disney's well-known antipathy to blacks and Jews, moreover, underscored his tribute to small-town whiteness at Main Street, USA.[80]

The thematic emphasis on race at Disneyland demonstrates not only a line of continuity between Disneyland and its cultural antecedents of the industrial metropolis, but also an ongoing preoccupation with racial distinctions across time. However, stereotypes of blacks, Indians, and other nonwhite racial groups held different meanings for different generations of ethnic and WASP Americans, who negotiated their white identity in different historical and spatial contexts. For Americans at the turn of the twentieth century, stereotypical depictions of these groups in the popular culture reinforced an emergent racialized nationalism that underlay the reconciliation between the North and the South in the aftermath of the Civil War, and largely inspired the U.S. involvement in the Spanish-American War and its imperialistic thrust into the Philippines.[81]

In postwar America, the contours of race relations had changed significantly. After World War II, which brought unprecedented levels of racial cohabitation in American cities, a new generation of white Americans sought various measures to maintain separate and not necessarily equal communities within the nation's sprawling cities. In the aftermath of the Supreme Court's ruling against racially restrictive covenants in *Shelley v. Kraemer*, and amid an explosion of civil rights activism, cultural stereotypes of nonwhite racial groups affirmed the racial distinctions that defined American social relations prior to the dawning of the civil rights era. In celebrating the opening of the Great Moments with Mr. Lincoln exhibit, Disney officials emphasized the need to return to traditional patterns of race relations: "Here a century has been erased. No better advice can be given to America of the 1960s."[82]

Thus, while civil rights activists touted their victories against racial segregation as social progress, Disneyland asserted a very different notion of progress, one predicated on an embrace of consumer abundance and technological advancement and a simultaneous rejection of more equitable relations between white and nonwhite. Removed from the "darker" shades of the inner city, yet permeated with representations of racial otherness, Disneyland provided a space where white Southern Californians could affirm their whiteness against a set of racial stereotypes. Such stereotypes recalled earlier discourses about race and race relations yet suited the new spatial and racial paradigm that overtook American cities during the postwar period. In Southern California after World War II, where chocolate cities and vanilla suburbs became a tangible reality, Disneyland cradled a racialized conservatism that informed the nascent political struggles of the New Right.

In a world where blacks were escalating their demands for civil rights and becoming more integrated into public life, Walt Disney took measures to safeguard his theme park from the fate that had befallen Coney Island and its generation of amusement parks. Placing his theme park in a suburban location, removed from the inner-city concentration of racialized poverty, Disney used racial representations to underscore the sense of whiteness that took shape along the suburban periphery of the metropolis. Thus, the same processes that exacerbated Coney Island's plight bolstered Disneyland's popularity. While Coney Island had fallen victim to the settlement of blacks in and the departure of whites from Brooklyn after World War II, Disneyland thrived in a setting removed from urban concentrations of racialized poverty and one increasingly identified with a white suburban identity.

If the presence of Aunt Jemima at Disneyland signaled the subordinate position of blacks in Walt Disney's vision of social order, it also symbolized the subservient position of women in that order. Disneyland's delineation of a social order appropriate to the tastes and values of an embourgeoised working class also included an emphasis on patriarchal social relations and the centrality of the nuclear family. Suburbanization provided a spatial context in which postwar Americans could confront their anxieties about the changing position of women in American society, seeking comfort in cultural representations of domesticated housewives and stable nuclear families. Disney's effort to position the "typical family of four" at the center of the Disneyland experience signaled yet another departure from amusement parks of Coney Island's generation. The *New York Times,* for example, described Disneyland "not as a place where anyone would casually go to take a roller coaster ride or buy a hot dog, but as the goal of a family adventure."[83]

Kathy Peiss has argued that Coney Island and other forms of urban commercial amusement offered single women a momentary escape from the surveillance of family members and employers and the opportunity to revel in the anonymous, heterosocial spaces of the modern industrial city.[84] Disneyland, by contrast, posited a privatized vision of public life that under-girded the patriarchal culture of the decentralized urban region, one that centered on the nuclear family and suburban home ownership. After the cri-sis of World War II and amid the threat of an expanding Soviet empire, Americans became "homeward bound," setting their sights on the family and its domain. The ideology of "containment," which sought to contain the spread of "subversive influences," not only informed American policy in the public arena of foreign relations, but also structured domestic relations in the private realm of home and family. According to the domestic version of containment, women, and the subversive influences they exerted on men, could be contained within the confines of the suburban home.[85] Betty Friedan condemned the postwar "incarceration" of women in *The Feminine Mystique*, a book that sparked an upsurge of middle-class feminist opposi-tion to suburban patriarchy in postwar America.

Disneyland reflected and reinforced the primacy of the suburban nuclear family and the centrality of the single-family home in postwar American culture. To return to an example discussed earlier, the centerpiece of Tomorrowland's "show world of the future," the Monsanto House of the Future, invited park visitors to preview "how the typical American family of four will live ten years from now." Promotional materials for the House of the Future reiterated popular conceptions of suburban domesticity that highlighted postwar American culture. When the house opened on June 12, 1957, models Helen Bernhart and John Marion acted the part of the model couple at home in their "showcase of modern living." Photographs depict the husband relaxing in the "psychiatric chair," which afforded "therapeu-tic relief after a hard day at the office," and the wife standing in the Atoms for Living Kitchen. In accordance with the dominant vision of family living during the postwar era, the House of the Future's interior "was divided into areas that reflected a modern approach to living." The home's cruciform floor plan ensured "added privacy for various family activities," separating the children's room from the master bedroom. A "step saver" kitchen opened onto the family/dining room, an arrangement "convenient and per-fect for party entertainment." This organization of interior space conformed to the regnant models of family life that guided the construction of subur-ban tract houses and infused the cultural landscape of Cold War America.[86] The House of the Future proved an immediate success. In its first year of operation, "an unending line of visitors from morning until long after dark had run up an attendance total of 1,405,248 viewers."[87]

The House of the Future denoted the concept of family entertainment that defined the image of Disneyland. Since Disney's initial description of Disneyland as a "kind of family park where parents and children could have fun together," park officials have invoked the family on more than one occasion to regulate behavior in and around Disneyland.[88] When Disneyland's neighbor, the Melodyland Theater, wanted to host the Las Vegas Topless Revue, park officials appealed successfully to the Anaheim city council, arguing that such a revue would spoil the "family entertainment" image created by the park. Similarly, in 1980, Disney security guards evicted two homosexual men from the park for violating the park's long-standing ban on members of the same sex dancing together. One guard justified his action based on the official conviction that "this is a family park. There's no room for alternative lifestyles here."[89] In contrast to the incubation of "alternative lifestyles" in spaces such as Coney Island at the turn of the twentieth century, such lifestyles clashed with the brand of family entertainment that defined the Disneyland experience.

Disneyland's emphasis on family entertainment reflected more general spatial transformations. Urban working-class families at the turn of the twentieth century, lacking the privacy of a townhouse or unable to occupy an apartment without the financial assistance of boarders, had relied on the public spaces of the city for sociability and entertainment. Private life and the emphasis on home and family thus had become hallmarks of urban middle-class identity, embraced by those whose social life tended to revolve around the home, restaurants, or private clubs. By the postwar era, however, as greater numbers of Americans acquired the means to own their own homes, the cultural focus of the United States gradually shifted away from the public venues of the city toward the private spaces of the home. That shift entailed profound consequences for the design and experience of popular culture after World War II. The cultural emphasis on family entertainment not only asserted an adherence to traditional models of gender relations, but also reflected a more general valorization of home and family among growing numbers of Americans who entered (or at least aspired to) the ranks of the middle class after World War II.

Other cultural entrepreneurs of the postwar period marketed their products as family entertainment. Corporations, eager to target both the family and its constituent parts, hired advertisers who could situate their products alongside compelling images of the nuclear family. Television manufacturers labored to install their product within the physical and cultural spaces of family life after World War II. Even the managers of historically working-class forms of entertainment endeavored to bring a modicum of respectability to their venues by appealing to families. Walter O'Malley built Dodger

Stadium on the premise that major-league baseball could shed its masculine, working-class image and appeal to a broader, family-oriented audience. The sum of these cultural efforts repositioned the white, middle-class nuclear family at the center of a new public life that took shape in the transition from the industrial, centralized city to the postindustrial urban region.[90]

One Disneyland exhibit in particular demonstrated how multinational corporations could reinstate traditional family values in the emerging patterns of postindustrial urbanization. General Electric sponsored Progress City, an exhibit that debuted in the Tomorrowland section of the theme park in 1967. Progress City showcased a futuristic city where "the latest in all electric ideas help cities look better, and make them better places to live and work in." Progress City invited audiences to marvel at the spectacle of "tomorrow's city," which marked a distinct contrast to the noir vision of urban life that circulated in postwar American popular culture. In contrast to the seedy disorder of the noir city, Progress City featured a "whole downtown completely enclosed," which afforded a "climate controlled environment offering dry and comfortable weather all year round." To narrate the spectacle of Progress City, the disembodied voices of the "typical American family of tomorrow" expressed their enthusiasm for the city of the future and its corporate sponsors. A mother's voice, for example, declares, "I just love getting around in my private transporter" and, unfettered by the inconveniences and dangers of public transportation, "it's not a chore to go downtown anymore!" The father, similarly, describes the reinvention of factory work in Progress City, upholding the traditional association of fathers with the public world of work. Unlike the dismal squalor of the urban factory that had so offended urban Progressives at the turn of the century, "companies have turned to attractive landscaping to make industrial areas more like city parks." And in response to the growing fear of public space that guided the postwar retreat to the suburban home and informed the brand of law and order politics that took shape in places such as Orange County, "brighter street lights have brought new safety to our suburbs." In short, with its emphasis on the corporate sanitization, or what we might call the Disneyfication, of the noir city, Progress City showcased how the spatial culture of suburbia could reinvent the nature of urban life in postwar America, offering a "safer" alternative to the noir city.[91]

Some early visitors to the theme park recalled their relief at finding a safe environment at Disneyland. Pamela Lawton, for example, grew up in South Gate during the 1950s. Historically a blue-collar suburb of Los Angeles that sheltered a community of Dust Bowl refugees during the 1930s, South Gate and its residents enjoyed a modicum of the prosperity that dawned upon suburban Southern California in the wake of World War II. Despite South Gate's newfound affluence, however, a number of concerns troubled local residents in their transition to the middle class. The proliferation of apartment complexes and dump sites, the increase in juvenile crime, and, most of all, the outburst of the civil rights movement and the expansion of black neighborhoods in South Central Los Angeles threatened the realization of the postwar suburban dream in South Gate. For Pamela Lawton, who recalled "a lot of rough kids" in her junior high school, juvenile delinquency remained a real threat in her universe. A shy girl, Pamela stayed mostly at home, where she listened to Elvis Presley and Johnny Otis on the radio. Occasionally, Pamela "saw things outside of South Gate" when she accompanied a neighboring family on visits to museums, the La Brea Tar Pits, or an Elvis concert at the Pan Pacific Auditorium, and she made a trip to Disneyland the week it opened in June 1955.[92]

Disneyland particularly enthralled Pamela, where she found "things . . . from your grandmother's day on Main Street . . . things about history," and "things that I'd only known about in books." At fourteen, Pamela moved to Orange County with her family, where she visited Disneyland more frequently. She found the theme park to be "immaculate and shiny and big," and she took an immediate liking to Disneyland's employees, who reminded Pamela of "the counselors at camp, who were so open, gregarious people." At a time when the price of admission to Disneyland was $1.25, Pamela went as often as she could. Her father would drop her off at the gates and she would roam the park alone. "I'd look at everything, look in all the windows, walk around looking in the stores . . . sometimes I would just sit there and watch people. I just loved being out in the world like that, and it was a safe environment."[93]

For some, Disneyland offered a way of "being out in the world" without the risks that typified urban life. For others, however, the park seemed to provide an entry into the "respectable" world of middle-class society. For example, Teresa Hernandez, my Mexican American mother, as a teenager made regular trips to the theme park with her family during the late 1950s and early 1960s. Teresa's mother, Mary Gonzales Hernandez, whom we have already met earlier in this chapter, had worked in the Firestone tire factory in the 1940s and occasionally visited the Pike amusement park in Long Beach. She met her husband, Gene, shortly before he enlisted in military service during the Second World War. As the children of Mexican immigrants growing up in Southern California during the 1920s and 1930s, Teresa's parents had experienced episodes of racial discrimination and, having four children between 1945 and 1959, resolved to oversee their children's entry into the middle class in spite of, or perhaps because of, such experiences. With loan assistance from the GI Bill of Rights, Gene and Mary purchased a modest home in a predominantly Mexican American working-class neighborhood of Redlands, some ninety miles east of Los Angeles. Although Gene and Mary occasionally spoke Spanish to each other, they encouraged their children to speak English in the home and stressed the value of education as a means of advancement, particularly for their son (my uncle). Buying their first television in 1954, the Hernandez family first learned of Disneyland by watching TV.

A trip to Disneyland became an annual ritual for Teresa Hernandez and her family. With new freeways completed by the early 1960s, the theme park was a mere hour's drive for Teresa's family. Despite Disneyland's emphasis on the nuclear family, Teresa's visits included not only parents and siblings, but also more distant relatives—aunts, uncles, and cousins—who would catch up during a day's visit to Disneyland. Close enough to visit occasionally, yet far enough to make each visit special, Disneyland earned its place in the childhood memories of a second-generation Mexican American family.

These are but two examples of how Southern Californians experienced Disneyland in the early years of its existence and they are, in and of themselves, insufficient to explain why the postwar public embraced Disneyland with such enthusiasm. They can, however, provide specific examples of the park's appeal. For Pamela Lawton, it seems, Disneyland offered a kind of safe haven—"a refuge like no other," as the *Los Angeles Times* described the theme park in 1970. For a resident of a white suburban neighborhood threatened by juvenile delinquency and racial succession, Disneyland offered a reassuring vision of domestic harmony and ethnic homogeneity and modeled the social order white suburban Americans sought to recreate within their own communities. And in its historical emphasis on the virtues of frontier democracy and small-town life, Disneyland's version of the American Way brought some relief to a public uneasy about the precarious balance of global power. For Pamela Lawton, Disneyland offered a new kind of public life, a way of "being out in the world" without risking the dangers that lurked beyond the fortified boundaries of the park.

Yet, like Dodger Stadium, as we shall discover in the following chapter, Disneyland's appeal also extended to members of minority groups, at least those who managed to enjoy a modicum of the new affluence bestowed upon Southern California's expanding middle class. The encounter between the Hernandez family and Disneyland illustrates some of the more complex negotiations between upwardly mobile minority families and the culture of suburban whiteness that overcame postwar America. Although Walt Disney himself originally envisioned an International Street at Disneyland, "where every American can find the home of his forebears . . . Italy or Ireland . . . France or England," and despite the park's emphasis on the otherness of Indians, blacks, and Mexicans, the Hernandez family managed to find aspects of the park that resonated with their middle-class aspirations. For a family unable to afford trips abroad yet craving the vacation experience requisite to middle-class identity, Disneyland's location in Orange County was but an hour's drive away on Southern California's new freeways, and its relatively inexpensive price of admission afforded a substitute for more elaborate vacation plans. And, typical of millions of Americans consumers who read, watched, and listened to advertisements and purchased the myriad commodities that promised at least a slice of the suburban good life, the Hernandez family recognized the familiar brand names that inundated the park landscape. For working-class families of color who labored to reap the fruits of the American Way, an annual trip to Disneyland may have signaled a rite of passage into the materially abundant universe of the middle class, and this suggests how the institutions of postwar popular culture encompassed the aspirations of racial and ethnic minority families, even as they upheld a dominant vision of suburban whiteness.[94] For Teresa Hernandez, Disneyland may well have been a means to "kill the slum tradition" that had defined the experience of her parents' generation.

By eradicating the "slum tradition" that endured in places such as Coney Island and its ilk, Disneyland allowed subsequent generations of immigrants to the United States to kill their own slum traditions and to revel in a respectable setting tailored to the suburban tastes of a sprawling public. The theme park's vision of suburban respectability conformed to earlier visions of "the better city," which upheld Southern California and its decentralized landscape as a moral alternative to the degraded culture of the modern city. Much like the Progressives' vision of suburban modernity, Disneyland reconciled modern progress with traditional social values and reflected a more selective embrace of modernity, one that rejected the more troubling aspects of the modern city: Its heterogeneity undermined the imposition of a singular culture; its impersonality precluded meaningful social relationships; and its relativism eroded established canons and social norms. By contrast, Disneyland insinuated nostalgic yearnings for a less complicated and more intimate time, upholding the small town and the nuclear family as cultural ideals. Yet by staging the wonders of technological innovation and the fruits of consumer abundance, the park simultaneously showcased a thoroughly modern lifestyle that held out the promise of the good life to all.

This fusion of modernity and tradition stood at the very center of a burgeoning political culture that took shape in the immediate surroundings of Walt Disney's new theme park. In the Orange County of the 1950s, a new generation of suburban homeowners began to plot its assault on the tenets of New Deal liberalism and found in Disneyland the themes and symbols that inspired their social vision. Davy Crockett and his Frontierland setting upheld the spirit of individualism that informed a growing assault on the "nightmarish collectivism" of the New Deal order, and the ubiquitous emphasis on family entertainment at Disneyland corresponded to a regional insistence on the nuclear family unit as the locus of moral authority. The park's jingoistic overtones saluted the region's expanding military-industrial complex and confirmed Cold War suspicion of Communists, and its emphasis on the subservient position of blacks, Indians, and Mexicans corroborated a growing backlash against racial minorities in their struggle for civil rights. In its physical design and its thematic imagery, Disneyland supplied the "political unconscious" of a grassroots social movement that took shape in Orange County and ultimately led to a decisive shift away from the hegemony of New Deal politics. In its specific form of economic growth, as well as in its racially exclusive patterns of suburban development, Orange County sheltered the critical nexus between the politics and culture of the New Right.

Suburbanization and freeway construction encouraged Walt Disney to build his theme park in Orange County. These processes, however, produced an unwieldy and highly unfamiliar spatial configuration that necessitated the imposition of new cultural models of order such as that proffered by Disneyland. If suburbanization destabilized the public's familiarity with their physical environment, so too did urban renewal, which marked another salient feature of postwar urbanization, destroying intimate and familiar urban spaces in the name of redevelopment. In this context, Dodger Stadium, hailed as "the most modern baseball temple in the world," opened on a site adjacent to downtown Los Angeles in 1962. Much like the transition from Coney Island to Disneyland, the westward migration of the Brooklyn Dodgers from Ebbets Field to Dodger Stadium reflected the shifting concentration of cultural capital after World War II and signaled the rejection of traditional patterns of city life that men such as Walt Disney personified. Although the stadium's location in the heart of downtown Los Angeles was diametrically opposed to the suburban setting of Disneyland, it demonstrated how the new spatial culture of suburban Southern California could rid the afflicted American city, or at least Los Angeles, of its noir connotations.

5 Suburbanizing the City Center

The Dodgers Move West

> If you were to lift the Dodger Stadium and its sprawling parking
> lots . . . replacing them with the hills, gullies, flatlands and homes
> that were there up to the 1950s . . . you would find la gente de los
> tres barrios traveling through their daily lives.
>
> MANZANAR GAMBOA, *Memories around a Bulldozed Barrio*

> Metropolitan Los Angeles, with its teeming millions, many of whom
> were raised on a diet of major league baseball before they came west,
> is considered the prize plum among cities not now having a major
> franchise.
>
> *Los Angeles Times*, 22 February 1957

From the newfangled spaces of suburban Orange County, our attention now
shifts to Southern California's urban core, which accommodated a cultural
transition similar to that effected by Walt Disney's reinvention of the
amusement park. The arrival of the Brooklyn Dodgers in Los Angeles in
1957 marked the incorporation of Los Angeles into the big league of American cities, and while that move signaled the public's expanding and enduring fascination with the national pastime, it also illuminated the shifting
paradigms of popular culture in the age of white flight. For it was not simply the negotiating skills of urban boosters or the profit-minded calculus of
one individual that prompted the move of the most famous ball club in
American history to the West Coast. Rather, the Dodgers' move to Los
Angeles was enmeshed within a larger set of social, economic, and technological changes that effected a transformation of the midcentury American
city and its culture. While the demolition of Ebbets Field in 1960 signaled
the end of a chapter in American cultural history, the opening of Dodger
Stadium in the heart of Southern California's sprawling urban region
marked the beginning of a new one.[1]

This chapter considers urban renewal as another episode in the history of
the postwar American city, in which the destruction of familiar urban spaces
begot a new cultural order, one that delivered an illusion of community
similar to that effected by the creation of Disneyland. If Disneyland and
Hollywood sanctioned a symbolic killing of the "slum tradition" that

defined the immigrant experience, Dodger Stadium evidenced a more literal enactment of that process. Although the Dodgers brought to Los Angeles the first racially integrated ball club in the history of the major leagues, the construction of Dodger Stadium signaled the destruction of a working-class Chicano community that became implicated within a noir vision of Los Angeles at midcentury. After a failed bid to resituate that community within an ambitious proposal for public housing, the Chavez Ravine ultimately fell into the hands of Walter O'Malley, who built Dodger Stadium at the very heart of Southern California's "black" city.

Although Dodger Stadium arrived as part of Southern California's "new downtown," it shared the spatial culture that defined the suburban periphery of the metropolis in places like Disneyland. In contrast to the old Ebbets Field, where the Brooklyn Dodgers had resided since 1913 and which epitomized the heterogeneous and rambunctious public life of the streetcar metropolis, the new Dodger Stadium ensconced baseball fans within a corporate arena tailored to the privatized, sanitized, and disciplined nature of public life after World War II. As Dodger Stadium facilitated the suburbanization of the city center, moreover, it promoted the racialization of the regional political culture, as the defeat of public housing and election of a prodevelopment mayoral administration commissioned the imposition of Dodger Stadium upon the remnants of a working-class Chicano community. These manipulations, though obscured by a fantasy of athletic competition and a spectacle of interracial cooperation, incited an outpouring of racial strife that disturbed Southern California during the 1960s. But three years prior to the eruption of the nation's worst race riot in Watts in 1965, Dodger Stadium, heralded as "the most modern baseball temple in the world," debuted as yet another landmark of popular culture in the age of white flight.

BUMS AND SLUMS

To fully grasp the scope of the transformation of major-league baseball after World War II, it is necessary to understand the experience of watching Dodgers games in Brooklyn. For some thirty years after its opening in 1913, Ebbets Field remained a vital institution within the Brooklyn community. At a time when cities such as New York were multiteam cities, cross-town rivalries between Dodgers, Yankees, and Giants fans reinforced the sense of a communal identity within the city's different boroughs. Before the national expansion of the major leagues after World War II, the Dodgers represented Brooklyn and offered a means by which baseball fans could identify themselves and their community to New Yorkers and Americans at large.

The patterns of urban life within industrial cities such as New York reinforced that relationship. In Brooklyn, the popularity of the Dodgers depended upon the close proximity of its fans. Although many Dodgers fans could walk to Ebbets Field, nine trolley lines served the ballpark, ensuring a steady supply of fans. The absence of the automobile on the streets of Brooklyn, moreover, bolstered the local popularity of baseball among younger Dodgers fans, who used the streets of their neighborhoods for occasional games of stickball. Even the name of the team suggested the absolute centrality of the streetcar to Dodgers players and fans, who allegedly had to dodge trolley cars on their way to Ebbets Field.[2]

The close proximity between fans and players bred a kind of familiarity unknown to the modern baseball aficionado. Unlike the massive Yankee Stadium, Ebbets Field seated only thirty-two thousand and was considered a "tiny comfortable park" by Brooklyn fans. It was not uncommon for fans to see each other regularly inside the park. One former Brooklyn Dodgers fan recalled, "You would go to the bleachers and sit in the same place every day and see and listen to the same people every day, and what you'd do literally would be to pick apart every Dodger that was down on the field."[3]

Although radio broadcasts had become a regular feature of Dodgers games by the 1920s, the technologies of twentieth-century mass culture had not yet fully impinged on the relationship between Dodgers and their fans. Before television, players remained local heroes whose fame did not extend far beyond the boundaries of their neighborhood. Of course, radio publicized the successes and failures of various teams and propelled a few outstanding players into national stardom, but it did not sever the intimacy between players and fans in the way that television would a few decades later. Knowing the players' faces, the shapes of their bodies, their physical prowess, as well as their idiosyncratic apparel, was the privilege of those who regularly attended Dodgers games and forbidden to radio listeners.

Although baseball fans came to the ballpark as spectators, they were able, to a certain extent, to participate in the spectacle about them. Some fans became as renowned as the players they came to watch. Even though other Dodgers fans may not have personally known these distinctive individuals, "they could count on them being there and adding to the noise and craziness." A few individual fans rose to celebrity status. After regularly attending Dodgers games at Ebbets Field for twenty years, Hilda Chester became a professional rooter of the team by the late '30s. Chester led the Dodgers

"Sym-phoney" Band and became an unofficial mascot of the Dodgers, exemplifying the integral role of the fans at Ebbets Field.[4]

Dodgers games reflected the vibrant and rambunctious nature of life in the industrial metropolis. Dodgers fans were not known for their gentility, and baseball at Ebbets Field historically included a note of violence. The umpire had not yet attained the kind of authority that went unquestioned after World War II. The "Sym-phoney" often played its version of "Three Blind Mice" when the umpires walked onto the field. While any Dodgers umpire was accustomed to such jeering, he also knew the risks of a controversial call, as Dodgers fans had the audacity to throw rotten fruits and vegetables at any umpire who called against the home team. Or the fans could follow the example of the players, who often fought with other players and attacked the umpire on occasion. Such conditions were tolerable so long as Ebbets Field remained a predominantly white, male, working-class domain.[5]

The prominence of a figure such as Hilda Chester at Ebbets Field, moreover, suggests that women actively participated in the spectacle of Dodgers games, but baseball nonetheless remained a fundamentally male endeavor, and as such it packaged a different kind of sexual culture than that which flourished with the turn-of-the-century amusement park, the nickelodeon, or the dance hall. As the cultural historian Michael S. Kimmel has demonstrated, baseball's institutionalization between 1880 and 1920 alleviated a crisis of masculinity in the United States, in which the collision of various historical forces—the closing of the frontier, accelerated urbanization, the ascendant women's suffrage movement, the mechanization of labor processes, and the surge of immigration—heightened anxieties about the flaccidity of white masculine identity within the national culture. The historical circumstances of the United States at the turn of the century wreaked havoc upon the hegemonic paradigm of white masculinity and necessitated a new set of social and cultural practices that restored the white male to his position at the summit of social hierarchies.[6]

Baseball thus emerged as a key component of a larger culture of sport that enveloped the nation at the turn of the century and offered a channel through which Americans sought to restore an order rooted in the social matrix of white patriarchy. Theodore Roosevelt, a man who posed as the very image of vigorous white masculinity, lauded baseball alongside boxing, football, wrestling, shooting, and riding as "the true sports for a manly race."[7] As a participatory sport, baseball could transmit such values to the broader public. Within the tumultuous milieu of the industrial metropolis, where traditional patterns of racial and sexual order seemed to dissolve, the baseball stadium centered on a regenerative vision of white male athletic prowess as mass spectacle and inculcated patriarchal civic culture into a broader working-class and middle-class audience.[8]

In its early-twentieth-century heyday, Ebbets Field thus showcased a restorative vision of white masculinity while catering to an ethnically heterogeneous and boisterous crowd of men and women. The 1930s and early '40s, however, inaugurated a new phase of urbanization in the United States, which fundamentally altered urban cultural life. The postwar suburbanization of the United States, which originated in the federal policies of the New Deal administration, disrupted the established patterns of neighborhood life in older cities such as New York, as people left their old neighborhoods in the city for greener pastures on the suburban frontier. The movement of people during and after World War II was not simply from city to suburb, but also followed the westward course of industrialization, which favored cities such as Los Angeles and Oakland. The demographic shifts initiated during the war years fell most heavily on older communities such as Brooklyn, which experienced a net decline in its population during the 1940s and '50s.

Such upheavals inevitably weakened the cultural ties that bound older urban communities together. Although the Brooklyn Dodgers remained a fixture in Brooklyn's cultural life through the 1940s, the team's standing in the community diminished amid the socioeconomic upheavals of the war years. Perhaps no one was more astutely aware of those changes than Walter O'Malley, who succeeded Branch Rickey as owner of the Brooklyn Dodgers in 1950 to become the third president of the ball club. His tenure as Dodgers owner constituted a chapter in the history of the organization that culminated in the celebrated and despised move to Los Angeles. Likened to a "cartoon of capital in a labour newspaper," O'Malley had a mind for business and showed little concern for the sentimental aspects of the game.[9] O'Malley ultimately based his decision to move his team west upon his acute business sensibilities and a clear estimation of the forces transforming communities such as Brooklyn during the early 1950s.

Upon assuming ownership of the Dodgers, O'Malley turned his attention to Ebbets Field, which by the early '50s paled in comparison to the more modern baseball facilities elsewhere. When Ebbets Field was built in 1912, it was surrounded by open fields and had an ample seating capacity of twenty-five thousand. By the 1920s, however, the stadium's seating and location had become cramped. The mass adoption of the automobile during that decade, moreover, abetted the congestion surrounding Ebbets Field and discouraged any attempt to renovate the stadium. By the late '40s, parking had become a serious problem as longtime fans who moved to the suburbs became increasingly dependent upon their automobiles to watch Dodgers games. Parking was available for only seven hundred cars at Ebbets Field, which O'Malley believed discouraged attendance.[10]

Increasing congestion on Brooklyn streets indicated some of the changes that that community faced at midcentury. Other changes included the darker shades of Brooklyn's incoming population during and after the war. The war forced Americans into a new era of racial integration, disrupting the patterns of community life in places such as Brooklyn. Like many urban communities at this time, Brooklyn experienced an increase in its black population and a decrease in its white population. The 1930s and '40s brought a new level of affluence to Jews and other white ethnics, who historically had populated Brooklyn's neighborhoods before World War II and who comprised the Dodgers' core constituency. After the war, however, these groups were able to participate in the mass suburbanization of the United States and left Brooklyn for Long Island, Staten Island, and New Jersey. Blacks and Puerto Ricans filled in the spaces they left behind. From 1950 to 1960, net migration from Brooklyn resulted in a decline of 476,094 white residents and an increase in 93,091 nonwhite residents.[11]

Although Brooklyn remained a predominantly white borough through the '50s, the beginnings of white flight nonetheless aroused the discomfort of many whites who remained in Brooklyn. Peter Golenbock's oral history of the Brooklyn Dodgers reveals the perceptions of many white residents of Brooklyn regarding the changing complexion of their community. One former Brooklyn fan recalled, "Blacks brought change. Puerto Ricans brought change. The language changed. The customs changed. Brooklyn was changing slowly from the solid Italian, German, Irish, Jewish that it had been to a tropical flavor." Amid such changes, longtime Brooklyn residents mourned the loss of the borough's most celebrated cultural institutions: "A lot of things changed. Coney Island wasn't Coney Island anymore. The Steeplechase closed. There was no more Luna Park." Ebbets Field would soon be another casualty of the racial transformation of Brooklyn during the 1950s.[12]

Inside the ballpark, the growing tensions between new and old residents became apparent. While Branch Rickey's decision to sign Jackie Robinson to the Dodgers in 1947 won favor with many African Americans, it also alienated many white Dodgers fans, who resented the growing presence of blacks within Ebbets Field. One former fan recalled, "In the '40s the crowds had been all white, but by the mid-'50s, after Jackie Robinson had been there a while, you go to a Sunday doubleheader, and the dominant smell in the ballpark was bagged fried chicken." Many whites resented how blacks favored black players while seeming to ignore other players: "When Blacks started coming to the game, a lot of Whites stopped coming. And the Black allegiance was only to Robinson and the Black ballplayers. They didn't have the history we had." The same fan insinuated that the changing complexion of the Ebbets crowd ultimately pushed the Dodgers to Los Angeles. "I guess O'Malley was like everyone else in Brooklyn. As long as you're not my neighbor . . . it was okay. But once they started to live in the neighborhood . . . it was time to move out."[13]

White flight and suburbanization aggravated O'Malley's dissatisfaction with Ebbets Field in other ways as well. For fifty years, the sixteen major-league teams were confined to ten eastern and midwestern cities. Only five teams, two in the National League and three in the American League, had no competition in their own towns. Most cities had both an American and a National League franchise. Boston hosted the Braves and the Red Sox; Chicago, the Cubs and the White Sox; Philadelphia, the Athletics and the Phillies; St. Louis, the Browns and the Cardinals; and New York had three teams, the Dodgers, the Giants, and the Yankees. As long as people remained concentrated within these cities, franchise owners could afford to share their hometowns with rival teams.

Postwar suburbanization, however, threatened that stability as it drastically reduced the base of financial support for teams that shared their city with other teams. By the early '50s, franchise owners sought new markets in which to expand their financial base. The Braves, the Browns, and the Athletics were the first to relocate to other cities between 1953 and 1955, and they profited tremendously. The move of the Braves from Boston to Milwaukee particularly captured the attention of Walter O'Malley, who marveled at the success of the Braves in their new home. The first nine games for the Braves in Milwaukee yielded an attendance equal to their entire 1952 season in Boston. In the first year of operations in his new home, the Braves owner Lou Perini realized a profit of a half-million dollars as the Braves finished third in 1953, only three games behind the Dodgers.[14]

Despite the Dodgers' continued success in Brooklyn during the early 1950s, the success of the Braves stunned O'Malley. As the Dodgers owner saw it, Milwaukee's record attendance would permit the Braves to sign the best young players available and within a short time eclipse the Dodgers and the rest of the league. O'Malley expressed his frustration at the success of the Braves in their new home: "We can't even afford a few years of this. The Braves will be able to pay bigger bonuses, run more farm teams and hire the best scouting talent." His premonitions were accurate—the Dodgers fell to third place in 1957 behind the Braves, who won the World Series that year and in 1958 repeated their league championship. The Dodgers would not prevail again until 1959, after their move to Los Angeles. That year, the Dodgers won a playoff game held in the Los Angeles Memorial Coliseum, drawing up to ninety thousand fans for a single game and easily surpassing the Braves' attendance and revenue.[15]

As historians have noted, television played no small part in changing the structure of major-league baseball after World War II. For former Brooklyn fans who retreated into the comforts of suburban life, television offered a more convenient alternative to watching Dodgers games at Ebbets Field. Most franchise owners resisted televised coverage of ball games, believing it discouraged live attendance. O'Malley rejected the conventional wisdom of his colleagues and anticipated the heightened revenue television could bring through advertising. The Dodgers owner was among the first to realize that sponsors would pay big money to affiliate themselves with teams like the Brooklyn Dodgers. His insights proved correct, as the team earned $787,155 in 1955 from radio and television broadcasts, while the Milwaukee Braves, by contrast, earned only $135,000 from radio broadcasts alone.[16]

Although television helped to offset the advantage Milwaukee enjoyed in gate receipts, it did not reduce O'Malley's dissatisfaction with Ebbets Field. On the contrary, television reinforced such dissatisfaction in more abstract ways. Certainly the mass adoption of television during the late '40s and early '50s did nothing to help attendance at Ebbets Field, which steadily declined after peaking in 1947. Although radio and newspapers did much to extend the popularity of baseball, television literally brought the game into the homes of millions of Americans throughout the nation, dramatically expanding and altering the traditional fan base of major-league teams after World War II. Television thus sensitized franchise owners and advertisers to untapped markets across the nation and abetted their eagerness to expand the scope of their enterprise.

The combined effects of television, suburbanization, and white flight put strains on older cultural institutions such as Ebbets Field, which could not cater to the changing demands of postwar Americans. Roger Kahn summarized the impact of World War II on Brooklyn, conveying the declining significance of Ebbets Field under the new conditions of (sub)urban life in postwar America:

> After World War II, Brooklyn, like most urban settlements, began a
> struggle to survive. Brooklyn had been a heterogeneous, dominantly
> middle-class community, with remarkable schools, good libraries and
> not only major league baseball, but extensive concert series, second-run

movie houses, expensive neighborhoods and a lovely rolling stretch of acreage called Prospect Park. For [all] the outsiders' jokes, middle-brow Brooklyn was reasonable secure of its cosmic place, and safe.

Then, with postwar prosperity came new highways and the conqueror automobile. . . . For $300 down one could buy a Ford, a Studebaker or a Kaiser, after which one could drive anywhere. . . . Whole families left their blocks for good. They had been overwhelmed by the appeal of a split-level house (nothing down to qualified Vets) on a treeless sixty-by-ninety foot corner of an old Long Island potato farm. . . .

Exodus worked on the ethnic patterns and economic structure and so at the very nature of Brooklyn. As old families, mostly white, moved out, new groups, many Black and Puerto Rican, moved in. The flux terrified people on both sides. Could Brooklyn continue as a suitable place for the middle class to live? That was what the Irish, Italian and Jewish families asked themselves. The answer, like the American urb itself, [is] still in doubt.[17]

As the suburban periphery of older cities thrived at the expense of inner-city communities such as Brooklyn after World War II, older urban neighborhoods increasingly lost their appeal as an appropriate venue for professional baseball. Although historically baseball had suited male working-class demands for entertainment within the industrial city, the mass suburbanization of the United States after the war forced upon franchise owners a reconsideration of their constituency. Elaine Tyler May points out how postwar suburbanization positioned the nuclear family at the center of American life, and forced corporations to target the family and not the individual as the primary consumer unit of the postwar era. Franchise owners within the major leagues were no exception. As baseball appealed to new audiences that did not fit the mold of traditional baseball fans, owners sought to introduce into the game a measure of respectability that had not previously existed.[18]

Well aware of these changes, Walter O'Malley is often credited with bringing baseball into its corporate era. As a franchise owner, O'Malley sought ways to make professional baseball compatible with the new suburban ethos that defined American culture after World War II. He turned first to Ebbets Field, which seemed outdated and irrelevant amid the midcentury transformation of New York. As the patronage of Ebbets Field shifted from a prewar fraternity of white working-class men to an integrated audience of women, families, and blacks, the intimate atmosphere of Ebbets Field seemed inappropriate, even dangerous. Stan Lomax, a sportswriter and a college fraternity brother of Walter O'Malley, confirmed the owner's contention that Ebbets Field had become a forbidding place by the 1950s:

The scene at Ebbets Field was one of riding on the crest of a volcano. If they didn't get a new park they would have had a riot or some terrible disturbance. Especially at midweek games—there was too darn much drinking. There were narrow aisles, the seats were too close and you had a rough, tough bunch there. If somebody threw a bottle or stabbed someone—that's all that was needed—the dynamite was there . . . with too many people in too small an area.[19]

The Dodgers owner, with the help of the industrial designer Norman Bel Geddes, imagined an alternative to Ebbets Field, one better suited for the suburban age. Bel Geddes designed a new structure to replace Ebbets Field, making sure to include every amenity of baseball's modern age: a retractable roof, foam rubber seats, heating in cold weather, a seven-thousand-car garage from which fans could proceed directly into the ballpark, "automatic hot dog vending machines everywhere, including mustard," a new lighting system, and "a synthetic substance to replace grass on the entire field and which can be painted any color." So impressed was he with Bel Geddes's futuristic vision of major-league baseball, O'Malley displayed a drawing of the new stadium in the Dodgers' offices in Brooklyn. Although some derided the proposal as "O'Malley's pleasure dome," Bel Geddes's design foreshadowed a radical departure from the experience of watching and playing baseball at Ebbets Field, one that eventually debuted in Southern California in 1962.[20]

Before O'Malley could realize baseball's Tomorrowland, he took steps to find an alternative site for Ebbets Field. In August 1955, the Dodgers owner announced that the Dodgers would play seven of their home games in Roosevelt Stadium in Jersey City, New Jersey. This facility accommodated only twenty-five thousand spectators, some seven thousand fewer than Ebbets Field, dramatizing O'Malley's intolerance of the old Brooklyn facility. The owner capitalized upon the uproar that this announcement incited by pressing New York officials for their assistance in clearing a site for a new stadium. In contrast to the emerging trend in the 1950s to finance stadium construction with public funds, O'Malley insisted that he would finance construction costs with private funds, declaring before the Antitrust Subcommittee of the House of Representatives in 1957, "I don't want to be a tenant in a political ball park."[21]

Despite his declared unwillingness to use public funds for the construction of a new stadium in Brooklyn, O'Malley found little sympathy among New York officials. In particular, the mighty Robert Moses, commissioner of parks and recreation, persistently refused to invoke eminent domain—the authority to acquire private land for a public purpose—for the construction of a privately owned stadium. His reluctance to assist O'Malley heightened the owner's dissatisfaction with his situation in Brooklyn and further piqued his interest in the possibility of moving elsewhere.

LOS ANGELES: BASEBALL AS URBAN RENEWAL

Meanwhile, in Los Angeles, an explosive suburban boom alerted corporate executives throughout the nation to rapidly expanding new markets that held the possibility of unimaginable profits. Leaders of the housing, automobile, and television industries looked not to the congested, deteriorating communities of cities such as New York to market their products, but rather to the spacious, booming cities of the West, which seemed to hold the promise of unlimited expansion. Like other corporate executives of the time, O'Malley and his cohort of baseball owners took an interest in the burgeoning markets of Southern California, sensing that the timing was right for expanding the major leagues. Urban elites in growing western cities did much to encourage that supposition. As baseball's stature as the national pastime flourished after World War II, western cities sought to attain their own major-league franchises. In Los Angeles, a city desperate to enter the big league of American cities, city officials began to pursue their own major-league franchise. County supervisor John Anson Ford, who played a key role in bringing the Dodgers to Los Angeles, lamented that his constituents "suffered from an inferiority complex because their city, the third largest in the nation, did not possess a major league ball club."[22]

To understand the depth of the enthusiasm with which Los Angeles officials pursued a major-league franchise, it is first necessary to comprehend the nature of growth in postwar Southern California and its impact on the historic downtown of Los Angeles. Ultimately, O'Malley based his decision to move west not on the mass suburbanization of Southern California, but rather on the ambitious proposal to revitalize a deteriorating downtown district. In Los Angeles, the decentralized patterns of housing and industry, underpinned by the construction of a regional highway system, threatened to undermine the historic hegemony of the downtown within the larger urban region. The acceleration of "urban sprawl" generated acute anxiety among the downtown's elite, whose voice echoed forcefully in the pages of the *Los Angeles Times* from the late nineteenth century on. The *Times* and its allied institutions, such as the Los Angeles Chamber of Commerce, the Downtown Businessmen's Association, and the Merchants and Manufacturers Association, sought ways to maintain the centrality of downtown amid Southern California's postwar suburban boom.

Such plans flourished during the Cold War, a period that brought the end of twenty years of New Deal progressivism in Southern California and a return to some of the former glories of the Republican, expansionist *Times*. The public relations firm Baus and Ross "had been working with the business establishment hand in glove" and won numerous campaigns on behalf of downtown interests to enforce its agenda. Their first victory came in the 1953 mayoral election, when, as Herb Baus recalled, "we found our man, Norris Poulson, and ran him and won." The *Times*, which "gently tapped Norris Poulson on the shoulder and pointed to City Hall," decided in conjunction with other business leaders that Poulson, a third-term Republican congressman, would faithfully execute their progrowth agenda for downtown expansion. During Poulson's tenure as mayor, city hall developed a close working relationship with the downtown establishment to aggressively pursue downtown redevelopment.[23]

A concerted attack on public housing became the cornerstone of Poulson's campaign, as subsidized housing within the vicinity of downtown did not suit elite visions of privatized redevelopment. The previous mayoral administration had secured federal funding for the construction of public housing in Los Angeles under the Taft-Ellender-Wagner Bill of 1949. With the help of a cooperative city council, Bowron had authorized the City Housing Authority (CHA) to build ten thousand low-rent "slum clearance" units on sites to be selected by the CHA. Among the sites approved for the construction of public housing, the Chavez Ravine had been identified as the most "blighted" area in the city in need of "rehabilitation." In 1951, the city approved the construction of some 3,360 units of public housing for the eight-hundred-acre parcel of land one mile north of the city hall.[24] Between 1952 and 1953, the CHA cleared residents from the Ravine with the promise that "this project is going to be built for you, we'll give you temporary housing. . . . [Y]ou'll have first priority, you can have whatever you want."[25]

That promise went unfulfilled as the new mayor canceled the plans for public housing in the Chavez Ravine after most of its residents had already been removed. Poulson extended his attack on public housing by promising to remove the "communists from the Housing Authority" and by sanctioning the blacklisting of several CHA officials. The *Times* bolstered Poulson's effort, exploiting Cold War hysteria to campaign against "socialistic" public housing.[26] After the blacklisting of thirty members of the CHA and the cancellation of public housing in the Chavez Ravine, the *Times* gloated, "The *Times* is proud of its part in crying the alarm against this creeping socialism and in supporting the Mayor who found the way to stop the creep."[27]

The death of public housing in the Chavez Ravine cleared the path for the corporate reincarnation of downtown Los Angeles during the late '50s and throughout the '60s. With the cancellation of plans for public housing, large-scale, private redevelopment came to the forefront of downtown's political agenda. The construction of Dodger Stadium in the Chavez Ravine must be viewed within this context. The election of Norris Poulson, the blacklisting of CHA officials, and the cancellation of the Chavez Ravine project were among the first battles in what Poulson would later describe as "the hottest battle in California since the war with Mexico." These events put Los Angeles officials in a position to argue that baseball was the more "American" alternative to public housing.

During their campaign against public housing in the Chavez Ravine, the proprietors of the downtown organized themselves to advance their agenda for downtown redevelopment. Neil Petree, head of Barker Brothers furniture store and president of the Downtown Businessmen's Association in 1940, expressed the concern with which his peers looked upon the rapid suburbanization of Southern California: "The city has to have a center to it, you have to have a hub like a wheel. If you let the hub deteriorate, you haven't got much to be suburban to."[28] Poulson affirmed that view: "We've got to support and strengthen the downtown area. . . . [N]o city can be a great city without a strong central core." This view informed the establishment of Greater Los Angeles Plans Incorporated (GLAPI), which included Petree, the insurance executive Asa Call, the *Times*'s publisher, Norman Chandler, and P.J. Winant of Bullock's department store. GLAPI's ultimate goal was to push the idea that upgrading downtown would benefit the entire region.[29]

GLAPI, with the aid of the Community Redevelopment Agency, a downtown-based city planning agency governed by a board of corporate allies with the powers of eminent domain, land write-downs, and autonomous planning, turned to the production of culture to ensure the political and economic centrality of downtown Los Angeles. Centering Los Angeles through the placement of hefty cultural institutions such as opera houses and museums within the vicinity of the downtown became a key tactic by which downtown elites sought to reinforce the economic vitality and political significance of the central business district.[30] As Los Angeles grew in stature after World War II, the *Times* grew increasingly self-conscious about the lack of "culture" in Southern California:

> Critics of Los Angeles and Southern California . . . can no longer refute the census figures. Already we are one of the biggest cities in the world and we are still growing. . . . Now Los Angeles needs a civic auditorium and music center. Faced with the facts, the critics of Los Angeles have to fall back on the old insinuation that we have no culture, that nothing

really important ever happens here, that there is no metropolitan "feeling" to the town, that we are a mere collection of suburbs in search of a city. Of course they are wrong. We know that. We like it here.[31]

The self-consciousness with which the *Times* addressed the criticism of Los Angeles as a city without culture underpinned GLAPI's efforts to establish an opera house atop Bunker Hill, which would have been the centerpiece of a new cultural acropolis in downtown Los Angeles. Those efforts, however, went unrealized as the electorate twice refused to finance its construction.

Even without opera, the vicinity of the downtown core was not the cultural void that GLAPI seemed to think it was. In downtown communities such as Bunker Hill and the Chavez Ravine, a working-class and immigrant culture flourished within the neighborhood venues of streets, porches, sidewalks, bars, dance halls, churches, and markets. One former resident of the Chavez Ravine recalled the vitality of her neighborhood before the intervention of the CHA:

> There were dances in the churchyard. Pageants held in the streets. Weddings in which the whole community joyously participated. . . . Flowers, gorgeous blooms, dahlias fit to grace any show display. Gardens, orchards, livestock. Cow's and goat's milk—cheese of every color, kind and consistency. Cactus broiled, baked, preserved. At night, bonfires—music wafted over the air. Chavez Ravine was the only place in the city that had not over-crowded school accommodations . . . and without traffic hazards to eat out the hearts of mothers.[32]

Part of the vitality of the Ravine's three neighborhoods—Bishop, La Loma, and Palo Verde—depended upon their accessibility to public transportation. The Ravine's central location afforded transportation to disparate sites within Southern California's expanding urban region via the streetcar. From the Chavez Ravine, for example, residents could ride the red cars to distant places such as San Dimas, Long Beach, and Santa Monica, all for a fare of ten cents. For seven cents, they could use the yellow cars to travel to more local sites such as Eagle Rock, Lincoln Park, and downtown Los Angeles. Like Bunker Hill, Boyle Heights, and Watts, the neighborhoods of the Chavez Ravine were a part of Southern California's streetcar metropolis that, as chapter 6 considers, began to fade as the era of highway construction ensued.[33]

It was not until 1961, with the publication of Jane Jacobs's *The Death and Life of Great American Cities,* that the American planning community began to appreciate the virtues of the kind of community that thrived within the Chavez Ravine. In 1950s Los Angeles, city officials remained intent upon pursuing a grand civic vision that depended upon the eradication of working-class communities of color in places such as Bunker Hill and the Chavez Ravine. Mexican Americans posed a particular obstacle to that vision. By 1950, the heart of Chicano Los Angeles had not yet completed its shift to East Los Angeles and remained in communities such as Bunker Hill and the Chavez Ravine. These neighborhoods, in the aftermath of the Zoot Suit Riots in 1943, which conferred a distinct notoriety upon the streets of downtown, were considered "pachuco zones," where a twisted combination of poverty and pathology allegedly repelled the city's more respectable white middle class. The "revitalization" of neighborhoods such as Bunker Hill and the Chavez Ravine thus demanded the eviction of Chicano people and Chicano culture from the vicinity of the downtown, enforcing what Mauricio Mazón described as the "psychology of symbolic annihilation."[34]

Eventually, high culture did come to downtown Los Angeles, albeit through a slightly different strategy than that pursued by GLAPI. Dorothy "Buffy" Chandler, the wife of the *Times*'s publisher, Norman Chandler, looked to one of the city's older working-class communities to help build a "music center" atop Bunker Hill. Although Jews in Los Angeles initially "made good" through the rise of Hollywood during the 1920s and 1930s, the postwar era saw the ascendance of Jewish nouveaux riches through the success of the savings and loan industry. Aware of this burgeoning source of wealth, Chandler "crossed over" to the Westside to enlist the support of savings-and-loan titans Mark Taper and Howard Ahmanson. In fundraising for a music center on Bunker Hill (after the neighborhood's demolition by bulldozers in the early '50s), Chandler tapped into multiple sources of wealth: new and old, Westside and downtown, Jewish and gentile. To the consternation of the anti-Semitic old guard, Buffy Chandler oversaw the construction of Los Angeles' answer to Lincoln Center: the Dorothy Chandler Pavilion, the Mark Taper Forum, and the Ahmanson Theater.[35]

Dodger Stadium, therefore, would arrive as the popular counterpart to the temples of high culture erected upon the remnants of Bunker Hill. Downtown's elite reasoned that although baseball did not suit their quest for high culture, to bring the Dodgers from New York to Los Angeles would underscore the heightened prominence of their city within the national culture. The growing popularity of major-league baseball during the postwar era coincided with the aggressive campaign of Los Angeles officials to place their city within the ranks of big-league American cities. The Dodgers became an instrument by which downtown elites promoted both Los Angeles within the national culture and downtown within the larger urban region. Ultimately, the campaign to bestow the Chavez Ravine upon Walter O'Malley exemplifies the growing importance of sports teams and stadia to city promotion and urban (re)development during the postwar era.[36]

Southern California's establishment was especially captivated by "the modern miracle of Milwaukee." The franchise move of the Boston Braves to Milwaukee, which marked the first major franchise shift, alerted Los Angeles officials to the advantages of acquiring their own major-league franchise. In 1957, the Downtown Businessmen's Association, whose members led Southern California's most prominent businesses, including Title Insurance and Trust, Bullock's, Mutual Life Insurance, and Security First Bank, reported to the Los Angeles city council the many benefits the Braves had brought to Milwaukee. The members of the Association marveled at how "overnight, big league baseball transformed a dull Midwestern city into blazing, dancing, fairy tale headlines." The report also pointed out the promotional value a major-league franchise would bring to Los Angeles: "Constantly flashing the name of our city throughout the nation creates more interest in our products and our varied industry . . . interest translated into real sales."[37]

The report also noted "the terrific psychological value" of acquiring a major-league franchise. As baseball grew in popularity after World War II, ownership of a major-league ball club became requisite for any American city wishing to enter the "big league" of U.S. cities. Norris Poulson reiterated the therapeutic value of luring the Dodgers to Los Angeles for downtown elites anxious about their city's stature: "Psychologically, it was a great boost to Los Angeles and the West that we had taken this team right out of New York under their own noses."[38]

Still, downtown's elite valued the material rewards of bringing the Dodgers to the Chavez Ravine over the psychological ones. Given the decline of the downtown as a center of manufacturing during the war years, the downtown establishment struggled to steward downtown's transition to a corporate-based, service-oriented economy in which tourists and tourist attractions became increasingly central. The *Times* and its allied institutions recognized that the Dodgers could play an important role in that makeover. Sidney Hodemaker, chairman of the Los Angeles Chamber of Commerce, recognized that "the addition of major-league baseball to the already imposing list of tourist attractions will have a definite stimulus on the hotel and restaurant business in the area." Similarly, the Merchants and Manufacturers Association anticipated that the Dodgers would bring a new influx of tourists into the area, who would "leave a great deal of cash behind in the restaurants, night clubs, bars, hotels, gas stations, stores and in many other places."[39]

Within the sprawling, decentralized context of postwar Los Angeles, placing Dodger Stadium within the regional metropolis became an issue of critical importance. That issue was especially critical for downtown elites, who sought to anchor the regional metropolis by placing such hefty cultural institutions as music centers and baseball stadia within the vicinity of downtown. Their campaign to bring the Dodgers to the Chavez Ravine reveals the important relationship between culture and place, a relationship that became critical in the evolving cultural matrix of Southern California during the postwar era.

"THE HOTTEST BATTLE IN CALIFORNIA SINCE THE WAR WITH MEXICO"

By no means was the effort to place the Dodgers in the Chavez Ravine smooth or easy. It is well to provide a reminder here that all cultural production involves struggle, even if that struggle involves the most powerful groups of a society. Los Angeles elites, whose social position depended upon the vitality of the historic downtown, faced an uphill battle in their effort to place Dodger Stadium in the Chavez Ravine. Ultimately, they won that battle but made many enemies along the way. The determination with which downtown interests pursued the Dodgers for the Chavez Ravine demonstrates their investment in that endeavor. While New York officials balked at O'Malley's requests for a new home for his team, *New York Times* sports columnist Arthur Daley recognized that "Los Angeles desperately wants the Dodgers and will go to almost any length to woo them to the Coast."[40] In February 1957, as if to provoke New York officials, Walter O'Malley purchased the Los Angeles Angels and Wrigley Field in South Central Los Angeles, commenting, "If it becomes necessary for us to play [in] any place other than Brooklyn, I think the final location is obvious." Norris Poulson handed O'Malley a key to the city, and the *Times* speculated, "All the evidence points to a move to Los Angeles."[41]

Amid the hearsay, Chavez Ravine reentered public debates as a possible site for the construction of a new stadium. In the months following his purchase of the Los Angeles Angels, O'Malley made a clandestine visit to the Ravine to survey its potential as a future home for his franchise. City and county officials in Los Angeles aided his efforts by forming a joint committee to investigate those possibilities. The parcel of land, taken from the CHA and cleared of its former inhabitants, struck many city officials as the ideal place for a new baseball stadium, one that suited the ambitions of both O'Malley and downtown elites.[42]

Despite the desirability of the Chavez Ravine, however, city officials could not simply give the land to Walter O'Malley. The city's deed to the land explicitly stated that the land was to be used "for public purposes only." This restrictive clause remained in the deed after the housing contract had been canceled and prevented the transfer of public property to private hands. So determined was he to hand the Ravine over to the Dodgers owner, Poulson later recalled in his memoirs, that "a few strings had to be pulled" in order to circumvent the exact wording of the deed. With the help of an obsequious CHA, thoroughly cleansed of any "subversive" opposition, Poulson simply changed the wording of the deed, eliminating the public purpose restriction. With the omission of this clause, the mayor and his clique in city hall could confidently promise the Chavez Ravine to Walter O'Malley.[43]

This clandestine action demonstrated the extent to which city officials in Los Angeles valued the addition of major-league baseball to Southern California's public culture. While New York officials interpreted the Federal Housing Act as precluding the use of their slum-clearing powers for the construction of a baseball stadium in Brooklyn, Los Angeles officials concluded that simply rewording an existing agreement could surmount such an obstacle. As Neil Sullivan points out, the key difference was not the relative power of city officials, but rather their willingness to use those powers to accommodate the demands of Walter O'Malley. In New York, a city with three major-league teams, officials concluded that a privately owned baseball stadium did not merit the use of government authority to acquire land. In Los Angeles, city and county officials felt otherwise and invoked their authority to situate Dodger Stadium within the Chavez Ravine.[44]

A formal agreement between Walter O'Malley and Los Angeles officials took shape by the end of 1957. Poulson appointed Harold "Chad" McClellan, a local business leader, to conduct negotiations with O'Malley on behalf of the city. A skilled negotiator familiar with the complexities of the downtown real estate market, McClellan represented the interests of downtown's business establishment. McClellan designed a contract under which O'Malley would receive 315 acres in the Chavez Ravine, worth anywhere between two and six million dollars, in return for the nine-acre Wrigley Field purchased earlier by O'Malley. In addition, O'Malley would acquire mineral rights to the land, a ninety-year lease, all revenues from parking and concessions, and 4.7 million dollars in land preparation costs. O'Malley also agreed to finance the construction of a "youth center" adjacent to the stadium on forty acres of land set aside for that purpose. This requisite was inserted into the contract to qualify O'Malley's acquisition of the Ravine as a "public purpose."[45]

Opposition exploded following public disclosure of the city-Dodgers contract. According to Herbert Baus, "there were a lot of surviving political scars" over the public housing fight and the losers in that fight, who "never did swallow this Chavez Ravine matter gracefully," used their defeat to organize opposition against the city's efforts to place the Dodgers in the Chavez Ravine.[46] Critics of the "sweetheart deal," as they nicknamed the city-Dodgers contract, resented the overzealous effort to "give away" the Chavez Ravine to O'Malley, calling for a more advantageous deal for the city. "I'm for the Dodgers coming, and we should do everything we can," said councilman Ernest Debs, "but they are seeking to come not because they love Los Angeles, but to make more money. We should not give everything away." Councilman John Holland, who became one of the leading opponents of the Chavez Ravine deal, expressed his surprise at the amount of property O'Malley had requested. "First it was 200 [acres], now 350. I shall oppose any deal giving them a tremendous bargain."[47]

Surprisingly, critics of the contract failed to point out the inconsistencies in the city's handling of the Chavez Ravine. During the effort to build public housing in the Ravine, the *Times* and other private interests decried government-subsidized housing as "socialistic." After the defeat of public housing, however, "city officials were willing to act like Marxists for the moment" by subsidizing O'Malley's bid for the Chavez Ravine.[48] The delivery of 315 acres of publicly owned downtown property for nine acres of Wrigley Field struck no one at the time as government subsidy. Asked by a journalist long after the opening of Dodger Stadium, "How can you justify the government subsidizing your stadium?" O'Malley replied in a paternalistic fashion, comparing his stadium with another civic enterprise built with government subsidy. "Son, look what the government did for the railroads to help develop this country."[49]

In comparing Dodger Stadium to the railroad, O'Malley situated his franchise within the history of urban expansion in Southern California. Shortly before the city council's vote to approve the city's deal with O'Malley, Mayor Poulson "traced the growth of the city and described this as another great step forward." Addressing critics of the city-Dodgers contract, the mayor recalled the "opposition that had prevailed when water was first brought here from Owens Valley; the dredging of the Los Angeles harbor and the development of the Colorado Aqueduct." The mayor described Dodger Stadium as another "work" in the history of public works in modern Los Angeles. The *Times* followed suit, arguing that the Dodgers would "restore to the city the sense of common enterprise it once had when all the citizens would join to tap a water supply far away in the mountains."[50]

Such rhetoric of progress contrasted sharply with disingenuous descrip-

FIGURE 10. Walter O'Malley proposes his new stadium to the Los Angeles public, 1958. (Courtesy of the Los Angeles Public Library.)

tions of the Chavez Ravine, a centrally located neighborhood that once housed more than eighteen hundred families, as a "wasteland." Walter O'Malley, for example, called the Ravine "two hundred and ten taxable acres of hill ground . . . of interest only to goats."[51] The *Times* described the area as a "half-forgotten wilderness in the very center of the metropolitan area." Frank Finch, sports editor for the *Times*, offered a more caustic characterization: "300 acres of steep hills, eroded gullies, weeds, stunted trees and a few ramshackle dwellings . . . densely populated by skunks . . . rusty tin cans, rotting tires, moribund mattresses, and broken beer bottles . . . an eyesore only a mile from the imposing Civic Center." Ironically, such characterizations of the Chavez Ravine echoed the conclusions of several planning reports from the 1940s, which identified the Chavez Ravine as a "blighted" community. By the mid-1950s, however, "blight" became invoked as a strategy for privatized, downtown redevelopment and not, as it once had been, for improving the living conditions of the urban poor.[52]

On October 9, 1957, the Los Angeles city council approved the city-Dodgers contract. "At long last, we've got the Dodgers!" roared the *Los*

Angeles Times. Such exuberance, however, was premature. The council's nearly unanimous ratification of the contract incited the opposing council-men to collect signatures on a petition that would place the contract on a referendum, subjecting it to voter approval. Opposition to the contract among the public at large was sufficient to subject Proposition B to a city-wide vote on June 3, 1958, asking voters to approve the city-Dodgers con-tract. A "yes" vote on B approved the contract, while a "no" vote would nul-lify it and allow its revision.[53]

The *Times* escalated its crusade to place the Dodgers in the Chavez Ravine by quickly organizing a "yes on B" campaign. The thrust of that campaign rested on the false insinuation that the Dodgers would abandon Los Angeles if voters rejected the proposition at the polls. In a remarkable admission, Poulson stated, "I suggested a scare campaign that would strike home with low income people who didn't belong to country clubs and social groups and who wanted big league baseball for entertainment. The referen-dum, we led them to believe, was a yes or no vote for baseball."[54]

The "Taxpayers' Committee for Yes on B" turned to television to an-nounce their campaign. Shortly before the election, KTTV aired a "Dodger-thon" to rally support for Proposition B. Eager to broadcast Dodgers games, KTTV, a Times Mirror subsidiary, generously donated production assis-tance and airtime to the Dodgers and their supporters. "The program went over like a ton of bricks," recalled William Ross of the Baus and Ross pub-lic relations firm, who engineered the fight against public housing for the *Times* and orchestrated the "yes on B" campaign.[55] Organizers of the Dodgerthon called on the support of local celebrities, who voiced their enthusiasm for the city-Dodgers contract. Stars such as Jack Benny, Debbie Reynolds, Groucho Marx, Lucille Ball, and George Burns all made appear-ances during the five-hour broadcast, bringing the glamour of the film in-dustry to O'Malley's cause. After starring in the opening telecast of Disney-land in 1955, Ronald Reagan appeared on the Dodgerthon, decrying the argument against proposition B as "one of the most dishonest documents I ever read in my life."[56]

The opposition cautioned voters not to be distracted by Hollywood's allure. The *Griffith Park News,* for example, warned TV viewers to "be wary of future emotional programs fostered by over-ambitious city fathers as tranquilizers to the public's normal alertness and common sense."[57] Councilman Edward Roybal of the city's Ninth District exposed what he perceived to be the central issue behind the celebrity of Hollywood and the popularity of baseball: "It is not morally or legally right for a governmen-tal agency to condemn private land, take it away from the property owner through Eminent Domain proceedings, then turn around and give it to a private person or corporation for private gain. This I believe is a gross misuse of Eminent Domain."[58]

Despite Roybal's poignant critique, Proposition B passed by a slim margin on June 3, 1958. "It is entirely possible," O'Malley opined after his victory at the polls, "that we can get going by July 5 if there are no road blocks such as problems of proper clearance or delays due to litigation."[59] O'Malley's qualifications were well founded; the opposition, inspired by its near success, took its crusade to court. Los Angeles taxpayers Julius Reuben and Louis Kirschbaum filed separate claims against the city-Dodgers contract in Los Angeles County Superior Court, where it was hoped the contract would meet its demise. On July 14, 1958, Judge Arnold Praeger overturned the voters' decision, handing the city council an injunction from proceeding with the contract. The judge ruled that land purchased with public funds could not "be transferred to a private corporation for the operation of a private business." This, the judge concluded, constituted "an illegal delegation of the City Council, an abdication of its public trust and a manifest gross abuse of its discretion."[60] The Civic Center News Agency celebrated Praeger's decision, chiding "the downtown newspapers and certain narrow thinking sportswriters and announcers who selfishly and irresponsibly promoted this illegal contract."[61]

Undaunted by this setback, city attorney Roger Arnebergh appealed the city's case to the U.S. Supreme Court, which upheld the validity of the contract in October 1959. The *Wilshire Reporter*, an outspoken critic of the city-Dodgers contract, cursed the ruling in bold headlines, "THE PUBLIC BE DAMN'D."[62] Mayor Poulson, of course, applauded the decision, turning the public's attention to the glories that lay ahead: "One world series in Los Angeles and every cent that Los Angeles has invested in this project will be repaid many times over. Progress must not be stopped in Los Angeles."[63]

Surmounting a referendum and a legal injunction, Los Angeles officials finally obtained a writ of possession for the remaining properties of Chavez Ravine, whose occupants had ignored the 1952 round of evictions initiated by the CHA. Eager to begin rapid construction of Dodger Stadium, Walter O'Malley and city officials underestimated the stubbornness with which those occupants would fight to keep their homes. Manuel and Avrana Arechiga, who had settled in the Ravine in the 1920s and had raised four children there, had managed to remain in their home after the conclusion of the public housing fight. Their residence upon that site ended abruptly on May 8, 1959, when county sheriffs evicted the Arechigas from their home. Emulating the limp bodies of southern civil rights activists who adopted the strategy of passive resistance to defy segregationist policy, one member of the Arechiga family forced authorities to carry her out the door before a crowd of news reporters and television cameras (see figure 11). The *Columbus Dispatch* reported the dramatic spectacle:

> As the sheriff's deputies moved in to carry out the evictions yesterday, Mrs. Arechiga shouted in Spanish, "Why don't they play ball in Poulson's backyard—not in ours!" Amid the shouting and cursing, deputies arrived and carried one of the women bodily out the door. The others went—but not quietly. One threw a stone. Ten minutes later, the roar of two giant bulldozers drowned out Mrs. Arechiga's sobs as she sat on a curb and watched the machine reduce the frail dwelling to rubble.[64]

American viewers, still enamored of the "magic" of television in 1959 and innocent of the televised wartime atrocities that would appear as "news" in the coming decade, expressed their horror at the images of the Arechiga evictions. The images incited resentment toward the Dodgers and the city of Los Angeles, auguring the ways in which television can subvert the intentions of dominant interest groups. Alice Ingersoll of Los Angeles wrote to Councilman Roybal after watching the Arechiga evictions in disbelief from her living room, "what a scene to be on t.v.—screaming children, women yelling and crying. Police carrying a woman down the front steps by arms and legs to a police car. We all sat there speechless. Free America . . . something like this makes you wonder."[65] "A Texas homeowner" wrote to the Los Angeles city council after the Arechiga eviction, wondering, "Can it happen in America? The pictures we saw on television today . . . shattered the . . . faith in a country where homeowners felt that only the omnipotent power would be able to turn our homes into a shamble."[66] The *Times* took a defensive position, attacking the veracity of televised images and blaming TV reporters for "shedding insincere tears up and down the picture tube without any effort to find out the true facts." Despite the *Times*'s counterattack, the official effort to enlist television on behalf of Dodger Stadium backfired, as images of the evictions reinforced popular opinion against downtown redevelopment.[67]

Reactions to the Arechiga evictions revealed the larger social tensions underlying the construction of Dodger Stadium and downtown redevelopment in general. The events of May 8, 1959, partially reignited Southern California's class tensions. Letters to the city council after the evictions express concern about the persecution of "the working man" or "the little fellow" by "big business" or "those rich bastards." O. J. Temple, secretary of the Federated Labor Council of California, commended Edward Roybal for

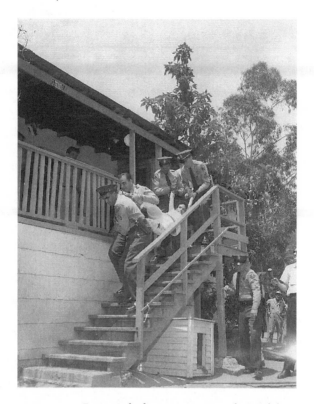

FIGURE 11.   Evicting the last remaining residents of the
Chavez Ravine, May 1959. (Courtesy of the Department
of Special Collections, Charles E. Young Research Library,
UCLA.)

his defense of working-class victims of downtown redevelopment: "You are
one of the very few in the city council that takes any interest for the taxpayers and the working man—just let that Walter O'Malley defend himself
as this man's greed knows no bounds; with cooperation of the Mayor he will
own city hall next. . . . This is the most brazen thing I have ever heard of."[68]
Ironically, such sentiments surfaced in spite of Poulson's pandering to the
working-class affinity for baseball. In his memoirs, the former mayor
recalled his pro-Dodgers campaign as doing something for "the low-income
people who didn't belong to country clubs and social groups."[69]

The mayor had reason to anticipate working-class support for placing the
Dodgers in the Chavez Ravine. While some union locals such as the Federated Labor Council, Local 123 of the Furniture Workers and Upholsterer's
and Woodworkers Union, protested the evictions of the Chavez Ravine, the

region's largest labor organizations threw their support behind city hall and its corporate allies. More typical of labor's position was the response of the larger Los Angeles Building and Trades Council, which described the Ravine as a "wasteland" and reprimanded the city for being "very slow in taking steps for needed improvements."[70] Although organized labor was an important part of the New Deal progressive coalition in Southern California and pledged its support for public housing, it betrayed its earlier alliances during the Cold War period by joining the progrowth coalition and supporting the construction of Dodger Stadium in the Chavez Ravine.[71]

The reluctance of organized labor to protest the Arechiga evictions shifted that burden to the city's minority groups, who suffered most directly from downtown redevelopment. In the public reaction against the Arechiga evictions, racial tensions eclipsed class struggle as people invested the images they witnessed on television with racial meanings. Elisa Garcia Lopez, "America's only woman Spanish-language newscaster," expressed her dismay at the Arechiga evictions: "We citizens feel very much ashamed because 'This is America.'"[72] Others compared the struggle of the Arechiga family to the struggle for integration in the South. "The people of Mexican descent are being treated worse than the colored!" complained Frank Wright of Los Angeles. "If this keeps up the Mexican people will all have to ask to enter a restaurant or public place like the coloreds are in the South."[73] The evictions also aroused racist sentiments against Mexican Americans. Some interpreted the defiance of the Arechiga family as indicative of the general barbarity of Mexican Americans. Mrs. Lota Barrett sarcastically ridiculed the evictees: "Those poor, poor Mexican people! (whom are you kidding?) . . . being hot blooded Mexicans they had to . . . go out feet first. What a touching sight—no one but Mexicans would think of that."[74]

The Arechiga evictions widened the growing racial gulf in postwar Los Angeles and set the urban stage for the late-'60s explosion of the Chicano movement. The strength of El Movimiento in Southern California drew upon the determination of local activists who had endured postwar urban renewal. Manuel Lopez, mayor of Oxnard in 1977, summarized the racialized legacy of the Arechiga evictions: "A lot of minority people are afraid of redevelopment. They see projects like the Chavez Ravine in Los Angeles, where a Mexican community was removed to build Dodger Stadium. Redevelopment has had a bad reputation among minorities that was well-earned."[75]

The Arechiga evictions shaped subsequent Chicana/o cultural production in Southern California. Rudolfo Acuña, among the first generation of Chicano historians, cited the Arechiga evictions to illustrate how the long history of land acquisition by the U.S. government continued to undermine the coherence of Chicano communities well into the twentieth century.[76] Judith Baca, a Los Angeles muralist, represented the episode in her *Great Wall of Los Angeles,* a mural spanning the Tujunga Wash in the San Fernando Valley (see the cover of this book). In the center of its section portraying the post–World War II moment in Los Angeles history, the mural presents the surreal image of an electric stadium hovering above a peaceful community. Playing with popular stereotypes of "alien invaders," Baca represents the Dodgers as the aliens who invade and destroy a peaceful settlement of indigenous Angelenos. The common reference to the Arechiga evictions in Chicana/o cultural production after the '60s demonstrates how postwar developments such as downtown renewal inspired different strands of Chicana/o activism.

Others recognized the racial implications of the Arechiga evictions. The mayor, for example, described the events of May 8, 1959, as "the hottest battle in California since the war with Mexico," comparing his pro-Dodgers campaign to another racialized struggle over land in California's history.[77] James Lin Beebe, former president of the Chamber of Commerce and a senior partner in the O'Melveny and Meyers law firm, made a similar comparison before the Chamber of Commerce. Upon the opening of Dodger Stadium in 1962, Beebe compared the westward migration of the Brooklyn Dodgers to "immigrant trains" that crossed the midwestern plains. The Dodgers, like California's white immigrants, "discovered there were a good many Indians in Los Angeles who were armed and . . . ready to shoot. So they did shoot." Both sides of the battle of the Chavez Ravine invested that struggle with racial meanings, but certain city officials viewed themselves as heirs to the white conquest of California and the West and foresaw an outcome that paralleled the racialized course of Western history.[78]

Whatever illusions the *Times* invested in the Dodgers as a civic endeavor, the effort to build Dodger Stadium in the Chavez Ravine further fragmented an already fragmented metropolis. Excluded from much of the growing housing and employment opportunities around the suburban periphery of Los Angeles, the city's minority communities were left vulnerable to the disruption unleashed by urban renewal programs such as the construction of Dodger Stadium. Downtown redevelopment galvanized opposition among the city's minority groups and inaugurated an era of racial politics during the 1960s. Chicano Power, particularly in Los Angeles, materialized in direct response to inner-city experience of aggressive redevelopment programs, growing police antagonism, and a failing school system. The Chicano response to the politics of urban growth in postwar Los Angeles, of which Dodger Stadium was an important part, led to Frank Wilkinson's astute observation: "Thus the Sixties reap the folly of the Fifties."[79]

"THE MOST MODERN BASEBALL TEMPLE IN THE WORLD"

Dodger Stadium opened to the public on April 10, 1962. The *Times's* publishers praised the new stadium as "the most modern baseball temple in the world," and their sports columnist, Jim Murray, wrote that Dodger Stadium "was not just any baseball park but the Taj Mahal, the Parthenon, and Westminster Abbey of baseball." The monumental stadium reflected O'Malley and Bel Geddes's collaborative design for a "pleasure dome."[80] New York architect Emil Praeger, who engineered the construction of the Tappan Zee Bridge spanning the Hudson River and served as a consultant for the construction of Los Angeles freeways, designed a stadium of three cantilevered tiers that could accommodate fifty-six thousand spectators. Ebbets Field paled in comparison, accommodating only thirty-two thousand. The design of Dodger Stadium suited O'Malley's earlier justification for coming to Los Angeles: "We came to California in the first place because . . . we wanted to build a new modern stadium. Chavez fits in perfectly with that plan."[81]

Architecturally, Dodger Stadium satisfied O'Malley's quest for something new and modern. As the corporate and civic structures of the "new" downtown familiarized Southern California elites with modernism and the international style, Dodger Stadium introduced a kind of popular modernism to the region's baseball fans. In the age of Ebbets Field, stadium designers used the building blocks of the industrial city: wood, brick, and stone. The architects of Dodger Stadium abandoned these materials in favor of newer, synthetic materials that defined commercial architecture after World War II: concrete, steel, and plastic. The result: a twenty-million-dollar concrete monolith that many believe suited O'Malley's calculated, if not cold, decision to move his franchise west.

Notwithstanding one's taste for architectural modernism, the new stadium eliminated the many inconveniences and idiosyncrasies that defined the experience of watching and playing baseball at Ebbets Field. For example, Praeger's substitution of brackets for columns to support the multiple tiers of Dodger Stadium offered spectators an unobstructed view of the game. *Sports Illustrated* noted that "there are no posts or columns" at Dodger Stadium, identifying such features with an outdated style of stadium architecture.[82] The playing field of Dodger Stadium, moreover, reflected a growing standardization in the shape of baseball diamonds across the country. The new stadium also featured "a field of balanced measurements in left and right field," unlike Ebbets Field, where right field extended three hundred feet from home base and left field extended more than four hundred feet.[83] In Los Angeles, the Dodgers no longer had to hone their abilities to fit the awkward shape of their home field. While many fans and players undoubtedly welcomed these changes, some critics derided what they perceived as a new monotony that informed stadium design after Dodger Stadium. The baseball historian David Voight, for example, cited Dodger Stadium as representative of the game's new "plastic style," describing its generation of ballparks as "utilitarian machines for sport."[84]

By the postwar era, the downtown itself had come to resemble a utilitarian machine for corporate investment, and the new stadium complemented that transformation. Dodger Stadium opened amid the initial construction of a corporate citadel in downtown Los Angeles, what Mike Davis later named "Fortress L.A." During the 1960s and '70s, the spaces of downtown became increasingly privatized, sealed off from the kind of public activity that animated New York's Central Park or Rockefeller Center, the quintessential spaces of urban liberalism. Given the heightened middle-class demand for social and spatial isolation that accompanied postwar suburbanization, the new downtown resembled a collection of single-use, not mixed-use, spaces. Thus corporate plazas and music centers displaced the older, heterogeneous public spaces that defined neighborhood life on Bunker Hill or in the Chavez Ravine.[85]

Dodger Stadium, a self-contained "sports center" resting alone on a man-made plateau, fit squarely within this transition. In moving from Ebbets Field to Dodger Stadium, the Dodgers sacrificed their organic connection to the cultural landscape of the city. The dimensions and design of the new stadium sealed off the park from its surrounding urban context and disallowed the kind of relationship that Brooklyn fans maintained with their Dodgers. Outside the concrete monolith, for example, there were no city streets upon which kids could loiter, as they did in Brooklyn, waiting to catch a fly ball or home run hit over the walls of the stadium. Gone too were the nicknames that drew upon the street vernacular of communities like Brooklyn. Few in Los Angeles referred to the Dodgers as "Dem Bums." And the vast parking lot surrounding Dodger Stadium, which *Sports Illustrated* described as a "corona of cars," further buffered the stadium from its surrounding urban context and discouraged the kind of intimacy that once characterized the relationship between the Dodgers and their Brooklyn fans.[86]

The stadium's parking lot even inspired a new artistic sensibility that emerged in Southern California during the 1960s, which asserted an iconography of daily life in postwar Los Angeles. Ed Ruscha, for example, catalogued the emergence of the parking lot as an increasingly prominent feature of the regional landscape in his 1967 work *Thirtyfour Parking Lots in Los Angeles*.

FIGURE 12. Aerial photograph of Dodger Stadium, 1967,
from Ed Ruscha's *Thirtyfour Parking Lots in Los Angeles.*
(Copyright Ed Ruscha.)

For this piece, Ruscha hovered over Los Angeles in a helicopter, taking photographs of empty parking lots to compile thirty-four black-and-white images into a forty-eight-page book. Parking lots were but one aspect of the Los Angeles landscape that caught Ruscha's eye. Swimming pools, palm trees, gas stations, and apartment buildings all became the subjects of the many nontextual books that Ruscha produced during the 1960s, which offered an alternative means of reading the city and its landscape. With one of the largest parking lots in Southern California, Dodger Stadium insinuated itself into Ruscha's aesthetic vision. The aerial photograph of the stadium in *Thirtyfour Parking Lots in Los Angeles* (see figure 12) exhibits not only the growing intricacy of parking lot design within the postwar urban region, but also the very centrality of the parking lot to its new cultural institutions.

Dodger Stadium marketed a different kind of public experience than that offered by Ebbets Field. That difference was largely contingent upon the primacy of the automobile and the freeway in decentralized, postindustrial Los Angeles, in contrast to the more public experience of walking or riding trolleys in centralized, industrial New York. Given the primacy of private automobile transportation in Southern California, the success of any cultural institution rested upon its accessibility to automobile traffic. Thus, in arguing to place the Dodgers in the Chavez Ravine, the *Times* pointed out that the Ravine "is just off the downtown Los Angeles confluence of all the major freeways and can be easily reached from any point in the Southland."[87] Similarly, in his arduous campaign for the city-Dodgers contract, Ronald Reagan asked sarcastically, "Where is a baseball stadium to go? In the suburbs? Away from the freeways?"[88] Walter O'Malley never gave serious consideration to any site in the Los Angeles region other than the Chavez Ravine for the construction of his stadium. Like Walt Disney, O'Malley predicated the success of his enterprise upon its proximity to the freeway.

The car-oriented culture of Southern California demanded a careful ordering of space in the Chavez Ravine. Dodger Stadium, like Disneyland and the freeways, demanded an almost complete surrender to a strict spatial order, designed to facilitate the smooth flow of cars and people. The parking lot alone constituted its own spatial regime. Outside the stadium, Los Angeles police officers directed the movement of car traffic. "Terraced parking" permitted fans to "drive to their section in the stands with practically no walking or climbing."[89] Others could ride a tram from the more distant reaches of the parking lot to the stadium entrance. Once inside, a uniformed legion of "ushers," "usherettes," and "hostesses" directed patrons to their seats.[90] Unlike at Ebbets Field, a new kind of spatial authority eclipsed the authority of the umpire in Dodger Stadium. The rigid spatial order of Dodger Stadium resembled that of Disneyland, which innovated spatial organization to process the crowd in an orderly and uniform fashion.

Perhaps a more striking difference between the experience of Ebbets Field and Dodger Stadium was the emphasis on the "wholesome" nature of Dodgers games in the Chavez Ravine. In contrast to the notoriously unruly crowd of Ebbets Field, Los Angeles officials introduced a modicum of middle-class respectability to Dodgers games. Walter O'Malley often reiterated his view that baseball's endurance as the national pastime depended on domestic harmony. "The future of all pro sports has to do with building a grass roots, starting with youngsters going to games with their parents."[91] The Downtown Businessmen's Association confirmed O'Malley's view of the Dodgers as family entertainment and even praised the team for displacing the criminal element that once troubled the establishment. "It has been said that nowhere can you see so much entertainment for so little—a healthy, wholesome diversion for the entire family. It is an ally against juvenile delinquency and an insurance against crime."[92] And during the city council debate over the city-Dodgers contract, the secretary of the Los Angeles Building and Trades Council urged the council to build Dodger Stadium, "bringing this type of entertainment [baseball] which is clean and wholesome."[93]

This last quotation is particularly revealing, as it suggests the changing standards of working-class entertainment after World War II. In a suburban metropolis such as postwar Los Angeles, which orbited around an ideal of the middle-class nuclear family, cultural entrepreneurs pandered to popular demands for family entertainment. The onus was thus on Walter O'Malley to clean up the image of major-league baseball, to sever the game from its historical affinity with working-class masculinity, and to make it more palatable for an expanding middle class comprising presumably stable nuclear families. During the postwar era, as the white working class entered the consumer lifestyle of suburban affluence, O'Malley discovered that he could meet his audience halfway. As O'Malley reinvented the image of baseball to meet the standards of middle-class respectability, Southern California's white working class, which increasingly resembled the region's new middle class, acquired its own taste for more family-oriented, "respectable" forms of entertainment. The pristine environment of Dodger Stadium, marketing order, homogeneity, safety, and respectability, satisfied the changing cultural appetite of an enfranchised, white, suburban working class.

During the Proposition B campaign, pro-Dodgers advocates argued that Dodger Stadium would "join Disneyland" among the ranks of Southern California's new attractions. A number of years later, *Forbes* magazine made a similar comparison between Dodger Stadium and "another entertainment success of the West Coast—Disneyland. Dodger Stadium is squeaky clean, beautifully landscaped and rests in a striking setting. As at Disneyland, Dodger Stadium attendants—even in the parking lot—are civil. The bathrooms are clean and safe."[94] The many comparisons between Dodger Stadium and Disneyland reveal a distinct pattern in the changing nature of public life after World War II. Both institutions constituted self-contained environments, which relied upon a careful organization of space to control the movement and vision of the crowd. Walt Disney and Walter O'Malley oriented their respective institutions toward the new freeway system and ensured their accessibility to motor traffic. And both entrepreneurs marketed a "wholesome" brand of entertainment that catered to an ideal of the white middle-class nuclear family.[95]

Of greater significance, however, is the common function of Disneyland and Dodger Stadium within the cultural order of postwar Southern California. Like Disneyland, Dodger Stadium offered a kind of "town square" for the new suburban metropolis. Dodger Stadium, like Disneyland, offered a point of public contact under the aegis of private, commercial capital. During its campaign to place the Dodgers in the Chavez Ravine, the *Times* recognized the potential of Dodger Stadium to become a core institution of a regional culture: "surely Los Angeles is not just the name of a large group of neighborhoods without common aims, with nothing to hold them together but the surrounding mountains." In the age of white flight, when communities such as Lakewood seceded from the city of Los Angeles, the placement of the Dodgers in the Chavez Ravine, elites hoped, would counteract municipal fragmentation. "The Dodgers," editorialized the *Times*, "might be expected to bind the neighborhoods together with a sort of communal glue. . . . The ball team will sow a new seed of civic consciousness and pride." Amid the suburban retreat from public life after World War II, private capital assumed the responsibility of providing the postindustrial city with a sense of community and civic pride.[96]

Unlike Ebbets Field and the Brooklyn Dodgers, which reinforced a tighter sense of community among residents of Brooklyn, Dodger Stadium and the Los Angeles Dodgers belonged to a more nebulous agglomeration of cities and communities within an ever-expanding, decentralized urban region. Within the postwar configuration of urban sprawl in Southern California, the advocates of a downtown stadium emphasized the ways in which that institution could impart a sense of regional identity to an amorphous collection of suburban communities connected only by an evolving freeway system. The cultural institutions of postwar Los Angeles were more suited to postwar patterns of urbanization in the United States, in which the decentralization of housing and industry undermined the sense of place that existed within the centralized industrial metropolis.

COMMUNAL GLUE

One might read the modernist design of Dodger Stadium as reflective of a larger effort to universalize the appeal of baseball among the diverse constituents of the postwar urban region, and if so, such efforts met with partial success. Clearly, the construction of Dodger Stadium in the Chavez Ravine exacerbated racial tensions throughout the postwar phase of urban redevelopment and modeled the racial and spatial order of chocolate cities and vanilla suburbs. Yet, in spite of the social fractures that opened upon the construction of Dodger Stadium, the team that occupied that stadium maintained a popularity that extended to the city's racial and ethnic groups, who shared an enthusiasm for watching and playing baseball as great as that of their white counterparts. Not unlike the way in which Disneyland appealed to both white and nonwhite families, the popularity of baseball among Southern Californians of all stripes was an island of commonality within a sea of social tensions.

Los Angeles' black community, for example, remained "Dodger Blue" since the team's arrival in the mid-1950s. Black enthusiasm for the Dodgers stemmed from a long interest in watching and playing baseball in Southern California since the turn of the century. African Americans, in response to the exclusionary practices of the all-white Pacific Coast League, formed their own semi-professional leagues and established various ballparks within the city's black neighborhoods. As baseball triumphed as the national pastime during the post–World War II era, moreover, African Americans shared the growing infatuation with the sport. While African Americans across the nation celebrated Branch Rickey's 1946 decision to break the color line in the National League, the black community of Los Angeles took special pride in the Dodgers' acquisition of Jackie Robinson, a local boy who had graduated from UCLA.[97]

Not surprisingly, the city's black community expressed its immediate enthusiasm at the prospect of a Dodgers move to Los Angeles. Throughout the 1950s and early 1960s, black support for the Los Angeles Dodgers and for the construction of Dodger Stadium in the Chavez Ravine remained unwavering. When the time came for Los Angeles voters to approve the city-Dodgers contract, black voters ratified that contract by an overwhelming margin of three to one.[98] Newspaper coverage within the black community reiterated neighborhood enthusiasm for the Dodgers and for the placement of Dodger Stadium in the Chavez Ravine. Beginning in 1958, African Americans frequently read about "their" team in community newspapers such as the *Los Angeles Sentinel* and the *California Eagle*. Both newspapers, while documenting white racism against black Angelenos in postwar Southern California, extensively covered Dodgers games—emphasizing the feats of their star players, Jim Gilliam, Charlie Neal, Johnny Roseboro, Maury Wills, Tommy Davis, and Willie Davis—and paid homage to retired Dodgers Jackie Robinson and Roy Campanella.

In fact, the sports editors of the *Eagle* and the *Sentinel* held these players up as role models for Southern California's black community. On one occasion, the sports editor of the *Los Angeles Sentinel*, "Brock" Brockenbury, scolded several black Dodgers for neglecting what many fans saw as their responsibilities to the black community. When the Dodgers celebrated their World Series victory in Chicago in 1959, Jim Gilliam and Charlie Neal were conspicuously absent from the festivities. "Where were you, Jim and Charlie?" demanded the *Sentinel*, which chided the players who "forgot their obligation to the fans who have made it possible for them to be where they are." The editor also reprimanded the same players for ignoring children's requests for autographs: "Do you ever think about the fans?" wondered Brockenbury.

> Has it ever occurred to you that the Negroes who for years prayed and cajoled and demanded and pleaded for a breakdown of segregation in baseball deserve something from you for their contribution? The kids worship you. Some of you are the idols of little children because you represent an opportunity for them as Negroes.... [W]hy do you let them down by your actions which sometimes seem ignorant and country? If all the Negroes had shown the type of selfishness you sometimes display, some of you would be picking cotton.[99]

Because black athletes dominate sports today, it is difficult to fully comprehend what the presence of black Dodgers must have meant to African Americans who were accustomed to their exclusion from the cultural mainstream of American life. In the postwar period, few within the black community took the presence of black players on major-league teams lightly. Indeed, as black participants in perhaps the most cherished ritual of white America, black Dodgers were held to the highest set of moral standards. The expectations heaped on black Dodgers exceeded the skills of catching, throwing, and batting and extended to a code of conduct usually assigned to the most prominent public officials. Clearly, within the black community of Los Angeles, among baseball fans and nonfans alike, Dodgers baseball was more than just a game.

Many Chicanos, however, maintained a more ambivalent posture toward the Dodgers. Although the Arechiga eviction alienated many Chicanas and Chicanos from Dodger Stadium, baseball was certainly not alien to the barrio. In fact, Mexican Americans did not discover baseball upon their arrival in U.S. cities such as Los Angeles. Mexicans and other Latinos had adopted the sport long before their immigration to the United States. Unlike other Latin American countries, which discovered baseball as one of the few fringe benefits of American economic and military intervention, the sport came to Mexico indirectly, by way of Cuba. Fleeing political turmoil at the end of the nineteenth century, many Cubans took their love of baseball to Mexico. Among Mexicans, the sport attained an immediate popularity among the elite and the working class alike.[100]

Mexican immigrants to the United States thus recognized baseball as one of the familiar rituals of American life. The sport flourished within barrios throughout the American Southwest, particularly in East Los Angeles, where Chicanos concentrated in greater numbers. The postwar period saw an unprecedented level of organization among Chicano baseball fans in East Los Angeles. There, clubs such as the Carmelita Provision "Chorizeros," the Los Angeles Forty-Six Club, and the El Paso Shoe Store, among others, competed against each other as well as other teams from other parts of the Southwest and Mexico.[101]

Sunday morning after church became baseball's prime time in the barrio. Neighbors would gather at various public parks not only to watch the ball game, but also to catch up with family and friends and to savor the home-made specialties of the barrio: tamales, tacos, tortillas, *aguas frescas,* and *cerveza.* Given the lack of public money for recreational facilities within the barrio, players made do with uneven diamonds, gopher holes, and rusting chain-link fences. Instead of an organ player, mariachis would often enter-tain the crowd with ranchera music. And on special occasions, the authority of the priest would exceed that of the umpire, as he blessed the players and the park before commencing play. Baseball in the barrios was much more than just a sporting event; it was a community gathering.[102]

Local teams in East Los Angeles maintained an active relationship with the larger community. For example, the Forty-Six Club, named after the fact that all of its players were between forty and sixty years of age, was not unlike other community institutions of East Los Angeles. The Mexican Political Association, the G.I. Forum, the Community Service Organization, and the Political Association of Spanish Speaking Organizations were com-mitted to enriching various aspects of barrio life in East Los Angeles. So too were ball clubs such as the Forty-Six Club, which sponsored fundraisers for local schools and parishes, held community dances, and solicited canned goods for local charities.[103] The influence of the Forty-Six Club in promot-ing community cohesion with the barrio demonstrated the overlap between political institutions and cultural institutions, as both served the Chicano community and its various needs.

Not unlike the way in which downtown elites adopted earlier progressive uses of baseball, Chicanos of East Los Angeles used baseball in ways that recalled the role of the sport within ethnic communities of other times and places. While many Irish or German immigrants found baseball a means of integration into the mainstream of white society, other immigrant groups adopted the sport as a venue for the promotion of ethnic identity. For exam-ple, baseball proved extremely popular among Bohemian immigrants in turn-of-the-century Chicago, as well as in the industrial towns of Penn-sylvania and Ohio. Czech Americans formed athletic clubs, or *sokols,* which encouraged various sports within the Bohemian community in the United States. Baseball was most popular within the *sokols.* Czech youth would learn about their ethnic heritage through the *sokol*, and participate with other Czech youth in ball games that were frequently covered by Czech newspapers.[104]

The popularity of baseball within the barrio of postwar Los Angeles, like its appeal among Czech Americans at the turn of the century, demonstrates the ways in which baseball became a means of preserving, and even enhancing, the particular ethnic identity of various immigrant groups. Historically celebrated for its all-American character (indeed, for its racial exclusivity), the national pastime proved popular among communities that did not consider themselves "all-American." Within the barrio of East Los Angeles, baseball offered the opportunity to preserve a sense of connection to Mexico. As one veteran ball player from the barrio recalled, "If it hadn't been for baseball, many of our families would have never met their relatives in Mexico or elsewhere."[105] Indeed, within the barrio, the national pastime became a venue not only for the strengthening of kinship and family ties, but also for the preservation of ethnic identity and the maintenance of communal traditions.

Given the popularity of baseball within the barrio, it is not surprising that many barrio residents welcomed the arrival of "Los Esquivadores" from Brooklyn. Before the Arechiga evictions, the Spanish-language newspaper *La Opinión* lent its support to the city-Dodgers contract, urging its readers to approve city hall's effort to hand over the Chavez Ravine to Walter O'Malley: "If you are a fan of baseball who can vote, you know what you have to do."[106] Similarly, *La Opinión* published the endorsement of José Castillo, a community leader from East Los Angeles, who "recommends to all Mexican Americans to vote in favor of Proposition B, which ratifies the concession of the Chavez Ravine to the major-league team, the 'Dodgers.'"[107]

The newspaper qualified its support for the Dodgers, however, by demanding greater Mexican and Latino representation in the ball club. For American Latinos, particularly Chicanos from Southern California, Latino ball players had been sorely missed on the team's roster year after year. It was not until the 1970s, with the success of Latino players such as Manny Mota and Pedro Guerrero, that Latinos held tenure in Dodgers lineups. At the outset of the Dodgers' career in Los Angeles, *La Opinión* reminded the team of its Chicano constituency, urging its managers to hire Mexican and Latino players. For example, a cartoon in the Spanish-language newspaper depicted "Doctor B.S. Ball" proudly prescribing a bottle whose label read "Jugadores Latinos—Vitaminas" (Latin Players—Vitamins) to his patient, Walt Alston. "What you need, Mr. Alston, is this type of vitamin to have first-class strength and energy." "Do I take it or leave it?" queried Alston. "If the attraction makes the audience," replied the doctor, "and the audience is a large percentage Latino, the attraction must have to be precisely Latino!"[108]

Despite *La Opinión*'s admonitions, however, the Dodgers remained overwhelmingly popular within the barrios of Los Angeles—so popular, in fact, that radio broadcasters in Los Angeles, at least those willing to broadcast in Spanish, discovered a healthy market for play-by-play coverage of Dodgers games. Rene Cardenas, a sports announcer in his native city of Managua, Nicaragua, came to Los Angeles in 1951 and immediately recognized the popularity of baseball within the Spanish-speaking community. When the Dodgers came to Los Angeles, Cardenas proposed a regular broadcast of Dodgers games in Spanish. Eager to tap into the Spanish-language market, William Beaton of KWKW radio acted upon Cardenas's proposal and sent the Nicaraguan Angeleno to Vero Beach, Florida, the site of the Dodgers' spring training, to try out the nation's first Spanish-language sports announcer. After a successful trial year, KWKW drafted Jaime Jarrin to join Cardenas in the broadcast booth. Jarrin, a native Ecuadorian, found immediate success as the voice of Dodgers *en español*. The success of the Jarrin-Cardenas team received an additional boost when the Federal Communications Commission permitted KWKW to increase its power to ten thousand watts, casting the popularity of the Dodgers well into the Spanish-speaking communities of Southern California, as well as into Mexico.[109]

Given the broad appeal of Dodgers games and Dodgers radio among diverse social groups, therefore, it is tempting to accept the proposition that the Dodgers arrived in Southern California's fragmented metropolis as "communal glue." But this proposition seems tenuous within a gendered framework, for in spite of Walter O'Malley's efforts to tailor his franchise to a burgeoning ideal of family entertainment, the game of baseball retained its historic affinity with men and masculinity. In whatever ways major-league baseball helped to solidify interracial alliances in Los Angeles, it did so around idealizations of male athleticism, competition, and camaraderie. Like all professional sports in contemporary society, baseball remains a fundamentally male endeavor and retains the capacity to incorporate men of diverse classes and cultural backgrounds within a broader culture of masculinity that excludes the contributions of women and persists within today's venues of professional sports. Whether within the cozy setting of Ebbets Field, the makeshift fields of East Los Angeles, or the ultramodern arena of Dodger Stadium, baseball showcased the athletic talents of men and provided a cultural arena for the celebration of masculinity.

Thus, even as the historic affinities between baseball and whiteness began to dissolve during the postwar period, the gendered connotations of the game retained their salience. When Jackie Robinson signed on with the Brooklyn Dodgers in 1946 amid great controversy, the color line in major-league baseball was broken, but the sport retained its association with men and masculinity. In the gendered context of sports, the inclusion of Robinson within the major leagues demonstrated how black men could model masculine identity alongside white men, and Robinson's iconic status as a symbol of black advancement in the United Stated hinged on the masculine qualities of athleticism and competition that he embodied. In this capacity, Robinson may reasonably be situated alongside Hazel Carby's "race men," whose successes in cultural endeavors such as sports, film, literature, and music have been lauded as the successes of an entire race. The problem with this tendency, from a black feminist perspective, is that racial consciousness, pride, and solidarity inspired by the talents of Jackie Robinson, W.E.B. DuBois, Miles Davis, and, in our age, Michael Jordan and Tiger Woods are rooted in an exclusive vision of black masculinity.[110]

Another way of looking at this historical problem is to suggest that the very act of building a ballpark at the city center with public and private monies reinforced the masculine underpinnings of civic culture in postwar Los Angeles. Even as the opening of the Music Center atop Bunker Hill proved that a woman, albeit a Chandler, could master the politics of culture in postwar Los Angeles, the city's gift of some 315 acres of public land to Walter O'Malley could be viewed as a kind of gender subsidy that appealed specifically to the cultural passions of men, not women. The beneficiaries of that transaction, after all, included not only male athletes and their predominantly male audiences, but also public and private corporations that sell male audiences to advertisers through broadcasting, as well as the advertisers and corporate executives who use sporting events to entertain political clients. Built at the literal and figurative center of civic culture in 1950s Los Angeles, Dodger Stadium, like most modern sports facilities, provided a "men's cultural center" that directed public and private investment and consumption toward largely male activities and, ultimately, buttressed male power and privilege.[111]

GOODBYE, "BUMS"

Despite the earnest exhortations of progress, competition, and civic pride that accompanied the campaign to place the Dodgers in the Chavez Ravine, that development encompassed a set of ironies too rich to ignore. That Dodger Stadium leveled the remnants of a tightly knit community to proffer its brand of "communal glue" illuminates the conflicting notions of community that accompanied the rise of Southern California's postwar urban region. That city hall reneged on its promise to subsidize public housing in order to subsidize Walter O'Malley's bid for the Chavez Ravine marked the beginning of the end for Southern California's New Deal moment. That Dodger Stadium, designed according to the principles of freeway construction, provided an "ultramodern" setting in which to showcase a sport that maintained historic affinities with an agrarian, rural past illuminates the reconciliation of tradition with modernity that surfaced elsewhere in places such as Disneyland. And that it incorporated Southern California's diverse racial groups into its fold—as players and spectators—even as its placement in the Chavez Ravine pitted those groups against each other illustrates the social antinomies that descended upon the region in the age of white flight.

A penchant for irony, however, should not obscure our comprehension of the real social tensions that accompanied this particular episode in the cultural history of postwar Los Angeles. Like the Martians who razed downtown Los Angeles in *War of the Worlds*, the bulldozers of first the CHA and then the county sheriff's department eviscerated a community that had managed to occupy the Chavez Ravine since the late nineteenth century. That community became implicated in a noir vision of Los Angeles at midcentury, which Dodger Stadium helped to eradicate by imposing the very spatial order that defined Southern California's new suburban culture. Much like the movie moguls who killed, or "screened out," the "slum tradition" in movies during the 1920s, Walter O'Malley and the Dodgers left behind a decaying community afflicted with white flight, depriving Brooklyn residents of their own "communal glue," and relocated to the West Coast to kill a lingering vestige of noir Los Angeles. And if the grand movie palace managed to wean a heterogeneous audience from the nickelodeon and its immigrant, working-class context, and to resituate that audience within a broader venue that reflected a prevalent notion of "respectable," middle-class entertainment, Dodger Stadium upheld a similar function, offering a monumental, family-friendly, and well-insulated environment that suited the classless fantasies of a suburban public fleeing Ebbets Field and its slumlike setting.

The postwar makeover of the national pastime in Los Angeles enforced the larger metamorphosis of Southern California's political culture. While film noir heightened the imperatives to suburbanization and urban renewal by emphasizing the blackness of the urban core, and while Disneyland upheld an idealization of suburban community that guided a burgeoning politics of white home ownership, the construction of Dodger Stadium facilitated the "whitening" of the city center by fueling a racialized political culture predicated upon a privatized, corporate version of downtown redevelopment. The upheavals that rocked city hall in the early 1950s resulted not only in the defeat of public housing, but also in public subsidies for private developers such as Walter O'Malley, who ushered the national pastime into its corporate era. Built upon a site originally designated for public housing, Dodger Stadium was both the product and producer of a shifting political culture that negated social programs such as public housing, favored public subsidies for private development, and heightened simmering racial tensions.

Perhaps a final irony to savor is that the name of O'Malley's team made very little sense in Southern California's freeway metropolis, where there were no speeding trolley cars that players had to "dodge" on their way to play ball. By the time of the Dodgers' arrival in Los Angeles, the streetcars were quickly becoming a relic of Southern California's noir past: a rumbling anachronism abandoned by a newly affluent and highly mobile public who sped along a newfangled network of freeways in pursuit of the suburban good life. Moving his team to Los Angeles and building his stadium at the convergence of an expanding regional network of freeways, O'Malley made sure that his team would not share the same fate as the streetcar, even if that meant sacrificing the relevance of his team's name. Not unlike the passage from Ebbets Field to Dodger Stadium, the postwar displacement of the streetcar by the freeway and the automobile inculcated a more expansive notion of a regional metropolis in a burgeoning white suburban consciousness and modeled the shifting paradigms of popular culture in the age of white flight.

6 The Sutured City

*Tales of Progress and Disaster
in the Freeway Metropolis*

In its mile-long narrative of Los Angeles history, Judith Baca's *Great Wall* renders its surreal depiction of Dodger Stadium alongside a similar image of destruction in postwar Southern California. In the section of the mural titled *Division of the Barrios* (see the cover of this book), a Chicano family is divided—mother and son on one side, father and daughter on the other. A writhing freeway enforces their separation, imposing a wide gulf between the family and crashing down on their barrio community. Not unlike its depiction of Dodger Stadium as an alien invader, Baca's mural presents an ominous vision of the Los Angeles freeway, conveying its constriction of family and community and its destructive impact on postwar Southern California's increasingly fragmented landscape.

Great Wall presents the history of highway construction in postwar Los Angeles from the perspective of the "slum," which became a target for California's corps of highway planners who built freeways in coordination with urban renewal programs. This perspective, however, clashed with a buoyant vision of Southern California's suburban good life, which upheld the freeway as a symbol of such middle-class ideals as physical mobility, individual freedom, and civic progress. To highlight the competing discourses surrounding an intense phase of highway construction, yet another facet of postwar urbanization alongside suburbanization and urban renewal, this chapter surveys the cultural responses to the implementation of a unified network of freeways in Los Angeles. The backdrop for this focus is the demise of the streetcar, which marked yet another passage from the public life of the industrial, centralized city to the privatized public experience of the postwar urban region.

The Los Angeles freeway accommodated the dawning political culture that found its mythic expressions in film, Disneyland, and Dodger Stadium.

Its insulated environment suited the growing mistrust of public life that permeated Southern California's suburban communities, and its removal from the social landscape of the city furthered a diminishing awareness of the city's social and economic diversity. Its expansive sprawl across the urban region, moreover, fed an insatiable appetite for growth and reinforced the accelerated patterns of private development in Southern California. In the interests of auto manufacturers, oil producers, and land developers, the freeway's displacement of the streetcar encouraged the public's addiction to cars and gasoline and heightened the centrality of these commodities within the region's expanding consumer economy. Its imposition on Southern California's aging inner-city communities, moreover, further excised the remaining vestiges of the noir city, and, in spite of its potential to suture the disparate communities of an increasingly fragmented metropolis, the freeway's destruction of communities such as Boyle Heights accelerated the racialization of the regional political culture.

Incorporating the disciplined spatial culture of Disneyland and Dodger Stadium into its own design, and presenting an edited view of the metropolis not unlike the narrative structures of film, the freeway channeled its "audience" along a concrete continuum that imposed a singular perception of the city and limited the possibilities for different perspectives. In the rush between on-ramps and off-ramps, the city's different neighborhoods blurred and the driver's experience of the city narrowed to those sites designated by an authoritative set of green-and-white signs. Highway construction implemented a new efficiency in the movement through urban space and processed the smooth flow of traffic across the city's variegated social landscape. Gliding over or sunken below the surface of the urban landscape, the freeway mediated a new view of the metropolis, one that suited the very kind of suburban idealizations that surfaced in places like Disneyland and Dodger Stadium.

WHEELED SLUMS

Although the rise of metropolitan Los Angeles coincided with the mass adoption of the automobile, the city's growth at the turn of the century did not depend on the automobile. Certainly the automobile had a profound impact on the pattern of urban development in twentieth-century Southern California, but that pattern had already been delineated by a previous mode of mass transportation. Between 1880 and 1930, most Angelenos depended on the Red Cars: the interurban system of streetcars that radiated outward from downtown Los Angeles, eventually extending west to Santa Monica, east to Riverside, and south to Long Beach. The mass adoption of the auto-mobile and the construction of the freeway system brought Southern California's age of the streetcar to an end. Before the freeway, however, the Red Cars offered Angelenos a semblance of the kind of public world that defined urban life in the United States before World War II.

The history of the interurban lines in Southern California at the turn of the century is, in its basic outline, quite familiar. The 1870s saw the initial development of streetcar lines in Los Angeles, which were propelled by horses, mules, cables, and, beginning in 1887, electricity. In 1895, Moses Sherman and Elihu Clark built the first interurban streetcar line in South-ern California, which ran from Pasadena to downtown Los Angeles, contin-uing west to Santa Monica. From this initial framework of interurban ser-vice, various streetcar lines began to serve neighboring cities. The key figure in this activity was Henry Huntington, who purchased Sherman and Clark's interurban line and opened a consolidated Pacific Electric (PE) Railway in 1901. The fifty-foot-long Red Cars were made of wood and steel, and painted crimson with gold letters and trim. Huntington also operated the Los Angeles Railway Company, the Yellow Cars, which served the central business district. At the company's peak, the PE Big Red Cars ran in trains traveling up to fifty miles per hour on eleven hundred miles of track. In 1910, Huntington sold his interest in the PE to the Southern Pacific Railroad and devoted himself to his art and book collections at his San Marino estate.[1]

The streetcar established the initial patterns of decentralized develop-ment in Southern California. Huntington, inheriting the entrepreneurial skills of his uncle, did not expect to profit by providing streetcar service to Southern California. Rather, his investment in the interurban system en-sured massive returns on his real estate investments. After purchasing large tracts of rural land, Huntington would build railway lines to connect his landholdings with downtown Los Angeles. Despite the losses Huntington incurred from his interurban and streetcar empire, the magnate made mil-lions by coordinating land development with the expansion of the interur-ban system. New communities sprouted beyond the parameters of the central business district, wherever Huntington was able to extend his inter-urban system. The sprawling tracks of the rail lines discouraged settlement within the city center, as the interurban allowed Southern California's new-comers to reside in far-flung communities such as Long Beach, Watts, Venice, Santa Monica, Hollywood, and Glendale.[2]

Huntington could profit from this activity only insofar as people were willing to live in newly developed communities on the periphery of the city center, and indeed they were. The construction of the interurban lines suited a growing demand for decentralized urbanization in Southern California at the turn of the century. The suburban ideal touted by Progressive reformers such as Dana Bartlett materialized in the region through the combination of geography, technology, and rising affluence among a growing consumer population. The streetcars played a pivotal role in the democratization of Southern California's suburban good life, as it sanctioned the dispersal of affordable housing. The interdependence of streetcar expansion and land development in Southern California allowed a vast influx of newcomers to combine the opportunities of urban life with a small-town sense of space and community.[3]

The sprawling streetcar lines also afforded access to employment opportunities among newcomers to Los Angeles. Mexican immigrants to Los Angeles, for example, depended on the streetcar to secure employment within the regional economy, even as greater numbers of Anglo Americans became wedded to the automobile. For newcomers already familiar with railroad travel in their journey north from Mexico, the commuter lines of Los Angeles put more control and accessibility in their hands, enabling them to pursue various work opportunities. Mexican farmworkers living within proximity of downtown, for example, could seek employment in agricultural fields far removed from the city center: east to the orange groves of Riverside and Redlands, west to the celery fields of Culver City, and south to the vegetable farms of the South Bay area. The combination of an extensive transportation network and a diverse regional economy made Los Angeles an attractive setting for Mexican newcomers in search of employment.[4]

The interurban lines also sustained leisure pursuits among working-class families. Early brochures for the interurban lines stressed how workers and their families could visit the region's attractions by streetcar. With links to Venice, Santa Monica, and Huntington Beach, the streetcar promoted the early development of the coastline in Southern California. The showpiece of the interurban system, for example, was the Balloon Route, so called because it followed a balloon-shaped circuit from downtown to the beach towns, then back again. In the teens, real estate developers circulated a colorful brochure for the Balloon Route, which advertised the beachside attractions for working-class families. The brochure described Venice as "the Coney Island of the West," Redondo Beach as the "happy medium for the masses and attractions," and Huntington Beach as the "rendez-vous for little families."[5]

The interurban system connected the disparate points of residence, work, and leisure, allowing Southern Californians to pursue the advantages of decentralized urbanization. People living in Watts, for example, were not confined to the boundaries of their neighborhood, but rather enjoyed access to more distant communities within the larger urban region. The musician Cecil "Big Jay" McNeely, who played saxophone in the bustling nightclubs of Central Avenue during the 1930s, recalled, "[We] had the 'big red' that would go out to Pasadena, big red to San Pedro, big red to Long Beach. They ran fast, so it didn't take you any time to get there."[6] Others rode the Red Cars downtown to explore its burgeoning nightlife. Mary Hernandez, who used the Red Cars in her daily commute between her home in Watts and her job at the Firestone Tire Factory in Florence, recalled, "They used to have the Red Cars go through Watts and into downtown Los Angeles. So I would always catch a Red Car and we'd go to the dances there in Los Angeles."[7]

The residents of Watts during the 1920s and '30s enjoyed easy access to the disparate points of work and leisure within the larger urban region. Although Watts began as a small station on the Southern Pacific line, it became a full-fledged community with the arrival of the PE in 1902. The Watts Junction marked the point of intersection among the system's busiest lines: the Long Beach–Santa Ana, the San Pedro, and the Redondo lines, drawing a multiethnic population of settlers to the area. By 1910, Watts had 1,922 residents of varying racial and ethnic backgrounds, including Germans, Scots, Mexicans, Italians, Greeks, Jews, Japanese, and African Americans. The community enjoyed a high profile up to the Second World War, as PE riders from the 1920s to the 1950s passed through the area on their daily commutes. The demise of the PE, as we shall consider, had dire consequences for communities such as Watts and Boyle Heights, which became isolated centers of racialized poverty in the subsequent age of the freeway.[8]

Southern California's interurban lines sustained a semblance of the heterosocial world that bustled in the public spaces of cities such as New York and Chicago. The experience of riding the streetcar invariably exposed riders to the city's great diversity, as people from all walks of life depended on the streetcar as their primary mode of transportation. In many ways, the streetcar and subway lines of American cities at the turn of the century constituted a part of the new mass culture that first took shape in cities such as New York. Within the crowded spaces of streetcars, sidewalks, subways, amusement parks, and movie arcades, the old distinctions that defined one's position in Victorian society diminished, as diverse peoples incorporated themselves into the new urban mass.[9]

As we have seen in the case of amusement parks at the turn of the century, the new mass culture, though it won immediate popularity with ordinary Americans, also aroused the consternation of middle-class reformers, who expressed their dismay at the rapidly changing conditions of urban life.

Encounters among the sexes, races, and classes, which seemed ubiquitous in the modern city, offended a deep-seated sense of a "natural" social order, which mandated the separation of such groups. Progressive reformers directed much of their efforts to combating the social dislocations wrought upon the new urban masses. "Experts" of various sorts, expounding the latest theories of social hygiene and racial purity, joined the Progressive campaign to "clean up" American cities, warning against what they believed to be promiscuous social interaction in the spaces of city life.[10]

In Los Angeles, Progressive reformers targeted the social spaces in which strangers crowded together, which seemed unbearably similar to patterns of daily life in cities such as New York and Chicago. In particular, the streetcar defied the Progressives' moral code, which maintained some adherence to Victorian notions of propriety and respectability. The *Los Angeles Record,* which voiced Progressive concerns, described the streetcar as "A Section of Hades in Los Angeles":

> Inside the air was a pestilence; it was heavy with disease and the ema-
> nations from many bodies. Anyone leaving this working mass, anyone
> coming into it . . . forced the people into still closer, still more indecent,
> still more immoral contact. A bishop embraced a stout grandmother,
> a tender girl touched limbs with a city sport, refined women's faces
> burned with shame and indignation—but there was no relief. Was
> all this an oriental prison? Was it in some hall devoted to the pleasures
> of the habitués of vice? Was it a place of punishment for the wicked?
> No gentle reader, it was only the result of public stupidity and apathy.
> It was in a Los Angeles streetcar on the 9th day of December, in the year
> of grace 1912.[11]

Although the streetcar promoted the suburban vision embraced by Progressive reformers, its crowded spaces undermined their quest for a new kind of urban life, one that offered a more salubrious alternative to the crowds and congestion of eastern cities. While Progressive reformers touted the healthful benefits of suburbs and sunshine, their suspicion mounted against the institutions of the new mass culture, including the streetcar, which sanctioned the kind of social mixing that conflicted with their ideals of suburban domesticity.

Social intermixing, however, did not always corrupt the innocent. Occasionally, the public spaces of the metropolis sustained spontaneous occurrences that imparted to strangers a fleeting sensation of their collective humanity. The passengers of a streetcar, for example, easily supplied an instant audience for the varied talents of the city's corps of artists and musicians. On board the interurban lines, one could sometimes hear the sounds of

Central Avenue. Red Callendar recalls hearing a jam session on the way downtown. As young men, Buddy Colette and Charles Mingus "used to ride the old Red Car together, the local streetcar from Watts into Los Angeles. Mingus would always take the cover off his bass and urge Buddy to jam with him during the ride. Instead of being bothered, the passengers loved it."[12]

Such instances of social harmony, however, diminished as Los Angeles approached the war years. In times of heightened social tension, contact sometimes bred conflict, or even violence, among competing social groups. In the early 1940s, when racial tensions ran high in almost every major American city, the streetcars of Los Angeles occasionally became venues for racial confrontations. After his stay in Los Angeles during the early '40s, Chester Himes wrote about the perils of public space for people of color. "I'll give you an illustration, and it wasn't in a bar," wrote Himes, who told of three white sailors who harassed a dark-skinned Mexican couple aboard a Red Car from Watts. The sailors, who boasted loudly "of how they whipped the Japs" in one of the Pacific skirmishes, began to flatter the "native gal" while provoking her boyfriend to a fight. Himes pointed out the futility of the situation for the boyfriend: "Should he go back and hit them [the sailors] in the mouth? The best he could expect . . . would be a whipping by the gang of servicemen, a whipping by the Los Angeles police, and then a charge in the courts of inciting a riot."[13]

Himes wrote this story in the aftermath of the Zoot Suit Riots, in which white sailors attacked Chicano youths whose clothing resembled the style of the zoot suit, popular among young, urban Chicanos and blacks in the early '40s. On the evening of June 3, 1943, as sailors patrolled the streets of downtown in "taxicab brigades," stopping to assault the conspicuous zoot suiters on the sidewalk, others ransacked a streetcar, attacking Mexican and black youths inside the car, while a crowd surrounding the trolley cheered the sailors on. The historian Robin Kelley notes how the design of streetcars and buses rendered them unique sites of contestation among African Americans who challenged segregation on board the vehicles of public transportation. By the same token, however, the anonymous, undisciplined spaces of public transportation also sanctioned brutal acts of racial violence, which served the tacit function of maintaining the racial status quo.[14]

Although we can easily mourn the loss of public space in contemporary urban life, such incidents and stories from the past serve to remind us that the public spaces of the industrial city harbored peril as well as pleasure. The streetcars, while providing a venue for social contact, sometimes became a stage for confrontation, which occasionally led to brutal acts of violence. As an institution of the modern industrial city, the streetcars bred awareness of the heterosociality of Southern California's public life. Such awareness could lead to tolerance and sensitivity, but also to suspicion and hostility. Whatever consequences followed social interaction in the public spaces of the city, such interactions could occur only as long as the city sustained its public realm.

Beginning in the late '20s, however, the gradual demise of the streetcar deprived Southern California of a vital social arena in which diverse peoples encountered one another. A combination of factors led to the streetcar's disappearance, including, if not especially, the mass adoption of the automobile. Southern California's love affair with the automobile commenced immediately. As early as 1915, when Los Angeles County had only 750,000 inhabitants, its 55,217 private cars made it the nation's leading county in automobile ownership. Three years later, vehicle registration in the county had risen to more than 441,000. Auto registration continued to skyrocket in the following decade, averaging 45,000 new vehicles per year in Los Angeles County.[15] Clearly the automobile allowed greater numbers of people to settle beyond the immediate proximity of the streetcar lines, enabling even broader access to suburban living than the streetcars afforded.

The broad appeal of car ownership complemented the active efforts of downtown business interests to replace public systems of transportation with the private automobile. The role of the *Los Angeles Times* in hastening the demise of the Los Angeles streetcar, as Robert Gottlieb and Irene Wolt demonstrate, should not be underestimated. As publisher and owner of the *Times,* Harry Chandler maintained early ties to the automobile industry, holding major investments in the Goodyear Tire and Rubber Company, the Western Construction Company, the Southern California Rock and Gravel Company, Union Oil, and the Consolidated Rock Products Company. By the early 1920s, the Chandler family had an economic interest in almost every aspect of automobile production.[16] The *Times* sought to generate public support for the automobile as the primary mode of transportation in Southern California. Beginning in 1920, the newspaper featured a new section of its Sunday edition, "The Pink Sheet," devoted exclusively to automobile news. While touting the importance of the automobile to Southern California's future, the *Times* also campaigned against the streetcar. In 1920, for example, as the automobile competed with the streetcar for space on the streets of downtown Los Angeles, city officials attempted to control congestion by enforcing a parking ban on weekdays. The *Times* vigorously denounced the ordinance, insisting that the rights of motorists take precedence over the streetcar's right of way. "Motor cars are essential," a *Times* headline declared; "Two weeks of no parking proves that business can't do without them." The *Times* argued that the city council's action "deprived motorists of the rights of citizens and taxpayers."[17]

The *Times* also championed the rights of motorists by crafting policy recommendations to make the automobile the primary means of transportation in Southern California. Chandler organized the Major Highways Committee (MHC), which became a subcommittee of the Traffic Commission of the City of Los Angeles. The MHC, controlled by Chandler and his associates, commissioned Frederic Law Olmsted Jr. to assess the traffic needs of the city. Olmsted summarized his findings in a 1924 report, *A Major Traffic Street Plan for Los Angeles,* which emphasized the removal of obstacles to the free flow of traffic in the region and suggested the use of grade separations to eliminate intersecting traffic. The *Major Traffic Street Plan* rested on the assumption that the automobile would become the dominant mode of transportation in Southern California and marked the first conception of a unified system of freeways in the region. The *Times* celebrated the findings of the plan. "The completion of this great street plan," the paper quoted one realtor, "will . . . draw people from all over the world at an even greater rate than in the past [and] you can readily understand what this constant influx of people must mean to the value of our real estate holdings."[18]

While the *Times* advocated municipal support for the construction of roads and highways in Los Angeles, it denounced proposals for subsidizing streetcar maintenance. As socialist and Progressive reformers lobbied to municipalize the interurban system during the 1920s, the *Times* mounted its attack. In 1920, the paper denounced a Progressive-backed initiative that called for public ownership of lines between Pasadena and Los Angeles. Foreshadowing its late 1940s criticism of public housing as "socialistic," the *Los Angeles Times* red-baited the initiative, proclaiming the "faddists are rebuked" when voters rejected the proposal at the polls amid the antiradical upsurge after World War I. Although the Progressives succeeded in establishing regulatory agencies to police corporate control of the streetcar lines and other public services, they were unable to enlist government support to maintain the adequacy of interurban service in Southern California.[19]

Well into a period of decline by the late '20s, the streetcar could not survive the Great Depression. Three years into the Depression, the rate of return for the PE fell from 2.3 to −0.2 percent, and for the Los Angeles Railway from 4.7 to 2.1 percent. By 1934, the former company's overall patronage had dropped by one-third from its 1929 figure of 107 million. Given the declining patronage, railway and interurban operators had less incentive to maintain the streetcar lines, further retarding the city's public transit system.[20] By 1941, a Works Progress Administration (WPA) guide to Los Angeles noted the decrepit state of public transit in Southern California: "Cumbersome, old-fashioned trolleys still rattle through the streets. The interurban service is incredibly slow and antiquated. Travel on public conveyances is often a distinct inconvenience because of long waits and overcrowding." One public official implicated the Los Angeles streetcars in the slum tradition that increasingly defined the streetcars' generation of cultural institutions, calling the PE "wheeled slums."[21]

By the late '40s, the streetcar was rapidly fading from the landscape of the city as many lines had been eliminated, forcing passengers to extend their commute by several hours or leaving them without transportation altogether. One regular patron of the Los Angeles streetcar described the decrepit condition of service: "People are jammed and packed into [the streetcars], there is little standing room, the exits are hard to get to and there are many people who therefore cannot reach the exit and are carried far beyond the stops where they want to get off." Some patrons collectively voiced their grievance against the demise of the streetcar. On October 7, 1947, citizens of South Central Los Angeles organized to protest the deterioration of streetcar service under the ownership of Los Angeles Transit Lines (LATL). The same day, the *Herald Examiner* reported on the "People's Revolt at Rotten Service," when LATL terminated its F line, which ran through South Central's commercial corridor. The F line was one of eight transit lines eliminated by LATL that year. Local businessmen presented councilman Kenneth Hahn, who represented South Central's Eighth District, with a petition of five thousand signatures, requesting that F line service be resumed. In a statement before the city council, Daniel Joseph Reagan, who owned a business at the corner of Hoover and Slauson Avenues, denounced the LATL. "The people along Hoover were classed as Reds because they had the audacity to protest . . . the L.A.T.L.," Reagan said. "We'll admit . . . we are red-blooded Americans and when we are shoved around by a Chicago outfit such as the L.A.T.L. we will protest and we will fight to get the service we are entitled to."[22]

The dramatic shift in the experience of moving through Los Angeles—from the heterosocial spaces of the streetcars to the insular, privatized cell of the automobile—was thus not inevitable. That transition resulted from a struggle among the region's most powerful interest groups to foster growth vis-à-vis the automobile, which was viewed as more conducive to regional development. The *Times* and its allies were clearly not alone in their conviction that the automobile was a more convenient and reliable form of urban transportation, as the public at large fell in love with the automobile

FIGURE 13. Streetcar junkyard: Los Angeles, 1956.
(Courtesy of the Department of Special Collections,
Charles E. Young Research Library, UCLA.)

immediately. The demise of public transit in Southern California, however, which had dire consequences for thousands of Angelenos, rested on the efforts of a public-private alliance dedicated to regional growth. Ultimately, the freeways symbolized the realization of a master plan for growth and development, celebrated as "progress" among Southern California's freeway planners, government officials, and private interests.

THE AGE OF THE FREEWAY

Although the age of freeway construction in Los Angeles did not begin until the early '40s, the previous decade had marked an era of intense planning for that undertaking. The 1930s saw an outpouring of reports and studies that confirmed the findings of the 1924 *Major Traffic Street Plan*. Southern California's business establishment championed the cause of freeways during the 1920s, and the federal government aided those efforts in the 1930s.

During the Great Depression, the federal government became a key advocate for highway construction and extended its highway building activities
into the nation's urban areas. Highway construction, New Deal officials
reasoned, could provide steady employment for thousands of workers in
American cities. Just when a federal blueprint for postwar suburbanization
was taking shape through the work of the Home Owners' Loan Corporation
(HOLC) and the Federal Housing Administration (FHA), a blueprint that
negated the heterosocial world of the public city, the federal government
forged a similar set of plans for highway construction, which furthered the
transition from the public life of the modern city to the private realms of the
postwar urban region.

In Los Angeles, certain individuals advocated joint efforts on the part of
public and private interests to construct a regional highway network in
Southern California. Lloyd Aldrich, the leading advocate for a freeway system for Los Angeles, provided an important nexus between private interests
and public monies in his effort to realize that system. Aldrich was appointed
city engineer of Los Angeles in 1933 and enlisted the support of P.J. Winant,
the president of Bullock's department store, who raised one hundred thousand dollars from the downtown business community to commission a
study of traffic needs in Los Angeles. These monies, coupled with funds from
the WPA, enabled Aldrich to establish the Citizen's Transportation Survey
Committee, which issued several reports articulating the need for freeways
in Southern California. These reports, including *A Transit Program for the
Los Angeles Metropolitan Region*, became the most influential studies leading to the establishment of a freeway system in Los Angeles.[23]

While most of these reports focused on the construction of individual
freeways, the 1937 *Traffic Survey*, issued by the Automobile Club of Southern California, marked the first proposal for a comprehensive freeway system. The survey recognized the patterns of movement that had already been
established by previous transportation systems, and suggested a radial pattern of freeways that followed the expanse of the interurban lines. A key
assumption underlying the *Traffic Survey* was the unquestioned acceptance
of the automobile as the primary mode of transportation in Southern
California. The report's conclusions echoed the assumption of the city's
business establishment that future growth in the Los Angeles urban region
depended on the unrestricted flow of automobile traffic. While the nation's
most extensive railway transit system crumbled, the authors of the *Traffic
Survey* lobbied for freeways based on their conviction that Los Angeles
lacked a regional system of mass transit: "The destiny of the Los Angeles
area has ceased to be a matter of speculation. It is now conceded by all who

watched its growth that it will become one of the largest population centers of the world. Future orderly growth is vitally dependent upon the establishment of a system of transportation lines serving all parts of the area."[24]

The social and political ramifications of urban highway construction in Southern California, particularly in inner-city neighborhoods, would not surface until the 1960s, when working-class Angelenos, blacks and Latinos in particular, targeted the disruptive effects of freeway construction in their protest against the conditions of inner-city life in Los Angeles. In the meantime, city planners and state engineers conducted their research, collecting "data" with which they could justify freeway construction as a rational necessity. The professionals who advocated freeway construction imbued their reports and studies with an aura of science and objectivity. They conducted numerous surveys of traffic flow in Southern California and recorded their findings in a voluminous array of graphs, flow charts, and tables. Their data became the raw reality, which, in the opinion of the regional planning community, mandated a total commitment to highway construction in Southern California. In emphasizing the priority of the data, planners were able to sidestep the political implications of their work and downplay their active role in the shaping of public policy.

Despite their insistence on scientific objectivity, planners invoked a popular consensus to advocate freeway construction in Los Angeles. A 1943 report from the County Regional Planning Commission, titled *Freeways for the Region*, began with the assertion, "ALL motorists in Southern California, and this means all of us, have for many years felt the need for some superior form of motorways in this region."[25] The assumption of consensus was reiterated throughout the 1950s and 1960s, when widespread freeway construction was under way. As David Brodsly points out, planners interpreted traffic, and especially traffic congestion, as a consensual demand for freeways. After surveying traffic congestion on a recently completed section of the Harbor Freeway in 1953, one highway official commended local planning agencies for their "wisdom . . . in anticipating a complete network of freeways to adequately serve the tremendous desire for motor vehicle travel in the Los Angeles metropolitan area."[26]

World War II marked a turning point in the history of highway construction in Southern California. Although freeway construction did not accelerate dramatically during the early '40s, economic and demographic expansion in Southern California heightened the demand for better highways. Los Angeles experienced a critical highway shortage, exacerbated by wartime migration, wartime restrictions on construction, a reduction of gas tax revenues due to fuel rationing, and roadway damage caused by heavy military vehicles. Local governments and special interest groups pressured the state to expand its highway building activities. The state legislature responded to such demands by forming the Joint Fact Finding Committee on Highways, Streets and Bridges, headed by senator Randolph Collier.

After three years of intensive study, the committee drafted the Collier Burns Highway Act, passed by the state legislature in 1947. Designed to amass new revenues for extensive highway construction, the Collier Burns Highway Act established a special highway tax fund from an increase in the state gas tax and various other highway-related taxes. The Act especially favored the construction of freeways within the state's metropolitan areas, as the legislature approved a higher tax increase than that proposed by many legislators, specifically to finance the construction of urban freeways. Los Angeles County stood to gain the most under the new Act, as the legislature also reshuffled the state funding ratio to apportion to Southern California, especially Los Angeles County, a larger piece of the pie. Collier himself defended this allotment by saying, "Some people don't seem to get the point . . . that one county in California produced 48 percent of the highway taxes in the state. That is Los Angeles county . . . they haven't been getting much back, so they are entitled to a great deal of consideration."[27]

The Collier Burns Highway Act prompted a massive surge in freeway construction in Los Angeles and inaugurated the city's age of the freeway. The Act initiated construction of most of the major freeways of the city's freeway system. Between the years of 1950 and 1955, total operating mileage of the Los Angeles freeway system increased four and a half times, as large segments of the San Bernardino, Hollywood, and Santa Monica Freeways opened. As freeway-to-freeway interchanges were completed, moreover, the skeletal framework of an integrated system of freeways began to take shape. The unprecedented four-level downtown interchange, celebrated in local and national media as "the Stack," was completed in 1954 with funding from the Collier Burns Act. By the late 1950s, images of the Stack even appeared on postcards, illustrating how Los Angeles' new freeway system became a familiar way of knowing the city in the popular imagination.[28] By financing the construction of freeways with taxes from gasoline consumption, the Collier Burns Act set in motion a self-generating mechanism by which automobile usage financed freeway construction and freeway construction encouraged the use of automobiles. Consumers were thus encouraged to buy automobiles and gasoline as a way of extending the freeway's reach across the state's expansive terrain. Under this scheme, alternatives to the automobile and the highway diminished.

At the same time many Angelenos protested the deterioration of streetcar service, others denounced the initial construction of freeways, auguring the outrage against freeway construction that erupted in the following decade. Weeks after the citizens of South Central staged a protest before the city council against the dismantling of the F line, the residents of that community gathered once again, this time before the State Highway Commission, to protest the proposed route of the Harbor Freeway, scheduled to extend south from downtown between Broadway and Figueroa avenues. Based on estimates that the proposed freeway would destroy between fifteen thousand and twenty thousand homes, local leaders from South Central's communities urged a rerouting of the Harbor Freeway. Significantly, city councilman Kenneth Hahn and his brother, assemblyman Gordon Hahn, who led the campaign against the proposed routing of the Harbor Freeway, also demanded the accommodation of a rapid transit line down the middle of the freeway. Highway officials responded to such protests by stating that Southern Californians "will just have to make up their minds that . . . freeways will help some property owners, hurt others and remove a lot of residents from their present homes."[29] With that, the Division of Highways proceeded with its original plan for the construction of the Harbor Freeway.

By the early '50s, the Division of Highways had become the principal force behind the construction of a unified freeway system in Los Angeles. That undertaking, which marked the largest public works project in the history of Los Angeles, lacked a single leading official with whom citizens could identify the freeway-building program. Postwar Los Angeles did not have its Baron Haussmann or Robert Moses, a Promethean figure that the public could either venerate as a hero of progress or despise as an executioner of urban communities. Instead, the Division of Highways became the "workhorse of the freeway planning team" by the mid-1940s. Its "highly trained professional planners, engineers, traffic and right of way experts, . . . whose only objective is the greatest public benefit," constituted the faceless bureaucracy that undertook the monumental task of implementing a regional network of freeways.[30]

The Division of Highways assumed the responsibility of justifying its disruptive impact on the fabric of neighborhood life in Los Angeles. It did so by invoking a familiar conception of "progress," which echoed a long-standing American faith in the promise of technological modernity. After clearing fifteen hundred homes for the Harbor Freeway south of Exposition Boulevard, the Division of Highways paused to assert its conviction that the displaced residents of South Central Los Angeles had willingly sacrificed their homes for "progress":

The freeway location is through an area of older houses that some of the occupants have owned for thirty years or more. Some of the occupants are older people who expected to live in their homes for the rest of their lives. It would be assumed, in approaching the owners of this type, that one would meet with tears, hesitation and reluctance and perhaps outright defiance when asked to move. This is not the case. The older folks seem to have resigned themselves to the fact that they should not stand in the way of progress and gladly cooperate. This is the rule rather than the exception. We have met with wholehearted cooperation and support many times where least expected.[31]

Such invocations of progress regularly appeared in *California Highways and Public Works*, a bimonthly publication issued by the Division of Highways, which chronicled the construction of freeways in Los Angeles and elsewhere in California. The series was largely devoted to chronicling each step made toward the completion of a unified freeway system in Los Angeles. As a cultural text, however, the pages of *California Highways and Public Works* reveal some of the official meanings ascribed to the new freeways. Despite the state's adopted stance of the objective and impartial government agency, enforcing the will of the people, its publications divulged some of the underlying cultural assumptions and social values that guided the work of the Division of Highways.

The state occasionally paused to celebrate its accomplishments, elaborating on its conception of progress. For example, in 1950 *California Highways and Public Works* issued its centennial edition, which situated the new freeways within a larger regional history of conquest and settlement. First, the editors paid homage to the "immortal padres, intent on planting the cross of Christendom among the heathen children of the wilderness," and went on to commemorate "California's first pioneers: Junipero Serra, Gaspar de Portola, and Juan Bautista de Anza." Renderings of the conquistadors were placed alongside portraits of high-ranking bureaucrats within the Division of Highways, represented as latter-day incarnations of California's "founding fathers."[32]

The centennial edition highlighted other examples of "progress" in its romanticized pageant of California history. After honoring "the early explorers in the service of His Majesty," the editors paid tribute to the explorations of "the fur traders and mountain men, restless and adventurous," and revered the "white covered wagons . . . answering the call of 'gold!'" The freeways, according to the editors of the centennial edition, marked the culmination of a "history fascinating and dynamic, tinted with romance and stained with pathos; sprinkled with the names of the immortal pathfinders [who laid] the foundation for a new and mighty empire on the shores of the Pacific." In the midst of the largest phase of highway construction in California history, the Division of Highways paused to create a usable past for its efforts. That history echoed not only the national rhetoric of manifest destiny, but also the regional myth of the Spanish Fantasy Past, which imparted a romantic gloss to the history of conquest in California.[33]

The state also used a familiar racial trope to represent the new freeways as progress. The opening of the Arroyo Seco Freeway in 1940, winding between downtown Los Angeles and Pasadena, marked the completion of the first freeway in Los Angeles. Built with WPA funds, the Arroyo Seco inaugurated the age of the freeway in Southern California. At the public ceremony for the freeway's opening on January 11, 1941, which included the mayor of Los Angeles, the governor of California, and the reigning queen of Pasadena's Rose Parade, was a man identified by local newspapers as "Chief Tahachwee." The "chief" appeared in a costume that resembled not the modest and functional apparel of Southern California's indigenous populations, but rather the wildly elaborate costume of an Indian in a Hollywood western. As if the feathered bonnet and excessive jewelry were not enough to convey authentic "Indianness," a photograph in *California Highways and Public Works* shows the Indian seated "Indian style" with the state director of public works (see figure 14). Together, the Indian and the bureaucrat smoked a peace pipe before news reporters.[34]

Why state officials chose to include "Chief Tahachwee" at the opening ceremony of the Arroyo Seco remains an open question. Nonetheless, the history of public cultural practices such as parades, museums, and expositions illuminates a larger pattern of representing otherness in the American public sphere. In a racialized democracy such as the United States, racial signifiers have been used to convey certain cultural ideals, including, if not especially, progress. Given that the realization of manifest destiny demanded the conquest of native America, the bodies of Indian men and women have figured prominently in the collective imaginings of progress throughout U.S. history. To dramatize the distance between the white American present and the nonwhite primitive past, Indians in their native garb have been photographed and painted alongside railroads, steam engines, telegraph wires, and automobiles. By 1941, such stereotypical images of the White Man's Indian were all too familiar. Freeways constituted the next stage of American progress, which required its own racial signifier.[35]

An alternative explanation might emphasize recurring representations of "friendly" Indians in the national culture, which exonerated the Anglo American conquest of North America. The presence of a friendly chief, who

FIGURE 14.   State director of public works Frank W. Clark smoking a peace pipe with "Kawie Indian chiefs," 1941, from *California Highways and Public Works*. (Original date of publication 1941; courtesy of CalTrans Library.)

shared a peace pipe with the chief executive of the Division of Highways, may have signaled the final surrender of Native Americans to the encroachment of Anglo American civilization. Indeed, *California Highways and Public Works* declared, "to the beating of tribal drums, Chief Tahachwee relinquished the rights of his people in the Arroyo and formally transferred the property to the State."[36]

Friendly, savage, or both, the Indian's representation at the opening ceremony of the Arroyo Seco underscored the racial meanings with which the city's first freeway was invested. One might imagine that the freeway materialized the Anglo American worldview, which saw history as a highway—an unbroken path of linear progress toward a utopian future. This worldview clashed with that of native Americans, who viewed the cosmos as cyclical and lived according to a principle of regenerative growth. Ultimately, Indians succumbed not only to the degenerative forces of guns, disease, and alcohol, but also to a linear conception of progress in which history pushed relentlessly forward, often over the peoples who stood in its path. "Thrown onto the highway of history," Indians could not withstand the force of

Anglo American progress.[37] Long after the conquest of Native America, however, and amid the very real predicament of relocated Indians in 1950s Los Angeles, the Indian's representation could periodically surface to commemorate the completion of grand civic works, including the Los Angeles freeway.

Other prominent Southern Californians bolstered the official connotations of Los Angeles' new freeways as progress. Walt Disney, for example, who marketed his own brand of Indian representations, went to great lengths to celebrate the advent of freeways in Southern California. Disney not only shared the popular faith in unrestricted auto mobility, but he also realized that the freeway, the new Santa Ana Freeway in particular, which ran south from downtown Los Angeles to Anaheim and Orange County, was crucial to Disneyland's success. Following the advice of the Stanford Research Institute, Disney strategically situated his theme park alongside the proposed route of the Santa Ana Freeway and built a parking lot twice the size of the park—the largest in the nation in the mid-'50s. Disney may well have been among the first to realize the importance of freeways to commercial success in Southern California.[38]

So confident was he in the promise of Southern California's new freeway system, Disney enlisted the financial support of the Atlantic Richfield Corporation (ARCO) to build a miniature freeway system in Tomorrowland, that section of Disneyland representing a "preview world of the future." Autopia was the centerpiece of Tomorrowland, "a real model freeway, [with] cars [that] are gas-engine automobiles powered with New Richfield Ethyl." In the car-oriented culture of Southern California, Autopia, and its counterpart for smaller children, the Midget Autopia in Fantasyland, introduced young people to the "real thrill [of getting] behind the wheel of one of the brightly-colored cars." While Disney's suburban audiences were still unacquainted with the inconveniences of traffic jams and the horrors of freeway shootings, they readily accepted his representation of the new freeways as futuristic symbols of American progress and modernity.[39]

By situating the new freeway within his "family-oriented" theme park, moreover, Walt Disney also suggested that the freeway and the automobile were compatible with the postwar emphasis on the family and the restoration of traditional gender roles. As the cultural construction of suburban whiteness during the postwar period included a set of gendered connotations, the new freeways acquired a set of meanings tailored to the particular needs of mothers and wives. The Automobile Club of Southern California, for example, an institution that historically extolled the virtues of automobile ownership, developed a series of short films intended as public service announcements to help Southern Californians, at least those who owned cars, adjust to the new order of the freeway metropolis. One series of such films, titled *Women at the Wheel*, took aim at women drivers, relying on a set of stereotypical assumptions about feminine behavior. In one short film titled *The Driver*, a young woman gets behind the wheel of a car. Uncertain about what to do first, she coyly looks to the camera for advice. "Safety first," a man's voice advises, and the woman responds by fastening her seat belt. Next she is asked, "Now, how about your rear-view mirror?" She immediately adjusts the mirror to check her hair. "Not that way," the narrator's voice chuckles. "We certainly want you to look your best, but let's pay attention to business, hmmm?"[40]

In the noir films *Mildred Pierce* and *The Reckless Moment*, Joan Crawford and Joan Bennett drive cars to pursue their personal ambitions, signaling the kind of sexual transgressions that surfaced within the disordered universe of the "black" city. The cultural order of the freeway metropolis, by contrast, tolerated women drivers, but only for activities deemed appropriately "feminine." In a promotional film titled *The Freeway*, created by the California State Chamber of Commerce to highlight the benefits of the new freeways, men and women are depicted enjoying the new freeways, but for very different reasons. With the "freedom to drive away from the city to work," a narrator's voice claims, "Father can pursue new work opportunities within the freeway's reach." His wife, by contrast, enjoys another use of the new freeway. "California women, like women everywhere," the narrator explains, "are dedicated shoppers." In the streetcar metropolis, the downtown department store aroused what Emile Zola described as "the happiness of women," but in the postwar urban region, "when one of the girls mentions a cute little shop just twelve miles away—twelve freeway miles—it's hats off to new shopping adventures. Isn't it great knowing how much safer, faster, and more convenient it is when she makes that shopping trip by freeway?"[41]

While the California Chamber of Commerce emphasized how women drivers could pursue consumer pleasures by driving the freeway, other women used the freeway to escape the ennui that accompanied such affluence. Radically divorced from husband, lovers, friends, and even her own past and future, Maria Wyeth, the troubled protagonist of Joan Didion's 1970 novel *Play It as It Lays*, finds a meaning on the LA freeway that numbs the pain of her existential predicament: "In the first hot month of the summer Carter left her, Maria drove the freeway." In the depths of a nervous breakdown, Wyeth clings to the remnants of her sanity by navigating the LA freeway:

Once she was on the freeway and had maneuvered her way to a fast lane she turned on the radio at high volume and she drove. She drove the San Diego to the Harbor, the Harbor up to the Hollywood, the Hollywood to the Golden State, the Santa Monica, the Santa Ana, the Pasadena, the Ventura. She drove it as a riverman runs a river, every day more attuned to its currents, its deceptions, and just as a riverman feels the pull of the rapids in the lull between sleeping and waking, so Maria lay awake at night in the still of Beverly Hills and saw the great signs soar overhead at seventy miles an hour, Normandie 1/4 Vermont 3/4 Harbor Fwy 1. Again and again she retuned to an intricate stretch just south of the interchange where successful passage from the Hollywood onto the Harbor required a diagonal move across four lanes of traffic. On the afternoon she finally did it without once braking or losing the beat on the radio she was exhilarated, and that night she slept dreamlessly.[42]

Play It as It Lays offers a glimpse into the postwar relationship between the metropolis and mental life. In the decentralized urban region of postwar Los Angeles, increasingly embroidered by a sprawling network of freeways, Maria Wyeth turned to the city's most accessible spaces to find some relief from the boredom of her existence. Sometimes "she fixed her imagination on a needle dripping sodium pentathol into her arm," but "when that failed, she imagined herself driving . . . the Hollywood to the San Bernardino and straight on out, past Barstow . . . driving straight on into the hard white empty core of the world."[43] A washed-up actress, a divorcée, and the mother of a brain-damaged daughter, Maria Wyeth recovers on the freeway a sense of purpose—which the characters of Joan Bennett and Joan Crawford claimed behind the wheel in the noir city (and were punished for it) and, as Betty Friedan lamented in *The Feminine Mystique*, which gradually slipped away from suburban women in postwar America.

Didion's portrayal of the Los Angeles freeway surfaced just after the completion of a rudimentary network of freeways that provided the basis for the future construction of more freeways. Her perspective is not mediated by the male voice of narrator, a film studio, or an institution such as the California State Chamber of Commerce, and as such, it presents a glimpse into the capacity of women to claim an independent space within a structure founded on racial and sexual hierarchies. Thus, Didion's description of the freeway might be considered an alternative perspective, like that of Judith Baca, which posits how women could use the freeway in ways different from the intentions of its designers. This discrepancy—between use and intention—is important to understanding the ambiguous dynamics of popular culture in the age of white flight. Just as women like Didion's Maria

Wyeth defied official meanings assigned to the new freeways, Southern California's racial groups also imposed a set of counterdefinitions on the new freeways—not as icons of progress, but as emblems of destruction.

MAKING WAY FOR WHITENESS

The year following the opening of Disneyland marked another windfall for freeway construction in the Los Angeles urban region. In 1956, the federal government lent its support to the construction of freeways in Los Angeles and other metropolitan areas of the United States. That year, Congress approved the Interstate and Defense Highway Act, which authorized the building of forty-one thousand miles of interstate highways, about eight thousand of them in urban areas, all to be completed by 1972. The cost was estimated at twenty-seven billion dollars, 90 percent of which would be shouldered by the federal government and the rest by individual states. Like the Collier Burns Act, the Interstate and Defense Highway Act reinforced public dependency on the automobile, establishing a highway trust fund, sustained by new excise taxes on gasoline, diesel fuel, and tires, and by special taxes on trucks and buses.[44]

The Interstate and Defense Highway Act entailed profound consequences for the reorganization of public space in Los Angeles and other American cities during the postwar era. Urban planners throughout the nation, in accordance with private interests, looked to the federal Highway Act as a means of renewing the deteriorating condition of American inner cities. With little or no official interest in providing inner-city housing for those residents displaced by freeway construction, huge sections of central-city land could be cleared for other uses. Downtown business leaders and real estate developers, anxious about the effects of suburbanization on their domain, clamored for central-city redevelopment. The architect Victor Gruen, whose Los Angeles–based firm, Victor Gruen and Associates, designed several noted buildings of postwar Los Angeles, summarized those anxieties: "The rotting of the core has set in in most American cities, in some cases progressing to an alarming degree."[45]

The Interstate Highway Act of 1956 struck many of the nation's leading planners as an opportunity to remedy the deteriorating condition of America's inner cities. The Urban Land Institute (ULI), a national organization for real estate developers, entrepreneurs, and builders, advocated urban freeway construction as a means of slum clearance and urban renewal. James W. Rouse, a Baltimore real estate developer involved with the ULI during the 1950s and later famous for building the "festival marketplaces" that became the hallmark of gentrification during the 1980s, argued that "major expressways must be ripped through the central core" as part of urban renewal efforts. Similarly, writing for the ULI in 1957, James Scheuer praised the "inner belt expressways" that would "inevitably slice through great areas of our nation's worst slums." And in its monthly newsletter, the ULI in 1956 urged planners and developers of American cities to consider "the extent to which blighted areas may provide suitable highway routes."[46]

Despite the Division of Highways' insistence that it routed freeways according to the "most direct and practical location," the pattern of freeway construction in 1950s Los Angeles followed the recommendations of the ULI to coordinate highway construction with slum clearance.[47] The freeways encircling Los Angeles' central business district are linked by four major interchanges, each of which stands on what used to be residential areas once identified as "slums" by the HOLC. The East Los Angeles Interchange, for example, linking the Golden State, Pomona, and Santa Monica Freeways, completed in the early '60s, stands on a former neighborhood of Boyle Heights, redlined by the HOLC and identified as a "melting pot area" of Los Angeles, "honeycombed with diverse and subversive elements." Similarly, the intersection of the Harbor and Santa Monica Freeways, in the southwest corner of downtown Los Angeles, displaced a "thoroughly blighted" neighborhood with a 50 percent African American population plus Mexicans, Japanese, and Italians.[48]

Throughout the postwar period, many of Los Angeles' multicultural communities succumbed to freeway construction. Before construction of the downtown segment of the Santa Monica Freeway began in the early '60s, Mateo—named for the street that ran through the southeast corner of downtown Los Angeles—sustained a tightly knit community of Mexican and Italian immigrant workers who found work in nearby factories and struggled to make ends meet during the Depression. Cabrini Church, a small Roman Catholic parish operated by the Missionary Sisters of the Sacred Heart, met the spiritual needs of the neighborhood's Catholic flock. Church records stated that the church was for "Mexicans only and all Italians living in the so-called Cabrini District," who used the church not only for worship, but also for a variety of services and classes. A freeway pillar now marks the site where the Cabrini Church once stood. With the coming of the Santa Monica Freeway in the early '60s, many of Mateo's Mexican immigrant families moved to larger Chicano communities such as Boyle Heights, Lincoln Heights, and Pico Rivera.[49]

Freeway construction in Los Angeles enacted a pattern familiar in the changing social landscape of the postwar American city. The defeat of public housing in the early '50s allowed downtown developers to pursue slum clearance and urban renewal without housing provisions for the displaced; thus highways could aid the city's effort to destroy "blighted" communities. Given that federal agencies such as the HOLC identified social diversity as "blight," the city's most heterogeneous communities were among the first slated for freeway construction. The people of Boyle Heights, dislocated by freeway construction, like those of Bunker Hill and the Chavez Ravine who abandoned their communities under similar circumstances, did not reproduce their diverse communities elsewhere. Some found the means to move to the suburbs, while others, lacking similar opportunities, remained concentrated within communities that increasingly resembled ghettos and barrios. The freeways played an important role in that process, wreaking havoc on the city's heterosocial spaces and accelerating the trend to postwar agglomeration of racially segregated communities.

Not unlike the residents of the Chavez Ravine who protested their displacement for the construction of Dodger Stadium, the residents of Boyle Heights and its neighboring communities spoke out against the imposition of the freeway. Various community leaders, among them newspaper editors, state assemblymen, city councilmen, religious officials, and small businessmen, led the fight against the freeway. The public at large also mustered opposition to the freeway by circulating petitions, holding community meetings, and organizing public demonstrations. The fight against the freeway in East Los Angeles did not belong to one particular social group, but rather reflected the cooperation of a multicultural community, albeit one that was becoming less multicultural because of the freeway's intrusion. Not that all community members were united in that effort. Some abandoned their homes without resistance, while others moved on to better living conditions. Those who did fight the freeway, however, challenged the official conviction that a consensus mandated the construction of freeways. Their efforts demonstrate one community's attempt to safeguard its well-being in the tumultuous age of the freeway.

When the Division of Highways announced its intention to route the Golden State Freeway through a dense neighborhood along the east side of the Los Angeles River in 1953, the *Eastside Sun*, serving the communities of Boyle Heights, Hollenbeck Heights, and Belvedere, reported, "Eastside Up in Arms over Proposed $32,000,000 Golden State Freeway."[50] Residents of Boyle Heights had the opportunity to voice their concerns about the coming of the Golden State Freeway in a hearing before the Division of Highways, one of several sponsored by the agency as part of its public relations program. More disrupted by freeway construction than any other area of

Los Angeles, East Los Angeles hosted several such meetings during the 1950s—their proceedings absent from the pages of *California Highways and Public Works* and the *Los Angeles Times*, but reported vigilantly by local newspapers such as the *Eastside Sun* and the *Belvedere Citizen.*

In December 1953, representatives of various community organizations of Boyle Heights, including the Jewish Homes for the Aged, the Japanese Methodist Church, the First Street Merchants, and the Daughters of the American Revolution, confronted the Division of Highways to voice their protest against the proposed construction of the Golden State Freeway. Episcopal bishop Donald J. Campbell and Monsignor Thomas J. O'Dwyer, both prominent crusaders for public housing in the 1940s, emphasized to state highway officials the destructive impact the freeway would have on the social institutions of the community, pointing out the many schools, churches, hospitals, and convalescent homes that lay in the path of the proposed freeway route. Also present at the hearing, councilman Edward Roybal, whose ninth council district included Boyle Heights, registered his protest before the Division of Highways, emphasizing the unique diversity of this community: "There is a population density in this area unequaled in the Southland. Some 15 language groups and nearly as many races are represented in this community, which, despite its variety, has been inhabited by good citizens for the last fifty years."[51]

The proposed route for construction of the Golden State Freeway also incited the formation of the "Anti Golden State Freeway Committee," which concocted strategies to disrupt official efforts to expedite freeway construction in Boyle Heights and its vicinity. The committee warned the readers of the *Eastside Sun*, "Watch Out! The Appraisers Are Busy Appraising!"— alerting citizens to the "Gestapo methods" of the Division of Highways, which sent its legion of appraisers into the neighborhoods of East Los Angeles to survey property values in that area. According to the committee, such "high handed action" on the part of the Division of Highways induced a "highly nervous state" among the residents of the Eastside, who dreaded that unexpected knock on their doors. The committee advised the citizens of the Eastside, "Please call . . . AN-5606 if the appraisers are bothering you. We would like to have all information concerning their activities."[52]

Despite the determination of Eastside residents to fight the imposition of the Golden State Freeway on their community, construction began as scheduled in January 1957. Joseph Eli Kovner, the editor of the *Eastside Sun*, devoted much of his daily column that year to decrying the disruption unleashed on Boyle Heights by the Division of Highways. A Jew fighting on behalf of a diverse community with an emergent Chicano majority, Kovner symbolized a long-standing partnership between Jews and Chicanos that had existed in Boyle Heights since the 1920s, which solidified through the establishment of such institutions as the Community Service Organization. "The eradication, obliteration, razing, moving, demolishing of Eastside homes continues as the Golden State Freeway pursues its tortuous path from the San Bernardino Freeway to the Santa Ana Freeway," wrote Kovner, who extended his sympathies to his readers: "Believe me, it is heartbreaking to see such old landmarks disappear." The editor coupled his lament with the assertion that "there must be a limit to the right of eminent domain," asking, "How long must urban dwellers of Los Angeles be subjected to fear and relentless mental torture by the State Highway Commission and our Los Angeles City Council in its rapacious, unflagging zeal to build more and more freeways?"[53]

The citizens of East Los Angeles, along with people in other areas of the city who experienced similar dislocations, questioned the dominant discourse of progress that surfaced in public ceremonies, government publications, and popular theme parks. A cartoon in the pages of the *Eastside Sun* illustrated the suspicion of progress that mounted in communities such as Bunker Hill, Boyle Heights, and the Chavez Ravine (see figure 15). The cartoon depicted a hand holding an array of technological innovations, each connoting "progress" as it was imagined during the '50s: rockets, missiles, satellites, jet aircraft, television, computers, trains, oil derricks, factories, and other symbols of postwar technological optimism. In the center of the illustration, a freeway united the disparate symbols into a world of technological progress, not unlike that created by Walt Disney in his Tomorrowland section of Disneyland. The caption, however, undercut the cartoon's optimistic veneer: "Look at this wonderful future! Look at this thundering progress! But . . . ," it continued, "who's going to enjoy it? What has happened to our homes?" Such skepticism emphasized the dark side of progress that surfaced amid the protest against freeway construction during the 1950s. The citizens of East Los Angeles could not stop the imposition of the freeway on their world, but they could contest, subvert, and mock the values and meanings that undergirded its construction.[54]

The construction of other freeways within East Los Angeles heightened public suspicion of progress and further incensed the local public toward the freeway and its builders. Upon the Division of Highways' disclosure that Belvedere residents would have to make way for construction of the Pomona Freeway in the fall of 1957, the *Eastside Sun* asked its readers, "Five freeways now slash through Boyle Heights, namely, the San Bernardino, Santa Ana, Golden State, Long Beach and now the Pomona. Question is, how do you

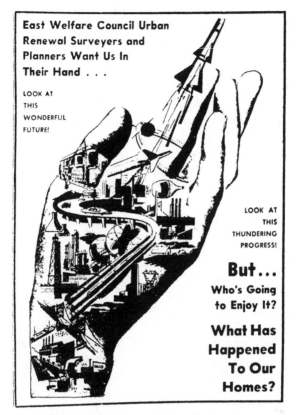

East Welfare Council Urban Renewal Surveyors and Planners Want Us In Their Hand . . .

LOOK AT THIS WONDERFUL FUTURE!

LOOK AT THIS THUNDERING PROGRESS!

But...
Who's Going to Enjoy It?

What Has Happened To Our Homes?

FIGURE 15. Cartoon from the *Eastside Sun*, 1959. (Courtesy of the *Eastside Sun*.)

stop the freeways from continuing to butcher our town?"[55] On October 19, 1957, some one thousand residents from the neighboring communities of Belvedere and Monterey Park packed the main auditorium of East Los Angeles Junior College to denounce the Division's proposal to route the Pomona Freeway through their communities. Throughout the hearing, people "listened intently and occasionally cheered the vocal protests of persons or institutions adversely affected by the proposed freeway route."[56]

East Los Angeles business leaders also decried the freeway's harmful impact on the local economy. John Askers, representing the small business interests of Belvedere as president of that community's chamber of commerce, voiced his opposition to the freeway's division of his community. "Belvedere shopping centers, schools, and churches are already difficult to get to from many areas," Askers declared before the Division of Highways in 1957, and "a freeway through the center would act as an even more formidable barrier to Belvedere residents."[57] Other local business leaders affirmed Askers's view of the coming freeways. The Brooklyn Avenue Businessmen's Association of Boyle Heights published its opposition to freeway construction in the *Eastside Sun*. The association's letter to the editor denounced "the projected [Golden State] freeway that would eliminate several hundred families who are now customers and would create a barrier between the Los Angeles River and our business district."[58] Despite the thriving regional economy of urban Southern California in the age of the freeway, the peak of economic prosperity for inner-city communities such as Boyle Heights had already passed. The freeway not only ravaged the housing stock of the communities of East Los Angeles, it also impaired the economic health of those areas.

Other East Los Angeles officials reiterated the economic threat posed by the new freeways. Ninth District assemblyman Edward F. Elliott decried the impact of the freeway on East Los Angeles. Recalling J. B. Priestley's famous description of Los Angeles as "sixteen suburbs in search of a city," Elliott described the "new" Los Angeles of the postwar era as "sixteen freeways in search of a suburb," insinuating that the new freeways favored suburban development at the expense of inner-city communities. Elliot presciently envisioned a dark future for Los Angeles, imagining a city with "the most impressive civic center in America," yet strangled by "one gigantic mass of parking lots traversed by a futuristic contanglement of expressways jammed with . . . compacts, smog-belching trucks and a few obsolete MTA buses."[59]

Elliot elaborated on the disastrous effects freeway construction entailed for his constituents in East Los Angeles. Citing a study that documented a decline in downtown retail sales by 57 percent between 1950 and 1960, Elliot blamed the freeways for the ailing health of the inner-city economy. Instead of accomplishing its original purpose of "routing traffic around areas of business concentration in order to facilitate the movement of traffic," the downtown vicinity and its inhabitants "had become encircled, cut up, and glutted with freeways." Elliot protested the fact that freeways had become "speedways to carry the buying public through instead of into the central business area."[60]

The arrival of the freeway in East Los Angeles thus coincided with a more general deterioration of the physical and economic health of Eastside communities. Citing a 1958 study issued by the Los Angeles County Committee of Human Relations, the *Belvedere Citizen* reported that, since 1940, the "Mexican American Population Shows 200% Increase in L.A.," and an even greater (500 percent) increase in the African American population.

"The implication of these facts is clear," warned the *Citizen*. "Throughout the central part of the city a tremendous ghetto is being created, into which the ever increasing number of these minority groups must go."[61] Superimposed on the neighborhoods of East and South Central Los Angeles, the freeway accelerated the trend toward increasing segregation by race, destroying the city's multicultural spaces.

Simultaneously, however, as freeway construction exacerbated racial tensions within the postwar urban region, the very experience of driving the new freeways diminished the public's awareness of such tensions. The freeway mediated a view of the metropolis, not unlike the way in which Disneyland's structured space mediated a view of a small-town past and a suburban future. Dense landscaping or concrete walls alongside freeway arteries, for example, obstructed the driver's passing glance at the sights of the city. This kind of visual screening sustained ignorance of, or indifference to, the surrounding built environment and negated the sense of passing through the city's landscapes of work and community. Certain critics recognized how the freeways mandated a forced perspective of the metropolis, not unlike that which Walt Disney's corps of designers implemented at Disneyland. Writing for *The Nation* in 1965, Carey McWilliams acknowledged how urban sprawl and freeway driving promoted ignorance of the Other:

> Los Angeles is the city of sprawl. To sprawl is to relax and feel comfortable. For most residents, Los Angeles is a comfortable city, psychologically as well as physically, because the unpleasant can be kept in its place—at a safe distance from most of the people. By accident more than design, Los Angeles has been organized to further the tendency towards social indifference. The freeways have been carefully designed to skim over and skirt around such eyesores as Watts and East Los Angeles; even the downtown section, a portion of which has become a shopping area for minorities, has been partially bypassed.[62]

McWilliams identified the freeway as a kind of protected space, insulated from the darker spaces of the inner city. In this capacity, the freeways extended the domestic space of the home into the city's public realm, affording a privatized public experience not unlike a trip to Disneyland or Dodger Stadium. In the construction of freeways, regional planners and state engineers applied a principal similar to that which informed the design of Disneyland. "At Disneyland," explained John Hench, the park's chief designer, "we program out all the unwanted elements, and program in all the wanted ones." Like walking Main Street, USA, driving Los Angeles' new freeways presented an edited view of the metropolis, cutting scenes of racial poverty, deindustrialization, urban renewal, and other unsightly features of the city's postwar metamorphosis. Like movies and theme parks, freeways mediated the relationship between the individual and his environment. But the logic of that relationship corresponded to the underlying impulse behind suburbanization: to claim a space of one's own—in homes and neighborhoods—and to abandon complex metropolitan realities. Reyner Banham implied this in his optimistic assessment that freeways could provide a respite from the demands of city life, offering Angelenos "the two calmest and most rewarding hours of their daily lives."[63]

In those instances when they did not eliminate the view of noir Los Angeles, however, the freeways inspired a new self-consciousness about the appearance of the city. On April 14, 1958, for example, councilman Edward Roybal received a letter from an upstanding constituent in his East Los Angeles district. Dr. T. Gordon Reynolds, an associate professor of medicine at White Memorial Hospital in Boyle Heights, wrote to Roybal to urge his support for urban renewal programs in the area, specifically because "our new freeways will all pass this section and unless we develop this section our visitors will enter our fair city receiving one of the most unfavorable impressions imaginable as they pass through the ragged back yard fences, the broken down garages and the sight of sagging kitchen doors."[64] Reynolds's plea illuminates the synergy between highway construction and urban renewal programs. To the doctor's chagrin, the slum tradition persisted in places such as Boyle Heights during the 1950s and remained evident from atop the new freeways. Urban renewal officials and their bulldozers could solve this problem, as they did in places such as Bunker Hill and the Chavez Ravine.

Highway construction, urban renewal, and their cultural manifestations reversed the fundamentally *urban* process by which the city's classes and races came to "know" each other by virtue of their mutual presence within public venues. In *All That Is Solid Melts into Air*, by contrast, Marshall Berman recites Charles Baudelaire's poem "The Family of Eyes" to illuminate the new social confrontations in Haussmann's Paris. The romantic solitude of a couple sitting in a posh café along a newly formed boulevard is disrupted by the presence of three onlookers: a family of beggars standing in awe of the lavish display of bourgeois wealth. Dismayed by his lover's antipathy to the loiterers, the narrator realizes that he cannot love the woman he is with. Berman recounts this literary scene to describe how the process of Haussmannization—routinely cited as the primordial experience of nineteenth-century urban modernity—created new social vistas by removing the walls that divided the isolated worlds of wealth and poverty.

However uncomfortable such new encounters might have been, modern boulevards fostered a new kind of democratic space that defined the public experience of parks, department stores, vaudeville houses, and other institutions of the modern city.[65]

The phase of modernization that wrought Southern California's postwar urban region, however, precluded such confrontations. Not unlike the way in which Disneyland minimized the gathering of crowds through its spatial "flow," the freeway eliminated the routine encounters between diverse peoples that defined the experience of public life in the modern city. Neither wholly public nor private, the freeway precluded the amicable and antagonistic confrontations that occurred within sites such as streetcars, boulevards, and city parks. By imposing new barriers between the city's various communities, the freeways lessened the possibility for social contact, fostering the kind of "social indifference" that troubled Carey McWilliams. While the boulevards and other public venues of the modern city demystified the presence of rich and poor and inspired a style of urban realism that dominated photography, literature, journalism, and film at the turn of the century, the freeway, like Disneyland and Dodger Stadium, sustained a cultural mystique of urban life that obscured the darker realities of the postwar American city.

FREEWAYS AND THE "NEW" LOS ANGELES

While the residents of inner-city neighborhoods railed against the destructive impact of highway construction, those communities situated within the region's growth centers, particularly those removed from the city center, emphasized the benefits of the new freeways and insinuated freeways into their vision of the suburban good life. "The Westside complex is soaring to new heights, both physically and culturally," reported *Los Angeles*, the "Magazine of the Good Life in Southern California." The editors of the upscale magazine credited the new freeways for this development: "Completion of the Santa Monica and San Diego Freeways . . . could create a remarkable, futuristic metropolis in the suburbs."[66] From the Westside, one could drive the 405 Freeway north, through the Sepulveda Pass, completed in 1962, into the San Fernando Valley, vaunted by local boosters as "America's great new industrial and leisure frontier," where "major highway projects are moving ahead."[67] South on the 405 would lead to Orange County, where, the Division of Highways optimistically reported, "Santa Ana Freeway Has Induced Industrial and Recreational Development."[68]

The California Chamber of Commerce added its own glowing assessment of the state's new freeways, emphasizing their decentralizing effect on the regional landscapes of industry, residence, and leisure. A short film produced by the Chamber of Commerce in the late 1960s, titled simply *The Freeway*, situated the state's new freeways within "our wonderful California way of life." The freeway, according to the film's producers, liberated Californians from the confines of the city, granting the "freedom to live in far-outlying residential areas" as well as "the freedom to drive away from the city to work." Reinforcing the postwar synergy between the new cultural institutions of the postwar urban region, the filmmakers also emphasized how the freeway granted access to new entertainment experiences, "with dad away at work, mom can use the new freeway to take the kids on a Disneyland outing." Above all, the Chamber of Commerce stressed the freeway's centrality to the region's decentralized society: "industry and satellite businesses move into new areas . . . and with them new homes and the people who enjoy our kind of living. . . . The growing network of freeways has a lot to do with this."[69]

While state business leaders welcomed the new freeways for promoting decentralization, corporate executives whose businesses resided in downtown Los Angeles lauded the new freeways for restoring economic prosperity to the city center and facilitating the corporate makeover of downtown Los Angeles. Neil Petree, president of Barker Bros. department store and president of the Downtown Businessmen's Association during the 1940s, praised the new freeways for "a resurgence in downtown business."[70] In fact, to celebrate the completion of the new Harbor Freeway through downtown Los Angeles, the Downtown Businessmen's Association held an al fresco luncheon for its 150 members atop a newly completed overpass extended into Fourth Street (see figure 16).

The Division of Highways emphasized the importance of freeways to the "L.A. Renaissance."[71] In its 1950 midwinter edition, the *Los Angeles Times* celebrated the "Panorama of Progress" in Southern California, highlighting the fact that the "new civic center is being hemmed by freeways."[72] *Westways*, a magazine published by the Automobile Club of Southern California and the region's equivalent to Charles Fletcher Lummis's *Land of Sunshine*, also saluted the new freeways for facilitating the "rejuvenation taking place in the downtown district."[73] Not unlike Dodger Stadium, the freeway reflected the suburbanization of downtown Los Angeles, implementing the spatial regimes of the new suburban society within the parameters of inner-city redevelopment.

Freeways sponsored promotions of postwar Los Angeles as the ultimate democratic city. Within the intense phase of boosterism that accompanied

FIGURE 16.   The Downtown Businessmen's Association, a major advocate of downtown freeway construction, dines atop a newly completed Harbor Freeway off-ramp. (Courtesy of the *Los Angeles Examiner*/Hearst Newspaper Collection, Department of Special Collections, University of Southern California Library.)

the frantic pace of development in postwar Southern California, the new freeways arrived as a conspicuous symbol of "the new Los Angeles," celebrated for the freedom bestowed on the citizen motorist to move about the city faster.[74] *Westways* celebrated the new freeways as "sinews of a supercity." The magazine posited the new freeway system as the very realization of Disneyland's Tomorrowland in Southern California while extolling the sacred American values of mobility and individualism: "Thus, Los Angeles is a kind of super metropolis with a downtown administrative core and a host of reasonably self-sufficient and self-reliant outlying communities, with its inhabitants driving to and fro as the spirit and the freeway system moves them."[75] Similarly, the State Division of Highways emphasized how the new freeways aided suburban decentralization. "The Los Angeles County area—and its neighboring counties, Orange and Ventura—is developing into a widespread, many centered, megalopolis linked together by increasingly scattered bands of freeways."[76]

The promotion of Los Angeles as the ultimate suburban metropolis emphasized the role of tourism and leisure and underscored a perception of the new freeway system as a key "attraction" among the region's many points of interest. Tourist guides to Los Angeles celebrated Southern California's new freeways as the "gateway to vacationland," while the Division of Highways situated the freeways within postwar Southern California's gentrified geography of play:

> Such widely scattered attractors of traffic as Dodger Stadium, the Los Angeles Civic Center, Disneyland, Marineland, the Griffith Park Zoo, the legitimate theaters of both Hollywood and the far-flung suburbs, the marinas along the coast, the Coliseum, the County Art Museum, the Music Center, and dozens of other centers can each operate at maximum capacity. They can do it without creating the sort of lethal competition for land and on access streets that has stricken so many other metropolitan centers.[77]

While *Look* magazine touted Disneyland as a "metropolis of the future," *Westways* packaged postwar Los Angeles as a veritable theme park, whose attractions were easily accessed by the new freeways. In another *Westways* article, "Where to Take Your Pleasure," the magazine featured a map of regional tourist attractions, connected by the new freeway system coming into place. In addition to Disneyland and Dodger Stadium, "one of the nation's best ballparks," the *Westways* map also emphasized the great cultural diversity of Los Angeles, at least those aspects of cultural diversity that lent themselves to tourist consumption. The "New Chinatown," for example, "a collection of import shops and fine restaurants," did not reflect the historic legacy of Chinese settlement in the "old" Chinatown, which had been demolished to make way for Union Station during the 1930s. Similarly, Olvera Street, following its Depression-era renovation into a commodified fantasy of "Old Mexico," came to "represent the best of the venerable Spanish and Mexican origins and traditions of the pueblo of Los Angeles." Finally, the Southwest Museum, just off the Arroyo Seco Freeway dedicated by "Chief Tahachwee" in 1941, featured "an outstanding collection of western Indian artifacts." Highlighting those tourist attractions most accessible by the region's new freeways as a means of experiencing the city's racial and ethnic diversity, the *Westways* map presented such diversity as spectacle, something occasionally and casually consumed by a sprawling suburban public.[78]

The map's likeness to Walt Disney's map of Disneyland underscored a more general conflation of the city and the theme park, and offered a friendlier vision of urban life than film noir's spectacles of urban blight. The city could be fun, but only from a safe distance. The freeway afforded such distance while providing access to the city and its many pleasures. By presenting the city as the sum of its attractions, the *Westways* map suggested how the freeways encouraged a view of the city as a collection of isolated sites, each severed from its sociohistorical context. After the debacle of the Arechiga evictions, the Chavez Ravine became more familiar as an exit off the freeway, significant for housing "one of the nation's best ballparks." Other sites in the postwar urban region also shed their distinct historical connotations: Venice has a nice beach, Pasadena a good museum, and Watts a good nightclub.[79] The freeways thus heralded a new view of the city, one that translated the complexities of urban life into a gentrified geography of play.

Freeways also inspired a new aesthetic vision of Los Angeles and its environs. The Los Angeles painter Roger Kuntz, for example, found a certain poetry in the bold graphics of freeway signs and translated that perception into his painting *Santa Ana Arrows* (ca. 1950s), which manifested a modernist appreciation for the urban built environment. Emil Kosa Jr., on the other hand, used watercolors to convey a transitional moment between the old and the new Los Angeles. His painting *Freeway Beginning* (ca. 1948) situates a half-finished freeway artery within a barren landscape cleared for highway construction. Above the freeway, the vaguely Victorian architecture of Bunker Hill serves as a visual reminder of the noir city that increasingly gave way to the whiteness of concrete freeways. Such images of the freeway resonated with the work of other contemporary artists such as Charles Sheeler, whose *California Industrial* (ca. 1957) posited the bold new look of a California downtown, rendering a celebratory vision of the state's new industrial landscape.[80]

While the circulation of such images within the region's cultural networks provided a way of seeing Southern California's new freeways, looking at paintings on a canvas or in the glossy pages of a magazine was far different from actually driving the new freeways. Initially, the new freeways seemed a strange, bewildering environment for many motorists, accustomed to the slower pace of surface streets and traffic signals. "The freeway is a relatively new facility," asserted the Division of Highways, acknowledging that many drivers "are not accustomed to the high speeds, the multiple lanes, and motorists entering on the freeway."[81] Southern California's decentralized urban region, though often touted as a more relaxed alternative to the frenzied chaos of the modern city, retained a key feature of modern life: speed. Essentially, the freeway democratized speed for its masses of motorists, but this aroused concern among certain public authorities. The *Los Angeles Examiner*, for example, confirmed to its readers: "Yep, You Can Go

Nuts Driving on the LA Freeways," quoting a health official from Camarillo State Hospital who compared the psychological dangers of freeway driving to the dangerous predicament of California's white pioneers:

> The strain of driving on Los Angeles freeways, surrounded by hurtling cars and trucks, is even greater than that faced by pioneering families who crossed the country in covered wagons and fought off Indians. These stresses undoubtedly work to trigger latent flaws in humans, either organic or psychic in nature, to produce full-blown mental diseases that would not have come to surface in other, more peaceful times.[82]

Echoing an earlier discourse that deplored the "fever of speed" and the hurried pace of modern life, certain public officials in Southern California expressed their concern about the freeway's potential to impair the mental health of the average motorist.[83]

Freeway driving forced new ways of negotiating urban space on the motorist. Traveling through the city at faster speeds, drivers had to master a bewildering array of signs in less time, identifying the names of unfamiliar streets and distant places within a span of seconds. The initial confusion wrought on drivers by the new freeways became something of a local joke. "The freeways really drive me crazy," declared Jack Benny in his opening monologue for CBS's *Jack Benny Show* that aired on February 19, 1961. The comedian recounted before his audience the hilarious confusion that ensued upon his first encounter with Southern California's new freeway system. "I get so mixed up with the signs," Benny told his audience, whose uproar indicated a familiarity with his bewilderment. Benny went on to describe his disorientation on the new freeways. "The other night, I was going to Palm Springs and all of a sudden I got on the wrong lane and I found myself in Pasadena. Then I left Pasadena and I got on another lane and I was in Anaheim! Then I went on another. . . . This went on for seven hours! And I still didn't get to Palm Springs!"[84]

To counter such confusion, the freeway's designers took careful measures to train drivers to master an elaborate array of signs and a tangled network of on-ramps, off-ramps, and interchanges. Herein lay a key paradox of the new suburban society that architectural critic Reyner Banham first discerned: that the private freedom afforded by the automobile demanded a public discipline imposed on freeway drivers. The freeway demanded a "lane discipline," in which drivers are forced into a "constant stream of decisions" on the freeway, ever attentive to speed, surrounding circumstances, and future intentions. Drivers also depended on a vast array of signs straddling the freeways, directing drivers to the lanes leading to their destinations. Jack Benny lost his way to Palm Springs because he failed to submit to the authority of the signs. Since "no human eye can unravel the complexities of even a relatively simple intersection" at sixty miles per hour, Banham saw no alternative to a "complete surrender of will to the instructions on the signs."[85]

Despite the widespread exaltation of Los Angeles' new freeways as the embodiment of democratic mobility, they were carefully monitored and regulated by an interlocking set of authorities. Driving the freeway meant not only surrendering one's will to the authority of signs, but also submission to and dependence on other forms of authority. By the mid-1950s, for example, the Los Angeles Police Department, under the command of Chief William Parker, implemented a new set of "interceptor cars," intended for use exclusively on freeways. Envisioned as the "nemesis of speeders," the new freeway patrol cars enforced the policing of freeway space.[86] The surveillance of freeway space had other purposes besides regulating speed, however. It also enabled awareness of unanticipated occurrences, such as accidents, landslips, or traffic snarls, which could be communicated to drivers through new channels of information, such as the Sigalert, established by local radio stations to broadcast information about traffic conditions. Freeway driving thus forced dependence on both public and private authority to maneuver through a situation "so closely controlled" that drivers would "hardly notice any difference when the freeways are finally fitted with computerized automatic control system that will take charge of the car at the on-ramp and direct it at properly regulated speeds and correctly selected routes to a preprogrammed choice of off-ramp."[87]

The new discipline imposed by freeways fit squarely within the culture of suburban whiteness that overcame Southern California during the postwar period. At various times and places in American history, becoming white required a willful submission to the disciplinary regimes of capitalist modernity. Initially, throughout the course of nineteenth-century urbanization, white workers were disciplined by their forced obedience to strict timetables. By the post–World War II period, however, the mass suburbanization of housing and industry (and the concomitant "whitening" of various ethnic groups) sanctioned the spatialization of capitalist discipline, which channeled white workers, families, and consumers through the regimented landscapes of postwar suburbia. If Hollywood film dramatized the disorder that surfaced within the undisciplined spaces of the "black" city, freeways, like Disneyland and Dodger Stadium, epitomized the new spatial discipline prerequisite to suburban whiteness.

In 1971, as the age of the freeway began to wane, the Los Angeles Department of City Planning conducted a survey to assess how ordinary Angelenos perceived their city and what features of the urban environment figured in their perceptions. To conduct their study, planning officials interviewed five citizens, each from a distinct Los Angeles community, and asked each individual to draw a mental map of the city. Three of the five maps, those representing the suburban communities of Westwood, the Fairfax District, and Northridge, presented a broad view of the urban region and included the city's major freeways. The other two maps, drawn by residents of Boyle Heights and Avalon, a working-class, predominantly black community of South Central Los Angeles, remained confined to a few streets and blocks that circumscribed their neighborhood and left out the city's new freeways.[88]

Why could residents from the suburban communities of Northridge and Westwood recognize the freeway system within their cognitive mapping of Los Angeles, while residents from Los Angeles' expanding ghetto and barrio could not? Contrary to Reyner Banham's assertion that the freeway constituted the "fourth ecology" of Angelenos and that it "is where the Angeleno is most himself, most integrally identified with his great city," the city planning report suggests how the freeways sustained a broader view of an expanding urban region, yet one that belonged to a newly formed suburban public whose affluence and mobility heightened their familiarity with sites beyond the immediate locale of home and neighborhood. For Southern California's great white middle class, suburbanization and highway construction unsettled previous ways of knowing the city by delivering new experiences of space and time. This enabled a more expansive view of the urban region and generated an affiliation with the suburban ideal that defined the image of Southern California during the postwar period.[89]

Yet the residents of Boyle Heights and South Central Los Angeles, though they remained on the margins of the "new Los Angeles," maintained what Southern California's sprawling public sacrificed in its high-speed pursuit of the suburban good life: community. An institution predicated on an ideal of unrestricted movement, the freeway symbolized the quintessentially American value of mobility. But mobility, as Alexis de Tocqueville realized some 130 years earlier, had its dark side. Southern California's freeway metropolis epitomized the "tumultuous and constantly harassed life" that defined American society as far back as its first encounters with modernity. In a society where "men are in constant motion" and where "rest is unknown," restlessness and mobility negate the sense of community that persisted within the older and compact spaces of the noir city. What remained of these neighborhoods in the age of the freeway did not belong to the "new Los Angeles," but their streets, sidewalks, markets, and bars sustained what Jane Jacobs described as an intricate "web of public respect and trust" that remained elusive in, if not altogether absent from, the mass-produced and highly privatized neighborhoods of suburban developers.[90]

Within the cultural system that took shape according to decentralized patterns of urban growth, therefore, highway construction virtually necessitated the creation of places like Disneyland and Dodger Stadium, which ostensibly anchored a highly mobile and transient population to a set of nodal points along the fluid space of the new freeways. With ample parking space, and for the small price of admission, Disneyland and Dodger Stadium invited commuters to pause in their rush between home and work to revel in a semblance of community tailored to the social values that informed the region's dawning political culture. To bask in the nostalgic warmth of Main Street, USA, or to witness the familiar ritual of masculine competition at Dodger Stadium was to find momentary relief from a world where "all that is solid melts into air," where the symbols of tradition, order, and progress countered the rush and transience of Southern California's new freeway metropolis.[91]

Epilogue

The 1960s and Beyond

After all the fanfare and spectacle that accompanied the post–World War II production of movies, theme parks, ballparks, and freeways, it seems by some accounts that the effort to reinvent Los Angeles as a new White City resulted in abject failure. Writing in 1963, for example, Remi Nadeau declared the region a "society of strangers." "In Los Angeles County," he wrote, "where the family moves an average of every four years, the movement of population works against community attachments." Nadeau predicted an ominous fate for the Southern Californian who, in spite of his best efforts to live out the suburban dream, finds himself lost within a "200 mile megalopolis," only to "succumb to the faceless existence that has overtaken man in other crowded cultures." That Southern California failed to deliver a communal haven for its suburban public was not lost upon D.J. Waldie, who recalls the vivid sense of isolation that pervaded his hometown of Lakewood in the early 1950s. In Lakewood, *neighborhood* did not imply *community:* "You rarely go across the street, which is forty feet wide. . . . [I]t is as if each house on your block stood on its own enchanted island . . . but the island is remote."[1]

In whatever ways the producers and consumers of suburban Southern California sought refuge from the dissipating forces of modernization, the vast scale and virtual instantaneity of the region's postwar suburban boom severely compromised that endeavor. For although Southern California's abundance of undeveloped land abetted a decentralized approach to the regional concentration of people and capital, it did not preclude the alienation, anomie, and isolation that remained endemic to the modern city and its culture. If the modern city inflicted these and other psychic wounds on its crowded, heterogeneous public, the sprawling postwar urban region, itself the product of yet another tumultuous phase of modernization, created a similar set of anxieties in its inhabitants.

Ultimately, suburbanization and its cultural manifestations marked the search for new remedies to the familiar consequences of urban modernity. With its tales of mishap and mayhem in the metropolis, film noir reminded postwar Americans of those consequences and heightened an imperative to create new models of community removed from the alienating confines of the modern city. Disneyland offered a privatized environment, intentionally shielded from the outside world and inundated with reassuring commercials for the corporations that manufactured the exclusive brand of community suburban Americans craved. Dodger Stadium situated a pastoral spectacle of athletic skill within a sanitized, regimented environment, suitable for "family entertainment," and freeways presented an edited view of the urban region, hiding the city's social complexity from sight and instead sustaining a momentary delusion of mobility among a public deeply infatuated with the automobile and its manufactured allure. White flight may not have entailed an easy departure from family, old neighborhoods, and childhood memories, but its cultural manifestations marked a collective effort to minimize the loss.

That effort, however, was more forceful than gentle and concealed motives perhaps more cunning than benign. If Disneyland packaged nostalgia and fantasy, it did so within a spatial regime crafted to induce consumption and maximize profit. Dodger Stadium, similarly, conditioned its captive audience according to a tedious and highly disciplined regimentation of space. Freeways, likewise, channeled Southern California's motorized masses through an intricate web of highways and fueled their addiction to gasoline, which satisfied their yearning for speed and mobility but diminished their cognizance of their social environment. Behind the spectacles of small-town nostalgia, masculine competition, and civic progress, which assuaged the discomfort wrought by the transition to a new and highly unfamiliar sociospatial configuration, the disciplinary structures of postwar popular culture enforced a set of power relations that accompanied the region's decentralized development. Such discipline aided workers in their adjustment to new working conditions and their contention with longer commutes between work and home. It sponsored familiarity with the mass-produced landscapes of the urban region. It enforced the maintenance of racially exclusive communities, and it encouraged the retention of traditional gendered divisions. Most of all perhaps, the disciplined spaces of the postwar urban region kept consumers buying houses, cars, television sets, and the myriad other commodities that sustained an ever-elusive suburban good life.

Such discipline, however, had its limits. Even residents of Southern California's whitest communities grew restless in their regimes of daily life. Offering a momentary escape into a world of moral degradation and sexual titillation, film noir issued its fantasies of urban decadence well into the 1950s, but the following decade witnessed an intensified search for more vital modes of experience beyond the plastic bubbles of theme parks and shopping malls. During the 1960s, Venice Beach, Silverlake, and the Sunset Strip surfaced as new cultural sites counterpoised against the homogeneous and regimented environments of Disneyland, Lakewood, and the freeway. Such were the spaces of difference that escaped the bulldozers wrought by highway construction and urban renewal programs and offered a respite from the disciplined landscapes of suburban Southern California. There, the children of Southern California's great white middle class reveled in an alternative set of sensations and experiences, smoking marijuana, dropping acid, and drowning in the rebellious sounds of The Doors and Jefferson Airplane.[2]

Southern California's youthful hippies, however, were not alone in their moral experimentation. Even their more respectable elders pursued pleasures not prescribed by Walt Disney and the purveyors of popular culture in the age of white flight. If Disneyland and Dodger Stadium connected their brand of entertainment to an ideal of the white nuclear family, subsequent media productions celebrated new forms of sexual experimentation among married couples. "Swinging" debuted as a fad among white, middle-class, married couples during the mid-1960s and captured the attention of magazines and movie studios alike. Los Angeles, for example, touted "the couples' contagion," declaring that "the extramarital affair has become a recognized art form."[3] Movies such as Bob and Carol and Ted and Alice (1969), with its story of two couples exchanging sexual pleasures in the hot tubs of the Hollywood Hills, also piqued the public's interest in swinging. Meanwhile, The Graduate (1967) explored the sexual idiosyncrasies lurking behind the posh facades of Beverly Hills, introducing Mrs. Robinson as an iconic fantasy of the boy next door, who seeks release from the plasticity and hypocrisy of bourgeois Los Angeles.

Moral apostasy loomed as but one threat to realizing the aspirations enshrined within the cultural landscape of Southern California's postwar urban region. By the latter half of the 1960s, Los Angeles itself seemed on the verge of a nervous breakdown. The "long hot summer" of 1965 echoed the chants of "burn, baby, burn!" emanating from South Central Los Angeles, shattering the illusory fantasy of a ubiquitous suburban good life that materialized within the insulated landscapes of tract developments, freeways, and theme parks. Other bouts of violence—racial or otherwise— further diminished the blissful ignorance that suburban Southern Californians pursued in their cultural endeavors during the 1950s. The 1968 assassination of Robert Kennedy at the Ambassador Hotel marked a violent end to the lingering myth of Camelot, and the following year brought the gruesome spectacle of the Manson family and its brutal slaying of a Hollywood starlet. In 1970, the killing of Ruben Salazar during the Chicano Moratorium outraged Southern California's Chicano community, who held Salazar up as a martyr in the struggle against Chicano oppression.

Beset with racial uprisings, moral implosions, mass murders, and political assassinations, suburban Southern Californians invested their hopes in a new political movement predicated upon a set of values embedded within the cultural landscapes of the postwar urban region. No one better embodied those values than Ronald Reagan, who by the mid-1960s had successfully translated his media celebrity into a new brand of conservatism aimed directly at the grievances of a decentralized public, which harbored growing animus against wasteful bureaucrats and angry minorities for obstructing their path to realizing the suburban good life. Reagan's popularity rested in part on a growing disillusionment with the brand of liberalism espoused by the Democratic Party during the years of Lyndon Johnson's Great Society, and Reagan was one among many conservative ideologues who heralded the New Right, but his postwar ascendance was also conditioned by the codification of more conservative social and political values within the symbolic architecture of Southern California's postwar urban region. His recurring presence in the preceding chapters underscores his affinity with the burgeoning institutions of the region's new "new mass culture" and his masterful use of media technologies—first film, then television—accustomed postwar Americans to his seemingly ubiquitous presence. In his very person, Ronald Reagan personified the merging of politics and popular culture in postwar America, and his entry into national politics from Southern California underscores the region's significance to the political shifts that ensued in the decades following World War II.

Reagan brought a decisive end to the New Deal order that dominated American politics throughout much of the twentieth century, but this book has shown how that order was already imploding within the cultural structures of Southern California's postwar urban region. Hollywood's pessimism at the outset of the postwar period reflected not only its financial troubles, but also the collective mood of a nation obsessed with security, privacy, and order: values inimical to the public spirit of the New Deal order. Film noir dramatized the imperative to retreat from the public spaces of New Deal urbanism, while the urban science fiction film leveled its indictment against the social actors who made substantial gains during the 1930s and into the subsequent decade. Walt Disney, meanwhile, strongly identified himself with the countersubversive tradition of 1950s America and built Disneyland as a reinstatement of traditional social values that seemed threatened by the hegemony of the New Deal and its brand of liberal modernism. Disneyland modeled a privatized, consumer-oriented subjectivity, predicated on notions of white supremacy and patriarchy and upheld by a new generation of political leaders who would come to constitute the New Right.

The negation of the New Deal order, however, was more than symbolic, and the emphasis on space and spatial relations in the preceding chapters illuminates the very material circumstances in which a new political movement took shape. White flight, suburbanization, highway construction, and urban renewal, which, ironically, had their origins in New Deal policy, destroyed the heterosocial spaces of urban life and cultivated new political constituencies that would ultimately turn against the collective and public premises of New Deal policy and ideology. If New York and its different neighborhoods epitomized the social world of New Deal urbanism, Los Angeles and its environs modeled a new spatial culture that bred a growing suspicion toward public life. Nothing better symbolized this shift than the transcontinental move of the Dodgers, who depleted Brooklyn of its most vital communal institution and landed in Los Angeles in the wake of defeated plans for public housing. The construction of Dodger Stadium illustrated the divisive politics of urban renewal and ignited racial opposition that undermined the liberal consensus of the 1960s. Highway construction brought a similar set of tensions, leveling the communal spaces that thrived in places such as Boyle Heights throughout the first half of the twentieth century and furthering the physical and psychological distance between white suburban affluence and racialized urban poverty.

The point here is not so much to mourn the passing of an idealized New Deal order, which was fraught with its own internal tensions and contradictions, but rather to underscore the linkages between politics and culture within the spatial reconfiguration of the American city during the postwar period.[4] Clearly, popular culture in the age of white flight prefigured the rightward shift of American politics during the postwar period. Its privatized milieu presaged a new political emphasis on ideals such as "law and order" and signaled a growing repudiation of the "nightmarish collectivism" of the New Deal order. Its linkages to an idealization of the white nuclear family foreshadowed a zealous preoccupation with family values that surfaced alongside the Reagan-era ascendance of the Christian right. Its arousal of racial opposition and its racialized representational fare upheld material and symbolic divisions among racial groups and provided a symbolic foundation upon which to oppose subsequent forms of civil rights legislation and policy toward immigrants. And in its elevation of a consumerist model of citizenship, popular culture in the age of white flight not only held up the theme park and the shopping mall as models for late-twentieth-century urbanism, but also anticipated the property tax revolts that railed against the evils of big government and aimed ultimately at preserving the consumption habits prerequisite to the suburban good life.[5]

If culture is the arena in which social identities are constructed, transformed, and destroyed, popular culture in the age of white flight codified the formation of a white suburban identity that encompassed the aspirations of diverse groups pursuing the fruits of postwar consumer affluence. Southern California during the postwar period cultivated a racialized vision of suburban modernity, a vision that, like Progressive aspirations a generation earlier, included every amenity of modern life, yet also sought relief from the dissipating effects of modernization on traditional notions of family, property, and community. That vision was neither the slick crafting of a Madison Avenue elite nor the authentic expression of a vox populi, but rather it took shape within a mutually constitutive relationship between cultural producers and their audiences, as well as between political luminaries and their constituencies. In Southern California during the decades following World War II, the distinctions between cultural audience and political constituency blurred and the region sheltered a nascent struggle to attain the promises of mobility, affluence, convenience, and stability built into the cultural landscape of its expanding urban region.

POSTSCRIPT: LOS ANGELES ANEW

That struggle, however, continues. In our present age of accelerated globalization, Los Angeles is undergoing yet another round of economic restructuring and demographic upheaval, and the cultural dynamics that gave birth to Southern California's versions of the White City have shifted to produce new cultural configurations. Whatever exhortations about the "new" Los Angeles circulated through the cultural networks of postwar America, another new Los Angeles has taken shape, and the cultural matrix of chocolate cities and vanilla suburbs is giving way to new social interactions that mirror the striking changes that have transformed the region since the postwar period. The city's capacity for rapid change and incessant innovation has perforated the physical and cultural boundaries that distinguished white space from black space, and although the noir city and its heterosocial interactions have made a certain comeback in recent decades, race continues to shape the cultural geography of the contemporary urban landscape in more powerful and less subtle ways. Once more, the cultural landscape of Southern California's ever-expanding urban region holds clues to the countervailing forces of twenty-first-century urbanism.

Furthering the extremes between white wealth and nonwhite poverty, the demographic transformation of Los Angeles and its environs poses a powerful challenge to the regional hegemony of suburban whiteness. Since 1970, the vast influx of immigrant populations into Southern California has transformed the region from a bastion of middle-class whiteness into a Third World citadel. In 1970, 71 percent of Los Angeles County's population was non-Hispanic white or Anglo, and the remaining 29 percent of the population was divided among Latinos (15 percent), African Americans (11 percent), and Asian/Pacific Islanders (3 percent). By 1980, the non-Hispanic white population had dropped to 53 percent, and ten years later it had fallen further to 41 percent. Throughout the 1970s, large-scale immigration from Latin America and Asia, coupled with a moderate growth in the African American population, inflated the region's nonwhite population. Immigration to the region continued to expand throughout the following decade as the population of Asians and Latinos swelled. By 1990, Latinos comprised 36 percent of the city's population; African Americans and Asians constituted 11 percent, respectively. Today's Los Angeles ranks among the most diverse urban regions in the world and the city once heralded as the "nation's white spot" now mirrors the polyglot diversity that defines the city and even its past.[6]

Fueling and fueled by demographic growth, economic restructuring in Southern California simultaneously enforces and enervates existing patterns of racial and ethnic inequality. Since the 1970s, the increasingly transnational currents of economic exchange have positioned the Los Angeles urban region to emerge as a "nodal point" within a new global economy. The manifestations of economic globalization in Southern California have furthered the sociospatial extremes of progress and poverty that have been manifest throughout every stage of capitalist urbanization. On the one hand, the region shelters a growing number of high-tech manufacturing districts, or "technopoles," which extend to the furthest corners of the urban region. In the southernmost portions of Orange County and the western fringes of the San Fernando Valley, where gated communities and high-end subdivisions guard the latest incarnation of suburban whiteness, high-tech manufacturers such as Hughes Aircraft Missile Systems Group, Micropolis, and Rocketdyne further the industrial and residential sprawl that began in earnest during the early 1940s. The region's high-tech economy, which has penetrated the entertainment industry to a certain extent, sustains the class standing of a highly skilled group of managers, business executives, scientists, engineers, designers, and celebrities who continue to reap the rewards of the region's economic prosperity.[7]

At the other end of the economic spectrum and concentrated within the region's multiple urban centers, a low-skill, low-wage, nonunionized workforce, comprising mostly women and undocumented Latino and Asian immigrants, has been taking shape alongside the growth of the manufacturing sector since the 1970s. In contrast to the high unemployment and economic decline that befell other major American cities through the phase of deindustrialization during the 1970s and 1980s, Los Angeles' manufacturing economy grew steadily throughout the 1970s and intensified during the following decade, when the infusion of Asian capital into the regional economy bolstered the production of manufactured goods such as apparel, furniture, jewelry, and machinery. Such growth, however, entails mixed consequences for Southern California's expanding immigrant populations, who are drawn by the prospects of job availability but face new depths of exploitation. The sweatshop has made a comeback within Southern California's industrial landscape in recent decades, providing an often overlooked reminder that the "new" Los Angeles runs on the sweat of immigrant labor.[8]

Between these extremes, the great white middle class, which dominated the image and reality of the postwar urban region, is making its departure. Throughout the Reagan era, the flight of major manufacturing firms from the region's industrial geography dislodged whites from their suburban neighborhoods, creating space for new concentrations of racialized poverty. This transformation was most visible in the communities of Southeast Los Angeles, which nurtured the suburban white identity explored in previous chapters: South Gate, Huntington Park, Maywood, Bell, Bell Gardens, Vernon, and Cudahy. The departure of industrial giants such as General Motors, Firestone Tires, Weiser Lock, Bethlehem Steel, Dial, and Oscar Meyer from this area during the 1980s entailed a set of profound social consequences that undermined the cultural order of the postwar urban region. White workers and their families, who enjoyed full benefits and union representation, have taken flight, and, in their stead, recent arrivals from Mexico and Central America find work in the expanding low-wage, nonunion sector and take shelter in cities crippled by shrinking tax bases and reduced services.[9]

While the brand of suburban whiteness that took shape within the cultural transition from the centralized, industrial city to the postwar urban region becomes a relic of the past, its legacy continues to shape California politics. The politics of white home ownership remains a powerful force in the state and its triumphs in recent decades have profound implications for the quality of race relations in the United States. In 1978, the passage of Proposition 13 marked a major victory for white homeowners and their brand of "identity politics" in California, much like the two-term presidency of Ronald Reagan. In the 1990s, California voters passed a series of measures that targeted immigrant groups and racial minorities. Looking back to the buoyant expressions of suburban whiteness that highlighted the cultural landscape of the postwar urban region, the current strategies to preserve white hegemony reflect a brazen attempt to maintain some semblance of the precarious social order that enjoyed a brief life span between the midcentury manifestation of the noir city and the current denouement of a Third World urbanism.

Film noir underscored the imperatives of suburban home ownership as a bulwark against the crisis of the public city; Proposition 13 surfaced in 1978 as a measure to secure that imperative for millions of California homeowners. The unbridled growth that swept across the region entailed a mixed set of consequences for suburban homeowners. On the one hand, the unceasing demand for homes generated higher property values, but, on the other hand, higher home prices brought higher property taxes, which basically doubled every few years. At the same time, the recession of the mid-'70s heralded a stagnation of real income and frustrated consumer efforts to live the suburban good life that California symbolized. Proposition 13, a measure that would lower property taxes by 60 percent, won by an overwhelming majority in California and inspired a similar set of homeowners' revolts in other states. In Los Angeles, Proposition 13 won by overwhelming majorities in white council districts, while it failed by a similar majority in the city's only black district.

Proposition 13 cannot be understood in isolation from the larger cultural context that dawned on Southern California during the postwar period. When Yvonne de Carlo warns Burt Lancaster in the climactic scene of the film *Criss Cross,* "You have to watch out for yourself; I can't help it if people don't know how to take care of themselves," she recites the creed that suburban homeowners adopted in their insular political outlook that disavowed any connection to other urban constituencies. Instead, the supporters of Proposition 13 campaigned with slogans such as "Vote for yourself! Vote for Proposition 13!" Proposition 13 upheld what Clarence Lo describes as a consumer model of citizenship, which is predicated upon the relentless pursuit of commodities that sustained popular idealizations of suburban domesticity. Such idealizations informed the dominant cultural narratives of Southern California's postwar urban region and guided the ascendance of tax-cutting conservatism that disavowed the interdependency of social groups and instead promoted self-interest as a primary goal of political struggle. Proposition 13 drastically reduced property taxes at the expense of public services such as schools, libraries, and police and fire protection, services that racial minorities have been increasingly forced to rely on. In this capacity, Proposition 13 continued the privatization of social life that began during the postwar period and widened the spatial and racial divide between chocolate cities and vanilla suburbs.[10]

Many proponents of Proposition 13 also endorsed the concurrent anti-busing movement, in which white suburban parents sought to preserve the postwar racial order by resisting state efforts to send their children to schools in black and Latino neighborhoods. In suburban communities of both the San Fernando Valley and Orange County, where Proposition 13 won overwhelming support, local organizations such as the PTA marshaled opposition to busing programs, sponsoring constitutional amendments to limit busing, challenging busing in court, and seeking to elect public officials who opposed busing. The racist underpinnings of the antibusing campaign during the mid-'70s were not self-evident, but against the official effort to elide the racial geography of the postwar urban region through school desegregation, white suburban families defended their distance from the racialized city and, with it, the right to maintain school policies that sent white middle-class children to white schools in white neighborhoods.[11]

The political culture that sustained both Proposition 13 and the antibusing movement is essentially the same as that which bestowed two consecutive presidential terms on Ronald Reagan, who championed the rights of homeowners and consumers in their pursuit of privatized self-interest. Reagan's victory in the White House confirmed Southern California's prominence within the national political culture, not unlike the proliferation of homeowners' revolts throughout the nation following the success of Proposition 13 in 1978. The triumph of the New Right by the late 1970s was made possible by the support of various regional constituencies, but the course of political events in Southern California—beginning with the 1950 defeat of Helen Gahagan Douglas, bolstered by the simultaneous victory against public housing, and gaining further momentum with the 1964 cancellation of the Rumford Fair Housing Act—prefigured the subsequent victories of a new brand of Republican conservatism predicated upon the values enshrined in places like Disneyland. By the mid-1980s, at the height of the Reagan era, the brand of suburban whiteness that first took shape within Southern California's cultural landscape had entered the symbol iconography of the American Way and remained under the stewardship of a countersubversive coalition that targeted civil rights crusaders, feminists, antiwar demonstrators, and gay activists as culpable for the social ills and economic malaise wrought by economic restructuring, deindustrialization, and the dismantling of the welfare state.[12]

Reagan's legacy endured through the 1990s and found powerful expressions in the culture and politics of California. One year after the end of the Reagan-Bush era and on the heels of the Rodney King uprising of 1992, the film *Falling Down* engendered controversy among national audiences for its neonoir portrayal of the white man's identity crisis in contemporary Los Angeles. "D-Fens," an unemployed engineer suffering a nervous breakdown, begins a killing spree as he walks from downtown Los Angeles to the beach. In the tradition of noir's white male antihero, D-Fens trudges through the racialized milieu of the city, attacking a Korean market, a fast-food outlet, a Chicano gang, and a neo-Nazi. The city that once resonated with compelling expressions of suburban whiteness is now alien territory for D-Fens, an inhospitable non-Anglo landscape that renders white male identity obsolete.

That filmmakers could market the fin de siècle crisis of white male identity as entertainment points to the very real challenge to whiteness posed by the demographic transformation of California and Los Angeles at the end of the twentieth century. In this context, California voters approved a series of measures that extended a note of nativist hostility to people of color. In 1994, Proposition 187 triumphed at the polls, denying public services to undocumented workers and their families. Although the measure's implementation has been indefinitely delayed by the courts, it targets California's immigrant population as a scapegoat for the economic woes that befell the state during the recession of the early 1990s. The specter of white identity politics surfaced twice again in the remainder of the decade. In 1996, as if the racial wrongs of the past had been righted, Proposition 209 brought a decisive end to affirmative action in both public service contracts and higher education, and in 1998, Proposition 227 terminated bilingual education programs in public schools to advocate "English only" as state law. The causes and consequences of these measures have been explored elsewhere; suffice it to say here that they signal last-ditch attempts to preserve what vestiges of suburban whiteness remain at the outset of the twenty-first century.[13]

Popular culture in the age of white flight thus maintains a powerful legacy, and although the future of that legacy is uncertain, the current phase of demographic upheaval in Southern California annihilates the racial identities imposed on the spaces of the postwar urban region. Watts, for example, no longer symbolizes the geographic core of black Los Angeles, as a massive in-migration of Latino immigrants dissolves the postwar boundary between white and black Los Angeles. South Gate and Huntington Park, where Southern California's Dust Bowl migrants reinvented themselves in the image of middle-class whiteness after World War II, are the current epicenter of *México de afuera*, as Mexican immigrants reestablish communal ties in the wake of deindustrialization and white flight. A large and expanding Koreatown lies just west of downtown Los Angeles, a new suburban Chinatown centered on Monterey Park has taken shape to the east, and a band of Cambodian and Vietnamese communities has grown to the south, extending from the older Japanese community of Gardena to Long Beach and into Orange County, where the city of Westminster is now known as Little Saigon.[14]

Perhaps even more striking, the San Fernando Valley now shelters a heterogeneous mix of Mexicans, Salvadorans, Guatemalans, Armenians, and African Americans. For a generation of white Americans in search of suburban domesticity, the Valley offered affordable housing and homogeneous neighborhoods, and its location on the northern side of the Santa Monica Mountains promised a comfortable distance from a Los Angeles mired in the mythology of film noir. The landscape of today's Valley, however, reveals a striking record of the demographic changes that have ensued over the past thirty years. On Van Nuys Boulevard, once the heart of white suburbia, Spanish has displaced English as the unofficial language of public signage. All around the Van Nuys business district, travel agents advertise discount tickets for international travel carriers such as Avianca and Aeroméxico. The native fare of El Salvador, Peru, India, Armenia, and a dozen other nations is served in the boulevard's myriad storefront diners. Most institutions that catered to the Valley's original white constituency are now gone: department stores have been replaced by *pupuserías* and *mueblerías*, the First Presbyterian Church closed after its English-speaking constituency plummeted, and the *San Fernando Daily News*, founded as the *Van Nuys Call* in 1911, left for tonier quarters in Woodland Hills. The "New Valley" harbors scant traces of the suburban good life that dominated the cultural imagery of postwar Los Angeles, and its public settings now echo the cultural dissonance of the polyglot noir city.

Amid the browning of the San Fernando Valley, homeowners there are mobilizing a campaign to authorize the secession of the Valley from the city of Los Angeles, in what would be the largest municipal divorce in national history. Valley VOTE (Voters Organized toward Empowerment), a grassroots organization established in 1998, has gathered sufficient signatures on petitions to push the secession drive to its most advanced stage ever. Whether or not the proponents of secession will have their way, the current move to secede from the city of Los Angeles inherits a tradition of municipal discord in Southern California and reflects a long-standing antipathy to the urban behemoth on the southern side of the Santa Monica Mountains.

The social, economic, political, and spatial transformations that engulf today's Los Angeles entail a set of cultural expressions that reflect both the extension and the extinction of popular culture in the age of the white flight. On the one hand, recent scholarship illuminates the cultural manifestations of contemporary urbanism by looking to Los Angeles as a window onto the "theming" of American culture and society. Through the disparate points of Southern California's urban expanse, scholars cite the most spectacular examples of the privatization of public life: From the self-contained citadel that has become downtown Los Angeles—including the cylindrical glass towers of John Portman's Bonaventure Hotel—to the gated communities of Orange County's "exopolis," to the ersatz urbanism of City Walk, Los Angeles and its environs support the many "variations on a theme park" that condition the experience of urban life at the outset of the twenty-first century. While generally eschewing the broader historical context that sanctions such cultural formations and often ignoring their immense popularity among white and nonwhite consumers alike, such observations generally deplore the corporate sponsors of contemporary public culture, emphasizing the manipulative and coercive strategies built into the design of contemporary public space.[15]

On the other hand, by looking "way, way below" the glass and neon facades of the contemporary metropolis, one can identify competing cultural expressions that emanate from the city's diverse neighborhoods. During the 1980s, amid the deindustrialization of South Central Los Angeles, black youth forged a cultural style that centered upon the distinctively West Coast sounds of hip-hop music. Gangsta Rap made its debut on the streets of Los Angeles through the innovative sounds of Ice-T, Eazy-E and NWA, Ice Cube, Snoop Doggy Dogg, and Dr. Dre, who drew upon African American cultural traditions such as descriptive storytelling and funk music, while utilizing samplers, drum machines, engineering boards, and other components of the latest in digital technology. Gangsta Rap of the late 1980s and early 1990s, as Robin Kelley and Tricia Rose point out, spoke to the realities of ghetto life for young black heterosexual men in postindustrial America, and proffered a genre of black popular culture that proved overwhelmingly popular not only in chocolate cities, but also, if not especially, in vanilla suburbs.[16]

Although the cultural palimpsest of contemporary urbanism supports the musical expressions of young black men, it also reflects the cultural stylings of the city's Mexican and Latino populations. A striking preference for big cities among Latinos brings a transformative energy to the texture of daily life in a "Latino metropolis" such as Los Angeles. As the old barrio of East Los Angeles gives way to the exponential growth of Spanish-speaking neighborhoods and subdivisions, the symbols and signs of *Mexicanidad* are visible throughout the urban region. Immigrant homeowners from Mexico and Central America are investing "sweat equity" in their homes, using paint and inexpensive landscaping materials to reverse the deterioration of urban neighborhoods crippled by deindustrialization and white flight. Bohemian enclaves of Chicano communities in East Los Angeles and the San Gabriel Valley support the proliferation of bilingual cafés and bookstores. Accustomed to the convivial spaces of *plazas* and *mercados* in Latin American cities, Latino immigrants and their children make vital use of playgrounds, parks, squares, libraries, and other endangered public spaces that their more affluent counterparts in the city tend to ignore. Amid the current re-Mexicanization of Los Angeles, with the addition of other Latino populations, we are witnessing an ethnic transformation of the urban landscape on a scale unparalleled in history.[17]

So what's left of popular culture in the age of white flight? What remains of the cultural institutions explored in this book, and how have they fared in light of recent social transformations? Hollywood continues to fixate upon Los Angeles in its dystopian spectacles of urban decadence, and film noir and science fiction maintain their popularity at the box office. In the early 1970s, at the outset of an economic recession and in the wake of the turbulent 1960s, Los Angeles occupied a starring role in a brief noir revival, climaxing with *Chinatown* by Roman Polanski, whose tragic and bizarre encounter with the Manson family in 1969 inspired his dark and morbid vision of Los Angeles and its past. Disaster films such as *Earthquake* and *The Towering Inferno* also kept the spotlight on Southern California, portraying Los Angeles as an epicenter of the moral catastrophe that dawned in the era of Watergate. The following decade witnessed *Blade Runner*, rendering its futuristic nightmare of a Los Angeles dominated by global capital and teeming with Third World populations, while a spate of neonoir films of the late 1980s and early 1990s, most notably *The Grifters, The Player, Reservoir Dogs, Pulp Fiction, Short Cuts,* and *L.A. Confidential,* keeps a tight focus on the darkness lurking behind the sunny façade of the Los Angeles landscape.

More striking, however, is the recent arrival of new voices that add their own distinct inflection to the canons of film noir and science fiction. With a nod to Chester Himes, Walter Mosley established his presence in American literature with the 1990 success of *Devil in a Blue Dress,* which portrays the investigations of Easy Rawlins, a black private detective in 1940s Los Angeles who unravels the depths of white racism at the core of Southern California's black city. In a similar vein, Octavia Butler brings a black feminist perspective to her futuristic vision of Los Angeles in *Parable of the Sower,* which renders a bleak portrait of a city overcome with violence and fear in the year 2027. Like all durable genres of American popular culture, film noir and science fiction have incorporated new perspectives that extend and broaden their appeal over time; while Los Angeles, ravaged by successive episodes of racial violence throughout the second half of the twentieth century, remains a favorite site for collective fantasies of urban despair.

Meanwhile, Hollywood finds new ways to recycle its former glory as a means to urban redevelopment. Responding to a cycle of decline throughout the 1980s and 1990s, Hollywood developers have enlisted the support of Los Angeles' Community Redevelopment Agency to bring consumers and tourists back to Tinsel Town. Their most recent *coup de main* has been the Hollywood and Highland Redevelopment Project, built by the Canadian developer Trizec Hahn, the nation's largest owner of downtown office space. At a price of 615 million dollars, the Hollywood and Highland complex occupies one and a half city blocks of downtown Hollywood, containing a mazelike 425,000-square-foot retail mall, a two-thousand-seat multiplex cinema, and an auditorium designed as a permanent home for future Academy Awards ceremonies. With architectural references to the glories of old Hollywood, including a partial reconstruction of the extravagant movie set from D. W. Griffith's 1916 film, *Intolerance,* Hollywood is now reclaiming its former glamour as a means of reversing decades of urban decline.[18]

Disneyland is alive and well, though its constant renovation and ongoing expansion illustrate the extent to which today's audiences have outgrown the thematic imagery and cultural stereotypes that dominated the park's landscape in its postwar heyday. Racial difference no longer supplies a central theme of Disneyland. Aunt Jemima's Pancake House is now the River Belle Terrace and the grinning mammy has been retired from the kitchen. Audio Animatronic animals singing country music have replaced the Indians who once performed at Frontierland. And though Disneyland remains a cornerstone of "family entertainment," this did not preclude park officials from ignoring the vehement protests of the Christian Right and extending domestic-partner benefits to employees in 1995. Moreover, the recent successes of Disney films such as *Mulan* and *Pocahontas* indicate an openness to new stories and images that include the perspectives of racial minorities and women.[19] Would Walt Disney have approved of these changes? That question is impossible to answer, but the business acumen and sensitivity to the changing moral climate that Disney exhibited throughout his career would seem to imply his willingness to make such modifications in the midst of a rapidly changing world.

The Walt Disney Company's more sensitive portrait of racial and ethnic diversity, however, parallels the ongoing Disneyfication of public and private space. Today, Disneyland rests alongside Downtown Disney, a shopping and entertainment complex that presents Southern Californians with a neon-lit simulacrum of the noir city that Orange County residents shunned a generation earlier. While Disney executives repackage the noir city as their latest "attraction," American cities and suburbs today increasingly weave the themed experiences of Disneyland into the fabric of daily life. The brand of suburbanism that took shape in locales such as Orange County during the 1950s now extends its reach into the archetypal noir metropolis. In New York City, under the patronage of Mayor Rudolph Giuliani, the Walt Disney Company spearheaded an effort to revitalize Times Square, investing thirty-two million dollars in the renovation of the New Amsterdam Theater on Forty-second Street. Enticed by a slew of tax breaks and zoning incentives, Disney and other entertainment conglomerates—Nike, Warner Brothers, Virgin—are struggling against the presence of homeless vagrants and porn dealers to rescue Times Square from its previous noir incarnation.[20]

An even more portentous example of how Disney continues to blur urban fantasy and reality, Celebration, U.S.A., reflects the Disney Company's latest effort to establish its definition of community. Celebration, U.S.A., south of Orlando, Florida, extends across five thousand acres, complete with its own school, post office, downtown, pool, and parks. There is also a "town hall" designed by the noted architect Philip Johnson, though it serves no political function since the Disney Company retains the powers of planning and governance for Celebration's first twenty years. Not unlike the planners of Lakewood and countless other suburban housing developments, Disney and Osceola County arranged a mutually beneficial deal to keep low-income housing out of Celebration, U.S.A. Such an arrangement allows for larger profits on the sale of homes and higher property tax revenues, but, in the suburban tradition, minimizes racial diversity and severely limits civic experience.[21] If Celebration, U.S.A., maintains some remnants of suburban whiteness in Florida, Southern California harbors other reminders of Disney's cultural roots. Recently, the Ronald Reagan Presidential Library in Simi Valley, California, featured the exhibit "Walt Disney: The Man and His Magic."

The Dodgers retain their popularity among diverse Southern California baseball fans, and Dodger Stadium endures in the Chavez Ravine. Whatever ill will lingered between the Dodgers and local Chicanos over the Arechiga evictions, the arrival of a rookie pitcher from Etchohuaquila, Sonora, in 1981 sparked an intense passion for Dodger baseball among Chicanos and Mexican baseball fans alike. In his first year of pitching for the Dodgers, Fernando Valenzuela led his team to its fifth World Series victory, and with that, "Fernandomania" descended upon the Spanish-speaking world. Valenzuela's overwhelming popularity demonstrated the new cultural flavor of major-league baseball and illustrated how popular cultural institutions can reinforce distinct cultural identities, even as they appeal to broader audiences. The particular appeal of Dodgers baseball for the city's diverse constituencies continues, as Asian Americans also enjoy a special claim to the Dodgers in recent years. Representing the recent advances by Korean players in the major leagues, Chan Ho Park signed a ten-million-dollar contract with the Dodgers in 2001. Park follows in the footsteps of Hideo Nomo, who pitched for the Dodgers between 1995 and 2000, arousing the loyalties of Southern California's Japanese American community, which maintains an enduring enthusiasm for the game of baseball, dating as far back as the war years, when baseball games provided a momentary distraction from the indignities of internment. Today, as during the postwar period, the Dodgers continue to model interracial cooperation on the field before the city's diverse constituencies in the stands.[22]

Meanwhile, civic officials elsewhere look to Dodger Stadium as an example of how not to build a ballpark. On April 11, 2000, San Franciscans celebrated Opening Day for Pacific Bell Park (now known as SBC Park), a throwback to Boston's Fenway Park and its generation of urban ballparks. In contrast to the sprawling, 250-acre site of Dodger Stadium, SBC Park sits upon a mere 13 acres in the city's South of Market neighborhood, a newly gentrified area adjacent to downtown. Designed by Joe Spear of HOK Sport, the architect of Baltimore's Camden Yards and Cleveland's Jacobs Field, SBC Park offers a more modest—albeit more nostalgic—alternative to the monumentality of Dodger Stadium. Garbed in ivy, brick, and limestone, SBC Park rejects the solemn gray concrete that clothes Dodger Stadium, and its expansive view of the San Francisco Bay delivers a scenic connection to the surrounding region. Most unlike Dodger Stadium, however, SBC Park maintains a mere five thousand parking spaces, one fifth of which are usually empty during any given home game. The park's accessibility to public transportation and its close proximity to the city's many neighborhoods diminish the necessity for the automobile. While it might be unfair to compare SBC Park to a stadium built four decades ago, its success suggests that the designers of Ebbets Field, Fenway Park, and Wrigley Field just may have had it right all along.

Finally, although Southern Californians continue to exercise their preference for the private automobile, the freeway's benefit to urban life is more suspect than ever. Traffic congestion remains an enduring civic nightmare, and with recent population gains and a growing number of commuters willing to drive longer distances to work, today's freeways now more than ever fail to provide rapid access to the disparate points of the urban region. Freeway construction continues, though the master plan for freeways established by the Division of Highways in 1958 remains only half completed. Local residents are far more vocal in their opposition to highway construction, as the recent controversy surrounding the extension of the 710 Long Beach Freeway through South Pasadena illustrates. In the 2001 mayoral campaign, candidate Antonio Villaraigosa won the support of that community by announcing his opposition to the completion of the 710 project, denouncing that freeway as "a throwback to another era."

Growing frustration with the freeway and the automobile has intensified the search for alternative forms of public transportation. Today, the Metropolitan Transit Authority maintains its effort to build an extensive rail transit system throughout the urban region. The Blue Line from Los Angeles to Long Beach opened in 1990, and parts of the Green Line (from Norwalk to Hawthorne) and the Red Line (from downtown to the San Fernando Valley) have followed suit. Whether the vast majority of Southern Californian commuters will relinquish their automobiles in favor of rail transit remains uncertain, but hundreds of millions of dollars continue to pour into a transit system that may or may not alleviate traffic congestion on the region's freeways. Meanwhile, working-class communities of color continue to depend on the city's overcrowded and inadequate bus system. The Bus Riders' Union, a grass-roots organization dedicated to improving bus service, continues its fight against fare increases and route cancellations. During the age of the freeway, Los Angeles has sustained a kind of "transit apartheid" in which the experience of moving through urban space remains contingent upon class and color.[23]

The age of the freeway may be passing, but the street is making a comeback within the city's diverse communities. Los Angeles' emergence as the nation's preeminent Latino metropolis brings the street-oriented culture of Chicanos and Mexican immigrants to the very center of a new civic life. The city streets support the informal economy that relies upon the public display of goods and services. Day laborers congregate on sidewalks or parking lots, looking for a day's work in the vicinity of paint and hardware stores. *Vendedores* and *vendedoras* sell produce and flowers at freeway off-ramps and along median islands. Although such public interactions are common-place within Latino neighborhoods, they are new to more affluent neighborhoods. Westside communities are taking their cue from their Eastside counterparts and learning to enjoy the pleasures of street life. Farmers' markets draw large crowds throughout the city's diverse neighborhoods, offering a weekly festival for adults and children. In the posh quarters of West Hollywood, planners have recently completed a massive redevelopment project to enhance street life along Santa Monica Boulevard. Sunset Strip and its more modest imitations throughout the Southern California metropolis continue to attract increasingly diverse crowds in search of the city's nightlife. Contrary to popular stereotypes about the freeway metropolis, the street is reclaiming its place at the center of a changing public life.

The cultural forms that nurtured a suburban white identity during the postwar period now include alternative perspectives and experiences. Since the postwar period, whiteness and white flight no longer have been the master narratives that shape the texture of American cultural life, at least in cities on the cutting edge of social transformations. Other narratives have been inserted into the built environment since the postwar period, and their vitality points to a new definition of urban life at the outset of the twenty-first century. Whether or not the recent appreciation of multiculturalism and diversity will empower marginal social groups, however, is an open question. If cultural expressions of suburban whiteness inaugurated a greater disparity between white suburban affluence and nonwhite urban poverty during the postwar period, can we expect the current incarnation of Los Angeles as a "world city" to bring about a more equitable reconfiguration of urban social relations? As whites have become a demographic minority in the Los Angeles urban region, new forms of urban popular culture model new configurations of race and space and encompass even more diverse cultural expressions. As the urban landscape mirrors the city's great diversity in more equitable ways, whiteness will lose its saliency as a defining principle of urban culture and identity. Once again, Los Angeles, a city often recognized as a cultural trendsetter, may be the first to model this development. Though the city once supported powerful expressions of suburban whiteness, it may be, in the not too distant future, that to imagine a white identity in a region teeming with nonwhite peoples will be to conjure a historical fiction from the city's past.

Notes

CHAPTER ONE. CHOCOLATE CITIES AND VANILLA SUBURBS

1. Martin Tolchin, "Coney Island Slump Grows Worse," *New York Times*, 2 July 1964. Throughout this book I have retained the original spelling in all primary texts except where the original spelling obscures the meaning; in these cases, I have corrected the spelling in brackets.

2. *Chicago Tribune Magazine*, 16 May 1976.

3. Quoted in David Nasaw, *Going Out: The Rise and Fall of Public Amusements* (New York: Basic Books, 1993), 252. For a deeper analysis of Shibe Park and its relation to its changing urban context, see Bruce Kuklick, *To Everything a Season: Shibe Park and Urban Philadelphia, 1909–1976* (Princeton, N.J.: Princeton University Press, 1991).

4. Quoted in Peter Golenbock, *Bums: An Oral History of the Brooklyn Dodgers* (New York: G. P. Putnam and Sons, 1984), 38.

5. Mark S. Foster, *From Streetcar to Superhighway: American City Planners and Urban Transportation* (Philadelphia: Temple University Press, 1981). For a more specialized treatment of the demise of Southern California's streetcar system, see Scott Bottles, *Los Angeles and the Automobile: The Making of the Modern City* (Berkeley: University of California Press, 1987); and David Brodsly, *L.A. Freeway: An Appreciative Essay* (Berkeley: University of California Press, 1981).

6. For general overviews of the history of nineteenth-century urbanization, see Sam Bass Warner Jr., *The Urban Wilderness: A History of the American City* (New York: Harper and Row, 1972); Eric H. Monkonnen, *America Becomes Urban: The Development of U.S. Cities and Towns, 1780–1900* (Berkeley: University of California Press, 1988); Raymond A. Mohl, *The New City: Urban America in the Industrial Age, 1860–1920* (Arlington Heights, Ill.: Harlan Davidson, 1987); and Howard P. Chudacoff and Judith E. Smith, *The Evolution of American Urban Society*, 5th ed. (Upper Saddle River, N.J.: Prentice Hall, 2000). For more specialized treatment of individual cities, see Gunther Barth, *Instant Cities: Urbanization and the Rise of San Francisco and Denver* (New

244 / Notes to Pages 3–4

York: Oxford University Press, 1985); and William Cronon, *Nature's Metropolis: Chicago and the Great West* (New York: W. W. Norton and Company, 1992).

7. John Kasson identifies Coney Island as exemplifying the "new mass culture" that emerged within the context of industrial urbanization, and Kathy Peiss describes the "heterosocial" nature of urban popular culture at the turn of the century, emphasizing the role of women within that culture. See John F. Kasson, *Amusing the Million: Coney Island at the Turn of the Century* (New York: Hill and Wang, 1978); and Kathy Peiss, *Cheap Amusements: Working Women and Leisure in Turn-of-the-Century New York* (Philadelphia: Temple University Press, 1990). Other scholars who have surveyed the history of the "new mass culture" include David Nasaw, *Going Out*; Gunther Barth, *City People: The Rise of Modern City Culture in Nineteenth-Century America* (New York: Oxford University Press, 1982); Neil Harris, *Cultural Excursions: Marketing Appetites and Cultural Tastes in Modern America* (Chicago: University of Chicago Press, 1990); Lawrence Levine, *Highbrow/Lowbrow: The Emergence of Cultural Hierarchy in America* (Cambridge, Mass.: Harvard University Press, 1988); Timothy Gilfolye, *City of Eros: New York City, Prostitution and the Commercialization of Sex, 1790–1920* (New York: W. W. Norton and Company, 1992); George Chauncey, *Gay New York: Gender, Urban Culture, and the Making of the Gay Male World, 1890–1940* (New York: Basic Books, 1994); and Karen Haltunnen, *Confidence Men and Painted Women: A Study of Middle-Class Culture in America, 1830–1870* (New Haven, Conn.: Yale University Press, 1982).

8. David Nasaw emphasizes the degree of racial segregation built into the public amusements of the modern city in *Going Out*. Others, however, have emphasized the racialized character of nineteenth-century urban popular culture. See W. T. Lhamon Jr., *Raising Cain: Blackface Performance from Jim Crow to Hip Hop* (Cambridge, Mass.: Harvard University Press, 1998); Eric Lott, *Love and Theft: Blackface Minstrelsy and the American Working Class* (New York: Oxford University Press, 1993); and John Kuo Wei Tchen, *New York before Chinatown: Orientalism and the Shaping of American Culture, 1776–1886* (Baltimore: Johns Hopkins University Press, 1999).

9. Kenneth T. Jackson, *Crabgrass Frontier: The Suburbanization of the United States* (New York: Oxford University Press, 1985), 238–45. See also Becky M. Nicolaides, *My Blue Heaven: Life and Politics in the Working-Class Suburbs of Los Angeles, 1920–1965* (Chicago: University of Chicago Press, 2002), 216–19.

10. The transition from the modern centralized city to the decentralized urban region rests on a set of generalizations about the changing patterns of urban life in the twentieth century and recalls a traditional distinction between city and suburb. It is important to acknowledge, however, that this distinction has never been fixed and that the boundaries between city and suburb have always been shifting and porous. There is what James Wunsch calls a "suburban cliché" that views suburbanization as the search for a simpler alternative to complex patterns of urban life. Suburban areas, however, in the past and present

include diverse political, social, and economic realities that often mimic typical urban complexities. Suburbanization, however, though it sanctioned the mixing of distinct ethnic, class, and religious groups, rested upon a set of historic assumptions that reinforced traditional patterns of racial segregation. See James L. Wunsch, "The Suburban Cliché," *Journal of Social History* 28, no. 3 (1995): 643–58; Richard Harris and Robert Lewis, "The Geography of North American Cities and Suburbs: A New Synthesis, 1900–1950," *Journal of Urban History* 27, no. 3 (March 2001): 259–61; and Matt Jalberg, " 'Burbs, Blockbusting and Blacks: Morphosis of the Postwar American City," *Radical Urban Theory* (www.rut.com/mjalbert/burbs/index7.html). For a historiographic debate on the nature of contemporary suburbia, see William Sharpe and Leonard Wallock, "Bold New City or Built-Up 'Burb? Redefining Contemporary Suburbia," in *The Making of Urban America*, ed. Raymond A. Mohl (Wilmington, Del.: SR Books, 1997), 309–31.

11. Nicholas Lehman, *The Promised Land: The Great Black Migration and How It Changed America* (New York: Random House, 1991); Jacqueline Jones, *The Dispossessed: America's Underclasses from the Civil War to the Present* (New York: Basic Books, 1992); Neil Fligstein, *Going North: Migration of Blacks and Whites from the South, 1900–1950* (New York: Academic Press, 1981); Kenneth L. Kusmer, "African Americans in the City since World War II," *Journal of Urban History* 21 (1995): 458–504; Reynolds Farley and Walter R. Allen, *The Color Line and the Quality of Life in America* (New York: Russell Sage, 1987); Dennis R. Judd and Todd Swanstrom, *City Politics: Private Power and Public Policy*, 2d ed. (New York: Longman, 1998); and Jon C. Teaford, *The Twentieth-Century American City*, 2d ed. (Baltimore: Johns Hopkins University Press, 1993), 115.

12. Kenneth T. Jackson, "Race, Ethnicity, and Real Estate Appraisal: The Home Owners' Loan Corporation and the Federal Housing Administration," *Journal of Urban History* 6, no. 4 (1980): 419–52. For the pax Americana between white labor and capital forged during the 1940s, see George Lipsitz, *Rainbow at Midnight: Labor and Culture in the 1940s* (Urbana: University of Illinois Press, 1994). See also Nicolaides, *My Blue Heaven*. On post–World War II patterns of racial resegregation in the United States, see Douglas S. Massey and Nancy A. Denton, "Suburbanization and Segregation in U.S. Metropolitan Areas," *American Journal of Sociology* 94, no. 3 (November 1988): 592–626; Douglas S. Massey and Nancy A. Denton, *American Apartheid: Segregation and the Making of an Underclass* (Cambridge, Mass.: Harvard University Press, 1993); Arnold Hirsch, *Making the Second Ghetto: Race and Housing in Chicago, 1940–1980* (Cambridge: Cambridge University Press, 1983); and Thomas Sugrue, *The Origins of the Urban Crisis: Race and Inequality in Postwar Detroit* (Princeton, N.J.: Princeton University Press, 1996).

13. National Advisory Commission on Civil Disorders, *Report of the National Advisory Commission on Civil Disorders* (New York: Bantam, 1968), 1. This report is also known as the Kerner Report, named after the chairman of the advisory committee, Otto Kerner, then governor of Illinois. For a specific

assessment of the 1965 race riots in Los Angeles, see California Governor's
Commission on the Los Angeles Riots, *Violence in the City—An End or a
Beginning? A Report by the Governor's Commission on the Los Angeles Riots*
(Los Angeles: Governor's Commission on the Los Angeles Riots, 1965).

14. George Clinton with Parliament, "Chocolate City," Casablanca Records,
3 May 1975. See also Robin D.G. Kelley, *Yo' Mama's Dysfunktional: Fighting
the Culture Wars in Urban America* (Boston: Beacon Press, 1997).

15. This dynamic among the creation, consumption, and contestation of cultural forms is key to understanding how cultural practices can be read as social
history evidence. See, for example, Stuart Hall, "Notes on Deconstructing 'The
Popular,'" in *People's History and Socialist Theory*, ed. Raphael Samuel (London: Routledge and Kegan Paul, 1981), 227–39.

16. Steve Fraser and Gary Gerstle, eds., *The Rise and Fall of the New Deal
Order, 1930–1980* (Princeton, N.J.: Princeton University Press, 1989). The political scientist James Q. Wilson also noted how Southern California harbored a
"Reagan point of view" throughout the post–World War II period. See James Q.
Wilson, "A Guide to Reagan Country: The Political Culture of Southern California," *Commentary*, May 1967, 37–45. See also Michael Paul Rogin and John
L. Shover, *Political Change in California: Critical Elections and Social Movements, 1890–1960* (Westport, Conn.: Greenwood Publishing Company, 1970),
153–212.

17. Dennis R. Judd and Todd Swanstrom make this point in structural terms,
arguing that urban and suburban development during the postwar period can be
understood only as a single, interdependent process. See Judd and Swanstrom,
City Politics.

18. Susan Sontag, "The Imagination of Disaster," in *Film Theory and Criticism*, ed. Gerald Mast and Marshall Cohen, 2d ed. (London: Oxford University
Press, 1979), 488–504.

19. Marshall McLuhan, *Understanding Media: The Extensions of Man*
(New York: McGraw Hill, 1965). On television and cultural implications, see
Lynn Spigel, *Make Room for TV: Television and the Family Ideal in Postwar
America* (Chicago: University of Chicago Press, 1992). See also Eric Barnouw, *A
History of Broadcasting in the United States*, vol. 3 (New York: Oxford Uni-
versity Press, 1973); and Eric Barnouw, *Tube of Plenty: The Evolution of Amer-
ican Broadcasting* (New York: Oxford University Press, 1975).

20. Lizabeth Cohen, "From Town Center to Shopping Center: The Recon-
figuration of Community Marketplaces in Postwar America," *American His-
torical Review* 101, no. 4 (October 1996): 1059; William S. Kowinski, *The
Malling of America: An Inside Look at the Great Consumer Paradise* (New
York: William Morrow and Company, 1985). For the suburbanization of shop-
ping in Southern California, see Richard Longstreth, *City Center to Regional
Mall: Architecture, the Automobile and Retailing in Los Angeles, 1920–1950*
(Cambridge, Mass.: MIT Press, 1997).

21. See Carl Schorske, *Fin de Siècle Vienna: Politics and Culture* (New York:
Vintage Books, 1981).

22. Mike Davis, *Ecology of Fear: Los Angeles and the Imagination of Disaster* (New York: Metropolitan Books, 1998), 392.

23. Alan Trachtenberg, *The Incorporation of America: American Culture and Society in the Gilded Age* (New York: Hill and Wang, 1982); R. Reid Badger, *The Great American Fair: The World's Columbian Exposition and American Culture* (Chicago: Nelson-Hall, 1979). See also Kasson, *Amusing the Million*. For a conceptualized approach to urban cultural history, see Warren Susman, "The City in American Culture," in *Culture as History: The Transformation of American Society in the Twentieth Century* (New York: Pantheon Books, 1984), 237–51.

24. John Findlay emphasizes the cultural models of order that took shape alongside the development of the Sunbelt in the post–World War II West. See John Findlay, *Magic Lands: Western Cityscapes and American Culture after 1940* (Berkeley: University of California Press, 1992). For more general surveys of Sunbelt urbanization after World War II, see Carl Abbott, *The New Urban America: Growth and Politics in Sunbelt Cities* (Chapel Hill: University of North Carolina Press, 1981); and Raymond Mohl, ed., *Searching for the Sunbelt: Historical Perspectives on a Region* (Athens: University of Georgia Press, 1993).

25. Kasson, *Amusing the Million*, 9.

26. Dana Bartlett, *The Better City: A Sociological Study of a Modern City* (Los Angeles: Neuner Company Press, 1907). For an exploration of Los Angeles and the emergence of modern consumer culture, see David Karnes, "Modern Metropolis: Mass Culture and the Transformation of Los Angeles, 1890–1950" (Ph.D. diss., University of California, Berkeley, 1991).

27. "Respectability" is a broad cultural category that encompasses a wide-ranging set of beliefs about how to be—or at least how to seem to be—in a public and highly impersonal environment. Whatever variations surfaced within that category at different times and in different places, "respectability" in the United States generally revolved around notions of being middle class, family centered, and white. These ideals surfaced with a vengeance in the new cultural settings of the postwar urban region, and they defined the parameters of a new, yet thoroughly familiar, identity that became affiliated with an ideal of the suburban good life. For a discussion of respectability in its nineteenth-century Victorian context, see Karen Haltunnen, *Confidence Men and Painted Women;* and John F. Kasson, *Rudeness and Civility: Manners in Nineteenth-Century Urban America* (New York: Hill and Wang, 1990).

28. For the distinction between "popular" and "mass" culture and its significance to the study of American history, see Lawrence W. Levine, "The Folklore of Industrial Society: Popular Culture and Its Audiences," *American Historical Review* 97, no. 5 (December 1992): 1369–99.

29. Academic judgments heaped upon Los Angeles tend to conflate the city with mass culture. Like movies, the primary elements of urban growth in twentieth-century Southern California—automobiles, water, and housing—are mass-produced commodities, manufactured and marketed by corporations and consumed by millions of consumers. This fundamental fact of Southern

California's growth arouses both consternation and celebration among scholars and intellectuals. The noir vision, to borrow Mike Davis's terminology, extends from the warnings of the Frankfurt School, most notably Theodore Adorno and Max Horkheimer, who as far back as the early 1940s sketched their ominous vision of the absolute power of capital. See Max Horkheimer and Theodor Adorno, *Dialectic of Enlightenment*, trans. John Cumming (New York: Continuum, 1995). From Horkheimer and Adorno's vantage point in wartime Los Angeles, modern society exhibited a profoundly undialectical relationship between an all-powerful cabal of capital and its dependent mass of passive consumers. This vision informed writing in and about Los Angeles throughout much of the twentieth century. Take, for example, Donald Worster's *Rivers of Empire*, which recounts the history of water acquisition in Southern California and the West. Los Angeles, to Worster, epitomizes the "hydraulic society," where "the common people become a herd" and, ultimately, "lifelong wards of the corporation and State." Donald Worster, *Rivers of Empire: Water, Aridity and the Growth of the American West* (New York: Pantheon Books, 1985), 57–58. See also Mike Davis, *City of Quartz: Excavating the Future in Los Angeles* (London: Verso Press, 1990).

30. In contrast to the noir vision, an "I love L.A." school has taken shape around the writings of Reyner Banham, who disregarded Southern California's patterns of racial and class inequality to emphasize Los Angeles as a "mobile, affluent, consumer-oriented society," in which "all its parts are equal and equally accessible from all other parts at once." According to this logic, Watts in the aftermath of 1965 was simply another "fashionable venue for confrontations." Reyner Banham, *Los Angeles: The Architecture of Four Ecologies* (London: Penguin Books, 1971), 25, 36, 124. Others who followed in this vein include David Brodsly, who wrote an "appreciative essay" about Los Angeles and its freeway system, which concludes that Los Angeles "has been, perhaps to an unprecedented extent, a reflection of choice." Brodsly, *L.A. Freeway*, 136. Additionally, Alan Hess documented coffee shop architecture in 1950s Los Angeles, which "made the images of the modern good life available to all." Alan Hess, *Googie: Fifties Coffee Shop Architecture* (San Francisco: Chronicle Books, 1984), 119.

31. Robin D. G. Kelley responds to Levine's description of popular culture as "the folklore of industrial society" with his injunction that "popular culture can simultaneously subvert and reproduce hegemony," emphasizing how popular culture audiences and texts are "gendered" and "raced." See Robin D. G. Kelley, "Notes on Deconstructing 'The Folk,'" *American Historical Review* 97, no. 5 (December 1992): 1400–1408.

32. Michael Danielson, *The Politics of Exclusion* (New York: Columbia University Press, 1976); Reynolds Farley, Howard Schuman, Suzanne Bianchi, Diane Colasanto, and Shirley Hatchett, "'Chocolate City, Vanilla Suburbs': Will the Trend toward Racially Separate Communities Continue?" *Social Science Research* 7 (1978): 319–44; William H. Frey, "Central City White Flight: Racial and Non-Racial Causes," *American Sociological Review* 44 (1979): 425–48; William H. Frey, "Black In-Migration, White Flight, and the Changing Economic

Base of the Central City," *American Journal of Sociology* 85 (1980): 1396–1417; and Karl E. Taeuber and Alma F. Taeuber, *Negroes in Cities: Residential Segregation and Neighborhood Change* (Chicago: Aldine Publishing, 1965).

33. Central to this discussion is Michael Omi and Harold Winant's theory of racial formation, which asserts that race "is constructed and transformed sociohistorically through competing political projects, through the necessary and ineluctable link between the structural and cultural dimensions of race in the U.S." *Racialization*, accordingly, denotes the process by which social, political, and economic practices are invested with racial meanings through a set of discursive or representational practices. Michael Omi and Harold Winant, *Racial Formation in the United States: From the 1960s to the 1990s*, 2d ed. (London: Routledge, 1994), 71. Other scholars explore the process of racialization in American history, emphasizing the structural and cultural formation of a white identity within various historical and regional contexts of the United States. See, for example, Reginald Horsman, *Race and Manifest Destiny: The Origins of American Racial Anglo-Saxonism* (Cambridge, Mass.: Harvard University Press, 1981); David Roediger, *The Wages of Whiteness: Race and the Making of the American Working Class* (London: Verso Press, 1991); Noel Ignatiev, *How the Irish Became White* (New York: Routledge, 1995); Alexander Saxton, *The Rise and Fall of the White Republic: Class Politics and Mass Culture in Nineteenth-Century America* (London: Verso Press, 1990); and Matthew Frye Jacobson, *Whiteness of a Different Color: European Immigrants and the Alchemy of Race* (Cambridge, Mass.: Harvard University Press, 1998).

34. The literature on the historical patterns of racial segregation in Los Angeles is slim. For general patterns of racial and ethnic community formation in Southern California, see James P. Allen and Eugene Turner, *The Ethnic Quilt: Population Diversity in Southern California* (Northridge: Center for Geographical Studies, Department of Geography, California State University, Northridge, 1997). Other scholars have focused on the historical development of specific ethnic and racial communities in the Los Angeles urban region. See Lawrence de Graaf, "The City of Black Angels: Emergence of a Los Angeles Ghetto, 1890–1930," *Pacific Historical Review* 39 (1970): 323–52; Ricardo Romo, *East Los Angeles: History of a Barrio* (Austin: University of Texas Press, 1983); George J. Sánchez, *Becoming Mexican American: Ethnicity, Culture, and Identity in Chicano Los Angeles, 1900–1945* (New York: Oxford University Press, 1993); Timothy P. Fong, *The First Suburban Chinatown: The Remaking of Monterey Park, California* (Philadelphia: Temple University Press, 1994); and Max Vorspan and L.P. Gartner, *History of the Jews of Los Angeles* (San Marino, Calif.: Huntington Library, 1970).

35. Chudacoff and Smith, *Evolution of American Urban Society*, 125.

36. Edward W. Soja, "History: Geography: Modernity," in *The Cultural Studies Reader*, ed. Simon During, 2d ed. (New York: Routledge, 1993), 113–25.

37. Richard Dyer, "White," *Screen* 29, no. 4 (1993): 1; Marlon Riggs, *Ethnic Notions* (San Francisco: California Newsreel, 1986), videocassette. Phillip Deloria recognizes a similar role played by representations of Indians in American

culture. See Philip J. Deloria, *Playing Indian* (New Haven, Conn.: Yale University Press, 1998); Roediger, *Wages of Whiteness*, 95–97; James W. Cook, *The Arts of Deception: Playing with Fraud in the Age of Barnum* (Cambridge, Mass.: Harvard University Press, 2001), 118–62; and Lott, *Love and Theft.*

38. Elaine Tyler May, *Homeward Bound: American Families in the Cold War Era* (New York: Basic Books, 1988); Joanna Meyerowitz, ed., *Not June Cleaver: Women and Gender in Postwar America* (Philadelphia: Temple University Press, 1994). For an analysis of the mutually constitutive relationship between whiteness and patriarchy, see Ruth Frankenburg, *White Women, Race Matters: The Social Construction of Whiteness* (Minneapolis: University of Minnesota Press, 1993).

39. Roland Marchand, "Visions of Classlessness, Quests for Dominion: American Popular Culture: 1945–1960," in *Reshaping America: Society and Institutions, 1945–1960*, ed. Robert H. Brenner and Gary W. Reichard (Columbus: Ohio State University Press, 1985), 163–90.

40. George Lipsitz, *The Possessive Investment in Whiteness: How White People Profit from Identity Politics* (Philadelphia: Temple University Press, 1998).

41. Several scholars have illuminated the heightened salience of race in Southern California's political culture during the 1960s and beyond. See David O. Sears and Donald R. Kinder, "Racial Tension and Voting in Los Angeles" (Institute of Government and Public Affairs, UCLA, January 1971, photocopy), 1–51. See also Rogin and Shover, *Political Change in California*, 198–201; Lisa McGirr, *Suburban Warriors: The Origins of the New American Right* (Princeton, N.J.: Princeton University Press, 2001), 183–85; Raphael J. Sonenshein, *Politics in Black and White: Race and Power in Los Angeles* (Princeton, N.J.: Princeton University Press, 1993); and Nicolaides, *My Blue Heaven*, chapter 7.

42. Raymond Williams, *Marxism and Literature* (Oxford: Oxford University Press, 1977), part II, chapter 9, "Structures of Feeling."

CHAPTER TWO. THE NATION'S "WHITE SPOT"

1. Douglas Monroy, *Rebirth: Mexican Los Angeles from the Great Migration to the Great Depression* (Berkeley: University of California Press, 1999); Lawrence de Graaf, "The City of Black Angels: Emergence of the Los Angeles Ghetto, 1890–1930," *Pacific Historical Review* 39 (1970): 323–52; Marc Weiss, *The Rise of the Community Builders: The American Real Estate Industry and Urban Land Planning* (New York: Columbia University Press, 1987); George J. Sánchez, *Becoming Mexican American: Ethnicity, Culture, and Identity in Chicano Los Angeles, 1900–1945* (New York: Oxford University Press, 1993).

2. Carey McWilliams, *The Education of Carey McWilliams* (New York: Simon and Schuster, 1979), 114–15.

3. Robert De Roos, "Los Angeles: Colossus of the West," *National Geographic,* October 1962, 452.

4. Joseph Widney, *Race Life of the Aryan Peoples* (New York: Funk and Wagnalls Company, 1907); Mike Davis, *City of Quartz: Excavating the Future*

in Los Angeles (London: Verso, 1990), 28; Carey McWilliams, *Southern California: An Island on the Land* (Salt Lake City: Peregrine-Smith, 1994); Carey McWilliams, *North from Mexico: The Spanish-Speaking Peoples of the United States*, ed. Matt S. Meier (New York: Praeger, 1990), 44–47. See also David H. Thomas, "Harvesting Ramona's Garden: Life in California's Mythical Mission Past," in *Columbian Consequences*, vol. 3, *The Spanish Borderlands in Pan American Perspective*, ed. David H. Thomas (Washington, D.C.: Smithsonian Institution Press, 1991), 119–57; and William Deverell, "Privileging the Mission over the Mexican: The Rise of Regional Consciousness in Southern California," in *Many Wests: Place, Culture and Regional Identity*, ed. David Wrobel and Michael Steiner (Lawrence: University Press of Kansas, 1997), 235–58.

5. James T. Lemon, *Liberal Dreams and Nature's Limits: Great Cities in North America since 1600* (Toronto: Oxford University Press, 1996), 192; Robert Fogelson, *The Fragmented Metropolis: Los Angeles, 1850–1930* (Berkeley: University of California Press, 1993), 63–68; McWilliams, *Southern California*, 165–82.

6. Douglas Flamming, "African Americans and the Politics of Race in Progressive-Era Los Angeles," in *California Progressivism Revisited*, ed. William Deverell and Tom Sitton (Berkeley: University of California Press, 1994), 207; Sánchez, *Becoming Mexican American*, 98–102.

7. Dana Bartlett, *The Better City: A Sociological Study of a Modern City* (Los Angeles: Neuner Company Press, 1907), 20, 74.

8. Quoted in McWilliams, *Southern California*, 157–58.

9. Bartlett, *Better City*, 24.

10. Janet L. Abu-Lughod, *New York, Chicago, Los Angeles: America's Global Cities* (Minneapolis: University of Minnesota, 1999), 245.

11. James P. Allen and Eugene Turner, *The Ethnic Quilt: Population Diversity in Southern California* (Northridge: Center for Geographical Studies, Department of Geography, California State University, Northridge, 1997), 67; Sánchez, *Becoming Mexican American*, 74–75; Ralph Friedman, "U.N. in Microcosm," *Frontier*, March 1955, 11–14.

12. Patricia Adler, "Watts: A Legacy of Lines," *Westways* 58 (August 1966): 22–24. See also Allen and Turner, *Ethnic Quilt*, 80–81.

13. Quoted in Clora Bryant, Buddy Collette, William Green, Steven Isoardi, Jack Kelson, Horace Tapscott, Gerald Wilson, and Marl Young, eds., *Central Avenue Sounds: Jazz in Los Angeles* (Berkeley: University of California Press, 1998), 103.

14. Vicki Ruiz, *Cannery Women, Cannery Lives: Mexican Women, Unionization, and the California Food Processing Industry* (Albuquerque: University of New Mexico Press, 1987); Monroy, *Rebirth*, 213–14; Sánchez, *Becoming Mexican American*, 234; Kevin Leonard, "Brothers under the Skin: African Americans, Mexican Americans, and World War II in California," in *The Way We Really Were: The Golden State in the Second Great War*, ed. Roger W. Lotchin (Urbana: University of Illinois Press, 2000), 190–92.

15. Sánchez, *Becoming Mexican American*, 224–25.

16. Josh Sides, "Working Away: African American Migration and Community in Los Angeles from the Great Depression to 1954" (Ph.D. diss., University of California, Los Angeles, 1999), 109; Louis Erenberg, *Swingin' the Dream: Big Band Jazz and the Rebirth of American Culture* (Chicago: University of Chicago Press, 1998), 148. Quotation from George Lipsitz, *Time Passages: Collective Memory and American Popular Culture* (Minneapolis: University of Minnesota Press, 1990), 138.

17. Don Parson, "Urban Politics during the Cold War: Public Housing, Urban Renewal, and Suburbanization in Los Angeles" (Ph.D. diss., University of California, Los Angeles, 1985), 98.

18. Beatrice Griffith, "Viva Roybal—Viva America," *Common Ground* 10, no. 1 (autumn 1949): 64. See also Martin Hall, "Roybal's Candidacy and What It Means," *Frontier,* June 1954, 5.

19. David Gutiérrez, *Walls and Mirrors: Mexican Americans, Mexican Immigrants, and the Politics of Ethnicity* (Berkeley: University of California Press, 1995), 168–69; Sánchez, *Becoming Mexican American,* 250.

20. Parson, "Urban Politics during the Cold War," 62–64.

21. Gerald D. Nash, *The American West Transformed: The Impact of the Second World War* (Lincoln: University of Nebraska Press, 1985), 25.

22. U.S. Bureau of the Census, *Sixteenth Census of the United States, 1940,* vol. 2, *Population and Housing* (Washington, D.C.: Government Printing Office, 1942); U.S. Bureau of the Census, *Special Census of Los Angeles, California: Population by Age, Race, and Sex, by Census Tracts,* P-SC, no. 188 (Washington, D.C.: Department of Commerce, 1946); U.S. Bureau of the Census, *Census of the Population, 1950,* vol. 2, *Characteristics of the Population* (Washington, D.C.: Government Printing Office, 1952); U.S. Bureau of the Census, *Census of the Population, 1960,* vol. 1, *Characteristics of the Population* (Washington, D.C.: Government Printing Office, 1963); U.S. Bureau of the Census, *Census of the Population, 1970,* vol. 1, *Characteristics of the Population* (Washington, D.C.: Government Printing Office, 1973); Allen J. Scott and Edward W. Soja, eds., *The City: Los Angeles and Urban Theory at the End of the Twentieth Century* (Berkeley: University of California Press, 1996), 8.

23. Kevin Allen Leonard, " 'In the Interest of All Races': African Americans and Interracial Cooperation in Los Angeles during and after World War II," in *Seeking El Dorado: African Americans in California,* ed. Lawrence B. de Graaf, Kevin Mulroy, and Quintard Taylor (Seattle: University of Washington Press, 2001), 312.

24. Chester Himes, *Lonely Crusade* (1947; reprint, New York: Thunder's Mouth, 1975), 131.

25. John Anson Ford, *Thirty Explosive Years in Los Angeles County* (San Marino, Calif.: Huntington Library, 1961), 137.

26. U.S. Bureau of the Census, *Census of the Population, 1950,* vol. 2, *Characteristics of the Population,* part 5, 100–103; U.S. Bureau of the Census, *Special Census of Los Angeles;* U.S. Bureau of the Census, *Census of Population, 1970,* vol. 1, *Characteristics of the Population.*

27. Davis, *City of Quartz*, 163; Allen and Turner, *Ethnic Quilt*, 80; quotation is from Andrew Murray, interview by Sides, "Working Away," 269.

28. George Sánchez describes the World War II generation of white Americans, including second-generation European Americans, as a "welfare generation living off the hard work of others." See George Sánchez, "Reading Reginald Denny: The Politics of Whiteness in Late Twentieth-Century America," *American Quarterly* 47, no. 3 (September 1995): 390; and Becky M. Nicolaides, "Incubating the 'Silent Majority': Community and Political Life in a Working-Class Suburb of Los Angeles, 1945–1965" (paper presented at the Annual Meeting of the Organization of American Historians, San Francisco, April 1997). See also Becky M. Nicolaides, *My Blue Heaven: Life and Politics in the Working-Class Suburbs of Los Angeles, 1920–1965* (Chicago: University of Chicago Press, 2002). For a discussion of the Dust Bowl generation of migrants to California, see James N. Gregory, *American Exodus: The Dust Bowl Migration and Okie Culture in California* (New York: Oxford University Press, 1989). See also James N. Gregory, "Okies and the Politics of Plain Folk Americanism," in *Working People of California*, ed. Daniel Cornford (Berkeley: University of California Press, 1995), 159–80.

29. Jon C. Teaford, *The Twentieth-Century American City*, 2d ed. (Baltimore: Johns Hopkins University Press, 1993), 115.

30. Carl Abbot, "New West, New South, New Region: The Discovery of the Sunbelt," in *Searching for the Sunbelt: Historical Perspectives on a Region*, ed. Raymond A. Mohl (Athens: University of Georgia Press, 1993), 7–24; John M. Findlay, *Magic Lands: Western Cityscapes and American Culture after 1940* (Berkeley: University of California Press, 1992), 15–16.

31. Thomas Sugrue, *The Origins of the Urban Crisis: Race and Inequality in Postwar Detroit* (Princeton, N.J.: Princeton University Press, 1996), 140–41.

32. Dennis R. Judd and Todd Swanstrom, *City Politics: Private Power and Public Policy*, 2d ed. (New York: Longman, 1998), 201–5; Alan Lupo, Frank Colcord, and Edmund P. Fowler, *Rites of Way: The Politics of Transportation in Boston and the U.S. City* (Boston: Little, Brown, 1971), 184; Raymond Mohl, "Race and Space in the Modern City: Interstate 95 and the Black Community in Miami," in *Urban Policy in Twentieth-Century America*, ed. Arnold R. Hirsch and Raymond A. Mohl (New Brunswick, N.J.: Rutgers, 1993), 66–100.

33. Kenneth T. Jackson, "Race, Ethnicity, and Real Estate Appraisal: The Home Owners' Loan Corporation and the Federal Housing Administration," *Journal of Urban History* 6, no. 4 (1980): 435.

34. Kenneth T. Jackson, *Crabgrass Frontier: The Suburbanization of the United States* (New York: Oxford University Press, 1985), 197.

35. Home Owners' Loan Corporation, Los Angeles City Survey Files, Record Group 195, National Archives, Washington, D.C., 38, 40, 88, 255, 280, 401.

36. Quoted in Judd and Swanstrom, *City Politics*, 198.

37. Nash, *American West Transformed*, 63; Scott Bottles, *Los Angeles and the Automobile: The Making of the Modern City* (Berkeley: University of California Press, 1987), 108.

38. "City Hunting for Source of Gas Attack," *Los Angeles Times*, 27 July 1943, part 1, p. 1. Contrary to a common tendency to single out Los Angeles as smog-ridden, New York City experienced a similar crisis during the early 1950s. New York experienced a six-day siege of air pollution in November 1953, and subsequent episodes in 1962 and 1966. The smog that plagued New York and Los Angeles during the 1940s and 1950s ultimately led the federal government to enact new clean air standards and beef up enforcement.

39. Nash, *American West Transformed*, 63. Bowron is quoted in Sides, "Working Away," 120.

40. Greg Mitchell, *Tricky Dick and the Pink Lady: Richard Nixon vs. Helen Gahagan Douglas—Sexual Politics and the Red Scare* (New York: Random House, 1998); Larry Ceplair and Steven Englund, *The Inquisition in Hollywood: Politics in the Film Community, 1930–1960* (Berkeley: University of California Press, 1983). See also Lary May, "Movie Star Politics: The Screen Actors' Guild, Cultural Conversion and the Hollywood Red Scare," in *Recasting America: Culture and Politics in the Age of Cold War*, ed. Lary May (Chicago: University of Chicago Press, 1989), 125–53.

41. Parson, "Urban Politics during the Cold War," 86 (Fritz Burns quotation); Robert Gottlieb and Irene Wolt, *Thinking Big: The Los Angeles Times, Its Publishers and Their Influence on Southern California* (New York: G. P Putnam and Sons, 1977), 261 (other quotations in paragraph).

42. Don Parson, "Los Angeles' Headline Happy Public Housing War," *Southern California Quarterly* 65, no. 3 (fall 1983): 267.

43. Parson, "Urban Politics during the Cold War," 132.

44. Greg Hise, *Magnetic Los Angeles: Planning the Twentieth-Century Metropolis* (Baltimore: Johns Hopkins University Press, 1997), 153–95; Leonard Pitt and Dale Pitt, *Los Angeles A to Z: An Encyclopedia of the City and County* (Berkeley: University of California Press, 1997), 381.

45. Sides, "Working Away," 259.

46. "Confidential Report on United States Housing Authority and Federal Housing Administration in Metropolitan Los Angeles," ca. 1940, box 102, Records of the Federal Home Loan Bank Board, RG 195, National Archives, 260.

47. Editorial, *California Eagle*, 15 May 1959.

48. Quoted in D. J. Waldie, *Holy Land: A Suburban Memoir* (New York: St. Martin's Press, 1996), 160.

49. Waldie, *Holy Land*, 74.

50. Karen Brodkin, *How the Jews Became White Folks and What That Says about Race in America* (New Brunswick, N.J.: Rutgers University Press, 2000); Matthew Frye Jacobson, "Looking Jewish, Seeing Jews," in *Theories of Race and Racism: A Reader*, ed. Les Back and John Solomos (London: Routledge, 2000), 238–56; Michael Rogin, *Blackface, White Noise: Jews and the Hollywood Melting Pot* (Berkeley: University of California Press, 1996); "West Coast, Too, Has Its Race Problems," *U.S. News and World Report*, 29 July 1956, 37.

51. Davis, *City of Quartz*, 165–69.

52. "L.A.—A Crazy, Mixed-Up Metropolis," *Los Angeles Mirror News*, 23

January 1957; "Are Big Cities Obsolete?" *Los Angeles Mirror News,* 23 January 1957.

53. Gary Miller, *Cities by Contract: The Politics of Municipal Incorporation* (Cambridge, Mass.: MIT Press, 1981), 135.

54. Waldie, *Holy Land,* 12; Robert Fishman, *Bourgeois Utopias: The Rise and Fall of Suburbia* (New York: Basic Books, 1987).

55. Waldie, *Holy Land,* 34.

56. Ibid., 3.

57. Richard Longstreth, *City Center to Regional Mall: Architecture, the Automobile and Retailing in Los Angeles, 1920–1950* (Cambridge, Mass.: MIT Press, 1997), 336–40.

58. Warren Susman, "Did Success Spoil the United States? Dual Representations in Postwar America," in *Recasting America: Culture and Politics in the Age of Cold War,* ed. Lary May (Chicago: University of Chicago, 1989), 19–37; Thomas J. Sugrue, "Reassessing the History of Postwar America," *Prospects: An Annual of American Studies* 20 (1995): 493–509; Elaine Tyler May, *Homeward Bound: American Families in the Cold War Era* (New York: Basic Books, 1988); Norman L. Rosenberg and Emily S. Rosenberg, *In Our Times: America since World War II,* 6th ed. (Upper Saddle River, N.J.: Prentice Hall, 1999).

59. U.S. Bureau of the Census, *Census of the Population, 1960,* part 6, *California.*

60. Lisa McGirr, *Suburban Warriors: The Origins of the New American Right* (Princeton, N.J.: Princeton University Press, 2001), 94–95. For a general history of Orange County after World War II, see Rob Kling, Spencer Olin, and Mark Poster, eds., *Postsuburban California: The Transformation of Orange County since World War II* (Berkeley: University of California Press, 1991).

61. Quoted in McGirr, *Suburban Warriors,* 204.

62. Abu-Lughod, *New York, Chicago, Los Angeles,* 263. Ronald Reagan quoted in McGirr, *Suburban Warriors,* 184.

63. Steve Fraser and Gary Gerstle, eds., *The Rise and Fall of the New Deal Order, 1930–1980* (Princeton, N.J.: Princeton University Press, 1989), xx–xxiv.

64. Los Angeles County Commission on Human Relations, *Population and Housing in Los Angeles County: A Study in the Growth of Residential Segregation* (Berkeley: Institute of Governmental Studies, University of California, Berkeley, 1963), 3.

65. The proportion of blacks living in census tracts that were at least 60 percent black increased from a relatively low 39 percent in 1940, to 59 percent in 1950, and to a high 70 percent in 1960. See Sides, "Working Away," 250; and Fred E. Case and James H. Kirk, "The Housing Status of Minority Families, Los Angeles, 1956," Los Angeles Urban League (1956), Edward R. Roybal Papers, Special Collections, Young Research Library, University of California, Los Angeles. See also Keith E. Collins, *Black Los Angeles: The Maturing of the Ghetto, 1940–1950* (Saratoga, Calif.: Century Twenty One Publishing, 1980); and Patricia Rae Adler, "Watts: From Suburb to Black Ghetto" (Ph.D. diss., University of Southern California, 1977).

66. Gerald Horne, "Black Fire: 'Riot' and 'Revolt' in Los Angeles, 1965 and 1992," in *Seeking El Dorado: African Americans in California,* ed. Lawrence B. de Graaf, Kevin Mulroy, and Quintard Taylor (Seattle: University of Washington Press, 2001), 377–404.

67. Jonathan Rieder, "The Rise of the 'Silent Majority,'" in *The Rise and Fall of the New Deal Order, 1930–1980,* ed. Steve Fraser and Gary Gerstle (Princeton, N.J.: Princeton University Press, 1989), 243–68.

68. Allen and Turner, *Ethnic Quilt,* 67.

69. Quoted in Mary Pardo, *Mexican American Women Activists: Identity and Resistance in Two Los Angeles Communities* (Philadelphia: Temple University Press, 1998), 72.

70. Reynaldo Flores Macías, Guillermo Vicente Flores, Donaldo Figueroa, and Luis Aragon, *A Study of Unincorporated East Los Angeles,* monograph no. 3, Aztlán Publications (Los Angeles: Chicano Studies Center, University of California, Los Angeles, 1973).

71. Allen and Turner, *Ethnic Quilt,* 109.

72. The 1959 yearbook for San Fernando High, the *Orange Blossom,* illuminates the rich diversity of that high school during the 1950s. For a consideration of Valens and his significance to the musical culture of postwar Los Angeles, see Lipsitz, *Time Passages,* 143–45. See also George Lipsitz, "Land of a Thousand Dances: Minorities and the Rise of Rock and Roll," in *Recasting America: Culture and Politics in the Age of Cold War,* ed. Lary May (Chicago: University of Chicago Press, 1989), 267–84.

73. Anthony Macias, "From Pachuco Boogie to Latin Jazz: Mexican Americans, Popular Music and Urban Culture in Los Angeles, 1940–1965" (Ph.D. diss., University of Michigan, 2001), chapter 4; Lipsitz, "Land of a Thousand Dances."

74. Following Pierre Bourdieu, Thomas Sugrue rejects the conventional dichotomy between structure and agency in his revisionist interpretation of postwar American history and, while acknowledging the "resiliency of the oppressed," also emphasizes the "the tremendous self-replicating power of domination." See Sugrue, "Reassessing the History of Postwar America," 504.

75. Susan Anderson, "A City Called Heaven: Black Enchantment and Despair in Los Angeles," in *The City: Los Angeles and Urban Theory at the End of the Twentieth Century,* ed. Edward W. Soja and Allen J. Scott (Berkeley: University of California Press, 1996), 336–64; Horne, "Black Fire," 390–91; Davis, *City of Quartz,* 251.

76. Art Farmer, quoted in Bryant et al., *Central Avenue Sounds,* 272.

77. John Dolphin, quoted in ibid., 309.

78. Johnny Otis, quoted in Lipsitz, "Land of a Thousand Dances," 274.

79. William Parker, quoted in Gottlieb and Wolt, *Thinking Big,* 378.

80. Reyner Banham, for example, offers "A Note on Downtown" because he feels "that is all downtown Los Angeles deserves." Reyner Banham, *Los Angeles: The Architecture of Four Ecologies* (London: Penguin Books, 1971), 211; "How Los Angeles Is Growing," *U.S. News and World Report,* 16 September 1955, 52.

81. "The Story of Los Angeles," *U.S. News and World Report*, 16 September 1955, 48.

82. Works Progress Administration, *Los Angeles: A Guide to the City and Its Environs*, American Guide Series (New York: Hastings House, 1941), 145, 150.

83. Joan Weibel-Orlando, *Indian Country, L.A.: Maintaining Ethnic Community in Complex Society* (Urbana: University of Illinois Press, 1991); John A. Price, "The Migration and Adaptation of American Indians to Los Angeles," *Human Organization* 27, no. 2 (summer 1968): 168–75.

84. Judd and Swanstrom, *City Politics*, 358–60. For a theoretical overview of growth coalitions, see John R. Logan and Harvey L. Molotch, *Urban Fortunes: The Political Economy of Place* (Berkeley: University of California Press, 1987), 57–74.

85. John H. Mollenkopf, "The Postwar Politics of Urban Development," in *Marxism and the Metropolis: New Perspectives in Urban Political Economy*, ed. William K. Tabb and Larry Sawyers (New York: Oxford University Press, 1978), 134–39. Mollenkopf reiterates this perspective using San Francisco and Boston as case studies. See John Mollenkopf, *The Contested City* (Princeton, N.J.: Princeton University Press, 1983), 139–80.

86. Norris Poulson, "Elephant with a Headache: Los Angeles and the Poulson Administration," *Frontier*, September 1955, 18.

87. Quoted in Ray Herbert, "Results on Central City Will Be Seen in Decades," *Los Angeles Times*, 2 November 1959, part 3, p. 2.

88. See, for example, Norris Poulson, "Renaissance in Downtown Los Angeles," presentation before the 32d Annual Meeting of Downtown Businessmen's Association, 29 June 1956. Miscellaneous publication. Government and Public Affairs Reading Room, University of California, Los Angeles.

89. Home Owners' Loan Corporation, Los Angeles City Survey Files, Record Group 195, National Archives, 385.

90. Robert Alexander and Drayton Bryant, *Rebuilding a City: A Study of Redevelopment Problems in Los Angeles* (Los Angeles: Haynes Foundation, 1951), 6.

91. Parson, "Urban Politics during the Cold War," 122–27.

92. Anastasia Loukaitou-Sideris and Tridib Banerjee, *Urban Design Downtown: Poetics and Politics of Form* (Berkeley: University of California Press, 1998), 24–32.

93. Ibid., 31.

94. Logan and Molotch, *Urban Fortunes*, 76–79.

95. "Building the Pavilions of Culture," *Time*, 18 December 1964, 46–58.

96. Gottlieb and Wolt, *Thinking Big*, 308–14.

97. Quoted in Parson, "Urban Politics during the Cold War," 125.

98. "City of Angels: It's Still an Age of Miracles," *Newsweek*, 3 August 1953, 64–66; Charles Champlin, "Los Angeles in a New Image," *Life*, 20 June 1960, 74–90; De Roos, "Los Angeles."

99. "West Coast, Too, Has Its Race Problems," *U.S. News and World Report*, 29 July 1956, 36; Wesley Marx, "Our Negro Community," *Los Angeles:*

The Magazine of the Good Life in Southern California, March 1962, 38–41; Aubrey B. Haines, "Word—and Deeds: Racial Barriers beyond the Mason Dixon Line," *Frontier,* August 1956, 11–14; "The Los Angeles Negro," *Frontier,* June 1955, 6–16.

CHAPTER THREE. THE SPECTACLE OF URBAN BLIGHT

1. Harrison Carroll, "Mars Men Strike L.A.," *Los Angeles Herald Express,* 26 November 1953, 23. *War of the Worlds,* Production Files, Motion Picture Producers Association Records and Collection, Academy of Motion Picture Arts and Sciences Library, Los Angeles, California.
2. John Huston, *An Open Book* (New York: Ballantine Books, 1980), 67–68.
3. Siegfried Kracauer, "Hollywood's Terror Films: Do They Reflect an American State of Mind?" *Commentary,* August 1946, 132–36.
4. This chapter rests upon the theoretical premise that movies constitute important and often overlooked social history evidence, drawing on the theoretical insights of scholars who view film as a window onto larger social transformations. A model for understanding the relationship between film and social history derives from Michael Ryan and Douglas Kellner, who conceive of that relationship as a process of *discursive transcoding,* in which the discourses that determine the substance and form of the social world are transcoded into cinematic narratives. More than merely reflecting reality, films execute a transfer from one discursive field to another and thus become part of that broader cultural system of representations that construct social reality. Such representations not only influence psychological dispositions within the individual, but "also play an important role in determining how social reality will be constructed, that is, what figures and boundaries will prevail in the shaping of social life and social institutions. They determine, for example, whether capitalism will be conceived (felt, experienced, lived) as a predatory jungle or as a utopia of freedom." Ultimately, films play an important role in a larger system of cultural representations that are crucial to the maintenance of social power, but are also essential to progressive movements for social change. See Michael Ryan and Douglas Kellner, *Camera Politica: The Politics and Ideology of Contemporary Hollywood Film* (Bloomington: Indiana University Press, 1988), 12–14. See also Louis Althusser, "Ideology and Ideological State Apparatuses [Notes toward an Investigation]," in *Lenin and Philosophy and Other Essays,* trans. Ben Brewster (New York: Monthly Review Press, 1971), 127–86; and Frederic Jameson, "Reification and Utopia in Mass Culture," *Social Text* 1 (winter 1979): 130–48.
5. Leo Charney and Vanessa Schwartz, "Introduction," in *Cinema and the Invention of Modern Life,* ed. Leo Charney and Vanessa Schwartz (Berkeley: University of California Press, 1995), 1; Ben Singer, "Modernity, Hyperstimulus, and the Rise of Popular Sensationalism," in *Cinema and Invention of Modern Life,* ed. Charney and Schwartz, 72–102.
6. Charney and Schwartz, *Cinema and the Invention of Modern Life,* 4.
7. Lary May, *Screening Out the Past: The Birth of Mass Culture and the*

Motion Picture Industry (Chicago: University of Chicago Press, 1980), 167–99; Steven J. Ross, *Working-Class Hollywood: Silent Film and the Shaping of Class in America* (Princeton, N.J.: Princeton University Press, 1998), 121–22; Neal Gabler, *An Empire of Their Own: How the Jews Invented Hollywood* (New York: Anchor Books, 1988), 104–5.

8. Ross, *Working-Class Hollywood*, 16–24.

9. May, *Screening Out the Past*, 177.

10. Ibid., 186; Michael Rogin, *Blackface, White Noise: Jews and the Hollywood Melting Pot* (Berkeley: University of California Press, 1996), 73–120.

11. David Karnes, "Modern Metropolis: Mass Culture and the Transformation of Los Angeles, 1890–1950" (Ph.D. diss., University of California, Berkeley, 1991), 217.

12. Adolph Zukor, quoted in Rogin, *Blackface, White Noise*, 78.

13. The literature on film noir is extensive and growing. See Foster Hirsch, *Film Noir: The Dark Side of the Screen* (New York: Da Capo, 1981); Paul Schrader, "Notes on Film Noir," in *Film Noir: A Reader*, ed. Alain Silver and James Ursini (New York: Limelight Editions, 1997), 53–64; A. M. Karimi, *Toward a Definition of the American Film Noir (1941–1949)* (New York: Arno, 1976); Alain Silver and Elizabeth Ward, eds., *Film Noir: An Encyclopedic Reference to the American Style* (New York: Overlook Press, 1979); Spencer Selby, *Dark City: The Film Noir* (Jefferson, N.C.: McFarland, 1984); and James Naremore, *More Than Night: Film Noir in Its Contexts* (Berkeley: University of California Press, 1998). Frank Krutnik offers a unique perspective on film noir, emphasizing the gendered connotations of the genre and its implications for the construction of postwar masculinity; see his *In a Lonely Street: Film Noir, Genre, Masculinity* (London: Routledge, 1991).

14. Raymond Borde and Etienne Chaumeton, "Towards a Definition of *Film Noir*," in *Film Noir: A Reader*, ed. Alain Silver and James Ursini, trans. Alain Silver (New York: Limelight Editions, 1996), 17–25.

15. Hirsch, *Film Noir*, 73–74.

16. Karnes, "Modern Metropolis," 484; Mike Davis, *City of Quartz: Excavating the Future in Los Angeles* (London: Verso, 1990), 36–54. See also Anthony Heilbut, *Exiles in Paradise: German Refugee Artists and Intellectuals in America, from the 1930s to the Present* (Boston: Beacon Press, 1983).

17. Pressbook, *Criss Cross*, American Motion Picture Arts and Sciences Library, 9.

18. Two scholars in particular have explored the image of Los Angeles in film noir: Tina Olson Lent, "The Dark Side of the Screen: The Image of Los Angeles in Film Noir," *Southern California Quarterly* 69, no. 4 (winter 1987): 329–48; and Karnes, "Modern Metropolis," chapter 5. For a consideration of the relationship between the city and its representation in a historical framework, see Alan Trachtenberg, "Image and Ideology: New York in the Photographer's Eye," *Journal of Urban History* 10, no. 4 (August 1984): 453–65.

19. Home Owners' Loan Corporation, Los Angeles City Survey Maps, Record Group 195, National Archives, Washington, D.C., 385.

20. Norman M. Klein, *The History of Forgetting: Los Angeles and the Erasure of Memory* (London: Verso, 1997), 53.

21. City Housing Authority of Los Angeles, in conjunction with University of Southern California, *And Ten Thousand More,* graduate student film project, 1949. Videocassette. Thanks to Frank Wilkinson for bringing my attention to this documentary film.

22. Karnes, "Modern Metropolis," 480–81.

23. Ibid., 494; Reyner Banham, *Los Angeles: The Architecture of Four Ecologies* (London: Penguin Books, 1971), 207–8. The Bradbury Building also makes a cameo appearance in Ridley Scott's futuristic *Blade Runner* (1983), an oft-cited example of contemporary Los Angeles noir, which incorporates noir themes and imagery into a science fiction film about the bleak future of Los Angeles.

24. Eric Lott, "The Whiteness of Film Noir," in *Whiteness: A Critical Reader,* ed. Mike Hill (New York: New York University Press, 1997), 81–101.

25. The racial implications of noir's use of light and darkness reflect a representational tradition in Western culture. Film noir is part of a broader "culture of light" in the West, in which light and dark are invested with social meanings. In a racialized democracy that values "white over black," to borrow Winthrop Jordan's famous characterization of Anglo American social values, the delineation of light in the representation of the social world is structured by racial hierarchies that place a moral premium on whiteness and light. The cinematic combination of white skin and light evokes ethical connotations that associate whiteness with moral purity and spiritual hygiene and, conversely, the absence of light and the abundance of shadows convey a denigrated state of moral ambiguity. In the history of portraiture, photography, film (as D. W. Griffith proved), and other aspects of Western visual culture, the uses of light speak not only to Western notions of the racial other, but also to the West's conception of itself. See Richard Dyer, *White* (London: Routledge, 1997).

26. Lott, "Whiteness of Film Noir," 86.

27. Eric Avila, "Reinventing Los Angeles: Popular Culture in the Age of White Flight" (Ph.D. diss., University of California, Berkeley, 1997), 11–12. For a more general treatment of cultural perceptions of women and the automobile, see Virginia Scharff, *Taking the Wheel: Women and the Coming of the Motor Age* (Albuquerque: University of New Mexico Press, 1991).

28. On Asian American suburbanization during the 1950s, see Timothy P. Fong, *The First Suburban Chinatown: The Remaking of Monterey Park, California* (Philadelphia: Temple University Press, 1994), 20–26; and Donald Teruo Hata and Nadine Ishitani Hata, "Asian Pacific Angelinos: Model Minorities and Indispensable Scapegoats," in *20th Century Los Angeles: Power, Promotion and Social Conflict,* ed. Norman M. Klein and Martin J. Schiesl (Claremont, Calif.: Regina Books, 1993), 80–84. For a discussion of Chinese American "assimilation" in San Francisco after World War II, see K. Scott Wong, "War Comes to Chinatown: Social Transformation and the Chinese of California," in *The Way We Really Were: The Golden State in the Second Great War,* ed. Roger W. Lotchin (Urbana: University of Illinois Press, 2000), 164–86.

29. The most obvious example of this racial dynamic in film noir is *Chinatown*, which deploys a set of Orientalized themes and images to convey the corruption behind the sunlit facades of Southern California. See Liahna K. Babener, "*Chinatown:* City of Blight," in *Los Angeles in Fiction: A Collection of Original Essays,* ed. David Fine (Albuquerque: University of New Mexico Press, 1984), 243–56.

30. Karnes, "Modern Metropolis," 540.

31. Ibid., 516–27; Naremore, *More than Night,* 226–27.

32. William H. Parker, *Parker on Police,* ed. O. W. Wilson (Springfield, Ill.: Charles C. Thomas, 1957), 34. See also Martin J. Schiesl, "Behind the Badge: The Police and Social Discontent in Los Angeles since 1950," in *20th Century Los Angeles: Power, Promotion and Social Conflict,* ed. Norman M. Klein and Martin J. Schiesl (Claremont, Calif.: Regina Books, 1990), 153–94.

33. Peter Stallybrass and Allon White, *The Politics and Poetics of Transgression* (Ithaca, N.Y.: Cornell University Press, 1995), 138.

34. William Deverell, "Plague in Los Angeles, 1924: Ethnicity and Typicality," in *Over the Edge: Remapping the American West,* ed. Valerie J. Matsumoto and Blake Allmedinger (Berkeley: University of California Press, 1999), 172–200. See also Nayan Shaw, *Contagious Divides: Epidemics and Race in San Francisco's Chinatown* (Berkeley: University of California Press, 2001); Susan L. Craddock, "Sewers and Scapegoats: Spatial Metaphors of Smallpox in Nineteenth-Century San Francisco," *Social Science and Medicine* 41, no. 7 (1995): 957–68; Stuart Galishoff, "Germs Know No Color Line: Black Health and Public Policy in Atlanta, 1900–1918," *Societas* 6, no. 2 (1976): 121–38; and Kay J. Anderson, "The Idea of Chinatown: The Power of Place and Institutional Practice in the Making of a Racial Category," *Annals of the Association of American Geographers* 77, no. 4 (1987): 580–98.

35. Parker, *Parker on Police,* 8.

36. Howard Whitman, "Don't Go Out Alone at Night in L.A.," *Collier's,* 28 October 1950, 30–31.

37. Parker, *Parker on Police,* 49.

38. Larry Ceplair and Steven Englund, *The Inquisition in Hollywood: Politics in the Film Community, 1930–1960* (Berkeley: University of California Press, 1983); Gerald Horne, *Class Struggle in Hollywood: Moguls, Mobsters, Stars, Reds, and Trade Unionists, 1930–1950* (Austin: University of Texas Press, 2001); Lary May, "Movie Star Politics: The Screen Actors' Guild, Cultural Conversion, and the Hollywood Red Scare," in *Recasting America: Culture and Politics in the Age of Cold War,* ed. Lary May (Chicago: University of Chicago Press, 1989), 125–53; John Cogley, "HUAC: The Mass Hearings," in *The American Film Industry,* ed. Tino Balio, rev. ed. (Madison: University of Wisconsin Press, 1985), 487–509.

39. Tino Balio, "Retrenchment, Reappraisal and Reorganization, 1948–," in *The American Film Industry,* ed. Tino Balio, rev. ed. (Madison: University of Wisconsin Press, 1985), 401–47; Ernest Borneman, "United States versus Hollywood: The Case Study of an Antitrust Suit," in *American Film Industry,* 449–

62; Thomas H. Guback, "Hollywood's International Market," in *American Film Industry*, 463–86. See also Robert Sklar, *Movie-Made America: A Cultural History of American Movies* (New York: Vintage Press, 1975), 269–85.

40. John Houseman, "Hollywood Faces the Fifties: Part I, The Lost Enthusiasm," *Harper's*, April 1950, 50–59.

41. Balio, "Retrenchment, Reappraisal and Reorganization," 401.

42. Lynn Spigel, *Make Room for TV: Television and the Family Ideal in Postwar America* (Chicago: University of Chicago Press, 1992), introduction.

43. Balio, "Retrenchment, Reappraisal and Reorganization," 401–2.

44. "Trouble in Hollywood," *Life*, 23 February 1948, 55–61.

45. May, *Screening Out the Past*, 233–234; Otto Friedrich, *City of Nets: A Portrait of Hollywood in the 1940s* (New York: Harper and Row, 1986), 418–21.

46. John Houseman, "Hollywood Faces the Fifties: Part II, Batter over Television," *Harper's*, May 1950, 55.

47. Lary May, *The Big Tomorrow: Hollywood and the Politics of the American Way* (Chicago: University of Chicago Press, 2000), 170–71.

48. Melani McAlister, *Epic Encounters: Culture, Media, and U.S. Interests in the Middle East, 1945–2000* (Berkeley: University of California Press, 2001), 58–60.

49. Peter Biskind, *Seeing Is Believing: How American Learned to Stop Worrying and Love the Fifties* (New York: Pantheon, 1983); Patrick Lucanio, *Them or Us: Archetypal Interpretation of Fifties Alien Invasion Films* (Bloomington: University of Indiana Press, 1987); Michael Rogin, *Ronald Reagan: The Movie* (Berkeley: University of California Press, 1987), chapter 8.

50. James Robert Parish and Michael R. Pitts, *The Great Science Fiction Pictures* (Metuchen, N.J.: Scarecrow Press, 1977); Ralph Ellison, *Invisible Man* (New York: Vintage Books, 1980), 3.

51. *Ethnic Notions*, prod. and dir. Marlon Riggs, 58 min., California Newsreel, 1986, videocassette.

52. Carroll, "Mars Men Strike L.A."

53. Such anxieties recall, in particular, the films of D. W. Griffith, who popularized stereotypes of black male sexuality in films such as *Birth of a Nation* and *The Girls and Daddy*. See Daniel Bernardi, "The Voice of Whiteness: D. W. Griffith's Biograph Films," in *The Birth of Whiteness: Race and the Emergence of U.S. Cinema*, ed. Daniel Bernardi (New Brunswick, N.J.: Rutgers University Press, 1996), 122.

54. Michael Paul Rogin and John L. Shover, *Political Change in California: Critical Elections and Social Movements, 1890–1966* (Westport, Conn.: Greenwood Publishing Corporation, 1970), 196–97; Elaine Tyler May, *Homeward Bound: American Families in the Cold War Era* (New York: Basic Books, 1988), 11.

55. Dyer, *White*, 116–42.

56. Charles Ramirez Berg, "Immigrants, Aliens, and Extraterrestrials: Science Fiction's Alien Other as (among Other Things) New Hispanic Imagery," *CineAction!* 18 (fall 1989): 3–17.

57. "Socko Science-Fiction Thriller with Big B.O. Potential," *Variety*, 4 March 1953.

58. Susan Sontag, "The Imagination of Disaster," in *Film Theory and Criticism*, ed. Gerald Mast and Marshall Cohen, 2d ed. (London: Oxford University Press, 1979), 488–504.

59. James W. Cook, "Of Men, Missing Links and Nondescripts: The Strange Career of P. T. Barnum's 'What Is It?' Exhibition," in *Freakery: Cultural Spectacles of the Extraordinary Body*, ed. Rosemarie Garland Thompson (New York: New York University Press, 1996), 139–57.

60. Rogin and Shover, *Political Change in California*, 189.

CHAPTER FOUR. "A RAGE FOR ORDER"

1. John F. Kasson, *Amusing the Million: Coney Island at the Turn of the Century* (New York: Hill and Wang, 1978), 32–34.

2. Quoted in ibid., 38–39.

3. Quoted in Kathy Peiss, *Cheap Amusements: Working Women and Leisure in Turn-of-the-Century New York* (Philadelphia: Temple University Press, 1986), 126.

4. Quoted in ibid., 126–27.

5. Kasson, *Amusing the Million*, 38.

6. Jimmy Durante, quoted in George Chauncey, *Gay New York: Gender, Urban Culture, and the Making of the Gay Male World, 1890–1940* (New York: Basic Books, 1994), 35.

7. Lanier Bartlett and Virginia Stivers Bartlett, *Los Angeles in Seven Days: Including Southern California* (New York: Robert M. McBride and Company, 1932), 150.

8. Works Progress Administration, *Los Angeles: A Guide to the City and Its Environs* (New York: Hastings House, 1941), 354; Norman M. Klein, *The History of Forgetting: Los Angeles and the Erasure of Memory* (London: Verso Press, 1997), 36.

9. Works Progress Administration, *Los Angeles*, 248.

10. Mary (Gonzalez) Hernandez, interview by Anthony Macias, tape recording, Redlands, Calif., 11 June 1999.

11. Judith Adams, *The American Amusement Park Industry: A History of Technology and Thrills* (Boston: Twayne Publishers, 1991), 88. For an account of Disney's early life, see Richard Schickel, *The Disney Version: The Life, Times, Art and Commerce of Walt Disney*, 3d ed. (Chicago: Ivan R. Dee Inc., 1997). For Disney's hometown and its influence on the construction of Disneyland, see Richard Francaviglia, "Main Street, USA: A Comparison/Contrast of Streetscapes in Disneyland and Walt Disney World," *Journal of Popular Culture* 15 (summer 1981): 141–56; and Margaret J. King, "Disneyland and Walt Disney World: Traditional Values in Futuristic Form," *Journal of Popular Culture* 15 (summer 1981): 116–39.

12. Alan Havig, "Mass Commercial Amusements in Kansas City before World War I," *Missouri Historical Review* 75, no. 3 (April 1981): 316–45.

13. Jane Addams, quoted in Kasson, *Amusing the Million*, 100; Helen L. Horowitz, "Varieties of Cultural Experience in Jane Addams' Chicago," *History of Education Quarterly* 14, no. 3 (spring 1974): 69–72.

14. Fred R. Johnson, quoted in Havig, "Mass Commercial Amusements in Kansas City before World War I," 341.

15. Adams, *American Amusement Park Industry*, 87–93. See also Schickel, *Disney Version*, 67–75.

16. Schickel, *Disney Version*, 75–86. For the midwestern flavor of Southern California culture at the turn of the century, see Carey McWilliams, *Southern California: An Island on the Land* (Salt Lake City: Peregrine Smith, 1994), 165–82. See also Robert Fogelson, *The Fragmented Metropolis: Los Angeles, 1850–1930* (Berkeley: University of California Press, 1993), 72–73. For the racialized climate of Southern California, see George J. Sánchez, *Becoming Mexican American: Ethnicity, Culture, and Identity in Chicano Los Angeles, 1900–1945* (New York: Oxford University Press, 1993), 43.

17. "Under the Gaslight," *Disneyland News*, July 1955, 3. Disney Archives, Anaheim History Room, Anaheim Public Library.

18. Stephen Watts offers an insightful analysis of Disney's embrace of a "populist cultural politics," identifying populist themes that surfaced in the earliest animated short and feature-length films of Walt Disney Productions. Stephen Watts, "Walt Disney: Art and Politics in the American Century," *Journal of American History* 100, no. 2 (June 1995): 84–110. For the cultural insurgency of populism during the 1930s, see Michael Denning, *The Cultural Front: The Laboring of American Culture in the Twentieth Century* (London: Verso Press, 1997); and Warren Susman, *Culture as History: The Transformation of American Society in the Twentieth Century* (New York: Pantheon, 1984), chapter 9.

19. Walt Disney, quoted in Watts, "Walt Disney," 104–5. For Disney's many troubles at the outset of the post–World War II period, see Schickel, *Disney Version*, parts 8 and 9.

20. Disney, quoted in Watts, "Walt Disney," 104. See also Larry Ceplair and Steven Englund, *The Inquisition in Hollywood: Politics in the Film Community, 1930–1960* (Berkeley: University of California Press, 1983), 157–58.

21. Watts, "Walt Disney," 104; Schickel, *Disney Version*, 278–81.

22. Watts, "Walt Disney," 105–6.

23. Quoted in Gladwin Hill, "Disneyland Reports on Its First Ten Million," *New York Times*, 2 February 1958, section 2, part 2, p. 1.

24. Gladwin Hill, "The Never-Never Land Khrushchev Never Saw," *New York Times*, 4 October 1959, 22.

25. John Hench, interview by Jay Horan, 3 December 1982. Transcript. Walt Disney Archives, Burbank, Calif. Hereafter referred to as Hench interview.

26. Rollin Lynde Hart, "The Amusement Park," *Atlantic*, May 1907, quoted in Peiss, *Cheap Amusements*, 127.

27. "The Wisdom of Walt Disney," *Wisdom* 32 (December 1959): 76.

28. Karen Haltunnen, *Confidence Men and Painted Women: A Study of Middle-Class Culture in America, 1830–1870* (New Haven, Conn.: Yale University Press, 1982), 192–93.

29. Hench interview.

30. Quoted in Randy Bright, *Disneyland: The Inside Story* (New York: Harry N. Abrams, Inc., 1987), 41.

31. D. J. Waldie, *Holy Land: A Suburban Memoir* (New York: St. Martin's Press, 1996), 37.

32. Harrison Price, William S. M. Stewart, and Redford C. Rollins, "An Analysis of Location Factors for Disneyland," final report prepared for Walt Disney Productions, 28 August 1953, by Stanford Research Institute, 3. Disney Archives, Anaheim History Room, Anaheim Public Library. Hereafter referred to as SRI report.

33. SRI report, 4.

34. Quoted in Van Arsdale France, *Window on Main Street* (Burbank, Calif.: n.p., 1991), 17.

35. *Disneyland News*, 10 February 1958, 7. Disney Archives, Anaheim History Room, Anaheim Public Library.

36. SRI report, 7–8.

37. Hench interview.

38. Ibid.

39. Jack Boettner, "Disney's 'Magical Little Park' after Two Decades," *Los Angeles Times*, 6 July 1975, part 10, p. 1.

40. Carl Walker, speech to Urban Land Institute, 5 October 1975, quoted in John Findlay, *Magic Lands: Western Cityscapes and American Culture after 1940* (Berkeley: University of California Press, 1992), 84.

41. Hill, "Disneyland Reports on Its First Ten Million."

42. Quoted in George Lipsitz, "The Making of Disneyland," in *True Stories from the American Past*, ed. William Graebner (New York: McGraw Hill, 1993), 188.

43. Findlay, *Magic Lands*, 68–69.

44. Herman Wong, "Disneyland: Can It Top 15 Years of Success?" *Los Angeles Times*, 12 July 1970, C1.

45. Schickel, *Disney Version*, 318.

46. Quoted in "Tinker Bell, Mary Poppins, Cold Cash," *Newsweek*, 12 July 1965, 75.

47. *Los Angeles Times*, 6 July 1985.

48. Jon Carroll, "Adventures in Robotland," *San Francisco Chronicle*, 9 June 1968, 24–25.

49. Waldie, *Holy Land*, 2.

50. *Disneyland News*, January 1957, 4. Disney Archives, Anaheim History Room, Anaheim Public Library.

51. Hench interview.

52. Roy Disney, quoted in Schickel, *Disney Version*, 283.

53. Lipsitz, "Making of Disneyland," 179–96.

54. Walt Disney, quoted in Schickel, *Disney Version*, 313.

55. *Burbank Review*, 27 March 1952. Disney Archives, Anaheim History Room, Anaheim Public Library.

56. SRI report, 3.

57. Lipsitz, "Making of Disneyland," 186–87. See also Schickel, *Disney Version*, 313–15.

58. Press Release, "Spectacular Disneyland TV Unveiling to Be Mammoth July 17 Presentation," n.d. Disney Archives, Anaheim History Room, Anaheim Public Library.

59. Lipsitz, "Making of Disneyland," 180. According to the author, there were sixty-three engineers and twenty-four live cameras at this event.

60. Vince Jeffers, quoted in Lipsitz, "Making of Disneyland," 186.

61. "News from Disneyland," Public Relations Division, Disneyland, Inc., n.d., 4. Disney Archives, Anaheim History Room, Anaheim Public Library.

62. Karal Ann Marling, "Disneyland, 1955," *American Art* 5, nos. 1–2 (winter/spring 1991): 168–207.

63. Bill Walsh, quoted in Lipsitz, "Making of Disneyland," 187.

64. *Disneyland Holiday*, Walt Disney Productions, fall 1957, 2. Disney Archives, Anaheim History Room, Anaheim Public Library.

65. Lipsitz, "Making of Disneyland," 187.

66. Carroll, "Adventures in Robotland," 24.

67. "You're in Good Company: A Report to Disneyland Lessees," Walt Disney Productions, summer 1968. Disney Archives, Anaheim History Room, Anaheim Public Library.

68. "'House of the Future' Demonstrates Way People Will Live within Decade," *Anaheim Bulletin*, 6 September 1957. Disney Archives, Anaheim History Room, Anaheim Public Library.

69. Schickel, *Disney Version*, 265.

70. *News from Disneyland*, Walt Disney Productions, 1965. Disney Archives, Anaheim History Room, Anaheim Public Library.

71. *Disneyland News*, August 1956, 4–5. Disney Archives, Anaheim History Room, Anaheim Public Library. For a discussion of the Igorot Village at the St. Louis World's Fair and the politics of racial representation, see Christopher A. Vaughn, "Ogling Igorots: The Politics and Commerce of Exhibiting Cultural Otherness, 1898–1913," in *Freakery: Cultural Spectacles of the Extraordinary Body*, ed. Rosemarie Garland Thompson (New York: New York University Press, 1996), 219–33.

72. *Disneyland News*, August 1956, 4–5. Disney Archives, Anaheim History Room, Anaheim Public Library.

73. Hill, "Never-Never Land Khrushchev Never Saw."

74. *Disneyland News*, August 1956, 7. Disney Archives, Anaheim History Room, Anaheim Public Library.

75. "Romance of Disneyland," *Vacationland*, spring 1961. Disney Archives, Anaheim History Room, Anaheim Public Library.

76. *News from Disneyland*, Public Relations Division, Disneyland, Inc., n.d. Disney Archives, Anaheim History Room, Anaheim Public Library.

77. David Nasaw, *Going Out: The Rise and Fall of Public Amusements* (New York: Basic Books, 1993), 75–78. See also Robert W. Rydell, *All the World's a Fair: Visions of Empire at American International Expositions, 1876–1916* (Chicago: University of Chicago Press, 1984).

78. *Disneyland Holiday*, Walt Disney Productions, July 1957; *Disneyland News* July 1955, 3. Both at Disney Archives, Anaheim History Room, Anaheim Public Library.

79. Richard Hofstadter, quoted in Watts, "Walt Disney," 97.

80. Text of speech from Great Moments with Mr. Lincoln. Disney Archives, Anaheim History Room, Anaheim Public Library. In keeping with changing social mores, Disneyland officials have updated many of the park's original depictions of racial minorities. See Jim Rawitsch, "Moving Right Along: Disneyland Grows Ever More Sophisticated," *Los Angeles Times Magazine*, 13 July 1986, 8.

81. Cecilia O'Leary, *To Die For: The Paradox of American Patriotism* (Princeton, N.J.: Princeton University Press, 1999), chapter 8.

82. "Profile: Great Moments with Mr. Lincoln," News from WED Imagineering, n.d. Disney Archives, Anaheim History Room, Anaheim Public Library.

83. Hill, "Disneyland Reports on Its First Ten Million."

84. Peiss, *Cheap Amusements*, introduction. For the similar relationship between Mexican American women and urban popular culture in interwar Los Angeles, see Vicki Ruiz, " 'Star Struck': Acculturation, Adolescence, and the Mexican American Woman, 1920–1950," in *Building with Our Hands: New Directions in Chicana Studies*, ed. Adela de la Torre and Beatrice Pesquera (Berkeley: University of California Press, 1993), 109–29.

85. Elaine Tyler May, "Explosive Issues: Sex, Women and the Bomb," in *Recasting America: Culture and Politics in the Age of Cold War*, ed. Lary May (Chicago: University of Chicago Press, 1989), 154–70. See also Elaine Tyler May, *Homeward Bound: American Families in the Cold War Era* (New York: Basic Books, 1988), introduction.

86. " 'House of the Future' Demonstrates Way People Will Live within Decade." See also Jack E. Jantzen, "The Monsanto Home of the Future," *The "E" Ticket*, Walt Disney Publications, winter 1991–92, 12–19. Disney Archives, Anaheim History Room, Anaheim Public Library. For an analysis of how gendered assumptions permeated post–World War II housing design, see Dolores Hayden, "Model Houses for the Millions: Architects' Dreams, Builders' Boasts, Residents' Dilemmas," in *Blueprints for Modern Living: History and Legacy of the Case Study Houses*, ed. Elizabeth A. T. Smith (Cambridge, Mass.: MIT Press, 1989), 197–212. See also Dolores Hayden, *The Grand Domestic Revolution: A History of Feminist Design for American Homes, Neighborhoods and Cities* (Cambridge, Mass.: MIT Press, 1981).

87. "Monsanto Chemical Co.," *Disneylander,* March 1958, 2. Disney Archives, Anaheim History Room, Anaheim Public Library. See also Hill, "Disneyland Reports on Its First Ten Million."

88. "Here's Your First View of Disneyland," *Look,* 2 November 1954, 89.

89. Quoted in Findlay, *Magic Lands,* 115.

90. Lynn Spigel, *Make Room for TV: Television and the Family Ideal in Postwar America* (Chicago: University of Chicago Press, 1992), chapter 2.

91. "G.E. Carousel of Progress," narration transcript, WED Enterprises, Inc., 22 July 1967. Disneyland Collection, Anaheim History Room, Anaheim Public Library.

92. Pamela (Lawton) James, quoted in Becky M. Nicolaides, *My Blue Heaven: Life and Politics in the Working-Class Suburbs of Los Angeles, 1920–1965* (Chicago: University of Chicago Press, 2002), 270–71.

93. Ibid., 271.

94. Teresa (Hernandez) Avila, interview by the author, 11 April 2001, San Diego, Calif.

CHAPTER FIVE. SUBURBANIZING THE CITY CENTER

1. Lawrence S. Ritter, *Lost Ballparks: A Celebration of Baseball's Legendary Fields* (New York: Viking Press, 1992), 60.

2. Marshall Berman makes this claim about the naming of the Brooklyn Dodgers in *All That Is Solid Melts into Air: The Experience of Modernity* (New York: Simon and Schuster, 1982), 160.

3. Peter Golenbock, *Bums: An Oral History of the Brooklyn Dodgers* (New York: Putnam, 1984), 20.

4. Ibid., 60.

5. Ibid., 56–61.

6. Michael S. Kimmel, "Baseball and the Reconstruction of American Masculinity, 1880–1920," in *Sport, Men, and the Gender Order: Critical Feminist Perspectives,* ed. Michael A. Messner and Donald F. Sabo (Champaign, Ill.: Human Kinetics Books, 1990), 55–65.

7. Quoted in ibid., 60.

8. Gunther Barth, *City People: The Rise of Modern City Culture in Nineteenth-Century America* (New York: Oxford University Press, 1980), 190.

9. Quotation from Neil J. Sullivan, *The Dodgers Move West* (New York: Oxford University Press, 1987), 28.

10. Ibid., 37–41.

11. Ibid., 52.

12. Golenbock, *Bums,* 433.

13. Ibid.

14. Sullivan, *Dodgers Move West,* 42.

15. Ibid., 43.

16. Ibid., 35.

17. Roger Kahn, *The Boys of Summer* (New York: Harper and Row, 1971), xv–xvi.

18. Elaine Tyler May, *Homeward Bound: American Families in the Cold War Era* (New York: Basic Books, 1988).

19. Stan Lomax, quoted in Sullivan, *Dodgers Move West*, 38.

20. "New Ebbets Field to Have Hot Dogs and Hot Seats," *New York Times*, 6 March 1952, 34.

21. Walter O'Malley, quoted in Sullivan, *Dodgers Move West*, 127.

22. John Anson Ford, *Thirty Explosive Years in Los Angeles County* (San Marino, Calif.: Huntington Library, 1961), 201.

23. Herbert M. Baus, interview by Enid Hart Douglass, 1990, transcript, 55. UCLA Oral History Project, Special Collections, Young Research Library, University of California, Los Angeles. Hereafter referred to as Baus interview.

24. Robert E. Alexander and Drayton Bryant, *Rebuilding a City: A Study of Redevelopment Problems in Los Angeles* (Los Angeles: Haynes Foundation, 1951), 17; Thomas Hines, "Housing, Baseball, and Creeping Socialism: The Battle of Chavez Ravine, Los Angeles 1949–1959," *Journal of Urban History* 8, no. 2 (February 1982): 123–43.

25. Frank Wilkinson, interview by author, Los Angeles, Calif., 24 January 1996. Tape recording.

26. "Public Housing and the Brooklyn Dodgers," *Frontier*, June 1957, 7–9.

27. *Los Angeles Times*, 30 July 1953.

28. *Los Angeles Mirror News*, 8 April 1955.

29. Norris Poulson, "Elephant with a Headache: Los Angeles and the Poulson Administration," *Frontier*, September 1955, 13.

30. John R. Logan and Harvey L. Molotch, *Urban Fortunes: The Political Economy of Place* (Berkeley: University of California Press, 1987), 76–79. On GLAPI, see Robert Gottlieb and Irene Wolt, *Thinking Big: The Story of the Los Angeles Times, Its Publishers and Their Influence on Southern California* (New York: Putnam and Sons, 1977), 306–8.

31. Quoted in Gottlieb and Wolt, *Thinking Big*, 306.

32. *Torch Reporter*, September 1957, 11. Edward R. Roybal Papers, Special Collections, Young Research Library, University of California, Los Angeles. For a photographic essay on life in the Chavez Ravine prior to the arrival of the CHA and the Dodgers, see Don Normark, *Chavez Ravine, 1949: A Los Angeles Story* (San Francisco: Chronicle Books, 1999).

33. Gilbert Hernandez, former resident of Palo Verde, interview by Don Normark, in Normark, *Chavez Ravine*, 37.

34. Mauricio Mazón, *The Zoot-Suit Riots: The Psychology of Symbolic Annihilation* (Austin: University of Texas Press, 1984), 101.

35. Mike Davis, *City of Quartz: Excavating the Future in Los Angeles* (London: Verso, 1990), 72.

36. George Lipsitz, "Sports Stadia and Urban Development: A Tale of Three Cities," *Journal of Sport and Social Issues* 8 (summer/fall 1984): 1–18.

37. Letter, Downtown Businessmen's Association to Los Angeles City Council, City Council File 78067 S2, Los Angeles City Clerk's Office, Box A-1403.

38. Norris Poulson, *Who Would Have Ever Dreamed?* Poulson Memoirs, Bancroft Library, University of California, Berkeley. Hereafter referred to as Poulson memoirs.

39. "Southland Civic Groups Hail Dodgers' Switch," *Los Angeles Times*, 2 October 1957, 2.

40. Arthur Daley, "Baseball's Gold Rush," *New York Times*, 30 May 1957, 14.

41. Frank Finch, "Brooklyn Dodgers Buy L.A. Angels," *Los Angeles Times*, 22 February 1957, 1.

42. Sullivan, *Dodgers Move West*, 87.

43. Poulson memoirs, 143.

44. Sullivan, *Dodgers Move West*, 120.

45. Norris Poulson, "The Untold Story of Chavez Ravine," *Los Angeles*, April 1962, 16; Cary S. Henderson, "Los Angeles and the Dodger War, 1957–1962," *Southern California Quarterly* 63 (fall 1980): 261–89.

46. Baus interview, 96.

47. Al Wolf, "M'Clellan Optimistic on Dodger Move," *Los Angeles Times*, 27 August 1957, part 4, p. 1.

48. Sullivan, *Dodgers Move West*, 223.

49. Penelope McMillan, "O'Malley's Life: Variety, Vision," *Los Angeles Times*, 10 August 1979, part 1, p. 32.

50. Editorial, "A Vote in Favor of Everybody," *Los Angeles Times*, 1 June 1958, part 2, p. 4.

51. Ibid.

52. *Los Angeles Times*, 3 June 1958.

53. Frank Finch, "Dodgers Approve L.A. Deal, Will Play Here Next Season," *Los Angeles Times*, 9 October 1957, part 1, p. 1.

54. Poulson, "Untold Story of Chavez Ravine," 50. See also "Poulson Reveals Scare Campaign for Dodgers," *Los Angeles Times*, 4 April 1962, part 2, p. 1.

55. William Ross (of Baus and Ross), interview, 287. UCLA Oral History Project, Special Collections, Young Research Library, University of California, Los Angeles.

56. "5-Hour Telethon Supports Prop. B," *Los Angeles Times*, 2 June 1959, part 1, p. 7.

57. *Griffith Park News*, 15 January 1959. Roybal Papers, Special Collections, Young Research Library, University of California, Los Angeles.

58. *Local Reporter*, 15 June 1959. Roybal Papers, Special Collections, Young Research Library, University of California, Los Angeles.

59. "O'Malley Sees Start on Park by July 5," *Los Angeles Times*, 5 June 1958, part 4, p. 1.

60. *Reuben v. City of Los Angeles*, Los Angeles Superior Court no. 687210 (1958); *Kirschbaum v. Housing Authority*, Los Angeles Superior Court No. 699077 (1958). Both quoted in Sullivan, *Dodgers Move West*, 168.

61. Ridgely Cummings, Civic Center News Agency, n.d. Roybal Papers, Special Collections, Young Research Library, University of California, Los Angeles.

62. *Wilshire Reporter,* 20 October 1959. Roybal Papers, Special Collections, Young Research Library, University of California, Los Angeles.

63. Gene Blake, "High Court OKs L.A.-Dodger Pact," *Los Angeles Times,* 20 October 1959, 25.

64. *Columbus Dispatch,* 10 May 1959. Roybal Papers, Special Collections, Young Research Library, University of California, Los Angeles.

65. Alice Ingersoll, letter to Edward Roybal, n.d. Roybal Papers, Special Collections, Young Research Library, University of California, Los Angeles.

66. Unsigned letter to Edward Roybal, n.d. Roybal Papers, Special Collections, Young Research Library, University of California, Los Angeles.

67. Editorial, "Tears on the Picture Tube," *Los Angeles Times,* 14 May 1959, part 3, p. 4.

68. O. J. Temple, letter to Edward Roybal, 25 July 1959. Roybal Papers, Special Collections, Young Research Library, University of California, Los Angeles.

69. Poulson memoirs, 154.

70. *Los Angeles Citizen,* 13 May 1959. Roybal Papers, Special Collections, Young Research Library, University of California, Los Angeles.

71. Don Parson, "Urban Politics during the Cold War: Public Housing, Urban Renewal, and Suburbanization in Los Angeles" (Ph.D. diss., University of California, Los Angeles, 1985), 133.

72. Elisa Garcia Lopez, letter to Edward Roybal, n.d. Roybal Papers, Special Collections, Young Research Library, University of California, Los Angeles.

73. Frank Wright, letter to Edward Roybal, 9 May 1959. Roybal Papers, Special Collections, Young Research Library, University of California, Los Angeles.

74. Lota Barrett, letter to Edward Roybal, 9 May 1959. Roybal Papers, Special Collections, Young Research Library, University of California, Los Angeles.

75. Patrick McCartney, "Oxnard to Consider Renovation Study Redevelopment," *Los Angeles Times,* 24 July 1993, 1.

76. Rudolfo Acuña, *Occupied America: A History of Chicanos,* 3d ed. (New York: Harper and Row, 1988), 296.

77. Poulson, "Untold Story of Chavez Ravine," 15.

78. James Lin Beebe to Los Angeles City Council, Minutes of Los Angeles City Council, 8 March 1962. Regional History Archives, University of Southern California.

79. Frank Wilkinson, interview by the author, 24 January 1996.

80. "56,000 for Dodger-Red Opening Day," *Los Angeles Times,* 10 April 1962, 1.

81. Al Wolf, "O'Malley Confident Despite Ruling," *Los Angeles Times,* 15 July 1958, part 4, p. 3.

82. Walter Bingham, "Boom Goes Baseball," *Sports Illustrated,* 23 April 1962, 18–25.

83. E.J. Bavasi, "Los Angeles Dodgers," promotional letter, John Holland

Papers, Special Collections, University Library, California State University, Los Angeles.

84. David Voight, *American Baseball*, vol. 3 (University Park: Pennsylvania State University Press, 1983), 119–24.

85. Davis, *City of Quartz*, 226–28.

86. Bingham, "Boom Goes Baseball."

87. Ray Herbert, "M'Clellan Describes Chavez Ravine Development Plans," *Los Angeles Times*, 19 September 1957, part 1, p. 2.

88. "Notables Back Prop. B on T.V.," *Los Angeles Times*, 2 June 1958, part 1, p. 7.

89. E. J. Bavasi, press release, n.d. John Holland Papers, Special Collections, Young Research Library, California State University, Los Angeles.

90. "Boom Goes Baseball," 22.

91. *Baseball Digest*, May 1969, 11–12.

92. Letter, Downtown Businessmen's Association to City Council, 30 September 1957. Los Angeles City Council File 78067 S2, Box A-1403. Los Angeles City Clerk's Office.

93. J. J. Christian, letter to Edward Roybal, 27 September 1957. Roybal Papers, Special Collections, Young Research Library, University of California, Los Angeles.

94. John Merwin, "The Most Valuable Executive in Either League," *Forbes*, 12 April 1982, 129–38.

95. Downtown Businessmen's Association, letter to City Council, 30 September 1957. Chamber of Commerce Collection, California Historical Society Collection, Specialized Libraries and Archival Collections, University of Southern California.

96. Editorial, "Holding Together until Monday," *Los Angeles Times*, 2 October 1957, part 2, p. 4.

97. Robinson joined the minor-league ball club in Montreal that year, bringing the first African American into the farm club system. See Richard Whittingham, *The Los Angeles Dodgers: An Illustrated History* (New York: Harper and Row, 1982), 53.

98. "Negro Voters Back Dems, Favor Prop. B," *California Eagle*, 5 June 1958, 1. After Walter O'Malley purchased Wrigley Field in 1957, the editors of the *Eagle* anticipated the possibility that O'Malley would renovate the ballpark to create a permanent home for his franchise. In fact, shortly before the vote on Proposition B, the editor of the *Eagle* cautioned his readers that a vote in favor of the city-Dodger contract could jeopardize the possibility of expanding Wrigley Field for the purposes of housing the Dodgers permanently within the black community of South Central Los Angeles. However, Walter O'Malley opted not to enlarge Wrigley Field and instead remained focused on the Chavez Ravine, perhaps precisely because of Wrigley Field's location within an expanding black neighborhood.

99. L. I. "Brock" Brockenbury, "Where Were You, Charley, Junior, and Maury?" *Los Angeles Sentinel*, 15 October 1959, 6B, 6C.

100. Gilbert M. Joseph, "Forging the Regional Pastime: Baseball and Class in Yucatan," in *Sport and Society in Latin America: Diffusion, Dependency, and the Rise of Mass Culture*, ed. Joseph L. Arbena (New York: Greenwood Press, 1988), 33–34.

101. Samuel O. Regalado, "Baseball in the Barrios: The Scene in East Los Angeles since World War II," *Baseball History* 1, no. 1 (summer 1986): 48.

102. Ibid.

103. Ibid., 55.

104. Steven A. Reiss, *Touching Base: Professional Baseball and American Culture in the Progressive Era* (Urbana: University of Illinois Press, 1999), 191.

105. Quoted in Regalado, "Baseball in the Barrios," 57.

106. "Esquinázos," *La Opinión*, 3 June 1958, 5.

107. "José Castillo Pide Apoyo para la Proposicion B," *La Opinión*, 31 May 1958, 7.

108. Alberto Huici (cartoonist), "Los 'Dodgers' Vistos por Alberto Huici," *La Opinión*, 1 June 1958, 5.

109. Samuel O. Regalado, "Dodgers' *Béisbol* Is on the Air: The Development and Impact of the Dodgers' Spanish Language Broadcasts, 1958–1994," *California History: The Magazine of the California Historical Society*, fall 1995: 281–89; Samuel O. Regalado, *Viva Baseball! Latin Major Leaguers and Their Special Hunger* (Urbana: University of Illinois Press, 1988), 103.

110. Hazel Carby, *Race Men* (Cambridge, Mass.: Harvard University Press, 1998).

111. Bruce Kidd, "The Men's Cultural Centre: Sports and the Dynamic of Women's Oppression/Men's Repression," in *Sport, Men, and the Gender Order: Critical Feminist Perspectives*, ed. Michael A. Messner and Donald F. Sabo (Champaign, Ill.: Human Kinetics Books, 1990), 31–43.

CHAPTER SIX. THE SUTURED CITY

1. Leonard Pitt and Dale Pitt, *Los Angeles A to Z: An Encyclopedia of the City and County* (Berkeley: University of California Press, 1997), 373–75; Spencer Crump, *Ride the Big Red Cars: How the Trolleys Helped Build Southern California*, 5th ed. (Corona del Mar, Calif.: Trans-Anglo Books, 1970); Robert Fogelson, *The Fragmented Metropolis: Los Angeles, 1850–1930* (Berkeley: University of California Press, 1993); George W. Hilton and John F. Due, *The Electric Interurbans in America* (Stanford, Calif.: Stanford University Press, 1960).

2. Glenn S. Dumke, *The Boom of the Eighties in Southern California* (San Marino, Calif.: Huntington Library, 1944), 48; David Brodsly, *L.A. Freeway: An Appreciative Essay* (Berkeley: University of California Press, 1981), 68–71.

3. Brodsly, *L.A. Freeway*, 80.

4. George J. Sánchez, *Becoming Mexican American: Ethnicity, Culture, and Identity in Chicano Los Angeles, 1900–1945* (New York: Oxford University Press, 1993), 69.

5. Norman Klein, *The History of Forgetting: Los Angeles and the Erasure of Memory* (London: Verso Press, 1997), 36.

6. Interview of Cecil "Big Jay" McNeeley, in Clora Bryant, Buddy Collette, William Green, Steven Isoardi, Jack Kelson, Horace Tapscott, Gerald Wilson, and Marl Young, eds., *Central Avenue Sounds: Jazz in Los Angeles* (Berkeley: University of California Press, 1998), 180.

7. Mary Hernandez, interview with Anthony Macias, Redlands, Calif., 11 January 1998. Tape recording.

8. Pat Adler, "Watts, a Legacy of Lines," *Westways* 58 (August 1966): 22–24.

9. This perspective is informed by several studies, which delineate the historical context for the cultural transformation of the United States at the turn of the century. See Gunther Barth, *City People: The Rise of Modern City Culture in Nineteenth-Century America* (New York: Oxford University Press, 1980); John F. Kasson, *Amusing the Million: Coney Island at the Turn of the Century* (New York: Hill and Wang, 1978); Kathy Peiss, *Cheap Amusements: Working Women and Leisure in Turn-of-the-Century New York* (Philadelphia: Temple University Press, 1990); and Francis Couvares, *The Remaking of Pittsburgh: Class and Culture in an Industrializing City, 1877–1919* (Albany: State University of New York Press, 1984).

10. Kasson, *Amusing the Million,* 94–105.

11. "A Section of Hades in Los Angeles," *Los Angeles Record,* 11 December 1912, 4.

12. Red Callendar and Elaine Cohen, *Unfinished Dream: The Musical World of Red Callendar* (New York: Quartet Books, 1985), 37–38.

13. Chester Himes, "Zoot Riots Are Race Riots," in *Black on Black: Baby Sister and Selected Writings* (New York: Doubleday, 1973), 220–25.

14. Mauricio Mazón, *The Zoot-Suit Riots: The Psychology of Symbolic Annihilation* (Austin: University of Texas Press, 1984), 67–77; Robin D.G. Kelley, *Race Rebels: Culture, Politics, and the Black Working Class* (New York: Free Press, 1996), 55–62; Philip Brake, "Zoot Suit Riots in Los Angeles," in *Fighting Racism in World War II,* ed. Fred Stanton (New York, 1980), 254–55.

15. Mark Foster, "The Decentralization of Los Angeles during the 1920's" (Ph.D. diss., University of Southern California, 1971), 40; Mark Foster, "The Model T, the Hard Sell, and Los Angeles' Urban Growth: The Decentralization of Los Angeles during the 1920's," *Pacific Historical Review* 44 (November 1975): 459–84.

16. Robert Gottlieb and Irene Wolt, *Thinking Big: The Story of the Los Angeles Times, Its Publishers and Their Influence on Southern California* (New York: G.P. Putnam and Sons, 1977), 248–49.

17. Quoted in ibid., 250.

18. Los Angeles Traffic Commission, *A Major Traffic Street Plan for Los Angeles,* prepared by Frederick Law Olmsted Jr., Harland Bartholomew, and Charles Henry Cheney (Los Angeles: Traffic Commission of the City and County of Los Angeles, 1924); *Los Angeles Times* quoted in Gottlieb and Wolt, *Thinking Big,* 251.

19. Gottlieb and Wolt, *Thinking Big,* 320–22.

20. Brodsly, *L.A. Freeway,* 93; Fogelson, *Fragmented Metropolis,* 163; Scott Bottles, *Los Angeles and the Automobile: The Making of the Modern City* (Berkeley: University of California Press, 1987), 210–24.

21. Works Progress Administration, *Los Angeles: A Guide to the City and Its Environs,* American Guide Series (New York: Hastings House, 1941), 7; Robert S. Allen, *Our Fair City* (New York: Vanguard Press, 1947), 36.

22. *Los Angeles Herald,* 7 October 1947. Box 48, Fletcher Bowron Papers, Huntington Library.

23. Los Angeles Transportation Engineering Board, *A Transit Program for the Los Angeles Metropolitan Area* (Los Angeles: Transportation Engineering Board, 1939); Donald M. Baker, *A Rapid Transit System for Los Angeles, California,* report to the Central Business District Association (Los Angeles, 1933). On Lloyd Aldrich, see Gottlieb and Wolt, *Thinking Big,* 259.

24. Automobile Club of Southern California, *Traffic Survey* (Los Angeles: Automobile Club of Southern California, 1937), 12.

25. Los Angeles County Regional Planning Commission, *Freeways for the Region* (Los Angeles: Regional Planning Commission, County of Los Angeles, 1943).

26. C.G. Beer, "Traffic Studies: Need for Network of Freeways in Los Angeles Clearly Evident," *California Highways and Public Works* 32 (September–October 1953): 31.

27. Quoted in David W. Jones, "California's Freeway Era in Historical Perspective" (research report, Institute of Transportation Studies, University of California, Berkeley, 1989), 238.

28. "World Famous Los Angeles Freeway Interchange," Box 11, California Postcard Collection, Special Collections, Young Research Library, University of California, Los Angeles.

29. *Los Angeles Daily News,* 30 October 1947. Box 48, Fletcher Bowron Papers, Huntington Library.

30. Pamphlet, *California's Freeway Planning Team* (Sacramento: California State Printing Office, n.d.). Box 48, Fletcher Bowron Papers, Huntington Library.

31. "Rapid Progress on the Harbor Freeway," *California Highways and Public Works* 33, nos. 5–6 (May–June 1954): 15.

32. Centennial edition, *California Highways and Public Works* 29 (9 September 1950): 3.

33. Ibid, 41.

34. "Governor Olson Dedicates the Arroyo Seco Freeway," *California Highways and Public Works* 32 (January 1941): 3–8.

35. Robert Berkhoffer, *The White Man's Indian: Images of the American Indian from Columbus to the Present* (New York: Vintage Books, 1979); Philip J. Deloria, *Playing Indian* (New Haven, Conn.: Yale University Press, 1998), introduction.

36. "Governor Olson Dedicates the Arroyo Seco Freeway," 6.

37. Eric Avila, "The Folklore of the Freeway: Space, Culture, and Identity in Postwar Los Angeles," *Aztlán: A Journal of Chicano Studies* 23, no. 1 (spring 1998): 15–31; Douglas Monroy, *Thrown among Strangers: The Making of Mexican Culture in Frontier California* (Berkeley: University of California Press, 1990), 18.

38. Eric Avila, "Reinventing Los Angeles: Popular Culture in the Age of White Flight" (Ph.D. diss., University of California, Berkeley, 1997), 163.

39. Advertisement, *Disneyland News*, n.d.; *News from Disneyland*, Public Relations Division, n.d. Disneyland Collection, Anaheim History Room, Anaheim Public Library.

40. *Women at the Wheel*, Automobile Club of Southern California, n.d., filmstrip.

41. *The Freeway*, California State Chamber of Commerce, n.d., filmstrip. Archives, Automobile Club of Southern California.

42. Joan Didion, *Play It as It Lays* (New York: Noonday Press, 1990), 16.

43. Ibid., 162.

44. Raymond Mohl, "Race and Space in the Modern City: Interstate 95 and the Black Community in Miami," in *Urban Policy in Twentieth-Century America*, ed. Arnold R. Hirsch and Raymond A. Mohl (New Brunswick, N.J.: Rutgers University Press, 1993), 100–158; Marc Weiss, "The Origins and Legacy of Urban Renewal," in *Urban and Regional Planning in an Age of Austerity*, ed. Pierre Clavel, John Forester, and William W. Goldsmith (New York: Pergamon Press, 1980), 53–80.

45. Victor Gruen, "The City in the Automobile Age," *Perspectives* 16 (summer 1956), 48.

46. Quoted in Mohl, "Race and Space in the Modern City," 109.

47. California Assembly Interim Committee on Natural Resources, Planning and Public Works, *Highway and Freeway Planning* (Sacramento: Assembly of the State of California, 1965).

48. Residential Security Maps of Metropolitan Los Angeles, California, 1939, and City Survey Files, U.S. Home Owners' Loan Corporation, Record Group 195, National Archives, Washington, D.C.

49. George Ramos, "Seeking a Lost Neighborhood," *Los Angeles Times*, 2 December 1999, B1 (article written by the son of a couple who lived in Mateo during the 1920s and '30s).

50. "Eastside Up in Arms over Proposed $32,000,000 Golden State Freeway," *Eastside Sun*, 10 October 1953, 1.

51. "Hollenbeck Heights Cutoff between Freeways Opposed," *Los Angeles Times*, 16 December 1953, 1.

52. "Watch Out! The Appraisers Are Busy Appraising!" *Eastside Sun*, 6 January 1955, 1.

53. Joseph Eli Kovner, editorial, *Eastside Sun*, 3 June 1957, 1.

54. Editorial cartoon, *Eastside Sun*, 29 January 1959, 1.

55. Joseph Eli Kovner, editorial, *Eastside Sun*, 14 November 1957, 1.

56. "Officials Give Reasons for Freeway Route at Hearing, Protests Voiced,"

Belvedere Citizen, 24 October 1957, 1. The *Citizen,* a bilingual weekly newspaper printed in Spanish and English, catered primarily to Spanish-speaking readers in Belvedere and Monterey Park.

57. Ibid.

58. Brooklyn Avenue Businessmen's Association, letter to the editor, *Eastside Sun,* 30 September 1953, 3.

59. Edward F. Elliott, op/ed column, *Eastside Sun,* 26 January 1961, 1.

60. Ibid.

61. "Mexican American Population Shows 200% Increase in L.A.," *Belvedere Citizen,* 22 May 1958, 1.

62. Carey McWilliams, "Watts: The Forgotten Slum," *The Nation,* 30 August 1965, 89–90.

63. John Hench, interview by Jay Horan, 3 December 1982. Transcript. Walt Disney Archives, Burbank, Calif.; Reyner Banham, *Los Angeles: The Architecture of Four Ecologies* (London: Penguin Books, 1971), 222.

64. Dr. T. Gordon Reynolds, letter to Edward Roybal, 14 April 1958. Edward R. Roybal Papers, Special Collections, Young Research Library, University of California, Los Angeles.

65. Marshall Berman's use of Charles Baudelaire's poem "The Family of Eyes," in Marshall Berman, *All That Is Solid Melts into Air: The Experience of Modernity* (New York: Simon and Schuster, 1982), 148–55.

66. "The Westside Story," *Los Angeles: The Magazine of the Good Life in Southern California,* February 1962, 23–25.

67. Jackson Mayers, San Fernando Valley, Los Angeles, California Promotional brochure, Industrial Association of the San Fernando Valley, Van Nuys, Calif., October 1955.

68. W.L. Fahey, "Santa Ana Freeway Has Induced Industrial and Recreational Development," *California Highways and Public Works* 32 (September–October 1953): 31.

69. *The Freeway,* Public Service Announcement by California Chamber of Commerce, video recording, n.d. Archives, Automobile Club of Southern California.

70. David Rees, "200 Million in Downtown Boom," *Los Angeles Mirror News,* 8 April 1955, 2.

71. "L.A. Renaissance: Freeway Service Key Factor in Downtown Growth Renewal," *California Highways and Public Works* 40 (September–October 1961): 29–45.

72. "What of California's Future?" *Los Angeles Times,* 3 January 1950, 29.

73. Larry L. Meyer, "Sinews of a Supercity," *Westways* 57 (June 1965): 27.

74. "Closing the Gap," *Los Angeles,* August 1961, 33.

75. Meyer, "Sinews of a Supercity," 26–28.

76. "Report from District VII: Freeway System Taking Shape in Greater Los Angeles Area," *California Highways and Public Works* 41 (March–April 1962): 42–57.

77. "The Freeways: Gateway to Vacationland," *Vacationland* 8 (winter–

spring 1964): 5–22. Disneyland Collection, Anaheim History Room, Anaheim Public Library; California State Division of Highways, *How Los Angeles Was Unified by Freeways*, pamphlet (ca. 1968).

78. "Where to Take Your Pleasure," *Westways* 57 (June 1965): 16–17.

79. Brodsly, *L.A. Freeway*, 33.

80. Sheri Bernstein, "The California Home Front, 1940–1960," in *Made in California: Art, Image and Identity, 1900–2000*, by Stephanie Barron, Sheri Bernstein, and Ilene Susan Fort (Los Angeles: Los Angeles County Museum of Art; Berkeley: University of California Press, 2000), 164–65.

81. "The California Highway Story." Box 48, Fletcher Bowron Papers, Huntington Library.

82. "Yep, You Can Go Nuts Driving on the LA Freeway," *Los Angeles Examiner*, 29 May 1957, section 1, p. 1.

83. Stephen Kern, *The Culture of Time and Space, 1880–1918* (Cambridge, Mass.: Harvard University Press, 1998), 109–30.

84. *Jack Benny Show*, originally aired on CBS, 19 February 1961. UCLA Film and Television Archive.

85. Banham, *Los Angeles*, 219.

86. "New Police Interceptor Car in Use on Freeway," *Los Angeles Times*, 18 July 1955, part 1, p. 11.

87. Banham, *Los Angeles*, 220.

88. Los Angeles Department of City Planning, *The Visual Environment of Los Angeles* (Los Angeles: Los Angeles Department of City Planning, 1971), 8–11.

89. Banham, *Los Angeles*, 221.

90. Alexis de Tocqueville, *Democracy in America* (New York: Alfred A. Knopf, 1948), vol. 2, pp. 208, 257, 255; Jane Jacobs, *The Death and Life of Great American Cities* (New York: Vintage, 1961), 56.

91. Berman, *All That Is Solid Melts into Air*.

EPILOGUE. THE 1960S AND BEYOND

1. Remi Nadeau, "The New California: A Society of Strangers?" *Los Angeles*, October 1963, 44–45; D.J. Waldie, *Holy Land: A Suburban Memoir* (New York: St. Martin's Press, 1996), 12.

2. David McBride, "On the Faultline of Mass Culture and Counterculture: A Social History of the Hippie Counterculture in 1960s Los Angeles" (Ph.D. diss., University of California, Los Angeles, 1998).

3. Robert Buhrman, "The Couples' Contagion," *Los Angeles*, July 1968, 32–34.

4. Barton J. Bernstein, "The New Deal: The Conservative Achievements of Liberal Reform," in *Towards a New Past: Dissenting Essays in American History*, ed. Barton J. Bernstein (New York: Pantheon Books, 1968), 263–88.

5. Lisa McGirr, *Suburban Warriors: The Origins of the New American Right* (Princeton, N.J.: Princeton University Press, 2001), 261.

6. William A. V. Clark, "Residential Patterns: Avoidance, Assimilation and Succession," in *Ethnic Los Angeles*, ed. Roger Waldinger and Mehdi Bozorgmehr (New York: Russell Sage Foundation, 1996), 115.

7. Allen J. Scott, "High-Technology Industrial Development in the San Fernando Valley and Ventura County: Observations on Economic Growth and the Evolution of Urban Form," in *The City: Los Angeles and Urban Theory at the End of the Twentieth Century*, ed. Allen J. Scott and Edward W. Soja (Berkeley: University of California Press, 1996), 293.

8. Janet Abu-Lughod, *New York, Chicago, Los Angeles: America's Global Cities* (Minneapolis: University of Minnesota Press, 1999), 364–65.

9. Raymond A. Rocco, "Latino Los Angeles: Reframing Boundaries/Borders," in *The City: Los Angeles and Urban Theory at the End of the Twentieth Century*, ed. Allen J. Scott and Edward W. Soja (Berkeley: University of California Press, 1996), 374–75.

10. Clarence Y.H. Lo, *Small Property versus Big Government: Social Origins of the Property Tax Revolt* (Berkeley: University of California Press, 1990).

11. Ibid., 57–60; Abu-Lughod, *New York, Chicago, Los Angeles*, 379–82.

12. Michael Paul Rogin and John L. Shover, *Political Change in California: Critical Elections and Social Movements, 1890–1966* (Westport, Conn.: Greenwood Publishing Corporation, 1970), 173–78; George Lipsitz, *The Possessive Investment in Whiteness: How White People Profit from Identity Politics* (Philadelphia: Temple University Press, 1998), 136–38.

13. Abu-Lughod, *New York, Chicago, Los Angeles*, 383–85.

14. Edward W. Soja, "Los Angeles, 1965–1992: From Crisis-Generated Restructuring to Restructuring-Generated Crisis," in *The City: Los Angeles and Urban Theory at the End of the Twentieth Century*, ed. Allen J. Scott and Edward W. Soja (Berkeley: University of California Press, 1996), 443.

15. Michael Sorkin, ed., *Variations on a Theme Park: The New American City and the End of Public Space* (New York: Hill and Wang, 1992); Edward W. Soja, *Postmetropolis: Critical Studies of Cities and Regions* (Oxford: Blackwell Publishing, 2000), 233–63.

16. Robin D. G. Kelley, *Race Rebels: Culture, Politics and the Black Working Class* (New York: Free Press, 1996), 183–227. See also Tricia Rose, *Black Noise: Rap Music and Black Culture in Contemporary America* (Hanover, N.H.: University Press of New England, 1994).

17. Mike Davis, *Magical Urbanism: Latinos Reinvent the U.S. City* (London: Verso, 2000). See also Victor M. Valle and Rodolfo D. Torres, *Latino Metropolis* (Minneapolis: University of Minnesota Press, 2000); Gustavo Leclerc, Raul Villa, and Michael J. Dear, *Urban Latino Cultures* (Thousand Oaks, Calif.: Sage Publications, 1999); and Marta López-Garza and David R. Diaz, *Asian and Latino Immigrants in a Restructuring Economy: The Metamorphosis of Southern California* (Stanford, Calif.: Stanford University Press, 2001).

18. "Can Hollywood Get Its Glitz Back?" 12 November 2001, www.businessweek.com/magazine/content/01_46/b3757018.htm.

19. Jim Rawitsch, "Moving Right Along," *Los Angeles Times Magazine*, 13 July 1986, 1.

20. Samuel R. Delany, *Times Square Red, Times Square Blue* (New York: New York University Press, 1999); Ada Louise Huxtable, "Reinventing Times Square: 1990," in *Inventing Times Square: Commerce and Culture at the Cross-roads of the World*, ed. William R. Taylor (Baltimore: Johns Hopkins University Press, 1991), 356–70.

21. Dana Cuff, *The Provisional City: Los Angeles Stories of Architecture and Urbanism* (Cambridge, Mass.: MIT Press, 2000), 334–35; Andrew Ross, *The Celebration Chronicles* (New York: Ballantine Books, 1999); Douglas Frantz and Catherine Collins, *Celebration, U.S.A.: Living in Disney's Brave New Town* (New York: Henry Holt, 2000).

22. Samuel O. Regalado, *Viva Baseball! Latin Major Leaguers and Their Special Hunger* (Urbana: University of Illinois Press, 1988), 122–28.

23. Roger Keil, *Los Angeles: Globalization, Urbanization and Social Struggles* (New York: John Wiley and Sons, 1998), xxxi–xxxii; Kelley, *Race Rebels*, 232–33.

Selected Bibliography

Abbot, Carl. *The New Urban America: Growth and Politics in Sunbelt Cities.* Chapel Hill: University of North Carolina Press, 1981.

———. "New West, New South, New Region: The Discovery of the Sunbelt." In *Searching for the Sunbelt: Historical Perspectives on a Region,* ed. Raymond A. Mohl, 7–24. Athens: University of Georgia Press, 1993.

Abu-Lughod, Janet L. *New York, Chicago, Los Angeles: America's Global Cities.* Minneapolis: University of Minnesota Press, 1999.

Acuña, Rudolfo. *Occupied America: A History of Chicanos.* 3d ed. New York: Harper and Row, 1988.

Adams, Judith. *The American Amusement Park Industry: A History of Technology and Thrills.* Boston: Twayne Publishers, 1991.

Adler, Patricia. "Watts: A Legacy of Lines." *Westways* 58 (August 1966): 22–24.

———. "Watts: From Suburb to Black Ghetto." Ph.D. diss., University of Southern California, 1977.

Alexander, Robert, and Drayton Bryant. *Rebuilding a City: A Study of Redevelopment Problems in Los Angeles.* Los Angeles: Haynes Foundation, 1951.

Allen, James P., and Eugene Turner. *The Ethnic Quilt: Population Diversity in Southern California.* Northridge: Center for Geographical Studies, Department of Geography, California State University, Northridge, 1997.

Althusser, Louis. "Ideology and Ideological State Apparatuses [Notes toward an Investigation]." In *Lenin and Philosophy and Other Essays,* trans. Ben Brewster, 127–86. New York: Monthly Review Press, 1971.

Anderson, Kay J. "The Idea of Chinatown: The Power of Place and Institutional Practice in the Making of a Racial Category." *Annals of the Association of American Geographers* 77, no. 4 (1987): 580–98.

Anderson, Susan. "A City Called Heaven: Black Enchantment and Despair in Los Angeles." In *The City: Los Angeles and Urban Theory at the End of the Twentieth Century,* ed. Edward W. Soja and Allen J. Scott, 336–64. Berkeley: University of California Press, 1996.

Avila, Eric. "The Folklore of the Freeway: Space, Culture, and Identity in Postwar Los Angeles," *Aztlán: A Journal of Chicano Studies* 23, no. 1 (spring 1998): 15–31.

———. "Reinventing Los Angeles: Popular Culture in the Age of White Flight." Ph.D. diss., University of California, Berkeley, 1997.

Babener, Liahna K. "*Chinatown:* City of Blight." In *Los Angeles in Fiction: A Collection of Original Essays,* ed. David Fine, 243–56. Albuquerque: University of New Mexico Press, 1984.

Badger, R. Reid. *The Great American Fair: The World's Columbian Exposition and American Culture.* Chicago: Nelson-Hall, 1979.

Baker, Donald M. *A Rapid Transit System for Los Angeles, California.* Report to the Central Business District Association. Los Angeles, 1933.

Balio, Tino. "Retrenchment, Reappraisal and Reorganization, 1948–." In *The American Film Industry,* ed. Tino Balio, 401–47. Rev. ed. Madison: University of Wisconsin Press, 1985.

———, ed. *The American Film Industry.* Rev. ed. Madison: University of Wisconsin Press, 1985.

Banham, Reyner. *Los Angeles: The Architecture of Four Ecologies.* London: Penguin Books, 1971.

Barnouw, Eric. *A History of Broadcasting in the United States,* vol. 3. New York: Oxford University Press, 1973.

———. *Tube of Plenty: The Evolution of American Broadcasting.* New York: Oxford University Press, 1975.

Barth, Gunther. *City People: The Rise of Modern City Culture in Nineteenth-Century America.* New York: Oxford University Press, 1982.

———. *Instant Cities: Urbanization and the Rise of San Francisco and Denver.* New York: Oxford University Press, 1985.

Bartlett, Dana. *The Better City: A Sociological Study of a Modern City.* Los Angeles: Neuner Company Press, 1907.

Bartlett, Lanier, and Virginia Stivers Bartlett. *Los Angeles in Seven Days: Including Southern California.* New York: Robert M. McBride and Company, 1932.

Berg, Charles Ramirez. "Immigrants, Aliens and Extraterrestrials: Science Fiction's Alien Other as (among Other Things) New Hispanic Imagery." *Cine-Action!* 18 (fall 1989): 3–17.

Berkhoffer, Robert. *The White Man's Indian: Images of the American Indian from Columbus to the Present.* New York: Vintage Books, 1979.

Berman, Marshall. *All That Is Solid Melts into Air: The Experience of Modernity.* New York: Simon and Schuster, 1982.

Bernardi, Daniel, ed. *The Birth of Whiteness: Race and the Emergence of U.S. Cinema.* New Brunswick, N.J.: Rutgers University Press, 1996.

Bernstein, Barton J. "The New Deal: The Conservative Achievements of Liberal Reform." In *Towards a New Past: Dissenting Essays in American History,* ed. Barton J. Bernstein, 263–88. New York: Pantheon Books, 1968.

Bernstein, Sheri. "The California Home Front, 1940–1960." In *Made in California: Art, Image and Identity, 1900–2000,* by Stephanie Barron, Sheri

Bernstein, and Ilene Susan Fort, 147–92. Los Angeles: Los Angeles County Museum of Art; Berkeley: University of California Press, 2000.

Biskind, Peter. *Seeing Is Believing: How Americans Learned to Stop Worrying and Love the Fifties.* New York: Pantheon, 1983.

Blake, Philip. "Zoot Suit Riots in Los Angeles." In *Fighting Racism in World War II,* ed. Fred Stanton, 254–55. New York: Monad Press, 1980.

Borde, Raymond, and Etienne Chaumeton. "Towards a Definition of *Film Noir.*" In *Film Noir: A Reader,* ed. Alain Silver and James Ursini, trans. Alain Silver, 17–25. New York: Limelight Editions, 1997.

Borneman, Ernest. "United States versus Hollywood: The Case Study of an Antitrust Suit." In *The American Film Industry,* ed. Tino Balio, 449–62. Rev. ed. Madison: University of Wisconsin Press, 1985.

Bottles, Scott. *Los Angeles and the Automobile: The Making of the Modern City.* Berkeley: University of California Press, 1987.

Bright, Randy. *Disneyland: The Inside Story.* New York: Harry N. Abrams, Inc., 1987.

Brodkin, Karen. *How the Jews Became White Folks and What That Says about Race in America.* New Brunswick, N.J.: Rutgers University Press, 2000.

Brodsly, David. *L.A. Freeway: An Appreciative Essay.* Berkeley: University of California Press, 1981.

Bryant, Clora, Buddy Collette, William Green, Steven Isoardi, Jack Kelson, Horace Tapscott, Gerald Wilson, and Marl Young, eds. *Central Avenue Sounds: Jazz in Los Angeles.* Berkeley: University of California Press, 1998.

California Governor's Commission on the Los Angeles Riots. *Violence in the City—An End or a Beginning? A Report by the Governor's Commission on the Los Angeles Riots.* Los Angeles: Governor's Commission on the Los Angeles Riots, 1965.

Callendar, Red, and Elaine Cohen. *Unfinished Dream: The Musical World of Red Callendar.* New York: Quartet Books, 1985.

Carby, Hazel. *Race Men.* Cambridge, Mass.: Harvard University Press, 1998.

Ceplair, Larry, and Steven Englund. *The Inquisition in Hollywood: Politics in the Film Community, 1930–1960.* Berkeley: University of California Press, 1983.

Charney, Leo, and Vanessa Schwartz, eds. *Cinema and the Invention of Modern Life.* Berkeley: University of California Press, 1995.

Chauncey, George. *Gay New York: Gender, Urban Culture, and the Making of the Gay Male World, 1890–1940.* New York: Basic Books, 1994.

Chudacoff, Howard P., and Judith E. Smith. *The Evolution of American Urban Society.* 5th ed. Upper Saddle River, N.J.: Prentice Hall, 2000.

Clark, William A. V. "Residential Patterns: Avoidance, Assimilation and Succession." In *Ethnic Los Angeles,* ed. Roger Waldinger and Mehdi Bozorgmehr, 109–38. New York: Russell Sage Foundation, 1996.

Cogley, John. "HUAC: The Mass Hearings." In *The American Film Industry,* ed. Tino Balio, 487–509. Rev. ed. Madison: University of Wisconsin Press, 1985.

Cohen, Lizabeth. "From Town Center to Shopping Center: The Reconfiguration of Community Marketplaces in Postwar America." *American Historical Review* 101, no. 4 (October 1996): 1050–81.

Collins, Keith E. *Black Los Angeles: The Maturing of the Ghetto, 1940–1950.* Saratoga, Calif.: Century Twenty One Publishing, 1980.

Cook, James W. *The Arts of Deception: Playing with Fraud in the Age of Barnum.* Cambridge, Mass.: Harvard University Press, 2001.

———. "Of Men, Missing Links and Nondescripts: The Strange Career of P. T. Barnum's 'What Is It?' Exhibition." In *Freakery: Cultural Spectacles of the Extraordinary Body,* ed. Rosemarie Garland Thompson, 139–57. New York: New York University Press, 1996.

Courvares, Francis. *The Remaking of Pittsburgh: Class and Culture in an Industrializing City, 1877–1919.* Albany: State University of New York Press, 1984.

Craddock, Susan L. "Sewers and Scapegoats: Spatial Metaphors of Smallpox in Nineteenth-Century San Francisco." *Social Science and Medicine* 41, no. 7 (1995): 957–68.

Cronon, William. *Nature's Metropolis: Chicago and the Great West.* New York: W. W. Norton and Company, 1992.

Crump, Spencer. *Ride the Big Red Cars: How the Trolleys Helped Build Southern California.* 5th ed. Corona del Mar, Calif.: Trans-Anglo Books, 1970.

Cuff, Dana. *The Provisional City: Los Angeles Stories of Architecture and Urbanism.* Cambridge, Mass.: MIT Press, 2000.

Danielson, Michael. *The Politics of Exclusion.* New York: Columbia University Press, 1976.

Davis, Mike. *City of Quartz: Excavating the Future in Los Angeles.* London: Verso, 1990.

———. *Ecology of Fear: Los Angeles and the Imagination of Disaster.* New York: Metropolitan Books, 1998.

———. *Magical Urbanism: Latinos Reinvent the U.S. City.* London: Verso, 2000.

De Graaf, Lawrence. "The City of Black Angels: Emergence of a Los Angeles Ghetto, 1890–1930." *Pacific Historical Review* 39 (1970): 323–52.

Delany, Samuel R. *Times Square Red, Times Square Blue.* New York: New York University Press, 1999.

Deloria, Philip J. *Playing Indian.* New Haven, Conn.: Yale University Press, 1998.

Denning, Michael. *The Cultural Front: The Laboring of American Culture in the Twentieth Century.* London: Verso Press, 1997.

Deverell, William. "Plague in Los Angeles, 1924: Ethnicity and Typicality." In *Over the Edge: Remapping the American West,* ed. Valerie J. Matsumoto and Blake Allmedinger, 172–200. Berkeley: University of California Press, 1999.

———. "Privileging the Mission over the Mexican: The Rise of Regional Consciousness in Southern California." In *Many Wests: Place, Culture and Regional Identity,* ed. David Wrobel and Michael Steiner, 235–58. Lawrence: University Press of Kansas, 1997.

Didion, Joan. *Play It as It Lays.* New York: Noonday Press, 1990.

Dumke, Glenn S. *The Boom of the Eighties in Southern California.* San Marino, Calif.: Huntington Library, 1944.

Dyer, Richard. "White." *Screen* 29, no. 4. (1993): 63–83.

———. *White*. London: Routledge, 1997.

Ellison, Ralph. *Invisible Man*. New York: Vintage Books, 1980 [originally published 1947].

Erenberg, Louis. *Swingin' the Dream: Big Band Jazz and the Rebirth of American Culture*. Chicago: University of Chicago Press, 1998.

Farley, Reynolds, and Walter R. Allen. *The Color Line and the Quality of Life in America*. New York: Russell Sage, 1987.

Farley, Reynolds, Howard Schuman, Suzanne Bianchi, Diane Colasanto, and Shirley Hatchett. " 'Chocolate City, Vanilla Suburbs': Will the Trend toward Racially Separate Communities Continue?" *Social Science Research* 7 (1978): 319–44.

Findlay, John. *Magic Lands: Western Cityscapes and American Culture after 1940*. Berkeley: University of California Press, 1992.

Fishman, Robert. *Bourgeois Utopias: The Rise and Fall of Suburbia*. New York: Basic Books, 1987.

Flamming, Douglas. "African Americans and the Politics of Race in Progressive-Era Los Angeles." In *California Progressivism Revisited*, ed. William Deverell and Tom Sitton, 203–28. Berkeley: University of California Press, 1994.

Fligstein, Neil. *Going North: Migration of Blacks and Whites from the South, 1900–1950*. New York: Academic Press, 1981.

Fogelson, Robert. *The Fragmented Metropolis: Los Angeles, 1850–1930*. Berkeley: University of California Press, 1993.

Fong, Timothy P. *The First Suburban Chinatown: The Remaking of Monterey Park, California*. Philadelphia: Temple University Press, 1994.

Ford, John Anson. *Thirty Explosive Years in Los Angeles County*. San Marino, Calif.: Huntington Library, 1961.

Foster, Mark S. "The Decentralization of Los Angeles during the 1920's." Ph.D. diss., University of Southern California, 1971.

———. *From Streetcar to Superhighway: American City Planners and Urban Transportation*. Philadelphia: Temple University Press, 1981.

———. "The Model T, the Hard Sell, and Los Angeles' Urban Growth: The Decentralization of Los Angeles during the 1920's." *Pacific Historical Review* 44 (November 1975): 459–84.

Francaviglia, Richard. "Main Street, USA: A Comparison/Contrast of Streetscapes in Disneyland and Walt Disney World." *Journal of Popular Culture* 15 (summer 1981): 141–56.

France, Van Arsdale. *Window on Main Street*. Burbank, Calif.: n.p., 1991.

Frankenburg, Ruth. *White Women, Race Matters: The Social Construction of Whiteness*. Minneapolis: University of Minnesota Press, 1993.

Frantz, Douglas, and Catherine Collins. *Celebration, U.S.A.: Living in Disney's Brave New Town*. New York: Henry Holt, 2000.

Fraser, Steve, and Gary Gerstle, eds. *The Rise and Fall of the New Deal Order, 1930–1980*. Princeton, N.J.: Princeton University Press, 1989.

Frey, William H. "Black In-Migration, White Flight, and the Changing Economic Base of the Central City." *American Journal of Sociology* 85 (1980): 1396–1417.

———. "Central City White Flight: Racial and Non Racial Causes." *American Sociological Review* 44 (1979): 425–48.

Friedrich, Otto. *City of Nets: A Portrait of Hollywood in the 1940s.* New York: Harper and Row, 1986.

Gabler, Neil. *An Empire of Their Own: How the Jews Invented Hollywood.* New York: Anchor Books, 1988.

Galishoff, Stuart. "Germs Know No Color Line: Black Health and Public Policy in Atlanta, 1900–1918." *Societas* 6, no. 2 (1976): 121–38.

Gilfolye, Timothy. *City of Eros: New York City, Prostitution and the Commercialization of Sex, 1790–1920.* New York: W. W. Norton and Company, 1992.

Golenbock, Peter. *Bums: An Oral History of the Brooklyn Dodgers.* New York: Putnam, 1984.

Gottlieb, Robert, and Irene Wolt. *Thinking Big: The Story of the Los Angeles Times, Its Publishers and Their Influence on Southern California.* New York: G. P. Putnam and Sons, 1977.

Gregory, James N. *American Exodus: The Dust Bowl Migration and Okie Culture in California.* New York: Oxford University Press, 1989.

———. "Okies and the Politics of Plain Folk Americanism." In *Working People of California,* ed. Daniel Cornford, 159–80. Berkeley: University of California Press, 1995.

Guback, Thomas H. "Hollywood's International Market." In *The American Film Industry,* ed. Tino Balio, 463–86. Madison: University of Wisconsin Press, 1985.

Gutiérrez, David. *Walls and Mirrors: Mexican Americans, Mexican Immigrants, and the Politics of Ethnicity.* Berkeley: University of California Press, 1995.

Hall, Stuart. "Notes on Deconstructing 'The Popular.'" In *People's History and Socialist Theory,* ed. Raphael Samuel, 227–39. London: Routledge and Kegan Paul, 1981.

Haltunnen, Karen. *Confidence Men and Painted Women: A Study of Middle-Class Culture in America, 1830–1870.* New Haven, Conn.: Yale University Press, 1982.

Harris, Neil. *Cultural Excursions: Marketing Appetites and Cultural Tastes in Modern America.* Chicago: University of Chicago Press, 1990.

Harris, Richard, and Robert Lewis. "The Geography of North American Cities and Suburbs: A New Synthesis, 1900–1950." *Journal of Urban History* 27, no. 3 (March 2001): 259–61.

Hata, Donald Teruo, and Nadine Ishitani Hata. "Asian Pacific Angelinos: Model Minorities and Indispensable Scapegoats." In *20th Century Los Angeles: Power, Promotion and Social Conflict,* ed. Norman M. Klein and Martin J. Schiesl, 80–84. Claremont, Calif.: Regina Books, 1993.

Havig, Alan. "Mass Commercial Amusements in Kansas City before World War I." *Missouri Historical Review* 75, no. 3 (April 1981): 316–45.

Hayden, Dolores. *The Grand Domestic Revolution: A History of Feminist*

Design for American Homes, Neighborhoods and Cities. Cambridge, Mass.: MIT Press, 1981.

————. "Model Houses for the Millions: Architects' Dreams, Builders' Boasts, Residents' Dilemmas." In *Blueprints for Modern Living: History and Legacy of the Case Study Houses,* ed. Elizabeth A. T. Smith, 197–212. Cambridge, Mass.: MIT Press, 1989.

Heilbut, Anthony. *Exiled in Paradise: German Refugee Artists and Intellectuals in America, from the 1930s to the Present.* Boston: Beacon Press, 1983.

Henderson, Cary S. "Los Angeles and the Dodger War, 1957–1962." *Southern California Quarterly* 63 (fall 1980): 261–89.

Hess, Alan. *Googie: Fifties Coffee Shop Architecture.* San Francisco: Chronicle Books, 1984.

Hilton, George W., and John F. Due. *The Electric Interurbans in America.* Stanford, Calif.: Stanford University Press, 1960.

Himes, Chester. *Lonely Crusade.* New York: Thunder's Mouth, 1975 [first published 1947].

————. "Zoot Riots Are Race Riots." In *Black on Black: Baby Sister and Selected Writings,* 220–25. New York: Doubleday, 1973.

Hines, Thomas S. "Housing, Baseball, and Creeping Socialism: The Battle of Chavez Ravine, Los Angeles, 1949–1959." *Journal of Urban History* 8, no. 2 (February 1982): 123–43.

Hirsch, Arnold. *Making the Second Ghetto: Race and Housing in Chicago, 1940–1980.* Cambridge: Cambridge University Press, 1983.

Hirsch, Foster. *Film Noir: The Dark Side of the Screen.* New York: Da Capo, 1981.

Hise, Greg. *Magnetic Los Angeles: Planning the Twentieth-Century Metropolis.* Baltimore: Johns Hopkins University Press, 1997.

Horkheimer, Max, and Theodor Adorno. *Dialectic of Enlightenment,* trans. John Cumming. New York: Continuum, 1995.

Horne, Gerald. "Black Fire: 'Riot' and 'Revolt' in Los Angeles, 1965 and 1992." In *Seeking El Dorado: African Americans in California,* ed. Lawrence B. de Graaf, Kevin Mulroy, and Quintard Taylor, 377–404. Seattle: University of Washington Press, 2001.

————. *Class Struggle in Hollywood: Moguls, Mobsters, Stars, Reds, and Trade Unionists, 1930–1950.* Austin: University of Texas Press, 2001.

Horowitz, Helen L. "Varieties of Cultural Experience in Jane Addams' Chicago." *History of Education Quarterly* 14, no. 3 (spring 1974): 69–72.

Horsman, Reginald. *Race and Manifest Destiny: The Origins of American Racial Anglo-Saxonism.* Cambridge, Mass.: Harvard University Press, 1981.

Huxtable, Ada Louise. "Reinventing Times Square: 1990." In *Inventing Times Square: Commerce and Culture at the Crossroads of the World,* ed. William R. Taylor, 356–70. Baltimore: Johns Hopkins University Press, 1991.

Ignatiev, Noel. *How the Irish Became White.* New York: Routledge, 1995.

Jackson, Kenneth T. *Crabgrass Frontier: The Suburbanization of the United States.* New York: Oxford University Press, 1985.

————. "Race, Ethnicity, and Real Estate Appraisal: The Home Owners' Loan

Corporation and the Federal Housing Administration." *Journal of Urban History* 6, no. 4 (1980): 419–52.

Jacobson, Mathew Frye. "Looking Jewish, Seeing Jews." In *Theories of Race and Racism: A Reader,* ed. Les Back and John Solomos, 238–56. London: Routledge, 2000.

————. *Whiteness of a Different Color: European Immigrants and the Alchemy of Race.* Cambridge, Mass.: Harvard University Press, 1998.

Jalbert, Matthew. " 'Burbs, Blockbusting, and Blacks: Morphosis of the Postwar American City." *Radical Urban Theory* (www.rut.com/mjalbert/burbs/index.html), 1993.

Jameson, Frederic. "Reification and Utopia in Mass Culture." *Social Text* 1 (winter 1979): 130–48.

Jones, David W. "California's Freeway Era in Historical Perspective." Institute of Transportation Studies, University of California, Berkeley, 1989.

Jones, Jaqueline. *The Dispossessed: America's Underclasses from the Civil War to the Present.* New York: Basic Books, 1992.

Joseph, Gilbert M. "Forging the Regional Pastime: Baseball and Class in Yucatan." In *Sport and Society in Latin America: Diffusion, Dependency, and the Rise of Mass Culture,* ed. Joseph L. Arbena, 29–61. New York: Greenwood Press, 1988.

Judd, Dennis R., and Todd Swanstrom. *City Politics: Private Power and Public Policy.* 2d ed. New York: Longman, 1988.

Kahn, Roger. *The Boys of Summer.* New York: Harper and Row, 1971.

Karimi, A. M. *Toward a Definition of the American Film Noir, 1941–1949.* New York: Arno, 1976.

Karnes, David. "Modern Metropolis: Mass Culture and the Transformation of Los Angeles, 1890–1950." Ph.D. diss., University of California, Berkeley, 1991.

Kasson, John F. *Amusing the Million: Coney Island at the Turn of the Century.* New York: Hill and Wang, 1978.

————. *Rudeness and Civility: Manners in Nineteenth-Century Urban America.* New York: Hill and Wang, 1990.

Keil, Roger. *Los Angeles: Globalization, Urbanization and Social Struggles.* New York: John Wiley and Sons, 1998.

Kelley, Robin D. G. "Notes on Deconstructing 'The Folk.' " *American Historical Review* 97, no. 5 (December 1992): 1400–1408.

————. *Race Rebels: Culture, Politics, and the Black Working Class.* New York: Free Press, 1996.

————. *Yo' Mama's Dysfunktional: Fighting the Culture Wars in Urban America.* Boston: Beacon Press, 1997.

Kern, Stephen. *The Culture of Time and Space, 1880–1918.* Cambridge, Mass.: Harvard University Press, 1998.

Kidd, Bruce. "The Men's Cultural Centre: Sports and the Dynamic of Women's Oppression/Men's Repression." In *Sport, Men, and the Gender Order: Critical Feminist Perspectives,* ed. Michael A. Messner and Donald F. Sabo, 31–43. Champaign, Ill.: Human Kinetics Books, 1990.

Kimmel, Michael S. "Baseball and the Reconstruction of American Masculinity, 1880–1920." In *Sport, Men, and the Gender Order: Critical Feminist Perspectives*, ed. Michael A. Messner and Donald F. Sabo, 55–65. Champaign, Ill.: Human Kinetics Books, 1990.

King, Margaret J. "Disneyland and Walt Disney World: Traditional Values in Futuristic Form." *Journal of Popular Culture* 15 (summer 1981): 116–39.

Klein, Norman M. *The History of Forgetting: Los Angeles and the Erasure of Memory*. London: Verso, 1997.

Klein, Norman M., and Martin J. Schiesl. *20th Century Los Angeles: Power, Promotion and Social Conflict*. Claremont, Calif.: Regina Books, 1990.

Kling, Rob, Spencer Olin, and Mark Poster, eds. *Postsuburban California: The Transformation of Orange County since World War II*. Berkeley: University of California Press, 1991.

Kowinski, William S. *The Malling of America: An Inside Look at the Great Consumer Paradise*. New York: William Morrow and Company, 1985.

Kracauer, Siegfried. "Hollywood's Terror Films: Do They Reflect an American State of Mind?" *Commentary*, August 1946, 132–36.

Krutnik, Frank. *In a Lonely Street: Film Noir, Genre, Masculinity*. London: Routledge, 1991.

Kuklick, Bruce. *To Everything a Season: Shibe Park and Urban Philadelphia, 1909–1976*. Princeton, N.J.: Princeton University Press, 1991.

Kusmer, Kenneth L. "African Americans in the City since World War II." *Journal of Urban History* 21 (1995): 458–504.

Leclerc, Gustavo, Raul Villa, and Michael J. Dear. *Urban Latino Cultures*. Thousand Oaks, Calif.: Sage Publications, 1999.

Lehman, Nicholas. *The Promised Land: The Great Black Migration and How It Changed America*. New York: Random House, 1991.

Lemon, James T. *Liberal Dreams and Nature's Limits: Great Cities in North America since 1600*. Toronto: Oxford University Press, 1996.

Lent, Tina Olson. "The Dark Side of the Screen: The Image of Los Angeles in Film Noir." *Southern California Quarterly* 69, no. 4 (winter 1987): 329–48.

Leonard, Kevin Allen. "Brothers under the Skin: African Americans, Mexican Americans, and World War II in California." In *The Way We Really Were: The Golden State in the Second Great War*, ed. Roger W. Lotchin, 187–214. Urbana: University of Illinois Press, 2000.

———. "'In the Interest of All Races': African Americans and Interracial Cooperation in Los Angeles during and after World War II." In *Seeking El Dorado: African Americans in California*, ed. Lawrence B. de Graaf, Kevin Mulroy, and Quintard Taylor, 309–40. Seattle: University of Washington Press, 2001.

Levine, Lawrence W. "The Folklore of Industrial Society: Popular Culture and Its Audiences." *American Historical Review* 97, no. 5 (December 1992): 1369–99.

———. *Highbrow/Lowbrow: The Emergence of Cultural Hierarchy in America*. Cambridge, Mass.: Harvard University Press, 1988.

Lhamon, W.T. Jr. *Raising Cain: Blackface Performance from Jim Crow to Hip Hop.* Cambridge, Mass.: Harvard University Press, 1998.

Lipsitz, George. "Land of a Thousand Dances: Minorities and the Rise of Rock and Roll." In *Recasting America: Culture and Politics in the Age of Cold War,* ed. Lary May, 267–84. Chicago: University of Chicago Press, 1989.

———. "The Making of Disneyland." In *True Stories from the American Past,* ed. William Graebner, 179–96. New York: McGraw Hill, 1993.

———. *The Possessive Investment in Whiteness: How White People Profit from Identity Politics.* Philadelphia: Temple University Press, 1998.

———. *Rainbow at Midnight: Labor and Culture in the 1940s.* Urbana: University of Illinois Press, 1994.

———. "Sports Stadia and Urban Development: A Tale of Three Cities." *Journal of Sport and Social Issues* 8 (summer/fall 1984): 1–18.

———. *Time Passages: Collective Memory and American Popular Culture.* Minneapolis: University of Minnesota Press, 1990.

Lo, Clarence Y. H. *Small Property versus Big Government: Social Origins of the Property Tax Revolt.* Berkeley: University of California Press, 1990.

Logan, John R., and Harvey L. Molotch. *Urban Fortunes: The Political Economy of Place.* Berkeley: University of California Press, 1987.

Longstreth, Richard. *City Center to Regional Mall: Architecture, the Automobile and Retailing in Los Angeles, 1920–1950.* Cambridge, Mass.: MIT Press, 1997.

López-Garza, Marta, and David R. Diaz. *Asian and Latino Immigrants in a Restructuring Economy: The Metamorphosis of Southern California.* Stanford, Calif.: Stanford University Press, 2001.

Los Angeles County Commission on Human Relations. *Population and Housing in Los Angeles County: A Study in the Growth of Residential Segregation.* Institute of Governmental Studies, University of California, Berkeley, March 1963.

Lott, Eric. *Love and Theft: Blackface Minstrelsy and the American Working Class.* New York: Oxford University Press, 1995.

———. "The Whiteness of Film Noir." In *Whiteness: A Critical Reader,* ed. Mike Hill, 81–101. New York: New York University Press, 1997.

Loukaitou-Sideris, Anastasia, and Tridib Banerjee. *Urban Design Downtown: Poetics and Politics of Form.* Berkeley: University of California Press, 1998.

Lucanio, Patrick. *Them or Us: Archetypal Interpretation of Fifties Alien Invasion Films.* Bloomington: University of Indiana Press, 1987.

Lupo, Alan, Frank Colcord, and Edmund P. Fowler. *Rites of Way: The Politics of Transportation in Boston and the U.S. City.* Boston: Little, Brown, 1971.

Macias, Anthony. "From Pachuco Boogie to Latin Jazz: Mexican Americans, Popular Music and Urban Culture in Los Angeles, 1940–1965." Ph.D. diss, University of Michigan, 2001.

Macías, Reynaldo Flores, Guillermo Vicente Flores, Donaldo Figueroa, and Luis Aragon. *A Study of Unincorporated East Los Angeles.* Monograph no. 3,

Aztlán Publications. Los Angeles: Chicano Studies Research Center, University of California, Los Angeles, 1973.

Marchand, Roland. "Visions of Classlessness, Quests for Dominion: American Popular Culture: 1945–1960." In *Reshaping America: Society and Institutions, 1945–1960,* ed. Robert H. Brenner and Gary W. Reichard, 163–90. Columbus: Ohio State University Press, 1985.

Marling, Karal Ann. "Disneyland, 1955." *American Art* 5, nos. 1–2 (winter/spring 1991): 168–207.

Massey, Douglas S., and Nancy A. Denton. *American Apartheid: Segregation and the Making of an Underclass.* Cambridge, Mass.: Harvard University Press, 1993.

———. "Suburbanization and Segregation in U.S. Metropolitan Areas." *American Journal of Sociology* 94, no. 3 (November 1988): 592–626.

May, Elaine Tyler. "Explosive Issues: Sex, Women and the Bomb." In *Recasting America: Culture and Politics in the Age of Cold War,* ed. Lary May, 154–70. Chicago: University of Chicago Press, 1989.

———. *Homeward Bound: American Families in the Cold War Era.* New York: Basic Books, 1988.

May, Lary. *The Big Tomorrow: Hollywood and the Politics of the American Way.* Chicago: University of Chicago Press, 2000.

———. "Movie Star Politics: The Screen Actors' Guild, Cultural Conversion and the Hollywood Red Scare." In *Recasting America: Culture and Politics in the Age of Cold War,* ed. Lary May, 125–53. Chicago: University of Chicago Press, 1989.

———. *Screening Out the Past: The Birth of Mass Culture and the Motion Picture Industry.* Chicago: University of Chicago Press, 1980.

Mazón, Mauricio. *The Zoot-Suit Riots: The Psychology of Symbolic Annihilation.* Austin: University of Texas Press, 1984.

McAlister, Melani. *Epic Encounters: Culture, Media, and U.S. Interests in the Middle East, 1945–2000.* Berkeley: University of California Press, 2001.

McBride, David. "On the Faultline of Mass Culture and Counterculture: A Social History of the Hippie Counterculture in 1960s Los Angeles." Ph.D. diss., University of California, Los Angeles, 1998.

McGirr, Lisa. *Suburban Warriors: The Origins of the New American Right.* Princeton, N.J.: Princeton University Press, 2001.

McLuhan, Marshall. *Understanding Media: The Extensions of Man.* New York: McGraw Hill, 1965.

McWilliams, Carey. *The Education of Carey McWilliams.* New York: Simon and Schuster, 1979.

———. *North from Mexico: The Spanish-Speaking Peoples of the United States.* Ed. Matt S. Meier. New York: Praeger, 1990.

———. *Southern California: An Island on the Land.* Salt Lake City: Peregrine-Smith, 1994.

———. "Watts: The Forgotten Slum." *The Nation,* 30 August 1965, 89–90.

Meyerowitz, Joanna, ed. *Not June Cleaver: Women and Gender in Postwar America*. Philadelphia: Temple University Press, 1994.

Miller, Gary. *Cities by Contract: The Politics of Municipal Incorporation*. Cambridge, Mass.: MIT Press, 1981.

Mitchell, Greg. *Tricky Dick and the Pink Lady: Richard Nixon vs. Helen Gahagan Douglas—Sexual Politics and the Red Scare*. New York: Random House, 1998.

Mohl, Raymond A. *The New City: Urban America in the Industrial Age, 1860–1920*. Arlington Heights, Ill.: Harlan Davidson, 1985.

———. "Race and Space in the Modern City: Interstate 95 and the Black Community in Miami." In *Urban Policy in Twentieth-Century America*, ed. Arnold R. Hirsch and Raymond A. Mohl, 66–100. New Brunswick, N.J.: Rutgers University Press, 1993.

———, ed. *Searching for the Sunbelt: Historical Perspectives on a Region*. Athens: University of Georgia Press, 1993.

Mollenkopf, John. *The Contested City*. Princeton, N.J.: Princeton University Press, 1983.

———. "The Postwar Politics of Urban Development." In *Marxism and the Metropolis: New Perspectives in Urban Political Economy*, ed. William K. Tabb and Larry Sawyers, 117–52. New York: Oxford University Press, 1978.

Monkonnen, Eric H. *America Becomes Urban: The Development of U.S. Cities and Towns, 1780–1900*. Berkeley: University of California Press, 1988.

Monroy, Douglas. *Rebirth: Mexican Los Angeles from the Great Migration to the Great Depression*. Berkeley: University of California Press, 1999.

———. *Thrown among Strangers: The Making of Mexican Culture in Frontier California*. Berkeley: University of California Press, 1990.

Naremore, James. *More than Night: Film Noir in Its Contexts*. Berkeley: University of California Press, 1998.

Nasaw, David. *Going Out: The Rise and Fall of Public Amusements*. New York: Basic Books, 1993.

Nash, Gerald D. *The American West Transformed: The Impact of the Second World War*. Lincoln: University of Nebraska Press, 1985.

National Advisory Commission on Civil Disorders. *Report of the National Advisory Committee on Civil Disorders*. New York: Bantam, 1968.

Nicolaides, Becky M. "Incubating the 'Silent Majority': Community and Political Life in a Working-Class Suburb of Los Angeles, 1945–1965." Paper presented at the Annual Meeting of the Organization of American Historians, San Francisco, April 1997.

———. *My Blue Heaven: Life and Politics in the Working-Class Suburbs of Los Angeles, 1920–1965*. Chicago: University of Chicago Press, 2002.

Normark, Don. *Chavez Ravine, 1949: A Los Angeles Story*. San Francisco: Chronicle Books, 1999.

O'Leary, Cecilia. *To Die For: The Paradox of American Patriotism*. Princeton, N.J.: Princeton University Press, 1999.

Omi, Michael, and Harold Winant. *Racial Formation in the United States: From the 1960s to the 1990s.* 2d ed. London: Routledge, 1994.

Pardo, Mary. *Mexican American Women Activists: Identity and Resistance in Two Los Angeles Communities.* Philadelphia: Temple University Press, 1998.

Parish, James Robert, and Michael R. Pitts. *The Great Science Fiction Pictures.* Metuchen, N.J.: Scarecrow Press, 1977.

Parker, William H. *Parker on Police.* Ed. O. W. Wilson. Springfield, Ill.: Charles C. Thomas, 1957.

Parson, Don. "Los Angeles' Headline Happy Public Housing War." *Southern California Quarterly* 65, no. 3 (fall 1983): 251–85.

———. "Urban Politics during the Cold War: Public Housing, Urban Renewal, and Suburbanization in Los Angeles." Ph.D. diss., University of California, Los Angeles, 1985.

Peiss, Kathy. *Cheap Amusements: Working Women and Leisure in Turn-of-the-Century New York.* Philadelphia: Temple University Press, 1990.

Perloff, Harvey S. "Planning for Postindustrial Cities." School of Architecture and Urban Planning, University of California, Los Angeles, 1980. Photocopy.

Pitt, Leonard, and Dale Pitt. *Los Angeles A to Z: An Encyclopedia of the City and County.* Berkeley: University of California Press, 1997.

Price, John A. "The Migration and Adaptation of American Indians to Los Angeles." *Human Organization* 27, no. 2 (summer 1968): 168–75.

Regalado, Samuel O. "Baseball in the Barrios: The Scene in East Los Angeles since World War II." *Baseball History* 1, no. 1 (summer 1986): 47–59.

———. "Dodgers' *Béisbol* Is on the Air: The Development and Impact of the Dodgers' Spanish Language Broadcasts, 1958–1994." *California History: The Magazine of the California Historical Society,* fall 1995, 281–89.

———. *Viva Baseball! Latin Major Leaguers and Their Special Hunger.* Urbana: University of Illinois Press, 1988.

Rieder, Jonathan S. "The Rise of the 'Silent Majority.'" In *The Rise and Fall of the New Deal Order, 1930–1980,* ed. Steve Fraser and Gary Gerstle, 243–68. Princeton, N.J.: Princeton University Press, 1989.

Riess, Steven A. *Touching Base: Professional Baseball and American Culture in the Progressive Era.* Urbana: University of Illinois Press, 1999.

Ritter, Lawrence S. *Lost Ballparks: A Celebration of Baseball's Legendary Fields.* New York: Viking Press, 1992.

Rocco, Raymond A. "Latino Los Angeles: Reframing Boundaries/Borders." In *The City: Los Angeles and Urban Theory at the End of the Twentieth Century,* ed. Allen J. Scott and Edward W. Soja, 365–89. Berkeley: University of California Press, 1996.

Roediger, David. *The Wages of Whiteness: Race and the Making of the American Working Class.* London: Verso Press, 1991.

Rogin, Michael. *Blackface, White Noise: Jews and the Hollywood Melting Pot.* Berkeley: University of California Press, 1996.

———. *Ronald Reagan: The Movie.* Berkeley: University of California Press, 1987.

Rogin, Michael Paul, and John L. Shover. *Political Change in California: Critical Elections and Social Movements, 1890–1966.* Westport, Conn.: Greenwood Publishing Corporation, 1970.

Romo, Ricardo. *East Los Angeles: History of a Barrio.* Austin: University of Texas Press, 1983.

Rose, Tricia. *Black Noise: Rap Music and Black Culture in Contemporary America.* Hanover, N.H.: University Press of New England, 1994.

Rosenberg, Norman L., and Emily S. Rosenberg. *In Our Times: America since World War II.* 6th ed. Upper Saddle River, N.J.: Prentice Hall, 1999.

Ross, Andrew. *The Celebration Chronicles.* New York: Ballantine Books, 1999.

Ross, Steven J. *Working-Class Hollywood: Silent Film and the Shaping of Class in America.* Princeton, N.J.: Princeton University Press, 1998.

Ruiz, Vicki. *Cannery Women, Cannery Lives: Mexican Women, Unionization, and the California Food Processing Industry.* Albuquerque: University of New Mexico Press, 1987.

———. "'Star Struck': Acculturation, Adolescence, and the Mexican American Woman, 1920–1950." In *Building with Our Hands: New Directions in Chicana Studies,* ed. Adela de la Torre and Beatrice Pesquera, 109–23. Berkeley: University of California Press, 1993.

Ryan, Michael, and Douglas Kellner. *Camera Politica: The Politics and Ideology of Contemporary Hollywood Film.* Bloomington: Indiana University Press, 1988.

Rydell, Robert. *All the World's a Fair: Visions of Empire at American International Expositions, 1876–1916.* Chicago: University of Chicago Press, 1984.

Sánchez, George J. *Becoming Mexican American: Ethnicity, Culture, and Identity in Chicano Los Angeles, 1900–1945.* New York: Oxford University Press, 1993.

———. "Reading Reginald Denny: The Politics of Whiteness in Late Twentieth-Century America." *American Quarterly* 47, no. 3 (September 1995): 388–94.

Saxton, Alexander. *The Rise and Fall of the White Republic: Class Politics and Mass Culture in Nineteenth-Century America.* London: Verso Press, 1990.

Scharff, Virginia. *Taking the Wheel: Women and the Coming of the Motor Age.* Albuquerque: University of New Mexico Press, 1991.

Schickel, Richard. *The Disney Version: The Life, Times, Art and Commerce of Walt Disney.* 3d ed. Chicago: Ivan R. Dee Inc., 1997.

Schiesl, Martin J. "Behind the Badge: The Police and Social Discontent in Los Angeles since 1950." In *20th Century Los Angeles: Power, Promotion and Social Conflict,* ed. Norman M. Klein and Martin J. Schiesl, 153–94. Claremont, Calif.: Regina Books, 1990.

Schorske, Carl. *Fin de Siècle Vienna: Politics and Culture.* New York: Vintage Books, 1981.

Schrader, Paul. "Notes on Film Noir." In *Film Noir: A Reader,* ed. Alain Silver and James Ursini, 53–64. New York: Limelight Editions, 1997.

Scott, Allen J. "High-Technology Industrial Development in the San Fernando Valley and Ventura County: Observations on Economic Growth and the Evolution of Urban Form." In *The City: Los Angeles and Urban Theory at the*

End of the Twentieth Century, ed. Allen J. Scott and Edward W. Soja, 276–310. Berkeley: University of California Press, 1996.

———. *Metropolis: From the Division of Labor to Urban Form.* Berkeley: University of California Press, 1988.

Scott, Allen J., and Edward W. Soja, eds. *The City: Los Angeles and Urban Theory at the End of the Twentieth Century.* Berkeley: University of California Press, 1996.

Sears, David O. and Donald R. Kinder. "Racial Tension and Voting in Los Angeles." Institute of Government and Public Affairs, University of California, Los Angeles, 1971.

Selby, Spencer. *Dark City: The Film Noir.* Jefferson, N.C.: McFarland Publishers, 1984.

Sharpe, William, and Leonard Wallock. "Bold New City or Built-Up 'Burb? Redefining Contemporary Suburbia." In *The Making of Urban America,* 2nd ed., ed. Raymond A. Mohl, 309–34. Wilmington: SR Books, 1997.

Shaw, Nayan. *Contagious Divides: Epidemics and Race in San Francisco's Chinatown.* Berkeley: University of California Press, 2001.

Sides, Josh. "Working Away: African American Migration and Community in Los Angeles from the Great Depression to 1954." Ph.D. diss., University of California, Los Angeles, 1999.

Silver, Alain, and Elizabeth Ward, eds. *Film Noir: An Encyclopedic Reference to the American Style.* New York: Overlook Press, 1979.

Singer, Ben. "Modernity, Hyperstimulus, and Rise of Popular Sensationalism." In *Cinema and Invention of Modern Life,* ed. Leo Charney and Vanessa Schwartz, 72–102. Berkeley: University of California Press, 1995.

Sklar, Robert. *Movie-Made America: A Cultural History of American Movies.* New York: Vintage Press, 1975.

Soja, Edward W. "History: Geography: Modernity." In *The Cultural Studies Reader,* ed. Simon During, 113–25. 2d ed. New York: Routledge, 1993.

———. "Los Angeles, 1965–1992: From Crisis-Generated Restructuring to Restructuring-Generated Crisis." In *The City: Los Angeles and Urban Theory at the End of the Twentieth Century,* ed. Allen J. Scott and Edward W. Soja, 426–62. Berkeley: University of California Press, 1996.

———. *Postmetropolis: Critical Studies of Cities and Regions.* Oxford: Blackwell Publishing, 2000.

Sonenshein, Raphael J. *Politics in Black and White: Race and Power in Los Angeles.* Princeton, N.J.: Princeton University Press, 1993.

Sontag, Susan. "The Imagination of Disaster." In *Film Theory and Criticism,* ed. Gerald Mast and Marshall Cohen, 488–504. 2d ed. London: Oxford University Press, 1979.

Sorkin, Michael, ed. *Variations on a Theme Park: The New American City and the End of Public Space.* New York: Hill and Wang, 1992.

Spigel, Lynn. *Make Room for TV: Television and the Family Ideal in Postwar America.* Chicago: University of Chicago Press, 1992.

Stallybrass, Peter, and Allon White. *The Politics and Poetics of Transgression.* Ithaca, N.Y.: Cornell University Press, 1995.

Sugrue, Thomas. *The Origins of the Urban Crisis: Race and Inequality in Postwar Detroit.* Princeton, N.J.: Princeton University Press, 1996.

———. "Reassessing the History of Postwar America." *Prospects: An Annual of American Studies* 20 (1995): 493–509.

Sullivan, Neil J. *The Dodgers Move West.* New York: Oxford University Press, 1987.

Susman, Warren. "The City in American Culture." In *Culture as History: The Transformation of American Society in the Twentieth Century,* 237–51. New York: Pantheon Books, 1984.

———. *Culture as History: The Transformation of American Society in the Twentieth Century.* New York: Pantheon, 1984.

———. "Did Success Spoil the United States? Dual Representations in Postwar America." In *Recasting America: Culture and Politics in the Age of Cold War,* ed. Lary May, 19–37. Chicago: University of Chicago, 1989.

Taeuber, Karl E., and Alma F. Taeuber. *Negroes in Cities: Residential Segregation and Neighborhood Change.* Chicago: Aldine Publishing, 1965.

Tchen, John Kuo Wei. *New York before Chinatown: Orientalism and the Shaping of American Culture, 1776–1886.* Baltimore: Johns Hopkins University Press, 1999.

Teaford, Jon C. *The Twentieth-Century American City.* 2d ed. Baltimore: Johns Hopkins University Press, 1993.

Thomas, David H. "Harvesting Ramona's Garden: Life in California's Mythical Mission Past." In *Columbian Consequences,* vol. 3, *The Spanish Borderlands in Pan American Perspective,* ed. David H. Thomas, 119–57. Washington, D.C.: Smithsonian Institution Press, 1991.

Trachtenberg, Alan. "Image and Ideology: New York in the Photographer's Eye." *Journal of Urban History* 10, no. 4 (August 1984): 453–65.

———. *The Incorporation of America: American Culture and Society in the Gilded Age.* New York: Hill and Wang, 1982.

U.S. Bureau of the Census. *Census of the Population, 1950,* vol. 2, *Characteristics of the Population.* Washington, D.C.: Government Printing Office, 1952.

———. *Census of the Population, 1960,* vol. 1, *Characteristics of the Population.* Washington, D.C.: Government Printing Office, 1963.

———. *Census of the Population, 1970,* vol. 1, *Characteristics of the Population.* Washington, D.C.: Government Printing Office, 1973.

———. *Sixteenth Census of the United States, 1940,* vol. 2, *Population and Housing.* Washington, D.C.: Government Printing Office, 1942.

———. *Special Census of Los Angeles, California: Population by Age, Race, and Sex, by Census.* P-SC, no. 188. Washington, D.C.: Department of Commerce, 1946.

Valle, Victor M., and Rodolfo D. Torres. *Latino Metropolis.* Minneapolis: University of Minnesota Press, 2000.

Vaughn, Christopher A. "Ogling Igorots: The Politics and Commerce of Exhibiting Cultural Otherness, 1898–1913." In *Freakery: Cultural Spectacles of the Extraordinary Body,* ed., Rosemarie Garland Thompson, 219–33. New York: New York University Press, 1996.

Voight, David. *American Baseball,* vol. 3. University Park: Pennsylvania State University Press, 1983.

Vorspan, Max, and L. P. Gartner. *History of the Jews of Los Angeles.* San Marino, Calif.: Huntington Library, 1970.

Waldie, D. J. *Holy Land: A Suburban Memoir.* New York: St. Martin's Press, 1996.

Warner, Sam Bass Jr. *The Urban Wilderness: A History of the American City.* New York: Harper and Row, 1972.

Watts, Stephen. "Walt Disney: Art and Politics in the American Century." *Journal of American History* 100, no. 2 (June 1995): 84–110.

Weibel-Orlando, Joan. *Indian Country, L.A.: Maintaining Ethnic Community in Complex Society.* Urbana: University of Illinois Press, 1991.

Weiss, Marc. "The Origins and Legacy of Urban Renewal." In *Urban and Regional Planning in an Age of Austerity,* ed. Pierre Clavel, John Forester, and William W. Goldsmith, 53–80. New York: Pergamon Press, 1980.

———. *The Rise of the Community Builders: The American Real Estate Industry and Urban Land Planning.* New York: Columbia University Press, 1987.

Whittingham, Richard. *The Los Angeles Dodgers: An Illustrated History.* New York: Harper and Row, 1982.

Williams, Raymond. *Marxism and Literature.* Oxford: Oxford University Press, 1977.

Wilson, James Q. "A Guide to Reagan Country: The Political Culture of Southern California." *Commentary,* May 1967, 37–45.

Wong, K. Scott. "War Comes to Chinatown: Social Transformation and the Chinese of California." In *The Way We Really Were: The Golden State in the Second Great War,* ed. Roger W. Lotchin, 164–86. Urbana: University of Illinois Press, 2000.

Worster, Donald. *Rivers of Empire: Water, Aridity and the Growth of the American West.* Berkeley: University of California Press, 1983.

Wunsch, James. "The Suburban Cliché." *Journal of Social History* 28, no. 3 (1995): 643–58.

Index

Page numbers in italics indicate illustrations.

Text: 10/13 Aldus
Display: Aldus
Compositor: BookMatters, Berkeley